A Christian Social Perspective

A Christian Social Perspective

Alan Storkey

Inter-Varsity Press

Inter-Varsity Press
38 De Montfort Street, Leicester LE1 7GP, England

Quotations from the Bible are from the Revised Standard
Version (copyrighted 1946 and 1952, Second Edition
1971, by the Division of Christian Education, National
Council of the Churches of Christ in the USA), unless
otherwise stated.

First published 1979

ISBN 0 85110 593 9

Set in 11 pt. Times by Woolaston Parker Ltd., Leicester
Printed in Great Britain by
Billing & Sons Ltd., London, Guildford and Worcester

For Amos, Matthew and Caleb

*Inter-Varsity Press is the publishing division of the
Universities and Colleges Christian Fellowship (formerly the
Inter-Varsity Fellowship), a student movement linking
Christian Unions in universities and colleges throughout the
British Isles, and a member movement of the International
Fellowship of Evangelical Students. For information about
local and national activities in Great Britain write to
UCCF, 38 De Montfort Street, Leicester LE1 7GP.*

Contents

theories of knowledge: *nature and knowledge; empiricism; rational knowledge.* The twentieth century faith in method. The modified faith in method. Linguistic theories of knowledge. A fundamental critique. A Christian epistemology.

CHAPTER 4

Christian failure
The problem. Church politics. The sacred–secular division. Synthetic thinking. The solution.

CHAPTER 5

A Christian social perspective
Biblical exegesis: *How is the Bible to be interpreted? some Christian misconceptions; some non-Christian interpretations.* The word of God. A Christian philosophy of sociology: *A Christian perspective; scientific knowledge; scientific differentiation; sociology as a scientific discipline.* A Christian sociological perspective: *creation; sin; redemption.* Free societal relationships and communities. Basic social institutions. Structures of institutional authority. Free institutions. A critical perspective.

PRIMARY SOCIOLOGY
CHAPTER 6

Free relationships
Free societal relationships. The individualist pole: *the egocentric response; the possessive response; the competitive response; individual pressure; the manipulative response; the self-validating response; the comparative response; the self-righteous response; the privatized response; the hedonist response.*
The collectivist pole: *the image-creating response;*

extrinsic relationships; the acceptability focus; group identity; the other-directed conscience; the status response. The dilemma. The Christian perspective.

content of television. Non-dogmatic television. News.
See-through characters. Continuity. Variation and
change. The effects of television. The other mass
media. Diagnosis. The economics of the media. The
Dutch alternative. Humanism and communication.

SECONDARY ASPECTS
CHAPTER 11

British politics and parties
Faith and parties: *the Labour party; the Conservative
party; the Liberal party.* Power and parties. The current
political expedients. The present weakness of parties.

CHAPTER 12

A Christian view of the state
Christian involvement in politics. A biblical
perspective of the state: *God's sovereignty; the state is
instituted because of sin; the state and justice;
the state and coercion; the state and law; political office;
impartiality; redistribution of resources:
limitations on the activities of the state;
religious toleration; peacemaking.*

CHAPTER 13

Economic perspectives
Christian foundations of modern economics. Post-
Christian economic perspectives: *property; self-interest;
blind natural evolution; neutrality, power and socialist
economics; changing the system; means and ends.*
Conclusion.

Preface

The present deluge of works in the social sciences is marked by a dearth of Christian contributions. This book was begun about ten years ago partly to remedy this deficiency, but a lot more was involved than just filling a gap. Because the social sciences have developed in a largely post-Christian era, a Christian perspective will necessarily depart in many ways from the approaches normally adopted within these disciplines. For some the attempt to speak biblically into them may initially create something like culture-shock. They will hardly recognize the areas under discussion as being central to contemporary social science. Others will feel that the kind of theory used is alien, especially those not familiar with the normative basis. Others will find the integration of values, principles and an overt philosophy with actual social analysis difficult and unusual. This change of direction may be difficult for some readers to adjust to, but I hope by the end of the book the reader will understand more fully why it is needed and will accept the justification.

The book is divided into three sections. The first, after chapter one, is written mainly for those with previous contact with the social sciences. The main theme is that no area of life is 'neutral'; they are all shaped by religious or faith commitments, whether these be Christian, humanist or whatever. In the same vein it is similarly argued that an attempt to construct a 'neutral' sociology or economics is misconstrued; the disciplines must both acknowledge the centrality of faith to social behaviour and also their own religious roots. One problem with a book of this scope, which I regret, is that it is not possible to do full justice to the work of various social scientists when looking at elements in their approach. Indeed it is only possible in this section to suggest some of the underlying dilemmas and problems as an initial apologetic for the new Christian approach outlined mainly in chapter 5.

The other two sections assume much less previous knowledge of the social sciences. The first looks at various straightforward kinds of social relationship and institution, and the second at relationships which are primarily economic, political or worship-centred. Again the scope of the book means that each chapter, rather than offering a textbook coverage, can do little more than open up the kind of analysis that can grow out of a Christian perspective. Anything more would have meant that it exploded in size. One crucial feature of the analysis is that, because it is normatively based, it relates directly to the issue of how we live; it is not 'academic' in the sense of being detached from life, but continually generates signposts for living. An obvious problem is that, since little research has yet been done from within this perspective, it is difficult directly to substantiate points, and many of them depend on indirect evidence or are exploratory. Already there are growing numbers of Christians working in these areas who are and will be going into the issues in greater depth, and my hope is that this contribution will help them in their Christian academic work.

A final point of caution is that the social, economic and political stance of this book is not to be taken for, or identified with, the Christian faith. It is merely looking at some of the implications and outworkings of that faith, wandering in the foothills of Christian truth with the mud of error on our boots. It is to be hoped that some, seeing a little of the reflected light, may turn to the Source.

I am grateful to many for their help at various stages: to London Bible College for sponsoring the course of lectures at Bedford College which started the book; to those with whom I have worked and studied in the Shaftesbury Project, and especially to the Rev. Pat Dearnley, my successor, and also to members of that anarchic body, the Christian Studies Unit, for help in random ways. My thanks to Dr. Andrew Brockett, Sir Fred Catherwood, Dr. David Lyon and Dr. Tony Cramp for comments on specific chapters, and to Fred Jones and Richard Russell for wider comments. My father has been mainly responsible for the task of trying to improve the clarity of the text. My thanks also to Janet Parr for typing most of the second draft.

None of the aforementioned can be held responsible for any of the content, but Elaine, besides typing the first and some of the second draft, is effectively the co-author, for better or worse, and to her I will express my thanks privately.

Chapter 1

Faith and social relationships

Faith and social behaviour

It is not difficult to point out the ways in which Christianity has become more peripheral in the lives of most British people during the 20th century. Some churches have fallen into disuse; congregations in others have shrunk in numbers and fewer assent to the basic tenets of Christian belief. A process of secularization has been in train for at least a hundred years, and it is often tacitly assumed that this is a movement from faith to non-faith, from belief to unbelief. On the basis of this assumption it becomes pointless to look for religious convictions in contemporary secular society. They cannot exist, except as fringe or disappearing phenomena. This view will be challenged in this chapter and the contrary view argued, that *faith* is basic to people's lives, and therefore to their social relationships, however secular they are. Faith has not evaporated in the 20th century, but people have transferred their faith from beliefs related to Christianity to other life-anchors which have a different form. The society we live in is no less believing, but it is considerably more difficult to define the important beliefs in our complex secular culture. In this chapter we shall make an attempt to do this by looking not at ideologies, politics or attitudes, but at the underlying religious commitment which, we believe, helps to shape these more immediate responses and the general, social and economic patterns which have developed in our society. The first step is to define what is meant by faith in this context. In some ways the word is inadequate because of its close Christian connotations, but faith could be defined as the meaning which people give to their lives and by which they understand themselves and other people; it is the framework or perspective within which they live and act; it is their construction of reality, the sense of their lives. Alternatively, it could be described as the integration point of people's lives or that which gives their actions coherence. It could be argued that this process of creating meaning and coherence is part of the life of each one of us, whether it is successful or not. It follows that a person without faith in God is not devoid of faith as such, but seeks a different point of coherence for his life. This is not a neat definition, but precision is almost impossible with such an important term.[1]

It is evident that this definition of faith is rather uncomfortable, and does not fit at all into most conventional social analyses. It raises a whole range of deep philosophical or religious issues. What is my identity? How do I relate to other people? What values do I hold and why? What is wrong treatment of others? Whom do I like and why? What is worth doing and what is the purpose of my actions? How do I communicate? What will make me happy? What does the behaviour of other people mean? These are not abstract problems; every person faces them day in and day out, whether they are verbalized or not. The response may be in terms of acquired habits, or of holding to one point of view or the other, but the answers must necessarily be tested in the daily process of living and, if the test fails, the beliefs need to be modified; they need to carry weight. Moreover, these issues are not confined to a certain group of people who 'have faith'. Everybody, even if by default, has to give answers to these questions, and if these basic issues of meaning are raised in the lives of ordinary people, they must also be part of a sociological perspective.

So far we have not discussed the link between the various issues of belief and ordinary social activity. Many people do not and cannot state their most deeply held beliefs, but they flow into their every-

---

[1] This concept shows some resemblance to subjective definitions of social behaviour from Weber to the phenomenologists. It involves a point similar to that made by ethnomethodological analyses, namely that people's beliefs matter in all areas of life and cannot be reduced to, or explained away by, so-called 'objective' phenomena. However, far more than this is involved.

day attitudes. Husbands and wives see their marriage in terms of love, various ideals, mutual obligations, sexual gratification and comfort, or in terms of how their parents lived, and these attitudes, rooted in their religious viewpoint, help shape the marriage relationship. Because people see themselves in a certain way, they put a high value on respectability, with the consequence that their relationships with others remain distant. In factories and offices throughout the country, managers officiously pursue profit and expansion to the extent that it shapes relationships with their staff. These norms reflect beliefs about the purpose of activity and are developed into complex patterns of behaviour. At another level, restaurants, country houses, pubs, holiday resorts, shops, homes and cars reflect the popular view of the 'good life'. Basic values can even be reflected in such mundane items as the height of people's shoes, the shape of chairs, the games they play, or the appearance of their gardens. Generally, we can say that core areas of meaning are connected, however tenuously, with all the activities and relationships of life. The connection might not be straightforward or consistent, but it is nonetheless important.

So far the place of faith in people's lives has been largely presented in individual terms, but this does not mean that the viewpoint is individualistic. Because the need for meaning-coherence is universal, the normal pattern has been for groups to develop a set of common answers to the basic issues of faith. Thus, major religious perspectives such as Buddhism, Hinduism, Animism, Humanism, and Communism are shared by millions of people. At the same time, there are significant variations within these groups, either in different localities or among different age groups. We can easily see that an awareness of the social dynamic of belief allows a community of faith but does not presume societal consensus. The sterile sociological debate between conflict and consensus views of society is easily resolved if one recognizes the pattern of beliefs which are common and those which are inconsistent or in conflict. It is also evident that our concept of faith is much more dynamic than is the sociological concept of culture. The idea of culture has its roots in anthropological studies of largely homogeneous societies, in which the individual is passive. Faith neither assumes homogeneity nor the passivity of groups and individuals in the formation of attitudes.

We are now ready to examine some of the more important faith-responses of people in British society. If we can accurately identify these deeply-held beliefs, it will help us to understand more fully the attitudes that appear in the specific areas of social life that we shall look at later. Because of the complexities of different systems of measurement, it is hazardous to generalize about which attitudes are the dominant ones. Nevertheless, some beliefs are so widespread that it is worth attempting to describe them, even though it will not be possible to do so in rigorous detail, and even though it will involve simplification of complex and pluralistic belief patterns. Further, since people do not normally divulge their deepest beliefs we must of necessity infer them. This can be attempted by examining the literature, studying the views of those who were dominant shapers of faith and learning to interpret the various patterns of meaning of each era, but it is always a proximate process. If, therefore, we select various dominant religious viewpoints for consideration, it is not because others can be reduced to these, but simply because the complexities cannot be raised at this stage. Issues of faith have often been ignored in the social sciences, but they can be avoided no longer.

Our approach in this chapter is historical, in that we shall look at those faith-perspectives which have been dominant at different periods and try to assess what they have contributed to attitudes in our society. Current beliefs, it can be argued, are either developments of, or reactions to those that have gone before, and an historical sketch will set the background of the dynamic of faith within which we now live.

The Reformation

There are three reasons for beginning with the social philosophy characteristic of the Reformation. Firstly, as we shall later be concerned with a Christian social perspective, this period has obvious interest. Secondly, many of the principles, attitudes and norms developed during this period remain important in British culture in one way or another. Lastly, since we shall be looking in detail at the development of non-Christian beliefs, it is helpful to begin with a period when the Christian faith had a strong, easily recognizable influence. During the latter half of the 16th century Lutheran, Anabaptist and Calvinist forms of Protestantism spread into Britain, permeated in part the new Church of England and became a widespread basis of belief among all groups in early 17th century society. It can justly be said that a large proportion of the population saw themselves and their social relationships in terms of the Christian faith.

There were of course significant variations of attitudes among Christians. Issues of church government divided Anglicans, Presbyterians and Independents. Some Puritans concentrated on the way in which their faith changed their thought and emotional life.[1] Others were far more activist and visionary to the extent that they became involved in revolution and regicide. The early 17th century produced such a ferment of ideas that it would be inaccurate to posit any uniformity of belief; indeed, the wrongness of enforcing uniformity was one of the new principles to emerge. At the same time, Christian ideas were synthesized with others; for example, the Digger, Gerrard Winstanley, often identified God with reason,[2] Shakespeare shows a commingling of renaissance and protestant attitudes, and even Milton was influenced by some classical ideas. However, although there were these many variations, we suggest that they are variations on a theme which had coherence, and which bears examination as a faith perspective with important social implications. Those who were known as Puritans perhaps most closely represent this perspective, and some of the effects of their lives are of great interest.

Firstly, they changed the work patterns of the nation. They aimed at abolishing the hundred or more saints' days, established Sunday as a day of rest and worship, and saw work in terms of a calling or vocation which was performed before God. The idea of efficiency at work grew in the context of man's responsibility to God. They also opposed ostentatious consumption, encouraged thriftiness and saving and attacked the idleness of the aristocracy and the unemployed. They scorned those who lived off

[1] See, for example, some of the superb volumes from this period by Brooks, Burroughs, Flavel, Gurnall, Watson, *etc.*, published by The Banner of Truth Trust, The Grey House, 3 Murrayfield Road, Edinburgh, EH12 6EL.
[2] See G. Winstanley, *The Law of Freedom and other Writings* (Ed. C. Hill) (Pelican, 1963), pp. 79, 80, *etc.*

accumulated wealth, established the sanctity of contract, and opposed bribery, exploitation and speculation. We would argue that only with the development of these attitudes at the Reformation did a positive economic perspective emerge to replace the largely prohibitive, negative mediaeval attitude, and to prepare the ground for later industrialization.[1]

The changes were no less marked in the political arena. Great importance was attached to the doctrine of *office*, seen as a responsibility before God, leading to a very different view of political authority from absolutism, the divine right of kings and Machiavellian power politics. Further, with the establishment of the primacy of man's relationship with God, various groups like the Pilgrim Fathers, the Independents and the Levellers set up the principles of allowing religious freedom to political subjects, of abolishing censorship and torture, and of giving the vote to *people* rather than to *property*. During this period the idea of the rule of law, even over the king, was developed and fought for tenaciously by Chief Justice Sir Edward Coke, the Parliamentarians and others. Similarly it was a period when the doctrine of sin opened up the possibility of criticism of the ruler. That the ruler was subject to the law, and also potentially as much a sinner as anybody else, radically transformed the shape of politics. The doctrine of the equality of men before God undermined the hierarchical views of society that had existed before and, we would argue, provided the basis for what subsequently became known as democracy. This was a time of wars, cruelty and deliberate destruction, and there were many so-called Christian attitudes of which we might be critical, but there is little doubt that this short period in the middle of the 17th century was the seedbed of much British constitutional and political thought, and that its Christian basis was crucial.[2]

[1] The point made here is different from that of M. Weber in *The Protestant Ethic and the Spirit of Capitalism*,[2] (Allen and Unwin, 1977) which is ahistorical, telescoping events covering 200 years, and tends to identify the attitudes of such diverse people as Richard Baxter and Benjamin Franklin. For a summary critique see G. R. Elton, *Reformation Europe 1517–1599* (Fontana, 1969) pp. 312–18.

[2] See C. Hill, *Puritanism and Revolution* (Secker and Warburg, 1958); C. Hill, *God's Englishmen* (Weidenfeld and Nicholson, 1970; Penguin, 1972); W. Schenk, *The Concern for Social Justice in the Puritan Revolution* (Longmans, 1948); M. Walzer, *The Revolution of the Saints* (Weidenfeld and Nicholson, 1966).

Alongside these changes there were new directions in social life. Magic and witchcraft died out as social forces and have reappeared only within the last few decades. The reformers stressed the right of both men and women to choose their spouses freely. Ordinary households became centres of worship and teaching. Education became much less ecclesiastical and scholastic and was soon important for all people; Knox, for example, aimed at universal, subsidized, primary education in Scotland, and the men who pioneered the great scientific revolution which culminated in the work of Newton were filling the universities.[1] More generally, the biblical doctrines that all men were created by God and were sinners in need of salvation were the bases of a new egalitarian view of society which undermined status, hierarchic nobility and privilege. The institutional church was also transformed; it ceased to be politically dominated, the separation between clergy and people was broken by the doctrine of the priesthood of all believers, and there was a spontaneous and rapid growth in pulpit teaching. The fact that 2000 ministers were prepared by conviction to give up their livings in the Great Ejection of 1662 conveys something of the strength of faith that bred new institutional forms.[2] Whole areas of life were seen in a different way; for example, people's view of time was changed by the awareness of the 'great taskmaster's eye', the doctrine of providence and of judgment, so that their rhythm of life changed. We could list many more ways in which the puritan viewpoint was profoundly reflected in economic, political and social changes but we are more concerned at present with the key points in the social philosophy which undergirds them.[3]

There were at least four basic tenets of the reformed Christian perspective which influenced the way men and women under-

[1] See chapter 3.

[2] See Iain Murray, *Sermons of the Great Ejection* (Banner of Truth Trust, 1962).

[3] For social changes see C. Hill, *Society and Puritanism in Pre-Revolutionary England* (Secker and Warburg, 1964); M. James, *Social Problems and Policy during the Puritan Revolution, 1640–1660* (Routledge and Kegan Paul, 1966) and L. Stone, *The Crisis of the Aristocracy* (Oxford Univ. Press, 1965). This interpretation is obviously at variance with neo-Marxist attempts to see 17th century changes predominantly in class terms, but unfortunately we cannot pursue the issue in more detail.

stood themselves and their society. Firstly, they could only understand themselves and their society *in relation to God*. They were created by God in his image, and he had to be the meaning-focus of their lives and the one before whom they were accountable. John Calvin makes the point like this at the beginning of his *Institutes*:

'For in the first place no man can survey himself without forthwith turning his thoughts towards the God in whom he lives and moves, because it is perfectly obvious that the endowments which we possess cannot possibly be from ourselves; nay, that our very being is nothing else than subsistence in God alone'.[1]

This root belief was not only personal but social. The meaning of justice, mercy, faithfulness, love, peace and other social norms was rooted in the character of God. It was through obedience to God that attitudes were changed.[2] The command to love one's neighbour followed on from, and was rooted in, the command to love God. The creatures needed the Creator's guidance in their social relationships, and apart from God those relationships could have no coherence.

A second basic principle followed from this and was expressed throughout the Scriptures. Because men were creatures they were not self-governing, but were subject to the norms of the Creator which governed all social relationships, including those of marriage, family, work, church and political life, and it was considered foolishness to go against the laws of one's created existence. The moral law expressed truly what it meant to live with one another, and to act outside it was to create false and destructive relationships. Here, for example is some of Luther's practical teaching:

'A man should not say "I will sell my wares as dear as I can or please", but "I will sell my wares as is right and proper". For thy selling should not be a work that is within thy own power or will, without all law and limit, as though thou wert a God, bound to no-one. But because thy selling is a work that thou performest to thy neighbour, it should be restrained within

[1] J. Calvin, *Institutes, I. i. l.*
[2] See J. Packer, *Knowing God* (Hodder and Stoughton, 1973) for an important modern exposition of this.

22

such law and conscience that thou mayest practise it without harm or injury to him.'[1]

We should notice that norms or morals were an integral part of economic, political and social understanding; they were not separated off into different compartments, as is often the case in the 20th century, but were the warp on which life was woven.[2]

The third aspect of reformed Christianity was that it was *critical* or *transcendental*. During the mediaeval period the norm for living tended to be rooted in the past. Gothic architecture ripened over a period of 400 years or more. The grip of tradition, often fairly localized, was very strong. The church, seen as the on-going repository of Christian tradition, had great authority. With the new emphasis on the Bible, this situation changed, and standards became extrinsic to society instead of intrinsic. The Bible declared God's evaluation of man and required obedience to him rather than to existing habits. The very clear explication of man's sinfulness in the Scriptures was a social critique backed by the authority of the Creator. The Puritans found no difficulty in applying the condemnations of the prophets to similar situations in their own society. Hence they developed a critique of the monarchy, aristocracy, church and other institutions and spawned groups like the Levellers and Diggers who could be called the first modern radicals. Less spectacular was the new spirit of nonconformity which set in motion unprecedented patterns of development.

Lastly, the Reformation brought with it a certain view of knowledge. This was based neither on the classical tradition which had played such an important part in the Renaissance, nor on the authority of a particular institution like the church, nor was it seen as the autonomous product of man's own thinking. Because he was a finite creature, man, it was argued, was very limited in his potential for knowledge. Further, because he was a sinner, his understanding was necessarily misguided. The only

[1] Quoted in R. H. Tawney, *Religion and the Rise of Capitalism* (Pelican, 1938), pp. 103–4.
[2] This emphasis had a long tradition in mediaeval Christian teaching, but it did not have the directness or authority that came when the Bible was made the touchstone, nor did it have the scope seen, for example, in Richard Baxter's *Directory*.

certain route to knowledge was God's revelation. The Bible held the keys to knowledge and it taught that the fear of God was the beginning of wisdom. This meant that much scholastic and traditional knowledge had to be repudiated, and Comenius, Hartlib, Bacon and others set out to do this. At the same time, because the creation was directly God's work, its study showed the glory and the power of God, and was an area of work to be encouraged. It is also probably accurate to say that there was an element of demystification in the approach of the Reformers. Biblical truths were plain and simple, and the professional mysteries of the church were wrong if they kept people from the Scriptures. Finally, knowledge was not divorced from action in the way it has subsequently become; faith included both knowledge and actions.[1]

These four points were crucial to most of the changes that we described earlier. We are not yet in a position to be critical of some of the attitudes, but undoubtedly there were weaknesses. It was a period of rapid social change in which events often preceded thought about them. We cannot look to this era for a Christian norm. Nevertheless, a Christian response did have important social, economic and political repercussions, and this perspective was coherent, and has had consequences for the structure of our society which will be developed in later chapters.

The Enlightenment

Our method is to look at social philosophies of different periods, rather than to follow events through in a strictly historical pattern, but it is worth considering whether the Enlightenment involves the complete discontinuity with the faith of the Reformation that we seem to imply. The Restoration brought a return of a monarchy sympathetic to Roman Catholicism and marked a serious setback for the ideas that had been developed by the Puritans, not only because of the Great Ejection and the imposition of uniform religious practices, but also because Nonconformists were excluded from education and politics for

---

[1] See chapter 3 for a fuller treatment of what a Christian theory of knowledge involves.

more than 100 years. It is interesting to ask to what extent the decline of the universities from the beginning of the 18th century was associated with this exclusion. The monarchy and then the landed gentry effectively defused this rather dangerous and critical Christian perspective by reshaping the church. Its patronage was carefully controlled and the church leaders tended to be subservient to those with power. Although many Christians who had grown up in the puritan context lived on into the 18th century, the religious views they held had by then been eclipsed in English, although not in Scottish, society.

At the same time an alternative faith-perspective was developing. It had its origins in groups like the Cambridge Platonists, who in the mid-17th century had reacted against puritan views of human depravity by seeing reason as an inner light that was given to man. This developed after the Restoration into deism, which was essentially a belief that the existence of God was a reasonable conclusion.

John Locke's book *The Reasonableness of Christianity* (1695) was an important strand in this development. Locke, like Pierre Bayle, was a defender of the Christian faith who at the same time made reason his final arbiter. His followers, like John Toland, put more faith in reason, and Christianity dropped out of deism. 'God' became synonymous with the 'supreme being', 'the great architect' or the 'divine mechanic'; he was assumed to have set the universe in motion, but then he retired, and could effectively be excluded from human affairs. The main characteristic of deism was its vagueness. Various clergymen and philosophers tried to develop general moral concepts which followed from a belief in the deity. Not surprisingly they concluded that virtues like benevolence were rationally valid; they also proved to be relatively without content. Although people like Pope and Voltaire continued the deist tradition for a while, it soon decayed and was replaced by a radically different philosophical perspective in which God had no part. The change was immense. Whereas beforehand man had believed that he was in a creaturely relationship with God, now he believed he was his own master. Formerly the Bible was the decisive authority, now it was man's reason. The fundamentals of the earlier faith were being challenged and replaced and it is this that constitutes the great discontinuity between this period and the previous one.[1]

At this stage, it is worth considering the social background of this new perspective. The dominant group in 18th century society was the landed gentry. The division between Whig and Tory was more a question of local interests than of any fundamental political divide. The Court in Britain was unintelligibly German, and so the great landed houses held sway in Britain in a decentralized, pluralist way. However, this class did not have a *raison d'être*. It was not an established, feudally-based landed class; it had no strong links with church or state; and it was not a tightly-knit group which could make claims to nobility or greatness. On the contrary, it continually recruited from commercial and business families which were successful.

However, the landed gentry did develop a faith-perspective, even if it was in part that of self-made men. The great 18th century country houses were self-validating; they even created their own total environment through landscaping. They attested the virtue of success, which was normally based on income from rents. The place of the gentry in society was further established by offices like that of Justice of the Peace, by the extent of patronage, and by the extent to which the population at large were dependent on them. The faith-perspective of the gentry was also formed as part of a system of learning that grew up at the time. The gentry were the patrons of learning, only they could afford to buy books and employ tutors for their children. The philosophers of the era tended to be either members of the landed gentry, like Hume, or patronized by them, like Locke; many clergymen became amateur philosophers to keep their patrons up to date. In retrospect, many of the new ideas seem to have been merely a justification for the newly created establishment; many philosophers, for example, tended to see property as a natural, inalienable right. It was in this rather leisured, upper-class world that the revolution of faith took place, a change very different

[1] Peter Gay in his study, *The Enlightenment an Interpretation* (Wildwood House, 1973) accurately entitles Vol. 1 *The Rise of Modern Paganism*. See also Paul Hazard, *The European Mind, 1680–1715* (Penguin, 1963) and *European Thought in the Eighteenth Century* (Pelican, 1965), both translated by J. Lewis May, for a gripping account of the transition to the new world-view in Europe as a whole.

from that which was taking place at the same time under the Wesleys and Whitefield. 'It is monstrous', wrote the Duchess of Buckingham, 'to be told that you have a heart as sinful as the common wretches that crawl on the earth.'[1]

Another aspect of the change was its international nature. Upper class education was seen as being European. People on both sides of the Channel soon came to know of Locke, Voltaire, Hume, Diderot, Pope, Montesquieu, Johnson and Rousseau. In France, the decline of the absolutist court of Louis XIV left the salons as the main form of French society and culture, while in most other European countries elite society was still centred on the Court. Travel was easy for those with leisure and money, and it is therefore fair to claim that the new ideas generated were cosmopolitan in a way which has not been possible in a post-nationalist world.

What then was the content of this new faith? The first basic belief was in *man*. Man was the shaper of his own destiny; he had rights and freedom and was subject to no higher authority. He was his own source of meaning-coherence; he was autonomous. This basic belief was not stated explicitly; rather ideas and attitudes had a new hidden reference point which was human rather than divine. Whether it was the appeal of the American Declaration of Independence to the inalienable rights of life, liberty and the pursuit of happiness, or the new virtue seen in the motive of self-interest, the focus was man. The Enlightenment was a new age of humanism, at least among the upper classes and intelligentsia. This change from a world view centred on God to one which was centred on man was the most important change of modern history. Although in some ways it seems as though the crucial, initial transition took place during the Enlightenment, the consequences of this change are still with us today.

Secondly, there was a belief in the *goodness of man*. The puritan idea of human depravity, and even the Hobbesian view of men as brutish, belonged firmly to the 17th century. If, as Locke argued, man's mind was a *tabula rasa* at birth, how could it be claimed that original sin was a characteristic of the infant? Man must therefore be naturally good. The moralists put the argument in

[1] H. Nicolson, *The Age of Reason* (Panther, 1968), p. 499.

many forms; here, for example, is Lord Shaftesbury writing:

'On the other side, if the Affection towards private or self-good, however selfish it may be esteemed, is in reality not only consistent with public Good, but in some measure contributing to it; if it be such, perhaps, as for the good of the Species in general, every individual ought to share: 'tis so far from being ill, or blameable in any sense, that it must be acknowledged absolutely necessary to constitute a Creature good'.[1]

There were many variations of the argument, but the underlying form was always the same. If man is a law unto himself and knows no higher authority, then what he decides is right, or what is in his own self-interest must be right; therefore he must be good. The argument was circular, and it was not until the 20th century that the question was raised whether good had any meaning in this framework, but nevertheless it was compelling and was widely accepted at the time. The key words in this new morality were virtue, benevolence, self-love, happiness, self-interest, natural affections and, of course, a few years later, utility. If man was not evil, it was still necessary to explain the existence of evil, and this was done in a variety of ways. Firstly, evil was caused by ignorance and superstition, often encouraged by the church (this argument was used more in Roman Catholic countries), and the means of eradicating it was through enlightenment, the spreading of knowledge. Thus the intelligentsia saw themselves as occupying a key social role; they were the means of salvation for 18th century society. The *Encyclopédie*, published in 1776, was conceived in this spirit, and philosophers hired themselves out to rulers to make sure that despotism was 'enlightened'. A second line of argument was that the churches with their morbid fixation on sin had created chains of guilt and inhibition which prevented people from doing naturally what was best for them. It did not seem difficult to eradicate these causes of evil, and it is but a short step from this hope to a view of human progress, an optimism that all is working for the best. This element also finds a strong expression in the late 18th century world view.

However, there was a slightly more complex argument about the

---

[1] From *An Inquiry concerning Virtue or Merit* (1699) in *A Guide to the British Moralists* (Ed. D. H. Munro) (Fontana, 1972), p. 238.

origin of evil which we must also examine. If man is not evil, then his plight must be explained in terms of the conditions he lives in, the constraints that are placed upon him. The evil is externalized, and is located, to use a word from a later period, in the *system*. 'Man is born free; and everywhere he is in chains', cried Rousseau in 1762.[1] Man is not the problem, and the criticism must therefore be directed externally. This new creed found some expression in the French Revolution, but it was not until well into the 19th century that the ideology of revolution based upon this premise was fully developed. The conclusion was that, if the old system was overturned and its evils eradicated, the post-revolutionary situation had to be good.

Perhaps the most influential change in the Enlightenment was the new view of knowledge which it brought. Knowledge was seen to be very pervasive, shaping people's actions and attitudes in a way of which few were conscious. Yet there were some at this time who were more conscious. For the enlightened classes revelation no longer had much authority, and the primary key to human knowledge was seen as the human mind, 'reason', but it was by no means evident how the mind worked. Thus a serious search was started to discover how ideas were formed and on what their validity depended. The formulations of Locke and Kant and the problems discovered by Berkeley and Hume were crucial for the long-term development of rational humanism,[2] but at a more mundane level the weaknesses of faith in reason began to be evident from the contradictions of so-called rational conclusions. The rationalist tradition remained stronger in Germany (the Hegelian system even succeeded in transcending contradictions), but in Britain it was rescued from subjectivity by the concept of nature which was also basic to 18th century thought and attitudes.

As a result of Newton's work, a whole body of natural laws had been discovered. Although Newton himself saw these as the laws of the Creator, his philosophical interpreters and popularizers saw them as laws of nature. That is, the world was no longer seen as a

---

[1] J. J. Rousseau, *The Social Contract and Discourses* (Ed. G. D. H. Cole) (Everyman's Univ. Library, Dent, 1973), p. 3.
[2] See chapter 3.

creation, but as a self-governing system. What Newton was thought to have done was then made the norm for knowledge in most other areas. The assumption was that study would reveal the inherent *nature* of law, morality, the economy, the emotions and the understanding, and human *nature* would be revealed. This faith was strong. The natural parks (as opposed to the formal French ones) which were scattered across the British countryside during this era were the 'churches' of the 18th century. Later the difficulties involved in this idea became apparent, and it became transmuted into various forms such as romantic naturalism, but its importance as a framework for thought about man and society was, and is, great.

Although the Enlightenment produced a new, coherent set of ideas and attitudes, it has been argued that these ideas did not immediately permeate very deeply into British society. This was because of the Methodist revival, and because the attitudes were tied to a class which was beginning to be eclipsed by the newly emerging industrial classes. At the same time the French Revolution produced a reaction from freethinking rationalism into established forms of social organization, especially among the landed gentry, who in the 19th century could no longer be called the class of the Enlightenment. While there may be some substance in this argument, at the same time these ideas had cultural dominance and, although they were modified, it can be argued that the basic faith was transmitted to the new middle and working classes. The evangelical revival became a strong social force, but the Industrial Revolution matured in the social philosophy of the Enlightenment, and it has since become the dominant faith-perspective in our society.

The great dilemma

Before we look at that later development, it is worth pausing to consider again the crucial change that came with the humanism of the Enlightenment. Later it will be argued that many of the problems that we face in contemporary society had their roots there. If this is the case, it should now be possible to identify the problems in the social philosophy.

A summary of the social philosophy of the Reformation can be conveyed in the diagram below:

GOD

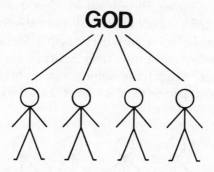

Each man's individuality rests in his relationship to, and his responsibility before, God. He is not autonomous but has identity in relation to the God who made him, an identity which is not dependent on his achievements, characteristics or the group he belongs to. At the same time, he is created to live in communion with his fellows in a whole range of relationships: family, marriage, neighbours, work and politics. Further, there are biblical laws, to which man is subject, which express what this communion should be. Thus man has both personal and communal identity. John Donne, as a Christian, can preach, 'No man is an island entire of itself; every man is a piece of the continent, a part of the main.'

However, with the Enlightenment's attempted dismissal of God the perspective changes. People become autonomous; that is, their meaning-coherence has to be found in themselves.

However, a dilemma emerges in this new situation. If each man asserts his own autonomous identity, what is the basis for community, and on what basis should people relate to one another? Who decides what norms should govern the relationship? Clearly, given the individualist starting point in which each man is his own master, there is no solution to this dilemma. On the other hand, if a collective identity and basis for community is asserted in terms of some unifying principle like race, nationhood or class, what then constitutes the identity of one individual over against another? Again this dilemma is insoluble for the unifying principle requires people to be identical. This is an over-simplified

summary of a basic dilemma which has burned through one area of modern society after another. And it is impossible to compromise between these alternatives; they are mutually exclusive. To the Christian the source of the problem is clear; it is a tension which results from the declared independence of man from God, and no resolution of the antinomy is possible until that step is reversed.

It is possible to see the dilemma working into social relationships and structures even during the 18th century. Here, for example, is the alternative that rests on the autonomous individual as expressed by the philosopher, d'Alembert. He writes:

'All questions that have to do with morals have a solution ready to hand in the hearts of each one of us, a solution which our passions sometimes prevent us from acting upon, but which they never destroy. And the solution of each particular question leads, by one or more branches, to the parent stem, and that, of course, is our own self-interest, which is the basic principle of all moral obligations.'[1]

---

[1] d'Alembert, *Eléments de la Philosophie* quoted in P. Hazard, *European Thought in the Eighteenth Century* (Pelican, 1965), p. 183.

Throughout the Reformation, selfishness had existed on a large scale, but now with the arrival of this man-centred faith it is changed from a sin into a legitimate self-interest, and is made a basis for morality.

In Britain this attitude expressed itself in the economic life of the country during the formative years of the Industrial Revolution. Mandeville in the *Fable of the Bees*, and many others, had argued that self-interest breeds communal wealth, because as everybody pursues his own ends he necessarily furthers the ends of society as a whole. This reflected attitudes which surfaced in the South Sea Bubble in 1720 and were directed to a commercial view of land tenure during the 18th century. It was further developed by Adam Smith and others into a *laissez-faire* approach to economics. In an incidental but famous comment in the *Wealth of Nations*, Adam Smith writes:

> 'As every individual, therefore, endeavours as much as he can both to employ his capital in the support of domestic industry, and so to direct that industry that its produce may be of the greatest value: every individual necessarily labours to render the annual revenue of the society as great as he can. He generally, indeed, neither intends to promote the public interest, nor knows how much he is promoting it . . . he is in this, as in many other cases, led by an invisible hand to promote an end which was no part of his intention.'[1]

Thus there was a general atmosphere which legitimized the weakening of norms and social responsibility; self-interest and lack of care received an ideological justification. Landowners accumulated more land through enclosure and made excessive profits through high war-time prices. New enterprises were developed, following the aristocratic example, with a deteriorating attitude towards the workpeople. The cruelty, neglect and lack of obligation to men, women and children which sometimes followed is too well documented to need further comment. Thus at a time when population growth, war, mobility, industrialization, and increasing complexity were creating all kinds of stresses in British society, a social philosophy was preached which

[1] Adam Smith, *The Wealth of Nations* (University Paperbacks, Methuen, 1961) Vol. I, p. 477.

destroyed the norms which were needed for communal development. New divisive patterns were set up which have characterized Britain's industrial structure ever since and have not yet been rectified. From the 1830s onwards there were attempts to correct the abuses that had grown up through economic self-interest, but permanent damage had already been done. As we see later, the British idea of an economic enterprise is still caught up in this early capitalist mould. An economic philosophy centred on the individual cannot solve communal and relational problems.

The collectivist horn of this dilemma was more evident in France during the revolutionary period. The development of this perspective was swift. The key figure was Rousseau, who lived on the edge of salon society and yet formed the ideological framework for the Revolution. In his *Social Contract* he developed the idea of a collective identity in the notion of the *general will*. He saw this as the result of an oath which all citizens would take, which goes as follows:

> 'Each of us puts his person and all his power in common under the supreme direction of the general will, and in our corporate capacity, we receive each member as an indivisible part of the whole.'[1]

As the Revolution gradually developed, the idea of the 'general will' caught hold of people's minds as an ideology which could be held up against the political absolution of the French monarchy and aristocracy. With the advent of war the collective sovereignty of the people became a more dominant idea which found its apotheosis in Robespierre. He dreamed of a legislative assembly with a gallery large enough to contain twelve thousand spectators, who would ensure that the general will was enacted in the chamber below. This rule of the people, unrealized though it was, was radically different from anything that had gone before. Here, for the first time in modern European history, the tensions of a manufactured social unity are manifest—mob rule, the extermination of minorities, the terror, the ebb and flow of people's views, manipulation of opinion, demagogy, the concentration of power and eventually the military dictatorship of

---

[1] J. J. Rousseau, *The Social Contract* (Everyman's Univ. Library, Dent, 1973), p. 13.

Napoleon. Not for the last time, the lives of individuals were treated as dispensable in the name of collective unity.

There was a recoil from the French Revolution as from the Industrial Revolution, when the problems of their philosophies became evident, but the underlying humanist faith still remained, and the dilemma we have just considered recurred in different forms throughout the 19th century.

Nineteenth century developments

The individualist and collectivist traditions of humanism developed during the 19th century, but not without Christian opposition. The Methodist and evangelical revivals shaped a wide range of responses to social issues, not just in areas like the Clapham Sect's work for the abolition of slavery,[1] but also in less dramatic areas like the development of Sunday Schools, missionary and medical work, factory reform and legislation, and colonial policy. The gathering of solid information to support proposed legislation was pioneered in the slavery campaign. The life of Shaftesbury was consumed in a pattern of practical, down to earth reform which was perhaps more effective than any subsequent approaches have been. Immediate, limited in aims and exactly locating the need, cheap but compassionate, his work oscillated between legal measures and direct action.

However, there were limits to these achievements. The first was that a majority of churchgoers cut themselves off from issues of social concern, so that Shaftesbury and others often had weak backing for what they tried to do. Secondly, the Christian reformers developed no systematic perspective on politics, economic and social life, so that their efforts came to have no long-term coherence. Their political stance tended to be that of a pressure group for one particular reform, and their loyalties were divided among the various parties, so that eventually the ideologies of those parties became definitive. Thus by the end of the century it was more accurate to talk of Anglican Tories, Nonconformist Liberals, and Methodist Socialists than it was to talk of a Christian presence in politics. All too often Christians

[1] See E. M. Howse, *Saints in Politics* (Allen and Unwin, 1971).

assimilated thought patterns and ways of living which were humanist in origin, and this further compromised their witness. Thus, although its influence was great, the extent to which a Christian perspective shaped society was limited and weakened as the century progressed.

The rival individualist tradition took a variety of forms which are worth examining. The first was the idea of individual achievement and success. With the rapid rate of change and geographical mobility in industrial society, there was a greater need for self-dependence and more isolation than in a more static society. The idea that the aim in life was achievement and success grew with this independence and with the competitive nature of economic activity. It was an era when units of capital were relatively small, and manufacturers or traders could achieve wealth in one generation through technological or organizational advances, but at the expense of others. Economic failure normally meant hardship and distress; groups like the Spitalfields silk weavers suffered intensely as the new cotton industry boomed.[1] Depending on a person's economic position, the goal in life was success, or at least survival. There were figures like Napoleon who had 'succeeded' from nothing, but normally success was defined in more immediate terms, like the style of clothes or house, or whether one had servants or land. Samuel Smiles' self-help books were written from this viewpoint. Success was self-justification, and within this framework it was easy to enjoy the praise and ignore the needs of those who had failed. Society had to be competitive; it was the natural order of things. Later in the century justification was transposed into evolutionary terms: the law of the survival of the fittest was inevitable to human progress. The idea of achievement was institutionalized into a system of status, which was reflected in clothes, houses, furniture and many other facets of life. It was not status based on a hereditary principle, although that was still some importance, but upon *worth*. We now regard it as part of the pomposity of the Victorians, for today 'success' is far more complicated.

[1] See, for example, the accounts in *Mayhew's London* (Ed. P. Quennell) (Hamlyn, 1969) and *The Unknown Mayhew* (Ed. E. P. Thompson and E. Yeo) (Pelican, 1973).

A second form of individualism was rather more theoretical. When Jeremy Bentham developed 'utilitarianism', his starting point was individual happiness, and he hoped that a rational calculus of pleasure and pain would be a universal spur to the kind of social policy that should be pursued. It is interesting that during the early decades of the 19th century, utilitarianism tended to dominate evangelical influence in many areas simply because it was an articulated social philosophy. The Benthamite aim was the greatest happiness of the greatest number, but the aim could not be realized. The subjective happiness of individuals could not be quantified and compared, without bringing in all kinds of value judgments which the 'rational' Benthamite system was supposed to avoid, and those value judgments could not but compromise the individual happiness which was the basis of the philosophical system. Sometimes the utilitarian reforms swept away a lot of traditional malpractice, but sometimes the rational calculus proved harsh and inhumane. When Chadwick, Wilson, Cameron and Coulson reformed the Poor Law on Benthamite principles in 1834, their calculations involved dealing with the lives of people in a way which was at odds with their individualist premises and this was deeply resented by the poor for generations. Although the weaknesses of the system became evident through the work of John Stuart Mill and others, the power of the utilitarian mode of thinking was tremendous, especially in the development of economic theory and practice. Throughout the 19th century the idea that consumption was a calculation of utility fermented in the economic textbooks, and gradually the idea became a social reality as consumer choice widened and advertizing developed. Although dead as a consistent philosophical system, utilitarianism has remained alive as a faith. People believe that their pleasure or satisfaction is their main aim in life and this belief is institutionalized in many different forms.

A third trend was that of romanticism. In reaction to the Enlightenment's stress on reason, there was a movement towards emphasizing the feelings or the emotions of the individual.[1] They

[1] For an analysis of the breakdown of man in his unity before God into the two warring aspects of reason and emotion see F. A. Schaeffer, *Escape from Reason* (IVF, 1968).

were the essence of a person. When his feelings identified with something, the romantic received a deep, inexplicable sense of the meaning of life. For the romantic poets the identification was with *nature*, not seen as in the 18th century, but as the trees, fields and rivers which were threatened by the new industrialism. Others found their forms of identification in the past, which resulted in developments like the Gothic revival, the Pre-Raphaelite Brotherhood, Guild Socialism and the Oxford Movement. Another identification was with other individuals in the all-encompassing emotion of *romantic love*. The Victorians expressed sentiments with a depth and length which is rarely equalled to-day, because the attitude has been echoed countless times until the sound of it is hollow.

Another important expression of romanticism was the idea of identifying with a collectivity, which might be the nation, the home-country or a particular class of people. From the time of the French Revolution onwards there were always leaders who were prepared to work on the feelings of identification to cement their own power. Palmerston was not above this ploy, but it had its weaknesses. The whole point of identifying with the object was that it excited certain feelings. The object was therefore instrumental to the feelings, and this meant that there was a danger that the individual would be caught up in subjective sentiment. It also meant that feelings were the arbiter. If a person followed the dictates of his heart, he could not be wrong; what he felt must be true. Christianity was affected by this humanist attitude. The man Jesus Christ, who cut through Jewish society proclaiming the Good News and offending many, was often romanticized into a soft meek figure of no consequence. The long-term consequences of this attitude were very serious. Firstly, it laid people open to manipulation of their emotions, whether on an interpersonal level or at the level of large-scale propaganda. Secondly, this view offers no basis for discerning between true and false emotions, so that genuine hate, anger, self-pity and lust were in principle justifiable. People's feelings were free to fly into areas which were destructive, subject only to the constraints of another form of individualism.

Moralism is an individualist perversion of Christianity. The Methodist and evangelical revivals were marked by a return to the central doctrine of Christianity, which meant an awareness of an individual's sinfulness and unworthiness before God, his need for forgiveness through faith in Jesus Christ and the help of the Holy Spirit to live a new life. As the living faith of converts gives way to conformity to a Christian pattern of behaviour, so moralism grows. It is Christian culture without Christian faith, but with humanist individualism at its heart. The moralist uses his good behaviour to buttress his own ego. The focus of his standards is man and not God. The moralist can develop into the Pharisee, confident in his own self-righteousness, and necessarily involved in judgments of other people to enhance that self-righteousness. However, it can take the less obviously unpleasant form of character building or of doing what is right. If we look at Victorian society, we see ample evidence of this attitude in various forms. One was the idea of Christian character building associated with Dr. Arnold of Rugby, which became basic to the ethos of many public schools. An important element in this was obedience to rules, as it was in the training of factory workers, and it is interesting that during this period the rules of cricket, boxing and other games were codified.

Another form of moralism was that which presented moral virtues as being the best policy for the individual. When Samuel Smiles wrote on *Thrift* in 1875, this was his theme. Victorian moralism did spill over into social judgment. One of the biggest barriers to reform and improvement was that the poor, unemployed and destitute were judged without accurate knowledge of their situation. There were many exceptions to this pattern, but it helped to give a certain moral stiffness to the era. Finally, although Victorian moral attitudes seem very rigid, it needs to be recognized that this was a symptom of their weakness. Their rules were often without a foundation, and therefore needed to be maintained by authoritarian attitudes. Thus the seeds for the 20th century retreat from moral consensus were already planted and growing. Moral norms were rooted in the individual not God or even in the 'reason' of the 18th century.

The last expression of individualism which we shall examine is political. Liberalism was a political ideology which had some links with Nonconformity and dissent, but during the first half of the 19th century the influence of utilitarianism, *laissez-faire* and free trade economic doctrines produced a new cluster of Liberal principles. They could be defined as a defence of the liberty of the individual (especially against the state), freedom of expression, and religion, trade and labour, and the principle of non-interference with the liberty of the individual where he did not interfere with the liberty of others. On the basis of these principles considerable progress was made towards freedom from political, economic, social or religious constraints.

However, this political philosophy had some weaknesses which were based on its individualistic starting point. The first was that it had no positive philosophy of the state. As a result, when all kinds of state activity were needed, Gladstone's budgets stayed at an incredibly low level of expenditure, and his main aim seems to have been the elimination of income tax. Secondly, the idea of liberty or freedom was anormative, in that what the individual wanted constituted his liberty. Since what one person did necessarily affected the lives of others in many ways, what the individual wanted often involved harm to others, and the Liberal definition of the limits of liberty tended to be inadequate to deal with issues of social injustice. In particular it could not deal with cases where the liberty of two contending persons or groups was mutually affected. Thirdly, its individual starting point tended to limit it to an atomized view of society, yet by 1900 British society was shaped mainly by corporate units and expanding institutions. An understanding of these could not easily be grafted on to classical Liberal philosophies. Thus even before Liberalism had reached the zenith of its power in the early 20th century, and while it remained the political credo of millions, its basic philosophy was constraining its response to the problems of the new century. Some, like Chamberlain, even moved out of Liberalism into imperialism and nationalism because of the barrenness of the old party ideology.

Thus we have traced the theories which, we would argue, contributed a great deal to the normal 19th century British citizen's world and life view. His economic life was in part shaped by utilitarianism and competitive individualism, his politics by Liberalism, and his social life by romanticism, achievement, status and moralism. These tenets of faith were ultimately rooted in the Enlightenment's religious commitment to man as the source of his own meaning-coherence. That they were inadequate is shown by the emergence of new collective objects of faith.

Collectivism

At first it seems rather an exaggeration to talk of people vesting their faith in the nation-state. Yet there is a strong case for arguing that nationalism was a religious commitment throughout much of Europe during the 19th century. The catalyst in this reaction was undoubtedly revolutionary and Napoleonic France, where freedom was France, but in the process other countries became nationally conscious. Italy and Germany slowly moved to unity and national identity. Britain grew proud of her industrial supremacy, and by the time of the Crimean War there was a marked contrast between the public fervour for a British victory and the way soldiers were treated as expendable. Earlier, the Opium War of 1839–42 had been a vindication of Britain's right to create opium addicts in China. National pride was evinced in another form during the Great Exhibition of 1851. Later in the century Britain's position came to be threatened by rivals, and national identity was associated much more strongly with the Empire. This competitive, patriotic imperialism was one of the major impulses behind World War I. Vague though the faith of nationalism was, insofar as it replaced reflection on the shortcomings of the nation, it allowed serious developments to take place: international exploitation, double standards and war.

Another example of a new collective identity was to be found in the churches. The Oxford Movement looked back to the time when the church was undivided and claimed the loyalty of all, and by ceremony and ritual it tried to rekindle this respect and revitalize the institution. At about the same time the Roman Catholic church, by emphasizing the doctrine of papal infallibility and by strengthening the Curia, aimed at strengthening the institution and giving it greater glory and respect. At the same time various denominations in Britain tended to emphasize their denominational loyalty. The secession of the United Methodist Free Churches in 1849 was not for doctrinal reasons, but because Methodism was so tightly held under the hand of Jabez Bunting. Denomination, or the Nonconformist/Anglican loyalty was a more important form of identification than that of being a Christian disciple.

Another collectivity which became an ideological focus was race. In 19th century Britain this was mainly expressed in a colonial context. We were the race that had built up the Empire and we also shared an inner circle racial identity with the white members of the Empire like the Canadians, Australians and South Africans. Without the assumption of racial superiority, colonial government would have been impossible. The attitude was boosted by the evolutionary ideas that followed Darwin's work. The fittest races survived in the same way as the fittest species, and the supremacy of Britain was therefore a vindication of her racial superiority. Racial identity did not have the strength in Britain that it came to have, for example, in Germany (where it was closely linked to the ideology of nationhood) but nevertheless at the turn of the century it was strongly suggested that a Teutonic alliance with Germany was the foreign policy that Britain should pursue.[1] In the United States, South Africa and many of the colonially-defined countries of the world the British pattern of racial superiority through commerce and economics was adopted and structured the subsequent development of much of the world. The violent racism that caused millions to die in the 20th century was localized compared with the more subtle British form.

Yet another form of collective identity was class-consciousness. A strong case can be made for arguing that class-consciousness developed with the landed gentry in the 18th century. For the first time in British society there was a group which had an identifiable economic situation, a national network of communication and a common culture; its members could articulate their political needs and get them implemented. At no other time has money so dominated British politics. The landed estate resulted in substantial isolation from other social groups. This cohesive group could be described as being elitist, paternalist and loyal to the Church of England; it believed in status based on wealth, stable relationships and various patterns of dependence, but its cohesion and its self-interest were divisive and induced other groups to identify their own separate economic interests. The new

[1] E. Halevy, *Imperialism and the Rise of Labour* (Benn, 1929), pp. 41–68.

industrial classes, and especially what came to be called the middle-class, began to identify their own power and self-interest. The latter tended to be against privilege; they were individualist, moralist, believed in hard work, rules, struggle, efficiency, thrift and the virtue of organizing people. Organizations were created which benefited this group at the expense of others, and rationalizations grew up which, although strongly challenged, justified the position of the middle class to the middle class and perhaps to the million or so servants whom they employed.

The growth of a working class identity during the 19th century has been thoroughly documented[1] and only a few points need to be highlighted. Firstly, this consciousness was a reaction to the prior assertiveness of the landed and middle classes. Secondly, the reaction was often dependent on the attitudes and perspective of the classes against which it was taking place. Thirdly, much working class activity was related to specific issues of injustice, so that the concept of class was not a basic ideology. However, there were some collectivist ideologies which became tied to the working class. One of these was Marxism. Marx was a romantic who identified himself with the working class to the extent that the collective group, the proletariat, was *ipso facto* right and was to be the source of identity of all of its individual members. This ideology never carried much weight in Britain. More important were various forms of socialism based upon the hope that working class expression in politics would be able to reform British society. The hopes of a political philosophy based on class are, to say the least, open to question.

However, the most important form of collectivism was not a great ideology like Marxism or imperialism. Rather, it consisted in the fact that a whole range of new institutions were growing up whose ultimate reference point was themselves. At this stage they were, of course, mainly economic, and the problems arose from the way monopoly power was used against the consumer and labour was used unfairly. Decision-making centred on the survival, growth and success of the empire, to which all else was subordinate. A major weapon in this process was the development of institutional power, which was to be used against other

[1] E. P. Thompson, *Making of the English Working Class* (Penguin, 1970).

sectors of society. We live in an era when the self-seeking and identity consciousness of institutions are so normal that we forget that their guiding philosophy could have been, and can be, wider.

These developments achieved nothing like so complete a grip on British culture as did the collectivist ideals of Germany, Russia, Italy and China in the 20th century forms of totalitarianism. Nevertheless, they did begin to contribute to a slow ideological squeezing of personhood which has continued and become expressed in a range of more acute problems in this century. The root of the problem was 18th century humanist autonomy. It has not been laid bare, and we are now structurally embedded in it up to our necks.

The twentieth century's insoluble problems

As we shall look later in detail at a range of contemporary problems, in this chapter we shall only deal with some examples of the deepening humanist dilemma. Humanism is 20th century dogma; it is the unquestioned faith of millions of people and they are hardly able to articulate their basic beliefs. For this reason few contemporary thinkers ever get outside the perspective in which the problems themselves are being nurtured.

During the 20th century the USA in particular has established a pattern of economic growth based on the creation of individual consumer demand. The pursuit of individual happiness has been encouraged through advertizing, the presentation of new goods in new ways and marketing in materialist directions. There has been a constant demand to satisfy pleasure in the form of mass media entertainment, holidays and luxury goods. The car-sprawled pattern of American city development has been shaped by the ideal of individual consumption. Wants multiply and, in satisfying them, new ones are created until people's lives are dominated by things. Hi-fi equipment and records are the extent of people's experience of music; cars are their travel, and food, drink, and drugs their pleasure. That this pattern of living is doomed because of scarce resources, pollution and basic human needs is now understood by many people, but faith in individual consumption is now as strongly rooted in Europe as it has been in the USA, and it cannot be dropped.

In another area the real significance of individualism was laid bare by the philosophical movement known as existentialism. This movement was an exploration of what followed when the autonomous existential ego was made the basis of a philosophical system. It was in effect an attempt to state consistently what the humanists of the Enlightenment had proposed, stripped of the Christian cultural clothes which had so long disguised it. Before World War II a few people began to develop these ideas, but in the postwar era existentialism constituted a faith-movement which, although centred in France, had a deep influence in Britain and other countries. The conclusions were devastating. For the autonomous existential ego there could be no stable values, no consistent right or wrong. There were no grounds for believing that the individual could communicate meaningfully, and in the end it was not even possible to have any assurance about one's own identity. For a while the creative artists in Britain and Europe faced the emptiness of this position and explored the absurd situation of the modern individual. The 'angry young men' ceased to worry about how they had been deceived by the previous generation and turned to the problems of their own. For a time they looked over the brink, but then they withdrew.[1] Meaningful communication might not be possible, but equally life is not possible without it, so by an emotive use of language you can at least convey that it might be meaningful. After a while people got over the stark honesty of existentialism and the down-to-earth British, recognizing that these problems were created when you asked such basic questions, returned to the ordinary business of living.

But things were not quite the same. A. J. P. Taylor could write of the inter-war period, 'England remained Christian in morality,

---

[1] Although the key book for humanist existentialism is probably Jean-Paul Sartre, *Being and Nothingness (Paris, 1943)*, the work of Heidegger, Jaspers, Camus and others fed into different strands of the movement. See F. H. Heinemann (who first used the term existentialism), *Existentialism and the Modern Predicament* (A. & C. Black, 1953); F. A. Schaeffer, *The God Who is There* (Hodder and Stoughton, 1968); S. U. Zuidema, *Sartre* (Presbyterian and Reformed Pub. Co., USA, 1960); J. Spier, *Christianity and Existentialism* (Presbyterian and Reformed Pub. Co., USA, 1953) and M. Esslin, *the Theatre of the Absurd* (Penguin, 1970) for further comment.

though not in faith.'[1] By the early 1960s it was evident that this shell was cracking under the pressure of the widespread, individualist viewpoint. A younger generation had caught their parents with a morality which they could not justify, because the parents were humanist in their faith even if they behaved in traditional patterns. The existentialist movement was the hammer that helped to crack the shell, and moral attitudes began to change quite rapidly. The freedom of the individual to use drugs, obtain a divorce, have an abortion, homosexual or extra-marital relationships was asserted and practised against parental and other forms of authority. Obligations and constraints were minimized and the pursuit of self-interest and rights became stronger. Professional workers went on strike, demands (whether from the trades unions or the women's liberation movement) became more strident, and the willingness of individuals to use power at the expense of others seemed greater. The position was complex and fluid, because norms were constantly being re-fashioned according to relative standards. People were unsure of what was right, and self-interest seemed to be one of the few fixed reference points. It was certain that, despite the actions of groups like the Festival of Light, moralism was dying, and that new forces would shape the norms of the next generation.

Another development was increased privatization. In our highly urbanized, closely packed, instant communication, mobile society it seems that people are becoming more and more isolated. Detached houses are self-contained except when the car issues from the drive; relationships are short-lived, superficial or means to another end, as families move around living incredibly busy lives. People together relate to an object such as a television or cinema screen, rather than to one another. Many individuals slip into loneliness because they are ignored or no longer 'useful'. School, work, shops, home, entertainment are vast empires into which the individual plugs himself for a while, but which have no personal meaning for him. But although privatization is a problem the depths of which few can assess, at the same time it is what individuals demand. Good fences make good neighbours,

[1] A. J. P. Taylor, *English History 1914–1945* (Vol. 15 of *Oxford History of England*) (Oxford Univ. Press, 1965), p. 169.

and privacy can be valued at thousands of pounds at the estate agent's.

The mass media, paradoxically, provide another example of individualization. Communication is provided on the basis of individual consumption through screen, radio, newspaper or magazine, while public meetings echo with absence and private correspondence declines. Yet is there any real communication? The existentialists and the artists who portrayed the breakdown of communication were never really answered; there was no answer from a humanist perspective. Nevertheless, the people who shaped the media found other ways of communicating at a less fundamental level. It was always possible to stir people's minds and emotions through suspense, sex, spectacle and human interest. In an era with uncertain foundations history was often drawn on by the media to provide more certain and less problematic subject matter. News provided an endless flow of events which could fill people's minds from day to day, give them ample opportunities of living vicariously as Prime Minister or football star, and prevent them from sitting back and asking what was the significance of all these events. There was another way in which communication was limited. Rarely did the recipients of programmes, films and magazines answer back; this flow was always one way, and the vast majority of the population had a passive role in the mass media forms of communication. Thus the individual is plugged into the mass media, and is condemned to be given what those responsible for producing mass communication think that he wants. Does this constitute a problem? Who can say?

In education individualism has also created deep problems. The dominant concern during the post-World War II period has been with *equality of opportunity, i.e.* that each individual should have the chance to succeed through the educational system irrespective of his home background and other conditions of his existence. Initially, this idea of individual achievement put the emphasis on competitive examinations, or academic hurdles, which not only created a generation labelled as successes or failures, but which also put a greater emphasis on the methods necessary for achievement than the content of the knowledge communicated. The great O and A level industries expanded. A later modification of this obviously inadequate view of education was to introduce *enforced equality of opportunity*. All children had to stay at school until the age of 16, and standardized schools promoted a standardized treatment of the individual, which was therefore unsuitable for important groups. Individual freedom in primary schools clashed with the rigours of individual equality of opportunity in secondary schools. The size of schools increased rapidly, so that they became remote from home and neighbourhood. In these conditions it was difficult for teachers to locate and understand children in a rounded way; they were isolated individual children. Thus in spite of the fact that money, resources, manpower and thought have been ploughed into education on a scale never seen before, many people are uneasy as the individualist ideal continues to yield its fruits.

Finally, we need to consider the part that this motive has played in politics. Twentieth century individualism is not primarily or even mainly associated with Liberalism. Rather it has affected the whole political system. In the British system tremendous emphasis has been put on the individual voter. To claim his vote a party needs to offer him what he wants in material and other terms. Increasingly the choice he faces resembles that which must be made at the supermarket between various well-packaged and presented goods. Because of this kind of appeal by the parties to the voter through the mass media, an element of unreality has crept into the British system of democracy. The choice is theatrical and over-dramatic compared with the political realities. At the same time a more dominant element in politics has been the tug-of-war between various economic and social interest groups whose aims are self-centred. At times it seems that the aim of the parties is rather to obtain power than to uphold principles. There is a feeling, encouraged by Watergate, that individual self-interest is a stronger motive than service among many politicians. The lack of a moral consensus on a whole range of issues makes solutions to political problems so much more difficult to find. Thus, although it is only part of the modern political response, individualism is opening up problems which, it seems, can only be solved by a stronger collectivist reaction.

In politics, economics and social life this faith is on the rampage. It is not just an idea which can be refuted; the refutations are all there for those who actually seek them. Rather it is a pattern of meaning-coherence in people's lives which is tenaciously rooted, even when the coherence is broken down. Yeats in his poem *The Second Coming* writes:

'Things fall apart; the centre cannot hold;
Mere anarchy is loosed upon the world.'

The 20th century has been marked in Europe by the fruition of some horrific collective ideals: the state socialism of Stalinist Russia, Hitler's Nazi Germany and Mussolini's Fascist Italy are the most obvious examples among many others. We do not know how many millions of individuals have been disposed of in the name of these collectivist ideals, but the penetration of humanist collectivism is far deeper than is suggested by looking at these extreme aberrations.

The three ideologies which dominate the modern world are class identity, racialism and nationalism. The first has become a framework of thought and faith which allows the totalitarian control of millions in China, Russia and the Eastern European countries. It is not merely a pattern for analysing iniquities and inequalities in British and other societies; rather it is a source of meaning-coherence for man and, as an ideology, it demands total allegiance. The logic of the faith includes revolution or industrial confrontation, and these therefore take place or are attempted. The human collectivity is justification for any kind of action. Racialism, similarly, is a world-wide phenomenon. Spreading from Europe through colonialism, it has taken root in the USA, South Africa and the Middle East, and has provoked the great black racialist reaction in Africa which began with negritude and continued with Amin. At the same time racialist attitudes continue to surface in social relationships throughout Europe. Nationalism, pride in national identity, was perhaps the most important ideological cause of World Wars I and II. In the post-colonial era rulers of the newly emergent nations laid hold of national identity and often made it a basis for a one party system of government. Britain's entry into the European Economic Community has aroused a considerable amount of latent nationalism, and the growth of Welsh and Scottish nationalism is no less a sign of the times. Thus these collectivist ideologies are loose in the world on a scale that continually provokes crises. They not only affect us directly or indirectly but they also have their origins quite close to home.

However, collectivism in Britain is rather more firmly established than these imprecise ideologies. One focus of it is in the socialist doctrines of the welfare state and state socialism. The faith these express is that the state, when it is controlled by the party which has the welfare of the working classes at heart, will itself control the economy and the provision of various services in a way which eliminates injustice and wrong. This is not the place for a detailed evaluation of these hopes. We are merely pointing out that state control has extended to nearly half the economy, and it includes empires of power which are not easily held to account. Yet the problem is not limited to the public sector. Throughout our society there are various institutions which constitute empires in their scale and in the independence of their identity. They may be national or multinational companies, professional groups such as doctors, lawyers, social workers, teachers, accountants or nurses, voluntary organizations like trades unions, political parties or churches, or a host of other important structures, but in all of them the possibility exists that they will take over or dominate a part of the lives of their members. For example, a company may require an employee to move or else accept demotion, a union may require a person to strike whatever he feels about the issue involved, or a professional worker may not be allowed to lower his fees although he thinks they are too high. The extent to which domination of this kind takes place is difficult to estimate, because the institutions themselves seldom make the information available and the evidence must necessarily be piecemeal. That it does take place, most people would recognize.

These macrosocial collectivities are not the only form of this kind of ideal. More immediate forms occur in interpersonal relationships. In our society people are constantly identifying with some group or other. It may be with a status group, a peer group, a consumption group, a social set, a church, or a gang. In each case it carries the idea of belonging, being 'with it', being accepted, respectable or 'in', being one of the boys or in the gang. There may be a great deal that is valuable in these groups, but insofar as they require people to identify with them and insofar as people are dependent on the group for identity, the relationship between group and individual becomes distorted and does damage in all kinds of ways. A man in the public house has spent enough, and hasn't yet given his wife the housekeeping money, but because he wants to be thought generous, he buys another round of drinks. This is one symptom of the religious dilemma of individual and collective identity which creates tensions in relationships in a whole range of situations.

There are many other ways in which this basic dilemma, and others, have grown in our society. There were grave problems in eras when Christianity was a more dominant faith, but we would argue that these were not intrinsic to the faith. The ones that we have just looked at are, on the contrary, *intrinsic* to humanism.

Chapter 2

Sociological perspectives

In chapter 1 we sketched the integral relationship between faith and social life. Now we carry the argument a step further by suggesting that sociology is also shaped by various religious viewpoints, not incidentally, but essentially and necessarily. The argument needs to be spelt out because many people would say that sociology has nothing to do with faith, and would therefore dismiss *a priori* the idea of a Christian sociology, and also because there is a lack of awareness of the religious viewpoints which have shaped sociology, which prevents them from being discussed. The fact that sociologists as varied as Comte, Marx, Durkheim, Weber and Parsons have all claimed some kind of scientific or objective status for their work while reaching vastly dissimilar conclusions should raise some questions in our minds. We shall argue that they, and other sociologists, have a perspective of society derived from the religious presuppositions which were dominant when the discipline first developed, and that these basic presuppositions are still built into the warp and woof of the academic discipline. The further and more basic issue of the non-neutrality of knowledge in the social sciences is examined in chapter 3.

The origins of sociology

During the Enlightenment social theory had a definite form. Firstly, it tended to be *a priori* and rationalistic. The theorists were characteristically philosophers who worked from first

52

principles to deduce various precepts about society. Secondly, their perspective was individualistic. Ideas like individual freedom, rights, happiness and self-interest shaped the way in which relationships were understood. Institutions were seen as relationships contracted between individuals. These views circulated in what seemed a very stable society among a class which rested on land, property and privilege, and they became out of touch with reality simply because they were so *a priori* and aristocratic.

In both Britain and France this kind of social theory was shattered by the Industrial and French Revolutions. When the rights of man were preached by Paine as well as by Locke, and when France was convulsed by warring groups who argued their case across Europe, a whole range of new issues had to be faced. What was the basis for order and national unity in a society? What changes had taken place and how had they altered things? What were the modern values? Rational individualism was bankrupt of answers to these issues, and there was a strong reaction against its pattern of thinking. Men like Malthus and Burke were far more immediate in their social and political theory, and their work was essentially problem-centred. It is no exaggeration to say that sociology (the substantive study of social relationships, not the previous social philosophizing) was born out of this reaction.

The new sociologists sought to provide an answer to these problems in terms of the religious viewpoints that were current in the early decades of the 19th century. Some, like Bonald and Le Play, worked largely within a Roman Catholic view of relationships and institutions. Others like de Tocqueville measured conditions in the USA and other countries in terms of modified traditional values. Yet others, like Marx, initially took their values from within the revolutionary framework. However, although there were these variations, the underlying new viewpoint which came to dominate within the sociological tradition was a *Humanist collectivism*. Theorists switched from the humanist belief in the autonomous individual to autonomous collectivity as the ultimate reference point. This was not difficult because, since Napoleon, the nation-state had emerged as a dominant form. In that context it was relatively easy to make 'society' the frame of reference. It needs to be emphasized, that we are not saying that sociology emerged because the social activities of men were investigated for the first time in a systematic way; rather we are highlighting the fact that it developed in a *humanist religious form*. The new assumptions were that the nature of man was essentially and ultimately social, and that society was a self-contained framework for analysing man's behaviour. No higher or other reference point was necessary. As a corollary 'society' could be seen in terms of a system, either mechanical or organic, of necessarily interrelated parts, and this reflected the naturalistic approach to knowledge that continued from the Enlightenment into this period. Such a view of the subject neither was, nor is, necessary for its development, and we shall argue that it is this religious perspective which has produced the contradictions and problems that are now evident in the discipline. Although there has been an attempt to modify and neutralize these basic humanist assumptions, sociology still operates within them, and few sociologists have been able to break away from them. As we briefly consider the positions of some of the most influential early sociologists, the new direction will become evident.

The French tradition

There were many contributors to the early development of sociology in France. We could look at the work of Bonald, Le Play, Abynaud, De Tocqueville and others to see the perspective within which they worked. However, because our main concern is with subsequent influences, we can without much loss concentrate on the conventionally important figures of Saint-Simon and Auguste Comte, who is often called the founder of sociology. Both were men of religious zeal; they were crusaders and visionaries. Here, for example, is Professor Nisbet's description of Comte's attitudes:

'Not for Comte the Enlightenment's conception of society as a collection of individuals, with institutions merely the projection of the intra-individual. Not for Comte, either, the view that Bentham and his followers made popular, of society likened to a vast arena of intersecting individual interests. For Comte society is substantive and primary; it precedes the

54

individual logically and psychologically, and it shapes him. Apart from his roles in society, man, as we know him, is not even conceivable. Carried away by his philosophical fervour, Comte makes society the 'Supreme Being' of Positivist worship. But beneath this veil of religiosity lies a penetrating view of the social sources of personality, language, morality, law and religion.[1]

This quotation is especially interesting in that it shows how Nisbet is embarrassed by the fact that Comte's position is a religious one. There is no 'veil' of religiosity. The emperor has no clothes. When Comte declared that the only real and complete religion involved the substitution of the love of humanity for the love of God and established a positivist religion complete with a priesthood and elaborate ritual, he was expressing the basis of his sociological perspective. To brush the faith under the carpet and pretend that Comte was a pioneer, neutral, social scientist is to misrepresent him. The point is that what to Comte was a matter of visionary faith has grown into the mainstream of sociology and has acquired the status of dogma.

Let us then try to state Comte's viewpoint briefly. He believed that the cultural development of man could be described roughly as a progression through the theological and metaphysical to the positivist stage, which would only arrive when the fullness of man's existence was explained scientifically. Since the ultimate meaning of man was to be found in society, positivism awaited the development of a science of society. This was the task that Comte set himself to fulfil, and it was the last crucial stage in the progress of humanity. The new positivist science, sociology, involved seeing society as a social *system* because, by analogy with the other sciences, the subject matter of sociology was characterized by its interconnectedness. The system was characterized by two aspects, the static and the dynamic, the former representing organic unity or social order, and the latter being broadly identified with human progress. When study of the social system yielded knowledge, this would lead to further progress of society.[2] A study of Comte's writings leaves no doubt that, for him, society

[1] R. A. Nisbet, *The Sociological Tradition*. (Heinemann Educational, 1970), p. 59.
[2] Faith in various theories of knowledge is discussed in chapter 3.

is autonomous, the arbiter of its own development and that which gives meaning to man.[1]

The same perspective continued to dominate French sociology and was taken up by, for example, Durkheim. The way it shaped his analysis can be seen in *Elementary Forms of Religious Life*, where he tries to give a unified explanation of the various forms of religion which are present in human societies. Although he does not reduce religion to the level of a mere social phenomenon, he does see it primarily as a totemic expression of the personality of a society.

'Thus there is something eternal in religion which is destined to survive all the particular symbols in which religious thought has successively enveloped itself. There can be no society which does not feel the need of upholding and reaffirming at regular intervals the collective sentiments and the collective ideals which make its unity and its personality.'[2]

He similarly arrived at a new view of morality.

'Society is not, then, as has often been thought, a stranger to the moral world, or something which has only secondary repercussions upon it. It is, on the contrary, the necessary condition of its existence. It is not a simple juxtaposition of individuals who bring an intrinsic morality with them, but rather man is a moral being only because he lives in society, since morality consists in being solidary with a group and varying with this solidarity.'[3]

It is easy to see that society is the ultimate frame of reference, and that this is a religious presupposition in that it shapes his perspective of the material, and in the Popperian sense that there is no evidence that could refute these interpretations of religion and morality. Again, although Durkheim claimed his own form of empirical neutrality, his perspective reveals his roots.

The metaphysical entity 'society' had become an ultimate concept in terms of which all phenomena could be explained.

[1] For a sympathetic analysis of Comte's views see R. Fletcher, *The Making of Sociology, Vol. 1 Beginnings and Foundations* (Michael Joseph, 1971) pp. 165–96.
[2] E. Durkheim, *The Elementary Forms of the Religious Life* (Trans. J. W. Swain) (Collier-Macmillian, 1961), p. 474.
[3] E. Durkheim, *The Division of Labour in Society* (Free Press, 1947), p. 399.

The British tradition

The growth of a discipline of sociology is an even more complex movement containing several different strands. One is the work done in the Scottish universities bv David Hume, Adam Ferguson, and John Millar alongside that of Adam Smith in economics. They achieved a general perspective on society through comparative studies and looked at issues like rank or class more thoroughly than had been achieved before. Another strand, often neglected, is the detailed work done by reformers like John Howard on prison conditions, the Clapham Sect on slavery, Sadler and others on factory conditions and Kay on education. This was often used as evidence in Parliament for legislative reform, and provided a pattern which was later followed by Rowntree, Booth, Bowlby and many others. It is interesting that this work, far from being neutral, was policy orientated, depended upon overt values, and involved establishing criteria by which the subject matter could be judged. For example, a definition of primary and secondary poverty or a good standard of education might be basic to the study. However, this approach, important though it has been in British public life, failed to develop into a coherent sociological perspective. Another strand is evident in the work of John Stuart Mill, struggling to move beyond utilitarianism into a social perspective. Again, no strong tradition followed from this work.

One which did survive more strongly is that which can be identified with radicalism and a critical view of capitalism. An early representative of this perspective was Robert Owen. He was not a great original thinker; many of his ideas were culled from others, but he did develop a strong critique of industrial society based upon a great deal of experience and evidence. Again, he was a man of faith and vision, expressed in his New Lanark factory and school, and in his New Harmony Community which did not succeed so well. The kind of premise from which Owen worked was made abundantly clear in his writing.

'every day will make it more and more evident THAT THE CHARACTER OF MAN IS, WITHOUT A SINGLE EX-CEPTION, ALWAYS FORMED FOR HIM: THAT IT MAY BE, AND IS, CHIEFLY CREATED BY HIS PREDE-

CESSORS; THAT THEY GIVE HIM, OR MAY GIVE HIM, HIS IDEAS AND HABITS, WHICH ARE THE POWERS THAT GOVERN AND DIRECT HIS CONDUCT. MAN, THEREFORE, NEVER DID, NOR IS IT POSSIBLE HE EVER CAN, FORM HIS OWN CHARACTER.'[1]

It is evident that Owen sees social systems as being determinative, and that he had an almost mechanistic view of society that grew out of the Newtonian world view. He was a social engineer, who had moved on from the utilitarian individualism of his Manchester days to a position of macrosocial engineering. Owen had a profound belief in the progress of society, and this introduced another element which is important to the sociological perspective of our era, that of evolution.

The first great, systematic, British sociologist was Herbert Spencer. He was discussing the idea of evolution well before Darwin wrote *The Origin of Species*, but whereas Darwin saw evolution as a theory of natural science, Spencer saw it as a universal law of development. Societies moved from incoherent uniformity, to coherent heterogeneity. This was the pattern of progress, of the growth of societies. In 19th century Britain there were all kinds of growth patterns—in population, communication networks, industrial output—which Spencer naturally responded to, but he was saying more than this in his perspective. Here, for example, is the conclusion to his *Principles of Sociology*:

'It seems that in the course of social progress, parts, more or less large, of each society, are sacrificed for the benefit of society as a whole. In the earlier stages the sacrifice takes the form of mortality in the wars perpetually carried on during the struggle for existence between tribes and nations; and in later stages the sacrifice takes the form of mortality entailed by the commercial struggle and the keen competition entailed by it.'[2]

It is clear that evolving society is the ultimate framework of Spencer's analytical thinking.

Allied with this presupposition was Spencer's concern with the organic nature of society. He used the analogy with care, and its

[1] R. Owen, *A New View of Society* (Pelican, 1970), p. 140.
[2] H. Spencer, *Principles of Sociology* (Ed. Stanislav Andreski) (Macmillan, 1969, p. 781. See also *The Evolution of Society* (Selections from Herbert Spencer's works) (Ed. Robert L. Carneiro) (University of Chicago Press, 1967).

importance was impressed upon him by the pattern of economic interdependence and specialization which industrialization exhibited. Nevertheless, at the same time the organic assumption was a necessary corollary of the evolutionary one, otherwise *what* was evolving, and to what could discrete social phenomena be related? That society as it was, and will have become, was Spencer's humanist norm is evident when we see the trends which he supported. For example, 'Complete individualization of ownership is an accompaniment of industrial progress' (*Principles*, p. 487) would not be argued too strongly now, but it is evident that it was an evolutionary norm for Spencer.

It is not difficult to see the perspective enlarged and given new direction by later British sociologists, like Hobhouse for example, who could say that 'the supreme purposes of religion and morals are to be found in the living process of evolution'[1] and could also criticize idealistic philosophy by subjecting it to a comprehensive social analysis. There are continual modifications within the perspective and contradictions begin to appear, but all the time the religious presuppositions of collective humanism shape the response.

The German tradition

In Germany, the assumptions of a humanist religious perspective took another form. Especially through the work of Hegel, the Enlightenment's faith in reason was given a social and an evolutionary dimension. Reason was not individualized in a Cartesian metaphysical sense, but ideas could be synthesized to produce new insights and the progress of a modern society was the progress of reason. The revolt of Feuerbach and Marx against this outlook is well known, but the reaction of the other German sociologists, such as Troeltsche, Weber, Burkhardt and Sombart, is rather more complex. To what extent was society shaped by ideas, and in what way could those ideas be said to be rational (spelt with even a small r)? These sociologists therefore, studied in depth the systems of ideas that were to be found in a whole range

[1] L. T. Hobhouse, *Sociology and Philosophy* (Essays introduced by Morris Ginsberg) (Bell, 1966), p. 79.

of different cultures and social situations. Judaism, Buddhism, Confucianism, Hinduism, capitalism, Lutheranism, the Renaissance, protestantism, the medieval and Roman Catholic churches all came under their scrutiny. They developed new methodological approaches for their work[1] and analysed the way in which these sets of ideas shaped the different societies which they studied.

However, the tensions of rationalism became more and more important. With the vast differences which these cultures exhibited, it was impossible to claim that they were all the product of reason, the sure guide to true knowledge of the 18th century and of Hegel. Rather, these different perspectives led to *ideologies* or ideal types; that is, the subjective product of different people's minds, which have no greater validity than that they affect social action. It was further disturbing that Weber found that all so-called rational systems seemed to contain an irrational core. Professor Eldridge writes of Weber's analysis:

'However, just as market capitalism was based on irrational foundations, so too is the bureaucratic apparatus whose permanent existence is dependent upon fully developed money economics.'[2]

In view of this it is not surprising that Weber was compelled to adopt *subjective meaning* as the basic character of social action.

'We shall speak of "action" insofar as the acting individual attaches a subjective meaning to his behaviour ...'[3]

There is a sense in which this commits Weber to a relativist position in that he cannot be critical of the meaning and ideas that are exhibited in different cultures, even though they might be contradictory, because there is no material basis of comparison. Although he believed that his business was to explain scientifically rather than to evaluate, this relativism left him with an eclectic language for analysing different cultures and also prevented him from criticizing his own society, although he suspected many of the roots of Nazism. Yet at the same time it is also a weakness of Weber's approach that his ideational emphasis excluded other

[1] See chapter 3.
[2] M. Weber, *The Interpretation of Social Reality* (Ed. J. E. T. Eldridge) (Michael Joseph, 1971), p. 67.
[3] M. Weber, *Economy and Society, Vol. I* (Bedminster Press, N.Y., 1968), p. 4.

aspects of human action from his study, even though he recognized that they were there. His categories were conceived in a rationalist framework and dominated his analysis, especially, for example, in his view of organizations.

Thus the sense in which Weber's position is humanist is different from the organic perspective of Comte, Durkheim and Spencer. It is humanist in that subjective meaning is not open to evaluation, so that in the end what people think is valid is an unchallenged building block of sociological analysis even if it is contradictory or does not seem to be true. Many sociologists have subsequently made this same root, non-critical, humanist assumption.

Marx

Marx drew elements of his thought from the German, French and English economic and sociological traditions, and was obviously rooted in post-Enlightenment humanism. He did not believe in God, did believe in man, but not in autonomous 18th century man.

> 'But the essence of man is not an abstraction inherent in each
> particular individual. The real nature of man is the totality of
> social relationships.'[1]

It is clear that Marx's commitment was also a religious one. He saw himself as a prophet, he had secular doctrines of sin and salvation, and his analysis was meant to touch all that mattered in the life of modern man. Again, we must emphasize that subsequent attempts to neutralize his analysis into acceptable sociological theories miss the point and misrepresent his perspective. He had moved on from rationalist 'truth' to humanist action to change things, and he was as much a journalist as an economist or sociologist for much of his life. In the summer of 1855 he writes of a demonstration against the Sunday Trading Bill.

> 'We witnessed the event from beginning to end and believe we
> can state without exaggeration that *yesterday in Hyde Park the
> English Revolution began*'[2]

[1] K. Marx, *Theses on Feuerbach*.
[2] K. Marx, *Surveys from Exile*: Political Writings Vol. 2 (Ed. D. Fernbach) (Penguin, 1973), p. 290.

This kind of prediction was born of hope rather than 'neutral' sociological study.

Marx's perspective meant a repudiation of the ideas of organic society and of the social system. These he saw as myths which were constructed by the dominant groups of the day to validate the social and political structures which supported them. His more historical perspective led him to focus on the typical socio-economic relationships which have structured society in different epochs. The forms of this relationship which interested him most were capitalism and the set of relationships which it embodied, and the system that he thought would succeed capitalism. The weaknesses of the market system and the process of increasingly concentrated wealth would, it was argued, polarize the classes into those who owned the means of production and those who had nothing more to sell than their labour, the proletariat. Gradually this latter group would become more cohesive, realize its common identity and, more important, would realize that the whole system of production depended on it. Moreover, the inherent weaknesses of capitalism, which Marx spent most of his later years analysing, would with time become more and more evident. Thus, inevitably, capitalism would be overthrown, and the injustices, divisions, alienations and false attitudes which accompanied it would, after a time, be eradicated.

This well-known programme was in part modified by events, but at this point we can consider the elements in the perspective which most concern us. Firstly, Marx revolted against making society the framework of his analysis; instead he made class into a similar ultimate concept. His explanatory schema was one in which all problems were in the end resolved in terms of class. Indeed it could be said that Marx's current popularity among sociologists is based on the fact that he discovered a collective basis for his theory which was outside the conventional organic one. Mainstream humanist sociology cannot be critical, because if society is its framework, it has no standard by which to criticize society. Secondly, we note that like other sociologists of the era, Marx, especially as interpreted by Engels, had to present his analysis as being scientific, realistic and pragmatic. Thirdly, he believed in his own particular form of progress or revolution, and in the eventual survival and ultimate triumph of the working class as the outcome of this progress. Fourthly, there was in addition a normative or moral element in this perspective. Marx believed that the proletariat was in the right and was exploited and alienated, while the capitalists were morally wrong. The strong implication is that if the capitalist class were eradicated, all cause of evil would be removed. Thus Marx is another apostle of humanism. The conflict between those who make collective society and those who make class their ultimate reference point is therefore rooted in the contradictions of the faith of collective humanism. It is not surprising that this radical division in sociology has continued to the present day.

Let us examine some of the conclusions that can be drawn from this brief survey of the views of society held by the dominant early sociologists. The key point is that all the sociologists had a religious commitment to humanism which was pre-theoretical and which shaped their perspective of society. The expression of humanism was that which was dominant in Europe after the Enlightenment, namely faith in collective man, progress, revolution, *etc.* That there were contradictions and different sociological starting points within this perspective has also been evident, and we have briefly discussed some of the problems associated with the ideas of society, class, culture and the other frameworks we have considered. Our arguments from this point onwards are, firstly, that these contradictions have become more and more evident as the humanist perspective has been explored, and, secondly, that there has been a continual attempt to neutralize the religious presuppositions while retaining a meaningful frame of discourse. The attempt has failed and had to fail.

The attempted neutralization of sociology

Why was this neutralization attempted? An answer can be given at a number of different levels. Firstly, the humanist faith in man's collective ability to progress and evolve was under severe strain by the end of the 19th century. That optimistic humanists like Sir Julian Huxley could still remain optimistic after World War II required great strength of will. However within sociology the problem was more the identity of the discipline. The various expressions of collective humanism developed by the early sociologists contradicted one another and gave no basis for coherent social theory. In no sense could a *discipline* of knowledge be said to exist at the beginning of this century. If sociology was to emerge as a coherent area of study it had to find a basis for its knowledge different from the substantive view of society which had failed to emerge. In chapter 3 we shall argue that the change that was made was in seeing the *method* of acquiring knowledge as the basis for true understanding, and the key issue, therefore, that emerged was how to define the epistemological basis for sociology. In part this seems to have been tied up with the status of sociological knowledge and sociologists. It was important to be able to speak with authority academically, but the only authority available early this century was that of science, objectivity and empiricism. Just at the time when the epistemological basis for empiricism was being undermined, sociologists made it the basis of the new scientific discipline of sociology.

However, although there was this change of emphasis, the content of sociology could not disappear. Analytical terms had to be used to describe and categorize society, and until the period following World War II nobody believed that these could be generated solely from within the research process. We can therefore trace the way in which the process of sterilization has been followed through in the attempt to achieve scientific sociology. Religious assumptions are buried like relatives who have discredited the family, but the ghosts will not rest.

Functionalism An obvious example of this process is the development of functionalism out of the Durkheimian tradition which we have already examined. The original belief was that society was an organic unity within which institutions and people functioned, in order to fulfil what were seen as the needs of society. Spencer's view of functionalism was different, focusing on the interdependence of specialized groups in a diversified market economy. That of Malinowski and Radcliffe-Brown was different again, pointing to the pattern of relationships existing in a closely-knit tribal unit. In other words their substantive views of what society was like were interpretations of the evidence which were open to question. But the religious fervour of these early functionalists, and the fact that people who did not share their assumptions about society would not share their interpretation led to refinement. Over the years this peculiar, indefinable entity called Society, which nobody had been able actually to identify, even though it had been given all kinds of sentient characteristics, became an embarrassing god to have in the sociological pantheon. The functionalist clothes had no emperor. As a result there were various attempts to stiffen the clothes so that they would support themselves or at least to make sure that they would fit whoever tried to wear them.

The first example of the latter response is the attempt by Parsons to construct a general, functional model applicable to all societies. The functions that need to be performed in every society are, we are told, those of pattern maintenance, integration, goal attainment and adaptation. These are needed to maintain the equilibrium of the social system. But what is equilibrium, and what is being equilibrated, and how? Parsons writes:

> 'For the population, a primary function of the social system is to create optimum situations for patterned regulation of behavioural processes through mechanisms like pleasure. This involves both giving pleasure and imposing the necessary controls on it, since evidence indicates that the pleasure mechanism, like money, easily gets out of hand. As regulator it also requires regulation.'[1]

Pleasure is therefore a mechanism for equilibrating, but who regulates: big brother, society or nobody? And what is meant by pleasure? It could include such diverse things as eating, making love, sadism, worship, acquiring fame or transcendental meditation, each with very different values underlying them. The answers that come back from these kinds of questions are always woolly, because Parsons' attempt to universalize functional theory must involve the assumption that abstract cross-cultural categories can be created. The coat must fit everyman. The mathematician would normally say that a term like $a + b + c + d + e$ could not be simplified; Parsons would say that they are all symbols. The results of this approach are either that the universalized categories have no meaning and do not communi-

---

[1] T. Parsons, An outline of the Social System in *Theories of Society* (Eds. T. Parsons, E. Shils, K. Nabgale and J. Pitts) (Free Press, 1961), p. 62.

cate or that they retain some of the metaphysics of the older functionalists, *i.e.* they support an organic, *status quo* view of society. Both of these complaints are often made.[1]

Another reformulation is to change the referent of functionalism from society to any social institution or structure like the family, the political system, the firm, the community or the educational system. The change in the functional reference point means on the one hand that the framework is no longer comprehensive, and on the other that there is a tendency to absolutize whatever becomes the new reference point. Teachers, pupils, caretakers, parents and administrators all function with reference to the educational system. Some local Education Authorities might actually behave this way, but this just underlines the folly of making a human institution the ultimate point of reference.

A further attempt to eradicate the metaphysical content has meant that functionalism is now seen not as a doctrine about society as an organic unity, but merely as a method of analysing the data, a holistic approach. This approach

> 'has tended to treat societies or social wholes as having characteristics similar to those of organic matter or organisms; it also stresses what might be called the "systematic" properties of social wholes.'[2]

This seems less ideological; it is merely a useful approach to social data which is nominalized rather than essentialized. It is, however, heuristic. However the approach is described, funtionalism as a method does not mean that basic presuppositions have been cast off. 'Society' might be replaced by 'the social system' but the latter term still shapes the analysis. However much sociologists try they will never succeed in making functionalism merely a neutral technique of analysis. It is rooted in an organic humanist perspective of society.

Conflict theory   We can similarly document the two obvious ways in which attempts have been made to divest Marx of his religious world and life view so as to make him innocuous enough

---

[1] See A. W. Gouldner, *The Coming Crisis of Western Sociology, Part II* (Heinemann Educational, 1971) for one broadside.

[2] P. S. Cohen, *Modern Social Theory* (Heinemann Educational, 1968), p. 14.

to be included in mainstream, scientific, neutral, academic sociology.

Firstly, the concept of class has been moved out of the framework in which Marx saw it, and has been used as a general explanatory tool in sociology. Everything, from eating habits to voting patterns, is explained in class terms, using the Registrar-General's or any other classification. More objective definitions of class have been developed, and the net result has been to trivialize the concept and divorce it from the context in which Marx, Weber and others set it.[1] Again, we have to recognize that class analysis without presuppositions does not exist.

A second secularized version of Marx is what is often called conflict theory. This developed as an antithetical, theoretical, movement to functionalism, and its core statement is that conflict cannot be reduced to friction within the social organism, but that it is often real to the extent that a social organism or consensus cannot be said to exist. The Marxist analysis of class gave weight to this perspective, but conflict theory tended to be empirical,[2] and the neutrality was one in which theory was seen as model-building in a language free of presuppositions. However, division, hostility, discensus, malintegration, coercion and other such value-free terms were not adequate when in-depth studies of conflict began to appear. Language was unable to straddle both sides of the conflict and the very different interpretations that each side gave to the issues. It was only logically possible for one or neither of the contradictory attitudes to be right. The sociologists had to fall off the fence and most of them fell where their hearts led them. Thus the neutral attack on non-neutral functionalism soon reverted to an avowedly value-laden attack and opened up the way for an approach to sociology with neo-Marxist perspectives. Members of this school, on the whole, hastily buried in Highgate cemetery all the claims to inevitability and an objective view of history, and concentrated on identification with the working class.

[1] For a thorough treatment of this issue see A. Giddens, *The Class Structure of the Advanced Societies* (Hutchinson Educational, 1973).

[2] See, for example, J. Rex, *Key Problems of Sociological Theory* (Routledge and Kegan Paul, 1961) especially chapters VII, VIII and IX, pp. 115–74.

Neutralized subjective meaning Another attempt to neutralize social theory developed from the tradition established
by Weber of treating subjective meaning as the basic framework
in which social actions were to be understood. If ideas were
subjective, how could any study based upon them be objective,
or claim status as sociological theory? The answer, which
was developed on the Continent within the phenomenological
perspectives of Husserl, Heidegger, Jaspers and Merleau-Ponty,
slowly filtered through from philosophy to sociology, and
was taken up by Alfred Schutz and others.[1] The central argument
is as follows: To judge ideas and attitudes as culture-bound,
subjective, and therefore in some sense wrong, is to fail to
appreciate the true nature of human experience. All experience
must be rooted in the consciousness of the subject, and the
experience must therefore be valid to the subject, otherwise he
would not have experienced things that way. What is required for
a scientific treatment of the experience is that the subjective
experience be treated as data or phenomena. If there is to be no
distortion, the full significance to the subject needs to be
recognized. The reality which the subject experiences must not be
translated into a sociological, official, establishment norm or into
any other framework which destroys the integrity of the
subjective experience.

Where does this perspective lead? Firstly, it has been valuable
in opening up the study of a whole range of subcultural life
expressions which have formerly tended to be dismissed or
labelled without careful study. Secondly, the phenomenological
approach has totally moved away from the previous pre-
eminence given to ideas as rational or as true in any *a priori* sense.
The Enlightenment's worship of reason is finally purged, and all
thoughts and experiences, whether of axioms or itches, are
reduced to the same status. Common sense is the most rational
category used. Thirdly, this approach does not involve the
concept of society, system or causality in a Weberian sense. Only
insofar as personal experience is shared or intersubjective is there

[1] A. Schutz, *Collected Papers I: The Problem of Social Reality* (Martinus
Nijhoff, The Hague, 1973); A. Schutz and T. Luckmann, *Structures of the Life
World* (Heinemann Educational, 1974); P. L. Berger and T. Luckmann, *Social
Construction of Reality: Treatise in the Sociology of Knowledge*[2] (Penguin, 1976).

any meaning to the term social, and to talk of society is to identify what are in fact different universes. There is no one system and no causality which can be isolated from personal experience.

This new perspective is, however, achieved at tremendous cost, the most obvious being that it effectively eliminates the discipline of sociology. All the sociologist can do is to bracket experience; he cannot interpret it, explain it, suggest that the experience was seen wrongly by the subject or develop a framework of analysis. The ultimate authority has to rest with the experience of the subject seen in his own terms. The perspective, although it emphasizes personal meaning without explaining it away, and although it does not assume *a priori* that sociological knowledge has a higher status, is tied to a subjectivity which does not allow systematic or critical analysis from an independent viewpoint. The sociologist becomes the tape recorder playing back the experience. Yet even this bracketing of experience does not allow the phenomenologist to be objective. The tape must be edited, the experience selected, and there must be priorities in research. Small wonder that the supposedly neutral framework has broken.

It has broken into ethnomethodology, where the concern is with practical reasoning and the immediate perspectives that individuals and groups develop to find their way around. It has also developed into the interactionist perspective and labelling theory which have as their main point that other people's (and especially official) interpretations of a person are often false to his own experience. which is special to his or her identity. Another development in the same direction is the concern with deviance and with deviant views of life which have hitherto not been taken seriously. Why, it is argued, should the judge, teacher, policeman, adult, doctor, prison officer or manager always be taken as arbiter of what the experience means. What characterizes these approaches, valuable though they have been in lifting the 'official line', is that they have espoused the subjective perspective they present. Sociology is representation with no claim to objectivity.[1] Another development which is in the same area is found in the work of Erving Goffman. Beginning in *The Presentation of Self in Everyday Life*, published in 1959, Goffman has explored human

[1] See R. Turner, *Ethnomethodology* (Penguin, 1974).

behaviour in terms of theatrical performance of the way in which people monitor their behaviour in the light of the expectations and attitudes of others. The vast and complex technical equipment which is used in ordinary social intercourse is opened up in Goffman's work, but so are some deeper metaphysical issues. Is it possible for people to be transparent in their relationships with one another? Are people's selves just the product of their interactions with other people? In this phenomenal world of images and presentation, what if anything, can be called real? These issues are opened up by the approach, but the implicit answer to these questions is that people's lives do not have meaning except in relation to other people. Life is public.[1] Phenomenology is rooted in the interpretation of social behaviour and subjective meaning, but Goffman twists this. The latter is reaction to the former. All the world's a stage, and all the men and women merely players in a more total sense than Shakespeare meant it.

Synthetic sociology   We have looked at attempts to neutralize various sociological perspectives by cutting off the pre-theoretical roots. Nevertheless, the existence of different and contradictory perspectives has been recognized in the traditions which these views have developed. However, a characteristic of much sociology is that the different traditions, which we have hardly had time to touch on, have been conglomerated. Theories have been picked up from here or there, the meanings of the terms used are ignored, and because it is assumed that the theories are neutral, they are gathered into the sociological fold. There is a synthesis of views which are just not compatible.

The sociologist most concerned in this development was Talcott Parsons. He aimed to develop sociology as a coherent body of knowledge, and to this end was prepared to synthesize the disparate views of various sociologists. The task is primarily undertaken in *The Structure of Social Action*. One of the 'verified conclusions' of this book is:

'That in the works of the four principal writers here treated

---

[1] See E. Goffman, *Stigma* (Penguin, 1970); *Relations in Public* (Penguin, 1972); *Frame Analysis* (Penguin, 1975).

(Marshall, Pareto, Durkheim, Weber) there has appeared the outline of what *in all essentials* is the *same* system of generalized social theory, the structural aspect of what has been called the voluntaristic theory of action.'[1]

This ability to combine different perspectives has been repeated in countless sociology texts, which treat them as contributions to the corpus of sociological theory. Sociological Readers, which are popular publishing forms for hungry students, also convey the same idea (although the commentary sometimes avoids this). A perspective becomes merely a useful conceptual framework for organizing data, and no integration of approach is considered necessary. One example of this attitude is conveyed in the following statement:

'The approach adopted in this text is eclectic—to present data within whichever theoretical frameworks appear most useful, and in this way to illustrate the explanatory use of theory. In general, functionalism and systems analysis is helpful at the macro-level, while the action approach and interactionism comes into its own at the micro-level.'[2]

The concept of the usefulness of theory is not easy to understand. How do sociologists judge when a theory is useful, and when theories conflict what criterion is used to weigh them? It can be argued that the mixture which the textbooks stir often curdles.[3]

If the argument of this section holds, and functionalism, conflict theory, interactionism and synthetic sociology cannot provide a neutral basis for the discipline of sociology, but have broken through into various value-laden viewpoints, then faith is not so alien to the subject as many textbooks suggest. Indeed the problem is that various sociologists with different faith-perspectives on their subject cannot communicate because the basis of their thinking has not been uncovered and brought into the discussion. There are, however, two responses which perhaps characterize the response to this situation. The first is to find some kind of integration point for the discipline in sociological method, which will be discussed in chapter 3. The second is to move into an

---

[1] T. Parsons, *The Structure of Social Action* (Free Press, 1949), pp. 719–20.
[2] S. Cotgrove, *The Science of Society*[2] (Allen and Unwin, 1972), p. 37.
[3] P. A. Sorokin has been a line critic of shallow American synthetic sociology in *Contemporary Sociological Theories, Fads and Foibles* (Harper, 1928).

avowedly radical sociology which does not disguise the faith barrier between it and the mainstream approach, but on the contrary actually articulates it. Let us therefore consider this obviously faith-based sociology.

Radical sociology

It is possible to identify various academic currents that contributed to the radical stream. The teaching of Harold Laski at the London School of Economics and Louis Althuisser at the Sorbonne are obvious examples. However, the most important characteristic of radical sociology was that it was produced by events, social crises and out of deeply felt commitment.

Moral issues faced the white American in his relations with blacks, the poor, and the Third World, and it was clear that on the whole the establishment was wrong and the underprivileged were right. At the same time, the optimism of the Eisenhower era was cracking and it was evident that the kind of society which was developing did not make sense. There was incessant talk of peace but acute international tension, and the economy seemed dependent upon armaments. The ideal of equality of opportunity seemed to lead to a rat-race and growing inequality. Affluence seemed to mean greed, meanness, isolation, waste and pollution. The so-called postwar economic miracle was based on deep divisions between management and unions and widespread patterns of exploitation of racial and economic groups and of the Third World. Love seemed to be more linked to divorce than marriage. People talked of freedom, but found themselves enslaved by money, popularity, status, pleasure and the social system. Men felt dominated by their own technology and alienated from their work. Authority was a cloak for self-interest and incompetence. Democracy seemed to obscure the areas where power and responsibility lay, and the political parties offered no real choice to the electorate. These contradictions became more and more evident, and the establishment was merely saying 'peace, peace' when so much was wrong.[1]

[1] For a thorough presentation of the issues in this development see O. Guinness, *The Dust of Death* (IVP, 1973) and N. Birnbaum, *Towards a Critical Sociology* (Oxford Univ. Press, New York, 1972).

As a result, the new sociologists saw themselves in a prophetic role. If their society was sick, they had a key position, because it was their task to uncover the basic causes of all the sickness. However, they realized that what was wrong could not be uncovered in bits and pieces, because the wrongs so interacted with each other that there was no area which could remain uncontaminated. Thus the need was for a radical, critical view which brought sociologists who held it into confrontation with the establishment sociologists who saw all social problems in terms of malfunction rather than as a morbid condition. These two metaphysical positions could not possibly meet on any neutral grounds of evidence, and they polarized the discipline. The main radical attack on the establishment position was through a sociology of sociologists, showing how the discipline was tied to its own sub-culture and social position. The rulers were relativized, and the way was open for a new approach.[1]

But if a critical view is to carry any weight, it needs a positive basis. An analyst diagnosing what is wrong, whether he is doctor or sociologist, must do it from an understanding of what is right. Without such a positive basis, the criticism cannot in the end be constructive and real, but must remain part of the conflict and destruction which it analyses. This can be illustrated from Herbert Marcuse's *One Dimensional Man* probably the most influential radical critique of the 1960s. Marcuse writes of his critical approach at the end of the book:

'The critical theory of society possesses no concepts which could bridge the gap between the present and the future: holding no promise and showing no success it remains negative. Thus it wants to remain loyal to those who, without hope, have given and give their life to the Great Refusal.'[2]

The criticism has no positive basis. There is no way in which he, or other radical sociologists, can be outside or transcend the situation. Humanist man cannot pull himself up by his own bootstraps. Marcuse realized that he could do no more than say

[1] I. L. Horowitz (Ed.), *The New Sociology* (Oxford Univ. Press, New York, 1964); A. W. Gouldner, *The Coming Crisis of Western Sociology* (Heinemann Educational, 1971).

[2] H. Marcuse, *One Dimensional Man*. (Sphere, 1972), p. 201.

'It is wrong' and participate in the 'Great Refusal'.[1] When man is the arbiter, what basis is there for criticizing that arbiter? Can a radical critique ever have an adequate positive basis?

Yet there are signs that this is beginning to happen. The criticism that Illich and others have mounted against various institutions of the West has a basis in Roman Catholicism and in the Third World, and it highlights something to which the whole radical movement has been straining. When Christ proclaimed that the poor in spirit, those who mourn, the meek, those who hunger for righteousness, the peacemakers, the persecuted were blessed, he was declaring truths that optimistic humanism could never absorb, because pride in man will not break into humility before God. But that pride has been battered and there are now some who find faith in man a played out theme.

[1] It is worth noting that where there is a positive basis for Marcuse's analysis, it is a return to the ideals of the Enlightenment, *e.g.* p. 20 'The individual would be free to exert autonomy over a life that would be his own.'

Chapter 3

What kind of knowledge?

We have suggested that sociology, because of its origins, has incorporated perspectives on society which are basically religious, but many will still feel that the case is not proven. It may be that the early sociologists had a faith behind their social analysis. It may be that a sociology of sociologists shows them to be culture-bound, and therefore tied to a certain perspective. It may be that theory at present is still unable to break completely free from ideological presuppositions. But this does not mean, they will argue, that sociology cannot develop an independent body of knowledge which has nothing to do with religious values and which can be tested by well established criteria. It can become a science in its own right, even if it has not yet fully made the transition. Is this hope justified? Clearly, we cannot answer this question without examining in detail the theories of knowledge which this and other views of sociology represent. What kind of knowledge do we expect from sociology? Many expectations exist, and a whole range of words is used like scientific, objective, value-free, empirical, logical or statistical, which give a certain status to the knowledge they describe. They are haloes which confer sanctity, authority and sometimes infallibility to the corpus of knowledge above which they sit. But is the status justified? This attitude leads to the standard response to Christian sociology, that it is 'just concerned with faith and religion and has nothing to do with scientific sociology'. Yet we have already seen that this response is less firmly based than many think, so we need to ask whether the claim that these words make is justified. Are we sure that current research and analysis produce the right kind of knowledge? And on what basis is it established?

The approach adopted in this chapter is a rather roundabout one. The aim is not to prove that Christian sociology is 'scientific'. That would not be very helpful, since, as we shall see, the idea of scientific sociology is littered with problems which have to be faced. Instead, we shall look at the weaknesses in the various views of what natural science and social science are, and look at a Christian restatement of the concept of science. The argument is that the very idea of science initially depended on a Christian religious perspective, and that when it was extricated from this parent tree of knowledge, it developed contradictions and problems which led the philosophy of the natural sciences into serious difficulties. Thus the idea of 'science', as often conceived, has become suspect because it has lost its Christian foundations. We shall then consider how sociology has borrowed its views of scientific knowledge from the natural sciences, normally just before they become obsolete, and has thereby imported a whole range of problems into the discipline. Related issues are why sociology has such a need to be 'scientific' and why so many of its practitioners have come to have faith in sociological method. Finally we shall look at the basic fallacies underlying these concepts of science and shall look at some initial points in an alternative Christian view of knowledge.

To some readers this may seem an unduly academic and roundabout way of studying social issues, but this is not so, for much is at stake. Understanding shapes action; academic knowledge shapes policy. The kind of knowledge sought today affects the way we shall live, make decisions and relate to each other tomorrow. Furthermore, many current views are given the status of objective or scientific knowledge and are therefore unquestioned; they are the new orthodoxy, the dogma which people believe subconsciously. Yet if these views are based upon religious presuppositions which others may or may not share, it is time they were brought out into the open so that they can contend with other views, and if their weak philosophical foundations are fully exposed rather than being propped up by the sociology textbooks, they can be examined unwrapped. The issue of the underlying theory of knowledge is therefore of fundamental importance. It was just at this point that Satan tempted Eve; so we should do well not to underrate its effect.

The natural sciences and their origins

The natural sciences have developed a considerable authority over the years as a form of knowledge which is certain and which can act as a paradigm for other forms of knowledge. Sociology, as a young immature science, has always been under the shadow of this older brother, and we shall find it necessary to examine first the philosophies of the natural sciences, because they have subsequently carried weight in the social sciences. The first step is a consideration of the origins of the natural sciences, and a substantial reinterpretation of the relationship between faith and science during the period when the latter was becoming established.

There are several different theses which we shall consider. The first is that the development of science was dependent on a predominantly Christian culture as opposed, for example, to a Hindu, Muslim, Confucian or Animist religious background. The second is that in varying degrees the natural sciences developed as a movement within the Christian faith, with Christian personnel, and without that basis they would not have developed to anything like the extent that they did. The third is that a Christian perspective was necessary for this development. Related to these historical points, but not of course directly dependent on them, is the claim that the Christian faith offers the only satisfactory basis for a comprehensive philosophy of science. We shall gradually try to substantiate this claim in a variety of ways throughout the chapter.

Christian culture and science Despite attempts by various scholars to establish the existence of scientific traditions in other cultures like the Chinese, Indian and African, there is little doubt that the Western European scientific tradition of the 16th and especially the 17th centuries was unique.[1] It achieved an

---

[1] See for example J. Needham (Ed.) *Science and Civilization in China* Vols. I–V (Cambridge Univ. Press, 1954–1976) for a contrary view.

understanding of different aspects of the world which was revolutionary, and it was the foundation for the technology which helped to produce another world-shattering revolution, the Industrial Revolution. It could be argued that in these other cultures the basic patterns of religious understanding were not congruent with what we call science. For example in a culture where nature is worshipped (and this would include African animist, Vedic, pre-Christian European and many other civilizations), it is impossible to examine analytically the object of worship. Similarly the relationship between man and nature is not seen in terms of control and technology, but in terms of magic.

Likewise, in cultures which are man-centred (West African and Chinese), there tends to be an anthropomorphic view of nature, and an inability to recognize relationships and order which is independent of man. Again, when there is an identification of man with nature (Upanishadic Hinduism and Buddhism), there is little possibility of the reflection on and categorization of nature which is basic to science. Further, where the god is seen in terms of the inscrutable or the fatalistic, or where the main human response involves correct behavioural patterns, there is no motive for scientific research and investigation is almost unholy. A thorough examination of all these cultures and the views of knowledge which they produce is not possible here, but a strong case could be made that the structure of their thought necessarily cramps, and historically has cramped, the growth of science.

Conversely, it is no accident that the unfolding of science occurred in Western Europe in an essentially Christian context. Belief in a creator who had made an ordered universe in harmony with man, and who required man to exercise responsible dominion over the creation, produced a predisposition to science, even though the actual pattern of development was rather complex, and involved challenging several non-Christian perspectives which were of considerable importance in Europe at that time. The first was a pattern of Aristotelian philosophy which tended to dominate much church thinking and that of many of the scholastics. It emphasised *a priori* thinking and was cut off from actual investigation of the natural world. It was also teleological in that it imputed human purposes and ideals to natural phenomena. Another perspective was Platonic or

Pythagorean in that phenomena were seen in terms of an ideal or a numerical harmony which was thought to be the essence of the world. This tradition was especially developed by Pico and Ficino, and Kepler among others felt the tension of this approach.[1] One of its characteristics was that it led to magic not technology. However the idea of magic was a stronger force than that associated with Neoplatonism, and had roots in pre-Christian West European religion. Witchcraft, astrology, alchemy and introchemistry all represented the penetration of magic into the life and thought of people of the time. The kernel of a magical perspective is that, through various processes or rituals, man is able to manipulate nature or unlock nature's secrets, so that she will do what man wants.[2] However, the alchemists' attempts at magical manipulation of elements did not, and could not, open up chemical science. Despite these various traditions, as the basic Christian doctrines of creation took root, especially after the Reformation, the foundation was laid for the development of the natural sciences, and they gathered coherence within a Christian world and life view.

Christian faith and science   As an introduction to a consideration of this stronger thesis, it is perhaps worth beginning with the evidence of R. K. Merton. In his book, *Science, Technology and Society in Seventeenth Century England* (1938), Merton suggests that the 'golden age' of science, was strongly associated with Protestants, especially Calvinists, in the countries of Britain, Holland and Germany. In Britain, the centre of the scientific revolution, Puritans numerically dominated Gresham College, the Invisible College and the early members of the Royal Society.

'Dean Dorothy Stimson, in a recently published paper, has independently arrived at the same conclusion. She points out that of the ten men who constituted the "invisible college", in 1645, only one, Scarborough, was clearly non-Puritan. About two of the others there is some uncertainty, though Merret had

[1] See W. P. D. Wightman, *Science in a Renaissance Society* (Hutchinson Educational, 1972), pp. 141–57; A. McLean, *Humanism and the Rise of Science in Tudor England* (Heinemann Educational, 1972), pp. 112–9.

[2] The obvious place to see the conflict between a Renaissance mediated magical tradition and a Christian one is in Shakespeare's work.

a Puritan training. The others were all definitely Puritan. Moreover, among the original list of members of the Society of 1663, forty-two of the sixty-eight concerning whom information about their religious orientation is available were clearly Puritan. Considering that Puritans constituted a relatively small minority of the English population, the fact that they constituted sixty-two percent of the "initial membership of the Society becomes even more striking".[1]

This was matched by a similar movement in the Netherlands, centred on the University of Leyden, and in Germany; it has also been shown that Huguenots were much more involved in scientific work than their Roman Catholic compatriots in France, until the Revocation of the Edict of Nantes in 1685 forced them to flee. The earliest notable scientific group in France centring round Claude de Peiresc, Gassendi, Mersenne, Pascal and others was also characterized by a strong Roman Catholic faith. The evidence is, therefore, that the people who were involved in science during this period were predominantly strong, usually protestant, Christians. Merton further points out the way in which faith and science intertwine in the lives of the great scientists of the era like Boyle, Ray, Grew, Oughtred, Barrow, Napier and Newton. The last two were serious theologians. Ray, Grew, Oughtred and Barrow were clergymen, and Boyle learnt Greek, Hebrew, Syriac and Chaldee so that he could read the Scriptures in the original. However, the main point is not just that they were zealous Christians and great scientists, but that their faith motivated, shaped and gave meaning to their science.[2]

Is this claim for the central role of a Christian perspective in the development of the natural sciences fully justified? There are one or two other theses which it contradicts, and which need consideration. One is that the 17th century scientists were developing the kind of empiricism suggested by Francis Bacon in *The Advancement of Learning* and *The Great Instauration*. This

[1] R. K. Merton, *Social Theory and Social Structure* (Free Press, 1966), pp. 574–606.
[2] See also C. Webster, *The Great Instauration: Science, Medicine and Reform, 1626–1660* (Duckworth, 1975); A. Kuyper, *Lectures on Calvinism* (Eerdmans, 1931); R. Hooykaas, *Religion and the Rise of Modern Science* (Scottish Academic Press, 1972).

view tends to be dependent on Thomas Sprat's first history of the Royal Society published in 1667, which was obviously a document tailored to the Restoration, and Bacon's role would perhaps not now be considered so important as it once was. However, the crucial point is that Bacon's empiricism, incomplete as a philosophy of science though it was, contains some important Christian insights. Direct study of the creation rather than Greek or Scholastic learning is held to be the route to knowledge, and it needs to be realized that this empiricism was in a completely different framework from 18th century and subsequent humanist empiricism. Another thesis is that there were important advances made in Italy during the period concerned, and these grew out of Renaissance humanism rather than a Christian perspective. The conflict of Galileo with the Roman Catholic church highlights this viewpoint, which undoubtedly has some weight. First the tradition of science was strongest in anatomy with Vesalino, Fallopius, Fabricius, Sanctorius and Eustachio doing work which was crucial for William Harvey's great breakthrough. Yet this was a special concern within the culture, reflected as well in the art of Michelangelo, and was not part of a general philosophy of science. Similarly, although the work of Galileo Galilei was so decisive, it is evident from his writing that he found it difficult to fight his way out of the Platonic and Aristotelian dominated philosophical perspective of the time, and it was in Archimedes that he found a justification for his methods. Thus, although the Italian tradition was important, it lacked coherence, and became less significant as the 17th century advanced.

If, then, it is accepted that the puritan philosophy of science was decisive, although it is impossible of course for the evidence to be fully considered here, we could ask what the principal elements of it were. The basic *credo* was that the universe was created by God and was completely subject to his ordered control which was faithful (consistent over time) and omnipresent (universal). Science, as the study of this order, was therefore an immediate possibility. The creation was diverse (Genesis 1), and this therefore suggested a plurality of sciences rather than the reductionism that has been preached from Thales onwards. More than this, the study of the natural world opened up the glory of God's creation; it evoked a response of worship and expressed the difference between the creature and the Creator. Also, because God had created man in his own image, it was possible for man to think God's thoughts after him, to learn his language, and therefore to penetrate and understand the creation order. Again, the command given to man 'to subdue the earth and have dominion over it' meant that an active involvement with nature was man's responsibility before God. Because the creation expressed God's providence for man, it was to be expected that science would reveal much which would be useful and helpful. Another important element in this general perspective was that because everything was created, it was relative and open to explanation, and need not be assumed to be an absolute and immutable entity. Within this general perspective observation, hypothesis, paradigm, experiments, the use of instruments and classification all had a place, and the impetus to science was considerable.

There were other puritan attitudes which predisposed them to science. They were not other worldly in the monastic sense, nor did they see higher knowledge as the domain of the church. They opposed scholasticism, abstract reasoning and book learning, and also were not tied to any concept of traditional authority. Their approach to work was that it was a calling before the Lord, a *profession* in the service of God and of their fellow men, and they were therefore less concerned with status, pleasure, and promotion. They formed a community, which although subject to strains (especially from Newton) worked in a very effective way. There were also conditions of political freedom and educational freedom, especially during the Commonwealth period, which were extended in the charter given to the Royal Society. Thus, in Britain, Holland and in other countries, an ethos was created based on faith in God's faithfulness, providence and order, which prompted many men to classify, experiment and seek laws. They looked beyond what was presented to them by their senses to the creation order, and natural science was their response.

The necessity of a Christian perspective   The third argument is that a Christian perspective was necessary to science. Here we go beyond historical explanation into the structure of the natural sciences. In particular, we shall consider the philosophy which

Newton developed, and the integral part that this played in his work. This is perhaps best done by contrast with Descartes. Descartes' cosmology as developed in the *Principles of Philosophy* and *The World* was of a self-subsistent universe in which matter was ubiquitous and in continuous motion in vortices. One weakness of Descartes' system was that it was self-subsistent. Once God had made the universe, he was supposed to have retired to leave the machine to run itself. The explanations that he gave, for example, for the law of inertia, which he first accurately stated, were therefore in terms of elements within the cosmos, in this case the aether. It was a materialist conception of the universe the limitations of which were soon evident, and which later became untenable. Newton, like Boyle, was however opposed to this perspective. His view of God was much more biblical than Descartes' rationalistic one. For example, he says:

'We are, therefore, to acknowledge one God, infinite, eternal, omnipresent, omniscient, omnipotent, the Creator of all things, most wise, most just, most good, most holy. We must love him, fear him, honour him, trust in him, pray to him, give him thanks, praise him, hallow his name, obey his commandments, and set times apart for his service, as we are directed in the Third and Fourth Commandments, for this is the love of God that we keep His commandments, and his commandments are not grievous (1 Jn. 5:3). And these things we must not do to any mediators between Him and us, but to Him alone, that He may give His angels charge over us, who, being our fellow servants, are pleased with the worship which we give to their God![1]

This view of God was fundamental to his view of science. It was within the *law* of God that the *Principia* was shaped. Rupert Hall states it thus:

'When he (Newton) wrote that gravity was not innate in matter "in the sense of Epicuros" he meant that neither matter nor gravity were independent of God, who need not have created matter in the first place, or could have created matter without

---

[1] Quoted in H. S. Thayer (Ed.), *Newton's Philosophy of Nature* (Hafner Press, 1953), pp. 65–6. Newton's theology is often described as unitarian. However, this is very different from what was later known as unitarianism, and it is explicable in terms of certain philosophical problems that Newton was trying to solve.

attaching gravity and other physical forces of nature to it. He could have created an inverse-cube law had he pleased. The existence of matter and the action of its forces alike depended on the continuous exercise of the divine will so that the cause of gravity, hidden in the divine plan of things, was as inscrutable as the cause of matter. For the cause of all the fundamental properties and laws of nature was to Newton the divine purpose that willed them.'[1]

Without such a creation-based perspective, Newton's system was incredible.[2]

Another example of the same kind of issue is the process of the discovery of chemical elements. Although Boyle and others went a considerable way towards systematizing a theory of elements, it was not completed, and it is generally agreed that the discovery and explanation of oxygen was retarded over a hundred years after the work of Boyle largely because of the theory of phlogiston. Basically this grew out of the Greek doctrine of the basic elements of earth, water, fire and air. The essential view of fire and air shaped phlogiston theory, and led to the situation where the chemists Priestley and Cavendish refused to draw the conclusions which their experiments made inescapable because of their love of phlogiston. Because an element within the creation was made absolute, scientific advance was severely curtailed.

These examples show something of the importance of the creation perspective on science. God and the law of God was basic to science. To absolutize any aspect of the creation and make it a 'prime mover' rather than something which was also subject to the law of God was to cramp science, and to move away from the perspective in which it necessarily grew.

Eighteenth century immanent theories of knowledge

Seventeenth century science was a success and was seen to be a

---

[1] A. Rupert Hall, *From Galileo to Newton, 1630–1720* (Collins, 1963), p. 316.

[2] It is interesting that Newton felt bound to absolutize time and space, by identifying them with God, and thus to put immanent limits on science which were not broken until Einstein. See S. F. Mason, *Main Currents of Scientific Thought* (Routledge and Kegan Paul, 1956), pp. 162–3.

success. But the same cultural transformation that we noted in chapter 1 was also operative in the area of science, and it was hastened by some socio-political changes. After the Restoration, Nonconformists were excluded from the universities, which in the long term meant that the recruitment of scientists to the universities waned and they became largely ecclesiastical institutions. The Nonconformists, especially the Quakers, moved into applied science, set up dissenting academies, and worked on a range of technological issues which became essential prerequisites of the Industrial Revolution. However, after 1688 the social initiative passed to the landed gentry, and they became the focus of patronage and learning. Although some of them were interested in experimental science, especially on the land, there is evidence that the momentum of advance in natural science slackened, and that the emphasis moved to philosophy. The context of this philosophy needs to be remembered; it was that of a leisured elite who enjoyed discussion and voicing their opinions but who did not need to give any practical expression to their views and rarely faced problems of stress or want. David Hume puts it this way:

'I dine, I play a game of backgammon, I converse, and am merry with my friends; and when, after three or four hours amusements, I would return to these speculations, they appear so cold, and strained, and ridiculous, that I cannot find it in my heart to enter into them any further'[1]

It was in this world of speculative philosophy that these non-Christian theories of knowledge were elaborated.

The basic change that took place was that, instead of a theory of knowledge which was centred on God, the new humanists developed various theories of knowledge which were rooted in man's ability to obtain knowledge or in some aspect of the creation, and this involved a marked revolution in the view of science that was held. As we have seen, science had been essentially a derivative of Christian faith. Now, cut off from actual scientific practice and free to speculate, the philosophers reinterpreted science. The argument, fundamentally at odds with the view of Newton, Boyle and others, went roughly as follows.

[1] D. Hume, *A Treatise of Human Nature* (Dent's Everyman's Library, 1911), p. 254.

Science exhibits a successful pattern of obtaining knowledge; a theory of knowledge must therefore mirror this pattern if it is to be successful. There were important variations in the way the pattern was interpreted, but the drift was general. Faith was no longer the basis of science; instead it was vested in science. The variations included seeing Nature as a self-subsistent system, seeing human reason as the basis of knowledge and making experience the basic component of knowledge. We shall argue, firstly, that this change of focus, from God to man and some aspect of the creation, was crucial, and that it is the underlying reason why these theories of knowledge open up so many problems. Secondly, we shall look at the way in which these epistemological problems were drafted into sociology.

Nature and knowledge   As God's direct creative control of the world was less and less recognized, the metaphysical framework which was put in its place was that of nature as a self-subsistent system. The paradigm was the solar system functioning continually in the Newtonian pattern. Everything that happened could be explained, it was argued, in mechanical terms. In an era when the most quickly advancing area of natural science was mechanics, this was adopted as the structural norm for knowledge. Thus von Holbach writes in his *System of Nature*:

'In short, Nature is but an immense chain of causes and effects, which increasingly flow from each other. The motion of particular beings depends on the general motion, which is itself maintained by individual motion. This is strengthened or weakened, accelerated or retarded, simplified or complicated, procreated or destroyed, by a variety of combinations and circumstances, which every moment change the directions, the tendency, the modes of existing, and of acting, of the different beings that receive its impulse. . . . Let us, therefore, content ourselves with saying . . . that *matter always existed; that it moves by virtue of its essence; that all the phenomena of Nature are ascribable* to the diversified motion of the variety of matter she contains and which, like the phoenix, is continually regenerating out of its own ashes.'[1]

[1] Noted in D. C. Goodman (Ed.), *Science and Religious Belief, 1600–1900* (John Wright, Bristol, 1973), pp. 284–5.

It is evident that this view is a response to Newtonian physics, but is at the same time a complete contradiction of Newton's philosophy of science. It could almost be called a Cartesian interpretation of Newton. The basic concepts—cause and effect, system, materialism, essential motion and regeneration—are all completely alien to the idea of a law of creation, and they all open up problems for both the natural and the social sciences. The model had a lot of influence and continued to be important in the popular mind for a long time, although with the development of biology, organic chemistry, electromagnetism, relativity and quantum theory it was seen to be a limited model which had been stretched too far.[1] Not only this, but as a metaphysical perspective, it offered no understanding of law, order, harmony or of why man was able to understand the world he lived in.

Nevertheless, this mechanistic paradigm was imported into the social sciences, because that was what was understood as science when sociology was first developing. The pioneer of this approach was Thomas Hobbes, who was influenced by Galileo and the materialism of Gassendi; he saw science as knowledge of consequences. He expressly sets out to see the body politic as an artifact or automaton, adopting a mechanical/organic model for his study. The crucial development was that the political, economic, social *system* was a self-subsistent entity, which had its own intrinsic rules, pattern of development and essential characteristics. Hobbes saw the anatomy of *Leviathan* in terms which included Christian insights, but later studies in the social sciences were far more secular. A whole range of problems arises when this model is transposed to the social sciences. The first is that it leads to a breakdown of co-ordination among the sciences. When the nature of society, the economy, the polity, the legal system, *etc.*, are studied, each is seen as being a law unto itself with its own intrinsic characteristics, and the study of human activity breaks down into autonomous empires of knowledge. Secondly, the mechanistic idea of cause and effect was essentially impersonal, and when used as a framework of knowledge for human activity it inevitably made people pawns or ciphers of non-

[1] See Peter Gay, *The Enlightenment: An Interpretation. Vol. 2 The Science of Freedom* (Wildwood House, 1973), pp. 126–66 for the development in the idea of nature.

personal forces. For example, Montesquieu saw laws as the necessary relationships which spring from the nature of things, and consequently confronted this problem.[1] Thirdly, the metaphysical perspective effectively limited the possibility of a critical understanding. The nature of social phenomena was described in their own essential terms, and there was therefore no possibility of an external standpoint. Thus the discipline of economics developed on the assumption that the economy was a natural self-regulating system in which markets were 'mechanisms' and prices were fixed by impersonal forces. Moreover, what was natural was right, and could not be seen critically. The perspective also led to the search for essential causes to give coherence to the explanations given, re-introducing the essentialist/nominalist antinomy; it also produced a distinction between 'material' causes and spiritual or rational causes, which had been absent in the thought patterns of the Reformation. For example, Marx is party to this way of seeing things:

'In considering such transformations, the distinction should always be made between the material transformation of the economic conditions of production which can be determined with the precision of natural science, and the legal-political religious, aesthetic, or philosophic—in short, ideological forms in which men become conscious of this conflict and fight it out.'[2]

Thus we see the way in which this 18th century mechanistic, causal paradigm became influential within sociology.

However, this view does not end with the early sociologists, but is now thoroughly enmeshed in the subject. The causal framework of explanation must stay. It is basic to Weber's view of science.

'Sociology ... is a science which attempts the interpretive understanding of social action in order thereby to arrive at a causal explanation of its course and effects.'[3]

[1] See R. Aron, *Main Currents in Sociological Thought, I* (Pelican, 1968), pp. 17–62 for an explanation of the problem in Montesquieu.

[2] K. Marx, *A Contribution to the Critique of Political Economy* (Trans. N. I. Stone) (New York. 1904) preface, pp. 11–3.

[3] M. Weber, *Social and Economic Organization* (Ed. T. Parsons) (Free Press, 1964), p. 88.

Many sociologists still see explanation as a process of impersonal causal analysis, which uncovers various social forces but excludes notions like values and responsibility. Others construct their theory on the idea that society can be considered as a mechanical or logical system.[1] Others expect that the results of their research can be generalized or repeated in the manner of a physical experiment. Others develop essential explanatory terms like attraction/repulsion, and see them as central to their theory.[2] Similarly, systems of equations and variables which yield a determinate solution are seen as valid knowledge. Thus in a whole variety of ways the paradigm of autonomous nature is still persuading people into thinking that sociological knowledge is 'scientific', when it is more accurately seen as a weak, obsolete and misapplied metaphysical framework.

Empiricism   Francis Bacon stressed direct observation of the creation rather than scholastic *a priori* reasoning, and this emphasis was reflected in the practice of 17th century scientists. However, this was not empiricism, that is, reliance on the senses for knowledge. The senses said, for example, that the sun rose in the east and set in the west, and those who fought for the Copernican system therefore had to fight against empiricism as a barrier to science. It is after the great revolution in science that empiricism appeared as a philosophic rationalization. Knowledge, including scientific knowledge, was seen as being based on sense experience. Once again, this was a humanist reaction; the God–creation–man context of knowledge was contracted into the narrower view which laid the whole weight of knowledge on *man's* sense experience. The epistemology was man-centred, and it failed, especially as a basis for natural science.

The development gains coherence with John Locke, who saw ideas as impressions made by the senses on the mind. Simple ideas are built up into more complex patterns of knowledge, which are always validated by the senses. The first weakness of this view was that if offered no understanding of mathematics, which Locke studiously avoids except in the simplest terms in *An Essay*

---

[1] See T. Parsons, *The Structure of Social Action* (Free Press, 1949), pp. 6–15.
[2] G. Homans, *The Human Group* (Harcourt, Brace, N.Y., 1950).

concerning Human Understanding. Secondly, as is evident in his section on 'Of Cause and Effect, and other Relations', Locke can offer no adequate understanding of causality in terms of sense experience. Hume later exposed this weakness before returning to backgammon.

> 'Thus, not only our reason fails us in the discovery of the *ultimate connection* of causes and effects, but even after experience has informed us of their *constant conjunction*, it is impossible for us to satisfy ourselves by our reason, why we should extend that experience beyond those particular instances which have fallen under our observation.'[1]

This conclusion, which was valid given the starting point, completely undermined what was then, and is now, understood by science. One cannot see, hear or smell the law of gravity. Nevertheless, the general idea that knowledge was built from the experiences of the human senses, or 'facts', continued to dominate, even though it was such an inadequate philosophy of science.

The authority which empiricism had gathered to itself as a basis for knowledge which was independent of opinion, revelation or reason was eagerly sought by the early sociologists. Comte saw positive science as seeking statements of the ways in which facts were linked; it was the method to replace theological and metaphysical opinions. Similarly, Durkheim in *The Rules of Sociological Method* sought to establish as the method by which sociological knowledge should be furthered, the gathering of objective social facts which yield self-evident conclusions that have a neutral scientific status. In his work on *Suicide* Durkheim tried hard to work within this framework, but all kinds of interpretations necessarily enter into his analysis. The strain of this empirical framework is even more obvious in *The Elementary Forms of Religious Life*, where the theory that the totemic forms which are worshipped in a community represent society was a totally dogmatic interpretation, in that there is no factual evidence which could refute the claim that the object of worship was *really* society. Empiricism, often weakly thought out, was

[1] J. Locke, *An Essay Concerning Human Understanding* (Dent's Everyman's Library, 1946), pp. 160–2; D. Hume, *A Treatise of Human Nature* (Dent's Everyman's Library, 1911), p. 94.

thus grafted into sociology, and continues to be important. Its structure changed at the beginning of this century, as we shall see later, but the confusion that surrounds the concept is considerable, as the following quotation shows:

'I am aware that the use of the terms empirical and non-empirical to refer to entities is problematic, since many abstract, scientific concepts such as gravitation and entropy, may be considered as non-empirical in that they are not themselves observable. However, every scientist recognises, at least intuitively, that there is a difference between the status of concepts like entropy and spiritual salvation.'[1]

Empiricism based on intuition is rather shaky.

Rational knowledge For Descartes, Malebranche, Leibnitz and others the key to knowledge was human thought. Science was essentially the product of the human mind exercising itself over the phenomena in the surrounding world. This theory of knowledge is again man-centred, and finds its fullest expression in Kant's *Critique of Pure Reason*, which attempts to develop a science of how the mind constructs knowledge. This transcendental understanding of knowledge aimed to give sure enough foundations to human thought to allow the continued rational accumulation of knowledge. This rationalist tradition continued, not necessarily in the form that Kant had suggested, especially in the work of Hegel, and once again the perspective on knowledge which it embodied was taken up into sociology.

The idea that society is subject to the analysis of the human mind is not the same thing as the proposition that society is essentially a rational system of relationships. The latter may not obtain, but it is still possible for the sociologist to construct a rational framework which allows this system of relationships to be understood. In the German tradition of sociology such a rational framework became the normal method of analysis. From Tönnies' analysis of Gemeinschaft and Gesellschaft onwards, the great conceptual tools were used to demarcate, divide, categorize and analyse social behaviour. Concepts and categories were seen as having explanatory power; terms like charisma, alienation,

---

[1] P. S. Cohen, *Modern Social Theory* (Heinemann Educational, 1968), p. 75n.

bureaucracy, *etc.*, were developed and became the stock in trade of most sociologists. They are the rational tools by which society is comprehended, and most people may use them after a short apprenticeship. Again, they are regarded as a normal part of scientific theory.

This conceptual sociology has moved out of Germany. The stream of emigrants from Russia and Eastern Europe, and then later from Germany as the Nazis took control, moved to the USA and especially into the newly forming sociology departments in universities. Some Americans, like Talcott Parsons, studied the work of the rationalist sociologists in Germany, with the result that in the post-World War II era this understanding of knowledge was widespread throughout the English-speaking world. It was this migration which was largely behind the development of 'grand theory' or 'macrosociology'. The idea is that the discipline requires basic categories in terms of which social phenomena can be expressed; these rational organizers are the necessary framework for knowledge.

It is impossible to begin a detailed critique of this kind of conceptualization. It always rests at some point upon the assumption that human thought could not but come to a certain conclusion. However, this assumption is rarely justified. Concepts are often based on differentiating criteria, but there is a limitless number of criteria which could be used to define social phenomena. What makes some 'rational' and not others? Further, the assumptions that people often think are irrefutable are very much open to challenge. 'Secularization' is a widely-used concept and most people assume that it is 'the decline of religion in society'. We have argued in chapter 1 that it is the replacement of one religion by another, and at the very least this reveals that there are basic presuppositions which are at variance, and which cannot be bridged by a rationale. The assumption that an *a priori* understanding of human relationships is possible is increasingly seen as too big a claim. As the categorizations proliferate, the assumption becomes weaker, and sociologists are forced to move into a post-rationalist phase.

Thus right from the foundations of sociology the subject was committed to several widely different and inherently weak theories of knowledge. In deciding what kind of sociological knowledge to seek and how to get it, sociologists diverged widely, especially when it is recognized that within each of the epistemological traditions that we have sketched there were also important differences. Yet it can be argued that these contradictions were not as crucial as they later became.

The 20th century faith in method

During the 19th century most sociologists had a theory of knowledge *and* a view of the nature of society. The view of society, whether functionalist or Marxist, tended to be the predominant concern but, as we saw in chapter 2, this view became a rather embarrassing commitment when the aim was to be a social scientist, and consequently there was a retreat into agnosticism and neutralism. At the same time there was a need for the discipline of sociology to have a basis of coherence, which could not be found in substantive agreement about the nature of society. Consequently, around the turn of the century there was a fundamental revolution in the meaning of knowledge which sociology shared with other forms of knowledge. The new pattern of belief was that if knowledge was obtained by the right method, then it would be true knowledge. The key was *how* it was obtained. Faith was no longer rooted in a metaphysical view of the world, and so metaphysics became an obsolete subject. It followed that the coherence of sociology as a science depended upon *how* its knowledge was obtained. If the correct methods, the right rules, were applied, they would guarantee the successful march of sociological knowledge. Or, to put it another way, the crucial issue in sociology was now epistemological. The change can be represented diagrammatically. (See next page.)

(A similar change can be observed in a whole range of other areas. For example, in art, Impressionism marked a concern with how one sees and paints—Monet painted over 100 pictures of a lily pond; obviously the subject was not his main concern, but how he saw it. In theology, the emphasis moved from exegesis to hermeneutics. In literature, the method of communication was the concern of Henry James, T. S. Eliot, Ezra Pound and Virginia Woolf. In music, Debussy and others were concerned with the means of communication, which found expression in chromati-

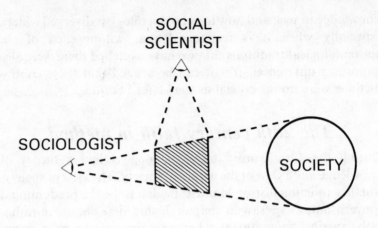

SOCIAL
SCIENTIST

SOCIOLOGIST

SOCIETY

cism and atonality. Methods of production were revolutionized. It is interesting to note where the changes occurred first, but why there was this fundamental shift around this time is difficult to understand.)

The development in the philosophy of science which corresponded to this change was the emergence of a new kind of empiricism through the work of Ludwig Wittgenstein and the Vienna Circle. These philosophers had the conviction that metaphysics was nonsense, and that science was the only means to knowledge. Further, they saw the crucial element in science as positivism, that is the building of knowledge from facts. However, the definition of propositions which were factually significant, the *method* of deciding what constituted meaningful knowledge, proved to be rather difficult. Wittgenstein in *Tractatus Logico-Philosophicus* identified the way in which meaningful propositions could be formulated about how knowledge is constructed. The Vienna Circle went further in trying to formulate a criterion for establishing the meaningfulness of any assertion. This criterion, or principle of verification, was stated by A. J. Ayer, the main British exponent of this position, in the following terms:

'We say that a sentence is factually significant to any given person if, and only if, he knows how to verify the proposition which it purports to express—that is, if he knows what observations would lead him, under certain conditions, to accept the proposition as being true, or to reject it as being false.'[1]

Once again, this is an attempt to make verification by the senses the only arbiter of what is true or false. But after many revisions and concessions, the verification principle turned out to be totally untenable for the following reasons.

An amusing if rather trivial problem was that in each of its formulations, the verification principle was self-refuting; it could not meet its own requirements as a meaningful proposition. A more substantial objection was that not only did the verification criterion exclude metaphysics, theology, *etc.*, but it also excluded what was most basic to science, namely statements of universal laws. Karl Popper's criticisms of the position have made the issue clear.

'It may appear as if the positivists, by drawing this line of demarcation, had succeeded in annihilating metaphysics more completely than the older anti-metaphysicists. However, it is not only metaphysics which is annihilated by these methods, but natural science as well. For the laws of nature are no more reducible to observation statements than metaphysical utterances.'[2]

Further, most propositions, especially scientific ones, contain terms which must be defined by universal criteria, and these cannot therefore be used within a strict positivist framework. The fact is that this view of science was wrong and obsolete; if Newton needed an apple (and that may have been an empiricist myth) it is certain that Einstein did not need one. Most areas of science at the time were moving well beyond dependence on data from the senses and methods which approximated to induction. Indeed, Heisenberg was showing that far from observation being an 'objective' method, it was necessarily part of the system under analysis. Thus, although it was not generally recognized, the various forms of logical positivism were discredited as definitions of natural scientific method.

[1] A. J. Ayer, *Language, Truth and Logic*[2] (Penguin, 1971), p. 35.
[2] K. Popper, *The Logic of Scientific Discovery* (Hutchinson, 1974), pp. 312–3. See also K. Popper, *Conjectures and Refutations* (Routledge and Kegan Paul, 1963), The Demarcation between Science and Metaphysics, pp. 253–92 for a discussion of Carnap's attempts at a criterion of demarcation. See also F. Suppe (Ed.), *The Structure of Scientific Theories* (Univ. of Illinois Press, 1974) for an account of the weaknesses of the 'received view'.

However, the popular appeal of positivism, that metaphysics was nonsense and we should concentrate on facts, was effective, and even though 'facts' had no sound basis, they became widely admired, especially in the social sciences. The transfer of positivism to the social sciences, however, raised a series of other problems which were a necessary part of this theory of knowledge, but which did not matter so much in the natural sciences. The first was the positivist conclusion that it was not possible to include within the area of meaningful knowledge any moral or ethical statements. It is impossible, it was argued, to derive what ought to be the case from what is the case (as decided by the senses). This 'is/ought' dichotomy, although it was only valid as long as the discredited positivist assumptions were accepted, was taken by many to be axiomatic as a definition of what knowledge in the social sciences was. Any kind of normative understanding was ruled out on this inadequate basis, and many textbooks began from this position. For example,

'Most philosophers would agree that we cannot derive an "ought" proposition from an "is" proposition. This is to commit what Moore called the naturalistic fallacy ... Sociology is then concerned with studying the nature of social systems, not with passing moral judgments about what it finds.'[1]

To express this position we merely need to consider that, as opposed to the sense data propositions which are the positivist court of appeal, most social behaviour is intrinsically moral. Thus, for example, to ask the question, 'Are you married?' is to raise a whole range of moral issues, although the issue is supposedly one of fact. Nevertheless, many sociologists have swallowed this dogma, and let it constrict the kind of knowledge which they think it can validly seek, on the authority of a philosophy of science discredited decades previously.

Other problems with positivism include the fact that it effectively rules out personal identity. 'The Philosophic Self', Wittgenstein tells us, 'is not the human being ... but rather the metaphysical subject, the limit of the world, not a part of it.'[2] This

[1] S. Cotgrove, *The Science of Society*[2] (Allen and Unwin, 1972), pp. 37–8.
[2] L. Wittgenstein, *Tractatus Logico–Philosophicus* (Routledge and Kegan Paul, 1961), p. 117.

makes interpersonal communication, except about verifiable propositions, also more or less impossible. As a consequence sociology has often been seen as a process of collecting hard, verifiable data. The ideal is the detached neutral observer, who does not communicate with his subjects for fear that he might bias the data he produces. Indeed some researchers have even been given strict instructions along these lines. This approach is confused in many respects. In sociology, data are not primarily sense-data, but are gathered through a system of communication involving the subject and the sociologist. For this communication to be meaningful there must be values and norms on both sides; the communication itself requires shared linguistic rules. The sociologist therefore cannot claim the position of detached observer that the positivist framework posits. Further, the *neutrality* of social facts is equally suspect when we recognize that what actually happens in a survey is as follows: the sociologist *chooses* a certain area of study, *selects* certain issues that he considers to be important, *defines* the groups that he is to study, *decides* what kind of questions to ask and how to ask them. The data are then analysed according to certain criteria that are *considered* to be important. Often answers are precoded to bring out what is *significant*. Clearly the framework of interpretation is already present, and the evidence is assessed within a perspective. Neutralism is impossible and any claim that facts are 'objective' is severely compromised. Again we see how this impersonal epistemological framework has both proved a lie in practice and also warped investigation. Many very important subjects remain untouched because they do not yield hard, quantifiable data.

Perhaps the most general expression of positivism in sociology has been the belief that, provided data were gathered in the right way and that they were reliable, knowledge was being furthered. Provided the heap was big enough, solid knowledge must emerge. The faith was in method, and all kinds of problems were therefore sublimated. Firstly, the data were normally seen as atomistic, but social behaviour is woven not granulated, and the data had therefore to be gathered together into knowledge, but how? Secondly, most sociologists had access to far more data than they could possibly understand. Thirdly, the observable data were the visible tip of the iceberg; what were all the buried non-verifiable issues? Fourthly, if the claim to be a detached observer was false, what assumptions and ways of seeing things had been illicitly introduced in the 'data' which had been collected? Even though the positivist method has had to be modified, the underlying faith that knowledge can be methodically gathered into the sociological barn is still very strong. Barns are continually being knocked down to build bigger ones.

The modified faith in method

There have been a number of restatements of the philosophy of science since the positivists, and perhaps the most important of these for the social sciences is found in the work of Karl Popper. He has a far more humble view of science in that he does not see scientific discourse as the only meaningful form of language, but allows that there are others. He also does not allow to scientific propositions the certainty that was previously attached to them; they only have the status of hypotheses which have not yet been falsified. This means that science can include the universal and general law statements which were excluded by logical positivism, and Popper therefore gives a much more satisfactory statement of scientific method, with important insights into the definition of experimental situations in the natural sciences. Indeed one could say that the idea of falsification is intimately related to the experimental method of the natural sciences; it involves making a certain scientific practice normative as the scientific method.

But what is the scope of the idea of falsifiability? It can be argued that there is much in science that cannot be directly tested; there are metatheories, presuppositions, or paradigms which form the framework within which theories are generated and terms defined. Although it may be possible to infer propositions or experimental situations which may be falsified, this need not invalidate the paradigm, since alternative inferences may be possible.[1] Falsifiability seems to assume that this larger framework is given. A further point is that different paradigms or even different theories, can generate different criteria for falsification,

---

[1] T. S. Kuhn, *The Structure of Scientific Revolutions*[2] (Univ. of Chicago Press, 1970).

so provided they are not self-refuting, there is no basis for comparison. Perhaps the essentially negative definition of falsification means that it does not say too much about what science is, but only defines how science can go on. This might not matter in the natural sciences, where it is relatively easy to delineate and test what is error, because so much is already experimentally tested, but in the social sciences the problems are rather deeper.

For example, in the social sciences the experimental method is far less powerful, for a variety of reasons. Firstly, social phenomena cannot usually be isolated, nor, since people's lives are involved, can the sociologist establish the conditions in which the process is examined. Secondly, there is no possibility of repetition. Thirdly, human knowledge of the analysis introduces a logical indeterminacy into the situation since there is always the possibility that people are reacting to the experiment and predictions of their behaviour.[1] Fourthly, since there are no universal laws like the law of gravity in sociology, falsification does not have the general significance that it does in the natural sciences. Fifthly, although atoms do not lie, human behaviour is an incredible mixture of true and false, and this makes the idea of falsification altogether more problematical than in the natural sciences. Lastly, in the human sciences the issue is one of different meanings or interpretations rather than of direct falsification. Thus we see that a range of problems arises when a definition of *the* scientific method, practically important though it is in some areas, is generalized as a method for all the sciences, including sociology.

Nevertheless, Popper does have faith in his critical method as a way to valid knowledge in most areas of life. He believes in the kind of knowledge which can be obtained by a trial and error process. In *The Open Society and Its Enemies* he attacks, through the writings of Plato, Hegel and Marx, the idea of a totalitarian utopia based upon irrefutable dogma. There is much in this attack which is valuable and justified, but the basis of his criticism is the idea of 'fallibilism'.

'By fallibilism I mean the view, or the acceptance of the fact,

---

[1] See D. M. MacKay, 'On the logical indeterminacy of a free choice', *Mind*, LXIX, 1960.

that we may err, and that the quest for certainty (or even the quest for high probability) is a mistaken quest. But this does not imply that the quest for truth is mistaken. On the contrary, the idea of error implies that of truth as the standard of which we may fall short.'[1]

Thus he believes that we shall approach more closely to truth through our understanding of error, and that this method should be universally adopted in social, economic and political policy. Again, we suggest that this faith in method may be justified in a closely defined area of natural scientific research, but not in other areas. Error is defined within a paradigm or perspective, and until that perspective is common, there is seldom agreement about what is to be falsified. The hope that the evolution of knowledge can proceed even by this open-ended method is one that involves a misplaced faith.

There is some evidence that faith in method has now come full circle. In *Against Method* Paul Feyerabend introduces two important new arguments. The first is that any scientific methodology which is not to stifle discovery must be anarchic since new discoveries are often associated with new methods. The second is that

'every methodological rule is associated with cosmological assumptions, so that using the rule we take it for granted that the assumptions are correct.'[2]

Once the point is made, it is obvious. The tests are formulated within a perspective on the world, and they implicitly validate that perspective. Nowhere is this more evident than in sociology. Consider, for example, the implications for a view of society that are involved in the following methods: a survey, a questionnaire, an opinion poll, sociometric tests, participant observation, rank correlation, the use of indices. Each method implies in a subtle way a great deal about social relationships and, not surprisingly, sociologists committed to certain views of relationships tend to favour a few methods and distrust the others. Thus the faith that many social scientists have vested in method as a route to

---

[1] K. Popper, *The Open Society and Its Enemies*. (Routledge Paperback, 1962), Vol. II, p. 375.

[2] P. Feyerabend, *Against Method* (New Left Books, 1975), p. 295.

sociological knowledge is now evaporating. It no longer offers any basis for the unity of the discipline, and once again the insistent question must be faced. What kind of knowledge should sociology seek?

Linguistic theories of knowledge

There is another important post-positivist perspective on knowledge which in some ways parallels developments in phenomenology and which is more dominant in Britain. Indeed it could be described as the dominant philosophical perspective on knowledge in Britain for several decades, although it is only slowly seeping into sociology. The movement began with Wittgenstein's break with his own earlier positivism into a radically different interpretation of the meaning of language and has since opened out into a range of different positions that we cannot hope to look at. Nevertheless there are some characteristics of the perspective that it is worth trying to sketch, because they have shaped, and will shape, the way sociological knowledge is seen.

We have seen how positivism was dogmatically attached to the idea of facts, propositions delineating states of affairs which existed in the real world and could be verified by the senses. These were the data of true knowledge, and all knowledge that could not be formed on this basis was seen as without meaning. Wittgenstein moved back from this dogmatism. 'Facts' could be seen in many different ways; they were always part of larger pictures of meaning; terms often had no strict empirical reference point; the use of language was ignored by positivism and there was obviously a whole range of different forms of discourse which were meaningful. Thus, instead of straight-jacketing knowledge, Wittgenstein allowed the great complexity and richness of ordinary experience and language to flood back in philosophy and overwhelm the tight formal structures that had been created by academic philosophers. He made language, the language of ordinary people in normal discourse, the focus of his perspective. In his *Philosophical Investigations* and other later works, Wittgenstein is engaged in an investigation into language in its ordinary use, and he comes to some conclusions about the pattern that discourse exhibits. For example, he sees that propositions have meaning only within the larger language networks, as a knight has meaning only within a game of chess. Further, these networks are complex and pluralistic, and it is more surprising that people share them than that they vary from person to person. Wittgenstein also recognized these patterns of meaning as being rooted in forms of life; they are woven into the ways in which people act and interact, so that these life circumstances often shaped the meaning of the language. It followed from this that the meaning was more in the use of the language than in an elaborate and uniform system of verification. Another crucial aspect of the use of language was the part that rules played in communication. These needed to be shared; they were complex; they varied during discourse, and if they were misinterpreted, language broke down. Wittgenstein also made the point that philosophical discourse often misses the point, because it abstracts language from the forms of life in which its meaning lies. Clearly, this is a far more open approach to what knowledge is, and opens up experience to the discipline of sociology in a way which is similar to the phenomenological impact.

It is interesting that, except in terms of what other philosophers should do, it is a very non-committal perspective;

'Philosophy may in no way interfere with the actual use of language; it can in the end only describe it. For it cannot give it any foundation either. It leaves everything as it is.'[1]

The position is described by David Pears thus:

'the whole point of answering philosophical questions in this way is that there is no discrimination against any of the modes of human thought. Each is accepted on its own terms, and justified by its own internal standards.'[2]

Why is this non-critical approach decreed? It is as if the philosopher is a person who is ordered to clean the house through and make everything neat, but he is not allowed to move objects or change the position of the furniture, for that is sacrosanct. Perhaps before we try to establish why this non-critical approach is adopted, we should do well to see how it is done.

[1] L. Wittgenstein, *Philosophical Investigations* (Trans. G. E. M. Anscombe) (Basil Blackwell, 1973), p. 49.
[2] D. Pears, *Wittgenstein* (Fontana, 1970), p. 172.

This is described by Gellner as the 'Third Person Approach' and by Pears as 'Subtle Positivism'.[1] The problem or theory of knowledge has usually been defined in terms of the relationship between man (me) and the world, and language has been either a conscious statement of this relationship (philosophy) or an unconscious one (actual knowledge). What Wittgenstein does, it is argued, is to move back from considering the issue, into the third person approach where the varying definitions of this relationship with the world are not treated as problematic, but are just seen as data which need to be tidied up. Thus epistemological problems are considered at one remove and are related to the meaning framework of those using the language. Not surprisingly, the problem of knowledge disappears, since it is not possible to have a theory of knowledge about language. It is true that Wittgenstein exemplifies problems with knowledge in many of his notes, but in principle the issue has been banished by linguistic empiricism.

When we return to the question of why this is done, it is perhaps most helpful to use Pears' assessment to illuminate the issue.

'It is Wittgenstein's later doctrine that outside human thought and speech there are no independent, objective points of support, and meaning and necessity are preserved only in the linguistic practices which embody them.'[2]

Pears describes this position as 'anthropocentrism' which is identical to the word 'humanism' that we have already used a great deal. What exactly is the form of Wittgenstein's humanism? His later philosophy does not allow him to be critical of people, their ways of life and attitudes, and the language which embodies these ways of life and attitudes. In its pluralism and tolerance, Wittgenstein's philosophy lifts ordinary people and makes them masters of their own meaning. The knowledge perspective is that of autonomous man.

The influence of this perspective on sociology is now great. Peter Winch in *The Idea of a Social Science* (Routledge and Kegan Paul, 1970) brought the idea of meaningful behaviour up against the causal/scientific conceptions of sociology, and since then

[1] E. Gellner, *Words and Things* (Pelican, 1968), p. 91f. and Pears, *ibid*, p. 173.
[2] *Ibid*, p. 168.

much sociology has both opened up the subtle and varied meaning networks in which people live and has also adopted as a norm the non-critical approach to the subjects who are studied. Their meaning and their linguistic forms are adequate to understand them, even if a little translation is needed to reach a wider audience. But are the meaning patterns of people's lives so unproblematic? Do they understand themselves and we ourselves? And is man's complacent definition of his own situation true?

A fundamental critique

We have looked at a whole variety of ways in which knowledge has been defined, and the definitions have conflicted and generated internal weaknesses which have eventually undermined the view of knowledge that was proposed. Each perspective took what seemed to be an important or key aspect of man's relation with the world, and made it the key to knowledge. The natural order, man's sense perceptions, man's reason and experimentation, were moved to a key position to define knowledge and establish once and for all how it was to be acquired. It is fair to say that all these definitions imposed restrictions on what was science or knowledge which in the end were untenable because they ruled out important areas of knowledge, and also that they proved false to what was generally understood by science. From a Christian viewpoint this pattern of failure and contradiction is understandable and even predictable. This is because the step in each case is to take some aspect of the creation, and to try to anchor knowledge in that aspect. The inevitable result of this attempt is that other aspects of the creation will be seen in a limited and twisted way, and that the identification of knowledge with one aspect will turn it into a lie, or at best a half-truth. Sociology is so enmeshed in these problems, looking at systems, causal explanations of behaviour, doing 'empirical research' and establishing its own autonomous kind of knowledge, that there is little coherence about what is seen as sociological knowledge.

But the various disciplines have developed on a large scale. They are industries producing knowledge, and every industry needs good production methods. Thus there has been continual pressure to have a method for producing knowledge in which people can put their faith. Sociology, as a rather loosely organized growth industry, has been especially under pressure in this direction. We now look on the confusion of this aim. The methods suggested, whether by positivists or Popper, do not and cannot provide an infallible method of producing knowledge. Knowledge cannot be produced like automobiles even in the best university department. Instead, throughout this great industry people are gradually being forced to recognize that (to continue our crude analogy) production methods have to be matched to the final product. One cannot make watches on a lathe. The methods imply a perspective and operate within it. This means, of course, that the tremendous momentum that has been generated within the subject by this faith in method is called in question. Nevertheless production cannot stop and the Social Science Research Council continues to invest. There must therefore be a search for a theory of knowledge which does not have such an obviously shaky foundation, and which is not so limited and restrictive.

Certainly both phenomenology and linguistic perspectives offer greater freedom. There are no constraints on the methods that can be employed, and the research can be more personal in its orientation. But what now is the coherence of the knowledge that is acquired? Is it just a process of bracketing experience and of tidying up various subcultural languages for general consumption? Is there nothing more to sociology than the opinions of the people who provide the data? Is there no possibility of a critical analysis of social behaviour? It may be the case that the problem of knowledge is effectively buried by these perspectives, but this does not solve the problem any more than the ostrich does by burying its head in the sand. The result is only that sociological knowledge is thoroughly heterodox and there is little agreement about what it is or should be. Sociology cannot be described as a discipline, let alone as a science, and the only coherence that the subject has is based on institutions, organizations and common practices.

It is possible that the way out of this dilemma involves recognition of why it has developed. It is the argument of this chapter that the false step is to move away from the Christian coherence of truth in God, and to seek a basis for knowledge in some aspect of the world. It is this step which has fractured and distorted knowledge, and all the fractured attempts at providing a secular basis for knowledge have rested on fallacy. The assumption that science and theoretical analysis were independent of a deeper religious perspective was shown to be false both in the origins and subsequent development of science. The idea that, by critical self-reflection, reason could attain an objective standpoint from which to analyse phenomena has failed the test; stating the parameters of reason could only be done from within a prior pre-theoretical religious perspective. Empiricism allowed nothing but data from the senses to be construed as knowledge but then found that the order which that data revealed and which was codified by the development of science was invalidated by its own definition of knowledge. The autonomous natural order which was assumed to be self-sustaining and systemic turned out to be both a misinterpretation of the Newtonian model and also a constraint on later science. The assumption that method is a reliable way of attaining true or even unfalsified knowledge is shown to be a localized one which is weak in the social sciences, and both phenomenological and linguistic perspectives support the patterns of knowledge of ordinary people, even when they happen to be contradictory. By contrast with this heterogeneous pattern, the rest of this chapter will be an attempt to move back into a Christian perspective on knowledge. That it is radically different from the theories of knowledge already presented will quickly be evident.

A Christian epistemology

It is probably helpful to introduce the various points made below by saying that a Christian perspective cannot be justified to a wider audience on 'rational' grounds. Indeed, one of the main points earlier in this chapter was that no 'rational' grounds exist independent of a prior religious orientation to life.[1] Thus, and this

---

[1] This point has been made far more comprehensively by H. Dooyeweerd, *A New Critique of Theoretical Thought* (Presbyterian and Reformed Pub. Co., USA, 1953) and C. Van Til, *The Defence of the Faith*[2] (Presbyterian and Reformed Pub. Co., 1963) and F. Schaeffer.

will be hard for non-Christian readers, no attempts are made to synthesize Christian and non-Christian views of knowledge. The simple fact is that a Christian perspective on truth and knowledge is cosmic in scale, and any such synthesis would be a contradiction of that perspective.

It is an incredible wrench for the modern mind to accept that the origin of all meaning in the universe is to be found with God. But this is so because he is the Creator of all things, he is the Giver of meaning to all things, and the ultimate significance or truth of anything can only be understood in relation to him. Thus everything in the creation is relative: relative first to God and then relative to the rest of creation. It is our confession that the human heart is restless until it finds its rest in God, and that 'in Him are hid all the treasures of wisdom and knowledge'. Knowledge which is isolated from God becomes a half-truth or less, because it is seen only in proximate terms. The claim is great, but the argument is that the evidence is also great; the creation is written in God's handwriting and man is made in his image. Would the figures on the canvas dispute the artist?

The nature of the creation gives us some insights into the shape of Christian knowledge. First of all, knowledge cannot be isolated or atomized, but must always be coherent, and the creation is coherently God's handiwork. Secondly, a great deal of knowledge will be relative to its situation in the creation; it will need to be placed in context and not be absolutized in any way. Thirdly, knowledge will not be autonomous or self-contained, but will always point beyond itself to God. So Swammerdam saw the glory of God revealed in the anatomy of a louse. Begone, damned neutral boring science! Fourthly, we can expect to understand God's language in the creation, whether in the forms of mathematics or the DNA code because, to use a totally inadequate expression, the creator is very articulate. Fifthly, God created the universe good, so that in many areas the creation provides us with an understanding of what good is. The natural sciences are therefore largely a response to what is good, and for that reason should be enjoyable, since what is good gives joy.

Further, the fact that man is part of the creation, is a creature, allows us insights into what his knowledge will be like. It cannot be omniscient, total or infallible, but must be relative to his

107

situation and bound by his limitations and finitude. Man as creature is culture-bound, socially bound spatially bound and logically bound, and not to recognize the creaturely limitations of knowledge is to pervert it. However, the unique position of man in creation points to some other characteristics of his knowledge. Firstly, it has a religious character, because man is created with an awareness of the meaning of the life which God has given him. Secondly, knowledge and life are intertwined as wisdom, and the former cannot be isolated from the whole of life in any rationalistic or 'objective' way. Thirdly, knowledge should be integrated in the life of man as knowledge of himself, others, the natural creation and God. It should not be disjointed: bits of life strung up on an intellectual washing-line.

Again, because the creation is diverse, with different kinds or orders of reality, we should expect knowledge of this diversity to vary. There should be no pressure to force all natural scientific knowledge into a single mould, or to require standard methods for the gathering of knowledge. Reductionist forms of knowledge and methodologies are trying to find a point of coherence within the creation and thereby distort its diversity. The pattern is much more that of a response to what is there, an openmindedness and receptivity which explore God's work, and this is very different from positivism. Science does not have to bear the onus of being the infallible route to knowledge. The power of science lies in the fact that it opens up a power-packed creation to the use of man, not in any intrinsic quality. Thus there is no reason why the human sciences should ape the natural sciences; rather they should know the freedom of response to the different aspects of the universe.[1]

Another basic point which relates to the nature of the creation is that it is controlled by law. The creative power by which God made and sustains all things has the nature of law, and all phenomena are subject to law; it is the frame of their existence. The forms in which the law or control is exercised vary, but the crucial point is that, while nothing is necessary for God, the

[1] For a statement of the full formal development of this point in the work of Hermann Dooyeweerd see J. M. Spier, *An Introduction to Christian Philosophy* (Craig Press, N.J., 1966) and L. Kalsbeek, *Contours of a Christian Philosophy* (Wedge, Toronto, 1975).

creation must be subject to God's law. This applies no less to human behaviour, although here the character of the law varies. Human behaviour is normative; that is, people are subject to norms which they can disobey even though they do not move outside them as a result. We shall look at this point in more detail in chapter 5, but the initial point is that human behaviour cannot move outside the structures of God's law and therefore cannot be seen anormatively.

These initial conclusions, that all knowledge coheres in God, that response to creation, or science, is meaningful, that man's creaturely position shapes the kind of knowledge he can attain, that the creation and therefore science is diverse, and that the creation is subject to law and normatively structured grow out of the biblical doctrine of creation. We can now look at some simple points in relation to man's sinfulness.

The first is that man's sinfulness radically affects knowledge. Because sin means alienation from God, it means that man is withdrawn from the coherence of knowledge. The way is opened up for all kinds of distortion, imbalance, fragmented areas of knowledge and false explanations. Sin means that pride focuses on human reason, or that nature is absolutized. It means that disciplines become independent citadels or that academic knowledge is unrelated to life. The blessing of the coherence of knowledge in God is lost as God withdraws his understanding and men grope in their own inadequacies. A long-term historical judgment on 20th century thought and knowledge is yet to be written, but it is likely that it will reveal more of the way in which sin has impoverished knowledge than most people to-day have an inkling of.

A second point relates especially to the human sciences, and to the view that is taken of the data or the behaviour that are studied. An empirical approach to human data has as an axiom that all behaviour should be given equal status, and theory is developed by ordering all the data of equal status into a uniform pattern. From the standpoint of the Christian doctrine of sin, however, this is a fatal false step. The crucial point is that the data are a mixture of good and evil, and unless the components in that mixture can be discerned, the behaviour cannot be understood. Unless there is a normative perspective on behaviour it is not possible to begin to discern the one from the other. Therefore, without an insight into the way sin affects human behaviour, fundamental false evaluations of human behaviour are likely to be made. If man is sinful and this affects his economic, social and political behaviour, then we are studying a conglomeration of true and false. It is unlikely that the fruit of the tree of knowledge of good and evil will be healthy.

It follows from this that a Christian perspective will be critical. That is, it will oppose the patterns of knowledge and behaviour which are perverted by sin and its effects. The stance of Moses, the Prophets, and the Apostles was just such a critical one. Their analysis of what was wrong in their societies, although they were not detailed sociological analyses, did reveal the pathological character of the relationships which were affected by sin, and they were critical in their approach. The critical stance was different from the humanist one. The latter is the pattern where one individual or group stands in judgment over another; it is intrinsically self-righteous. A biblical critical perspective has a totally different structure; it is a response to the question 'How does God judge us?' The question, if faced squarely, preempts any possibility of pride or self-righteousness. Indeed, it could be said that the kind of knowledge which results is humiliating for everybody.

A final point that follows from the biblical doctrine of sin is that knowledge is no longer self-evident. Christ and Paul point out that knowledge has been hidden from the wise. There is no natural or straightforward route to knowledge; it is not a production process, because the sinfulness of man means that his perspective on life must be distorted and false. Thus all the attempts at a straightforward approach to knowledge, whether by using reason, gathering facts or looking at the nature of man or society contain a fatal flaw. Until the distortion is recognized, there is necessarily a fundamentally unself-critical approach to knowledge. As we have already noted, the problematic character of understanding is compounded when the subject-matter is also distorted by sin. Thus, the biblical evaluation of the state of knowledge in the world, in spite of what so many think they know, is that it is darkness. The various theories of knowledge and views of society are all tainted with the vain imaginings of this world. This might be a harsh verdict, but the question is whether it will prove to be a substantial one.

We now move on to a central part of the Christian faith. If man is unable to reach knowledge independently and unaided, where is he to find help? The Christian answer is that the Bible is his guide; it is God's revelation of the central truths about himself, the creation, the nature of man and his sinfulness, and especially about the life, death and resurrection of Jesus Christ in the context of mankind's sinful, murky history. If the central coherence of knowledge is lost to man, then it is only through the revelation of God's Word and Jesus Christ that it can be recovered. Without this light on our situation, the lot of man is to become 'futile in his thinking and darkened in his senseless mind' (Rom. 1:21). In chapter 5 we shall discuss the way in which the Bible and the life of Christ are revelations to us, especially in the area of social life. At this point we just note this integral part of Christian teaching and the challenge that it makes to the contemporary patterns of intellectual life. Those who think that there is no need for this kind of help will obviously not read any further.

The final point of this chapter is one which will cause even more offence, but it is the offence that Christ himself caused when he came and died as the Saviour of the world. It would be possible to assent at various levels of intellectual sophistication to biblical teaching in a variety of areas, and yet to remain the arbiter of what is true and false, merely adjusting opinions. Yet the message of Christ is much more personally direct than that; it is that you and I are false and lost, and that he is the Way, the Truth and the Life. Unless we are prepared to admit that we cannot help ourselves or arrive at truth because we are already lost in deception and untruth, the need is not pressing. But it has been argued, 'if we say we have no sin, we deceive ourselves and the truth is not in us' (1 Jn. 1:8). If that is granted then our need of a renewed central, true relationship with God through Christ's love and sacrifice for us begins to be the answer to the key issue in the problem of knowledge.

Chapter 4

Christian failure

The problem

Thus far we have been looking at the dominant secular views of society, sociology and knowledge; we now turn to consider why there is no coherent Christian social perspective in Britain and much of the West to-day. Why has there been such a resounding silence from Christians in this area in the 20th century? Why has the process of secularization that we have examined been the dominant one? These are embarrassing, morbid questions and perhaps those who are not Christians would prefer tactfully to avert their eyes, but they must be asked. Now that more and more people are realizing 'the need for Christian involvement' it could be that the silence of recent decades will be succeeded by a jangle of voices with little in common. Some critical self-examination is therefore needed before we go further, however painful it may be.

What is the nature of the failure? It could be measured in a variety of ways: falling church attendances, disappearing Christian attitudes, loss of authority among the churches and moral decline. As we should expect, the indicator chosen to identify the problem also often reflects the diagnosis that is being made. Later we shall be looking at social aspects of church life and problems that occur, but the issue that we face here is bigger than any of the answers which are normally given. In the Sermon on the Mount, Christ said:

'You are the salt of the earth: but if the salt has lost its taste, how shall its saltness be restored? It is no longer good for anything except to be thrown out and trodden underfoot by men' (Mt. 5:13).

This surely is secularization; it is the failure of Christians, and the nature of the failure is that the saltness, or the content of the Christian faith, has been lost. In this chapter we shall attempt to sketch this development.

Church politics

It seems to be a fairly universal law that all human weakness begins as pride.[1] Nowhere is this more evident than in the attitudes of the churches in Britain in the past. It could be argued that the New Testament says relatively little about the church; its focus is on the life, teaching, death and resurrection of Jesus, and on the subsequent growth, teaching and empowering of the Christian community. The institutional churches which are addressed by Paul and Peter, or are the subject of the pastoral letters, are essentially seen as functional to the new Christian life. They are not institutions which are self-validating, but only make sense in the context of Christ.[2] The contrast between this view of the church and the pattern that grew up in the Roman Catholic church of the 15th and 16th centuries is stark. The institution has become powerful, self-glorifying, dependent upon its own resources, greedy, asserting its own authority and interfering wherever it could. The focus was not Christ, but the church. This was reflected in the baroque style of architecture, which was developed and used, especially by the Jesuits, to enhance the glory of the church.

The flavour of this attitude can be tasted from the papal bull against Elizabeth in 1570:

'He that reigns in the highest, to whom has been given all power in heaven and earth, entrusted the government of the one Holy Catholic and Apostolic Church (outside which there is no salvation) to one man alone on the earth, namely to Peter, the

---

[1] This is the obverse of the movement in 1 Peter 5: 6–11.

[2] Perhaps church-employed theologians have given an artifically church-centred interpretation of the New Testament.

chief of the Apostles, and to Peter's successor, the Roman pontiff, in fulness of power. This one man he set up as chief over all nations and all kingdoms, to pluck up, destroy, scatter, disperse, plant and build . . . we declare the aforesaid Elizabeth a heretic and abettor of heretics, and those that cleave to her in the aforesaid matters to have incurred the sentence of anathema . . . Moreover, we declare her to be deprived of her pretended right to the aforesaid realm, and from all dominions, dignity and privilege whatsoever, and the nobles, subjects and peoples of the said realm, and all others who have taken an oath of any kind to her, we declare to be absolved for ever from such oath and from all dues of dominion, fidelity and obedience . . .'[1]

It was an attitude bred in the context of war, the reign of Bloody Mary, persecution, the Inquisition, and compulsion of belief. Nor was the attitude limited to the Roman Catholic church; it was transmitted in a modified form to the Church of England and other British churches. There was compulsion to worship, the seeking of a monopoly position, the ambition for power, the rivalry, the exaggerated ecclesiastical issues, and the confusion of political and church issues which from our perspective look largely irrelevant, but which, from within the powerful insti- tutions of the time were the very *raison d'être* of their organization. During the 18th century the tendency towards power, privilege, status, a monopoly position, and political influence became even more marked. It was a worldly-wise and successful church, but it was dead, saltless. The leadership of the churches was in the hands of influential and promotion-conscious archbishops, not of Christ.

The results of this position were devastating. First, it necessarily involved churches in alliances with various political and economic groups, so that Christian teaching was modified to accord with the groups whose support was needed. It would not be inaccurate to say that the churches went a-whoring after landowners, the monarchy, the Tory Party, the capitalists, and whomever also could offer them influence. If the attitude of

<hr>

[1] H. Bettenson (Ed.), *Documents of the Christian Church* (Oxford Univ. Press, 1963), pp. 338–9.

Christ and the early church can be described as suffering for the truth, it was evident that the churches had in the intervening years found a better way. That this way comprised the teachings of the Christian gospel in a hundred different ways and cut large sectors of the population off from Christian teaching did not matter. The situation was met by the revival associated with Wesley and Whitefield, but in many ways the churches remained tied in their teaching by the alliances which they had developed.

Another result of this ecclesiastical self-glorification was that the Christian faith was made into a very church-centred system of belief. Issues like those surrounding vestments, order of church service, liturgy, the position of the clergy, ecclesiastical architecture, the communion, all assumed disproportionate emphasis, while broader issues of Christian faith and life atrophied by default. The Oxford Movement, essentially the attempt to defend the Christian church rather than the Christian faith, reinforced this tendency. The thought patterns of the church therefore became very ingrown and ecclesiastical, and unable to grapple with the issues that were being thrown up in every decade by the changing culture. The self-importance of the institutional churches helped to produce their irrelevance and to shut off the Christian faith from the main issues of life.

By the 20th century, the power of the institutional churches had waned considerably, but there was no decisive break with the pattern that had developed. They still craved influence, and one felt that it was the absence of power rather than a change of attitude which shaped the more recent responses. Similarly, the ecclesiastical emphasis has continued; for example, the recent development of the ecumenical movement has focused on institutional church unity. It is arguable, therefore, that the churches have been driving for several hundred years into an institutional cul-de-sac, and have lost contact with many aspects of the New Testament church.[1] Its irrelevance is rooted in its own institutional pride.

---

[1] Obviously this judgment needs qualification, which the reader can supply from his own experience. A much fuller explanation of the basis for the judgment is given in the chapter 15.

The sacred—secular division

It is commonplace for sociologists to talk about secularization, and to use the distinction between sacred and secular. It is also widely used by theologians, church leaders and others discussing Christian affairs, but few question the concepts or realize what a devastating effect they have had on Christianity in Britain. The concepts are not biblical, nor is it possible to identify the ideas in the teaching of Christ or the apostles. Christians are called to be holy, but there is no area of their lives which can then be labelled secular. There is a clear distinction between love of the world and love of God, but again this has a completely different meaning from that which secular and sacred have come to carry. This concept is essentially a compromise; it involves agreeing on a domain which is the concern of the church (and is therefore 'Christian')[1] and another which is the domain of the non-church powers. The compromise has its roots in the long power struggles of the mediaeval and post-Reformation Roman Catholic church to establish as strong a position as possible with respect to the various political and other powers that existed at the time. The counter-reformation can be seen as an attempt, especially by the Jesuits, to defend this sphere or domain against further erosion, to strengthen the church or the sacred against the attack of secular powers. In many largely Roman Catholic countries this position was regularized in that the chief secular institution, the state, agreed to support the church in all affairs within the sacred domain, while the church gave its sacred legitimization to the state.

For a time, during the Reformation, it seemed that Christians were breaking out of this straightjacket. In chapter 1, we saw how the faith of Christians was expressed in marriage, family, economic and political life, in education, art, science, music and literature. However, the pattern of constriction was never really thrown off and with the Restoration the Christian faith was once more squeezed into an institutional mould, and the sacred boundaries carefully drawn within an agreement between the

[1] This fallacy of identifying the Christian faith with the institutional church is crucial.

established church and the establishment. Nonconformists were legally excluded from universities, local and national government for a period of a hundred and fifty years, which helped ensure that all non-ecclesiastical concerns atrophied. Independent Christian thought and action became difficult as the church was cast into its role as custodian of the sacred and supporter of the establishment. During the Enlightenment, as we have seen, most of the important thinking became independent of Christian foundations and rooted in various forms of humanism, rationalism and naturalism. The sacred domain of the Church of England was still extensive, but the compromise implicit in the sacred/secular division, and the departure from the wholeness of the Christian faith soon took their toll on this seeming strength.

Again, with the Methodist and evangelical revivals there was an opening up of the scope of the gospel. Slavery, working conditions, education and missionary activity were within the orbit of the Christian faith, and many bridges were slung across the sacred/secular chasm, but despite this the divide remained; it had by then become too firmly entrenched in the culture. Many people brought up in industrial towns, or even on landed estates, regarded the church as sacred and therefore largely irrelevant to their secular existence. The Oxford Movement aimed to stress the sacred and reassert its importance. (It was the protestant counter-reformation). Thus the basic pattern of thinking remained. Now, however, it took a more malevolent form. The secular area was growing and the churches were weak against this erosion. Morals, the origins of man, religious education, marriage, miracles and many other areas were under attack, although they had previously been sacrosanct, and the process of secularization gathered momentum. At this stage, the 'secular' perspective became for most people the normal way of looking at things, and from this perspective the 'sacred' came to look peculiar. Isolated from the great Christian themes which are its rationale, Sunday observance became odd and out-dated. Many theologians, feeling the constrictions of the enclosed sacred framework, have tried to break out of it,[1] but the result tended to be a compromise with the secular forces that had become so dominant. The church is

[1] An obvious example was Harvey Cox's *The Secular City*.

hemmed in by the dominant secular forces, and is finding it difficult, if not impossible, to step outside this constriction into the fullness of the Christian gospel. This division, and the misstatement of Christianity that it involves, have further weakened the salting power of Christians in a variety of ways which we shall now examine.[1]

Synthetic thinking

At the same time as Christians were constructing a sacred citadel which would be immune against the attacks of those outside, they were also very much affected by the need to justify the Christian faith to others and recommend it to their assent. Moreover, the need became more acute the stronger the sacred/secular divide became and the more institutionalized Christianity became. Christian apologists needed to build long bridges across these chasms. Although there was a strong tradition during the Reformation which recognized that Christian thinking had a radically different basis from non-Christian thought, the pattern which became normal in the late 17th century was for Christian apologetics to involve a compromise with other thought forms and to accept them as legitimate. This was evident with the rational apologists like Lord Herbert of Cherbury, the Platonists and John Locke. The humanist concept of reason was seen as common ground on which the Christian appeal to non-Christians could be made. That reason and Christian faith are antithetical concepts was ignored, and the result was that Christianity was both perverted into a vague moralistic deism, and also that it was discredited with the fall of 18th century rationalism. Nevertheless, the same kind of apologetic alliance was forged between nature and the Christian faith, and it became the normal pattern for Christian thinkers to accommodate themselves to any new trend in secular thought that came along.

During the 17th and 18th centuries, this kind of apologetics seemed relatively easy, in theory, although in practice the apologia that claimed common ground became a lukewarm

[1] See D. Lyon, Sociology and Secularization in *Christian Commitment and the Study of Sociology* (Ilkley Study Group/UCCF, 1975) for a good review of the concept of secularization.

version of Christianity which commanded little respect. However, as secular humanism developed, the polarity between Christian and other thought forms became greater and the agility needed to find common ground became Olympian, but Christians still, and in more obvious ways, muddied their thinking with the perspectives of the day. This was evident at layer after layer of Christian thinking, even at the levels most central to the gospel. At one level Christians were Conservatives, Liberals or Socialists, and when Shaftesbury was silent, there was no longer a Christian political voice in any way independent of the secular party stances. At another level, by the middle of the 19th century the complex and very strong pattern of Christian and near-Christian education had begun to wither, so that by about 1870 education changed from being primarily religious to being primarily secular. At another level, various secular patterns of thought were introduced into biblical criticism, so that a mechanistic or naturalistic presupposition required 'reinterpretation' of miracles, or else the rich, *ordinary* documents of the Bible were subjected to the kind of academic analysis which distorted their meaning and questioned their validity. Higher criticism was like an art historian looking at the corner of a Michelangelo fresco through a magnifying glass, so that the brush-strokes did not make sense. The arrogance of human scholarship in various forms—historical, linguistic, scientific—was matched by the weakness of Christian thinking about the Word of God, which was defended with unnecessary and pathetic weapons. This is not a thorough theological study, and little evidence has been produced for this pessimistic judgment, with which many theologians would disagree, but the rapidity with which Christian thought was eclipsed and lost strength both outside and within the churches requires explanation. The explanation given here is that secular patterns of thought and life had so penetrated post-industrial Britain, that in many churches the Christian faith was choked and withered.

It is interesting to see this change in the context of a particular issue in late 19th century church history. The down-grade controversy was raised by C. H. Spurgeon, a great Calvinist preacher whose congregations were as big as football crowds. He took a position in the 1880s which has been described thus by Iain Murray:

'Spurgeon was unimpressed by the intellectual brilliance of German theologians and he was unmoved by the claims made by "science" where it impinged upon Scripture, because his basic viewpoint left no room for a Christianity which man's wisdom could trim or improve. For him, the only spiritual progress was a deeper knowledge of the Word of God, with a corresponding sanctification of the life, and whenever disbelief in divine revelation was tolerated under the name of "progress", it demonstrated, in his view, that man, in pride, was assuming a liberty to which he had no right. The new religion practically sets "thought" above revelation, and constitutes man the supreme judge of what ought to be true! He was equally certain that the "progressive theology" would lead to worldliness and not holiness in the church.

A rejection of Scriptural fundamentals, far from being a sign of superior knowledge, was evidence that man was not taught and called of God. Man's only true position before the Lord and His Word is one of humble submission. So the widespread agitation for a revision of the old theology was not for him a sign that accommodation and adjustments were needed, but rather that God and the authority of His Word must be asserted over against the wisdom of man.'[1]

In holding this position Spurgeon was left fairly isolated because the spirit of the age was enmeshed in synthetic thought. It is arguable that, whatever the details of the case, Spurgeon's was the prophetic voice of the era. He saw the collapse of the churches because of their own weakness, which has been the characteristic of the 20th century.

It needs also to be pointed out that there has been another widespread response to the non-Christian patterns of thought which encroach on the church. It is that islands of sacred thought have been constructed. Sometimes these have been mystical or devotional. At other times they have been ecclesiastical. At other periods they have been emotional or even intellectual. The characteristics of these 'islands' is that they are sets of ideas or attitudes which do not speak to the world at large, because they

[1] I. H. Murray, *The Forgotten Spurgeon* (Banner of Truth Trust, 1966), pp. 189–90.

are largely defensive in orientation. In this situation, Christian truth is largely reduced to subjective truth, which cannot act as salt and light.

The solution

The problems that we have briefly discussed may not be acknowledged by some Christians. If the church reorganizes and modernizes itself, things will soon improve, it is commonly argued. However, for those who do not succumb to this kind of optimism, there is no need to labour the point further. The self-glorification of Christians and of the church, the intellectual pride, the fear, the faithlessness, the weakness and social conformity which we Christians have displayed is obvious and requires repentance. However, this brings us again within hearing of the Word of God, because the Old and New Testaments are continually warning of exactly these dangers, and pointing the way back to Christian grace and truth.

Chapter 5

A Christian social perspective

We have already pointed out the failure of Christians to face and understand their social environment, and we now turn to this task. One caveat that must be mentioned at this stage is that understanding is needed at a whole range of different levels, and confusion can easily arise when too specific a point is considered too early. We cannot paint with a fine sociological brush until we have sketched out a perspective and established the important tonal values, so that the reader may have to wait before the issue with which he is concerned is approached.

Our perspective begins with the Bible. We are created, finite, sinful, fallible and mistaken in so many ways that we need guidance and revelation. This will cause offence to those who still pride themselves on their independent search for the truth, but in this chapter the Bible will be recognized not as just another book about which we have an opinion but as a book which examines us and discloses who we are. Our first task therefore is to look at this crucial position of the Bible in opening up a Christian understanding. How is the Bible to be interpreted? What is its message?

Biblical exegesis

How is the Bible to be interpreted? To some people this immediately brings to mind a whole range of technical and theological issues and, although these have some importance, they need to be seen firmly in context. The issue is not so much of a problem as it sometimes seems, since the Bible is comprehensive enough, covers so much history and so many literary forms, engages the lives of so many people, and is forthright and simple enough to establish what is said without too much room for variation. The understanding of God, the creation, mankind, sin and salvation which emerges and consistently develops throughout its pages is unequivocal, provided that the reader is not selective. As long as people do not interpret the Scriptures in the light of their own ideas, there can be substantial agreement about what it means.[1] Those who find they cannot assent to this should perhaps reserve judgment for a few paragraphs.

Some Christian misconceptions   One problem is that people have often brought their own ideas to the Bible, with the result that there have been as many different interpretations as there have been imported ideas. A rationalist, positivist, moralist, relativist, ascetic or materialist interpretation all produce very different results. Before we look at some positive principles of exegesis, it is therefore worth looking at some common, imported patterns of interpretation which cause problems. For example, it has sometimes been assumed that biblical teaching on social issues can be understood by applying texts to specific situations. 'Children obey your parents' or 'slaves be obedient to your earthly masters' are commands which are seen as defining parent/child or work relationships. These injunctions are important, but to 'apply' them directly is a dangerous method because it allows people to use verses to support their own opinions, especially when they are divested of their context. On many occasions unbiblical principles like 'the divine right of kings' have supposedly come from the pages of Scripture, and this pattern of imported meaning is clearly wrong.

Another pattern of interpretation is that which sees biblical social teaching as 'moral'. The emphasis is put on the Ten Commandments, the Sermon on the Mount, and the division between right and wrong. This is seen as the main thrust of the Bible, and as a result there is a good deal of selectivity in

[1] See D. Guthrie, J. A. Motyer, A. M. Stibbs and D. J. Wiseman (Eds.), *The New Bible Commentary Revised* (IVP, 1970).

approaching its pages. (Perhaps this emphasis arises because secular knowledge has claimed to be 'factual', 'neutral' and 'scientific' so that the only area of knowledge which clergymen and theologians have felt they have left to them is the moral or ethical area, which they have tended to overemphasize). This moralist emphasis is wrong. The scriptural focus is not on *rules* for living, but much more basically with the meaning of people's lives before God. The moral teaching follows from the meaning of people's lives and relationships. If, for example, we look at the teaching on marriage, we find a clear-cut rule, namely the forbidding of adultery, but this grows out of the teaching about the created pattern of marriage (Genesis 2), of the effects of bigamy (Genesis 16 and 30), about sexual love (Song of Solomon) peace in marriage (1 Peter 3), married and single life (1 Corinthians 7) and about the nature of a troth relationship (Ephesians 5). In other words the teaching is composite and to fasten just on moral commands is to distort its wholeness.

Another common misconception is to see biblical teaching as setting forth *ideals*. It is claimed that they may be unattainable, but at least they are a target at which people can aim. This approach allows biblical teaching to be put at a distance as impractical and unrealistic. However, biblical norms never allow this kind of dismissal; they are given into a sin-ridden situation, and exhibit a totally realistic assessment of life. Moses was given the Law, not when the children of Israel were living ideal lives, but when they were committing the sin of apostasy, and the Law was closely tailored to Israelite weaknesses. The norms, principles, prophecy and advice are given directly to people in their sinful, compromised, weak and mixed up lives, and in no way allow themselves to be held up as unattainable ideals.

Again there is sometimes a tendency to spiritualize or allegorize biblical narrative, so that hidden meanings are seen as more important than the plain meaning of the particular situation. One effect of this approach is to abstract it from the murder, war, rape, deceit, violence and destruction, which is the background for the scriptural revelation. It grows out of a personal devotional approach to the Bible which is a response to the individualistic streak in modern British Christianity. If all the world is secularized, at least the individual can hold on to these deep spiritual truths and allegorical meanings. This is similar to the Gnostic reaction in the first century, and although personal devotion is an important part of the Christian life it is not a complete response to the Scriptures.

Some non-Christian interpretations A more crucial form of interpretation is that which brings humanism in its various forms into the Bible. One humanist reaction is to present Christ as just a man, in defiance of all the evidence of the New Testament to the contrary. Another response is to 'demythologize' the Bible, by which is meant that all non-human agency is eliminated *a priori* from the narrative. Yet another is to present Christ as a radical revolutionary with attitudes similar to those of the Zealots. There has also been an emphasis on human experience as the focus of the Christian message: human *experience* of God and of grace is what is significant in a man-centred perspective on the Bible; the transcendent is seen merely as what people experience rather than as what is. Interpretation is shaped in a whole variety of ways by the kind of humanism that we looked at in chapter 1. That these assumptions are imported into much biblical study is often not realized by those who do the work. The supposed neutrality of their work reveals again how no perspective is free from a religious basis, and a non-Christian basis of biblical interpretation leads to the obvious results.

A further caveat is that we must not approach the Bible as a scientific, sociological or even theological textbook. Theoretical knowledge has its own structure and place, and it is wrong to bring these structural characteristics to the Scriptures, which are *pre-theoretical* writings in that they recount God's dealings and communication with ordinary people in concrete pre-scientific situations. Thus it is incorrect either to expect that a particular science will accurately and exhaustively analyse Scripture, or to expect Scripture to be directly relevant to a particular science like sociology. The Scriptures speak to humble men and women at an immediate day to day level and not to specialists *qua* specialists. Therefore it would be a denial of the nature or its revelation to treat it in a theoretical or scientific way. However, we argued in chapter 3 that all theoretical positions depend on pre-theoretical assumptions about the nature of mankind, and this means that in moving from biblical teaching to social analysis we need a Christian understanding of the relationship between pre-theoretical biblical writings and knowledge in the various sciences that depend on them.

We can also note that the Scriptures enclose a period of history that is contained in no other book. Its dimensions are vast. Within its pages the development of a nation under the hand of God spans thousands of years through tremendous social and political changes. There is nothing static about God's revelation of himself, and the changing context needs to be noted. Thus, for example, political revelation and prophecy is given into tribal societies, a totalitarian empire, a theocracy, anarchic, judge-ruled, monarchical and colonial situations. In transposing biblical principles and teaching, we therefore need to beware of too static and fixed a response.

These are just a few non-technical points relating to biblical exegesis. There are many more that can and will arise, and these will be dealt with in the chapters that follow. What is of general importance is the content of the Scriptures rather than the method of interpretation; the modern preoccupation with method is not a necessary commitment.

The word of God

The scope of the Bible is cosmic as it criss-crosses history showing God's dealings with mankind, but a crucial point is that it speaks to each person and demands a certain kind of response. The writer of the Epistle to the Hebrews bears witness to this when he says:

'For the word of God is living and active, sharper than any two-edged sword, piercing to the division of soul and spirit, of joints and marrow, and discerning the thoughts and intentions of the heart. And before him no creature is hidden, but all are open and laid bare to the eyes of him with whom we have to do.' (Heb. 4:12, 13)

The response is either to draw near to God in grace or a hardening of heart. Some of the most repeated words in Scripture are:

'Go to this people, and say,
You shall indeed hear but never understand,

and you shall indeed see but never perceive.
For this people's heart has grown dull,
and their ears are heavy of hearing,
and their eyes they have closed;
lest they should perceive with their eyes,
and hear with their ears,
and understand with their heart,
and turn for me to heal them.' (Acts 28:26, 27, *etc.*)
and they show the inevitable *personal* tension produced by the biblical message of man's creation, his sinfulness, his need to repent, to be forgiven and by faith know atonement for his personal pollution. This tension is not resolved when we examine the scope of the Christian perspective as it especially relates to social issues. It is a characteristic of the Word of God in the Law, Prophets, Gospels and Letters that it examines mankind, and so examines us, and this is not comfortable.

Let us therefore, inadequately, but as a timid start, summarize some of the themes that are developed within the Word of God and which Christians down the centuries have tried to define as doctrine. The statements may not be theologically nice, but they are substantially true, and that is more important; they state implicitly the way things are and why they are as they are.

God has created the universe in great verbal acts and has ordered and upheld it according to the laws and formulae which express this power. Nothing is independent or self-explanatory, but everything depends upon his creativity and providence. The creation is as diverse as the structure of a feather, a crystal, an atom and the solar system, and each part reflects and shouts God's glory.

Mankind was created, or structured, subject to the total law and order of God. He was made a creature with unique personal characteristics, palely reflecting his Creator, and able to live in a structured relationship with his Lord and God. His relationship with God was structured by the unconditional commands to have dominion over his environment, to steward, to love, to be holy, just, and to honour people. All these are focused in the great commandment to love and worship God outright. God has made people the pre-eminent creation of his world.

As man's history has lengthened, people have been tempted to exchange the reality of their own existence, and the nature of their relationships to God, other people and to their environments for various webs of lies. These have taken various forms: the worship of idols, gods, rulers, sets of ideas, aspects of human experience, or various propositions of man's ignorance, but they have the common characteristic that they are a rebellion against God and truth. They are denial, sin, perverseness, disharmony, strife, degeneration and eventually death both for persons and in terms of the general effect of these rebellious responses throughout history. The overwhelming conclusion to which the life history of the children of Israel witnesses is that mankind's independent efforts to shape his existence are doomed to total and abject failure; they are judged by God and the lie is continually given to the lie. The darkness in which men stumble is otherwise unrelieved, and there is no hope.

The predominant response of mankind, however, did not in any way change God's care and faithfulness to mankind, and he continually called men into a new, clear relationship with himself and provided witness to the true (historical) situation of mankind. The completeness of this love found expression in the birth of Jesus Christ, his Son, among us, to show and exemplify the truth and to be the light that enlightens every man. Jesus accomplished what mankind on its own could never do. He carried human sin and removed it from us by his own death, and restored the relationship between man and his Father for those with faith in him. Thus, new, not humanly conditional, life was and is given to those who are disciples and depend upon Christ's teaching, rescue and help. He has sent the Spirit of God to those who ask, to teach, guide and empower them to be obedient to the Lord Jesus Christ. The healing of the creation is under way and cannot be halted.

The victory over sin and death that was first evident in the resurrection of Jesus has been and is to be shared in and proclaimed by the church. It is the means of new life to all who believe, and where sin is not allowed to continue, it brings peace, love, joy, justice and grace. The tension between the rule of Christ (in the lives of Christians) and the other faiths that involve rebellion against God will continue through history until the return of Christ fully establishes his kingdom, and all that is not of God withers away under final judgment. The fulness of God's love and glory is to be revealed as the restoration of the creation is completed after the ravages of man's pride.

If these statements approximate, however inadequately, to some of the central themes of the word of God, their testimony to the reality on which our sociological perspective is founded is evident. The testament of God is present in the very structure of the creation and is open to mankind through his Spirit; for sinners who are distorted in understanding, motives and behaviour, the need for the revelation of God's Word and of his Son is unavoidable.

The Christian perspective presented below is therefore a response to this revelation. A basic point is that a *response* to the authoritative truth of the Word of God is in no way proof against error, since it is subject to all the limitations, weaknesses and sins of the author and other human beings.

A Christian philosophy of sociology

Although our main concern will be with the content of a Christian sociological perspective, it is important at this stage that we take up the issues considered in chapter 3 and look at the status of scientific knowledge and of sociological knowledge in particular. This also must be subject to a radical Christian re-interpretation, as we suggested at the end of chapter 3; we therefore start by recalling some of the basic points made there, and making them the basis for a more rigorous and detailed analysis.

A Christian perspective We stated that all theoretical or scientific knowledge presupposes a pre-theoretical starting point, and we therefore first consider some of the Christian doctrines that throw light on the nature of scientific knowledge. The primary point is that the creation is made and upheld by God's word of power; the whole creation is dependent on him. and it is therefore subject to his law. Nothing in the creation can by nature escape being structured by this law. Law, in this pre-theoretical sense, is the inescapable situation of man. All the sciences therefore respond to the prior or given order within which mankind exists. This is no less so with human sciences than with the natural ones, although the former involve human freedom and are therefore more complex. Thus there is a continuity and integration between human and the natural sciences in that they are a response to the given laws and norms of God's creation. Sociologists, in trying to be anormative, have missed one of the most fundamental points about their discipline.

A second major point is that because all theoretical analysis presupposes a pre-theoretical or religious perspective, we cannot find the meaning of any discipline within itself, nor can the meaning of science be established in scientific terms. The ultimate reason for this is that the creation is not self-contained but always depends on God and points beyond itself to God. All the inanimate universe is telling the glory of God and mankind is made in his image. The laws which structure creation are God's laws, not self-generated patterns. The disciplines must therefore always point beyond themselves and any attempt to 'contain' them or define scientific knowledge autonomously is doomed to failure. More particularly, sociology cannot just be defined as the study of society, for social relationships and institutions have a prior created structure and meaning. Thus a discipline must, and will in this perspective, cohere within a context of meaning which is religious.

The third main point is that the creation is diverse with a richness which is startling in contrast with some of our man-made environments. The account in Genesis 1 outlines the developmental process at the beginning of time by which God decreed this diversity. The consequence is obvious: the sciences that respond to reality must be pluriform. Each science therefore responds to a recognizable aspect of the creation and examines it. This means that each discipline is a partial framework of knowledge, in that it examines only one aspect of reality. We must, therefore, be careful to define carefully the partial nature of scientific knowledge.

Scientific knowledge   The first point that arises about scientific knowledge is the authority which it should be accorded. All attempts to give science some kind of ultimate authority by grounding it on an empiricist, positivist or behaviourist theory of knowledge are misplaced because they fail to recognize the nature of the process of scientific analysis. The order of the creation is prior and God given, and man's response is that reality is necessarily fallible, limited, inadequate, often misguided and subject to correction. The results obtained may often be dazzling, but this is no excuse for ignoring the very important limitations of human scientific activity. Empiricists who have hoped that from their data they can develop self-contained and 'objective' scientific explanations have always come up against the fact that no process of induction can generate statements of universal laws. Science cannot escape being a response of *faith*, seeking out structures determined by laws and all theories and predictions are implicitly or explicitly statements of faith. The argument of chapter 3 is that the only consistent scientific faith is in the creator, and that science could not have developed and cannot consistently be maintained without recognition of his law. Thus, scientific knowledge rather than being authoritative is always a tentative, falsifiable response to what is given.

Another important conclusion concerns the position of the scientist. A popular and tenacious model sees the scientist as the objective, omniscient eye looking down on his field of study. The Christian perspective by contrast sees the scientist as a creature necessarily subject to the laws of that which he is studying, and his observation and analysis is therefore relative to the subject matter being studied. Not surprisingly, therefore, in a variety of disciplines this necessary relativity has meant problems for an omniscient, universal model of knowledge. Einstein's work, Heisenberg's uncertainty principle, Gödel's second theorem and Taski's proof that every universal language is paradoxical show

the kind of problem that crops up, unless the scientist's creatureliness is recognized. The problem is acute in sociology. Many sociologists have ignored this creatureliness and have assumed the position of the omniscient, neutral eye looking down at the way society works. In fact, the sociologist cannot play god and faces a much more prosaic situation.

The sociologist is therefore a creature like the subjects of his study, and his position relative to them needs to be carefully considered. Only with the breakdown of 'objective' sociology has a more critical awareness of the problems of the relation between sociologist and subject developed, egged on by anthropologists.

Scientific differentiation The process of scientific differentiation or abstraction is the next crucial element in our view of scientific knowledge. It is in the nature of a science that it abstracts from the full complex of reality and analyses in a particular way. Thus, to take an example, when a physicist, a chemist and a botanist look at a tree, they do not look at three trees, but at three different aspects of one tree. Or, to take an example involving human activity, when a person goes to work on a bus there are mathematical, physical, chemical, biological, geographical, psychological, logical, linguistic, social, economic, aesthetic, legal, ethical and other aspects of his activity which can be analysed by a natural or human science, but no one analysis can claim to be the definitive one, for the process of abstraction

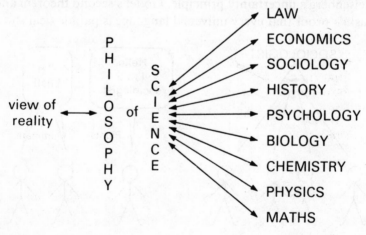

from reality means that scientific knowledge is a partial and limited form of understanding.

Because I may grasp the chemistry of dogs, it does not mean that I understand 'real' dogs which have many different aspects to them; indeed I may be incapable of looking after a pet properly. Thus the limited nature of scientific analysis should continually be recognized in the disciplines and the fallacy of *reductionism*, whereby one scientific analysis is taken to be the definitive view of reality, is laid bare. Prof. D. M. Mackay makes a similar point when he criticizes 'nothing buttery', the fallacy which arises when the nature of scientific differentiation is ignored and a particular scientific interpretation is made a total explanation.[1]

However, a Christian perspective involves more than acknowledging the plurality of disciplines and their necessarily partial perspective. The disciplines reflect aspects of coherent reality, and something of their interrelationships and interdependence can be understood by reflecting on the diversity of creation. Dr. Herman Dooyeweerd does this in his famous model analysis of the various law spheres of the creation order and, as we can use this interpretation later, the modalities from the most elemental to those most specifically human are detailed below.[2]

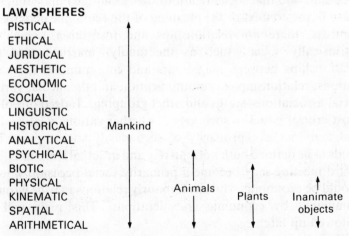

LAW SPHERES
PISTICAL
ETHICAL
JURIDICAL
AESTHETIC
ECONOMIC
SOCIAL
LINGUISTIC
HISTORICAL   Mankind
ANALYTICAL
PSYCHICAL
BIOTIC
PHYSICAL
KINEMATIC   Animals   Plants   Inanimate
SPATIAL   objects
ARITHMETICAL

[1] See D. M. Mackay, *The Clockwork Image* (IVP, 1974), Ch. 4., pp. 40–8.
[2] See H. Dooyeweerd, *The New Critique of Theoretical Thought*, Vols. I & II (Presbyterian and Reformed Pub. Co., USA, 1953) and J. Spier, *An Introduction to Christian Philosophy* (Craig Press, 1968) for a thorough development of this model framework.

This overall perspective and some of the conclusions that Dooyeweerd draws from this diversity can be used in our specific analysis of sociology as a science.

Sociology as a scientific discipline If sociology is a theoretical, limited, fallible study of an aspect of reality, what more can we say of it as a discipline and in relation to other areas of study? First and foremost, the study of social relationships is an independent area of study not because social facts exist, or society exists, or even subjective interpersonal meaning, but because God has created people in a variety of structured normative relationships which are inevitably an aspect of their existence. The subject will survive even without the support of sociologists.

Within the discipline we can note a distinction between *primary* and *secondary* sociology. The first denotes the study of relationships and institutions which focus on human interaction, *i.e.* there is no basically extrasocial meaning to the institutions or activity. Secondary sociology covers areas where the primary concern is not social, but legal, economic, educational or ecclesiastical. Some examples will make the point clear. In a boardroom one expects to find that the focus of activity is economic and that social relationships, although important, take place in the context of the meaning of the economic activity. By contrast, there are relationships and institutions which are intrinsically social, such as the family, marriage and sex; relationships between neighbours and communities, races and nations; relationships in communication and the media; various social associations, status and other groupings. Indeed one of the most crucial issues in sociology is whether various relationships and activities are primarily or secondarily sociological. This needs to be defined both normatively and in actual situations. The board meeting may become a primarily social occasion when it should be economic, while neighbourly relations may be wrongly dominated by economic considerations. This issue will be followed up later.

The domain of secondary sociology would include the following sub-disciplines, among others:
The sociology of religious institutions.
The sociology of law.

Social criminology.

Political sociology.

The sociology of morals.

The sociology of art, music, literature, *etc.*

The sociology of work.

Industrial sociology.

The sociology of organization.

The sociology of education.

Linguistic sociology.

The sociology of development.

Cultural sociology.

Historical sociology.

The sociology of thought.

The sociology of emotional life (not social psychology).

Demographic sociology.

The vital point in relation to these subject areas is that sociology cannot be neutral with respect to the meaning of the aspect of life which is the primary focus. It is not only that a church is primarily an institution for worship and not a community centre, or that a political party is not primarily a social club, but that the meaning of these other areas must be established. The sociologist cannot be politically or ecclesiastically value-free, but must try to penetrate the meaning of these other disciplines which are not merely extensions of the social, and cannot be treated in a reductionist manner. At the same time, it must be emphasized that secondary does not mean subsidiary or subordinate. The social aspects of work are not relegated to a subordinate position. The emphasis throughout the Bible is that treatment of other people should never be compromised to meet non-social claims. Non-social ends never justify wrong social means. Thus social norms are no less important in these secondary areas, but the interrelationships between different aspects of life need to be recognized. Secondary sociology is therefore in no way inferior, but requires an external reference point.

We are now also in a position to say something of the methods that can be used in sociology. Methodology is no guaranteed route to truth, and we are not therefore bound to any infallible method. We recognize that each science, because of the diversity of the creation, needs to develop its own methods of analysis and study, all of which must be qualified by norms of honesty. The concept of modal diversity would lead to the conclusion that there are many methods appropriate to social analysis apart from the obvious ones like the questionnaire, interview, case studies, participatory methods, social experiments, *etc*. These, corresponding to the modal spheres, would include statistics, analyses of social space, social dynamics, analysis of social movements, studies of organic units, attitude surveys, study of social philosophies, longitudinal studies, historical case studies, content analysis, semiology, systems analysis, critical path analysis, studies of social harmony and conflict, social jurisdiction analysis, analyses of social power and analysis of the moral and faith content of relationships. These methods can shed light on one facet of the phenomena that are studied, and if properly used help to achieve a more coherent sociological understanding. Now to the content of the subject.

A Christian sociological perspective

Now that the scope of sociology as a discipline has been defined in some respects, we are in a position to outline a Christian formulation of what sociology is. The various points are an elaboration of doctrines which most readers will readily recognize.

Creation

1. Social relationships are a created part of man's existence, and as such they are subject to a law which is not man-made, but rests in God's creative authority. Relationships are therefore no less subject to law than humans are subject to the law of gravity, although this law is not mechanical, but defines the true structure of human relationships. Social relationships are therefore to be understood basically in *normative* terms.
2. All human, and therefore social, activity is meaningful in God's eyes, and the true meaning of relationship can therefore only be established in the context of man's relationship with God.
3. Social and normative development is historically an ongoing process with the creation of new lives and the growth of

mankind. The meaning of relationships before God, and their normative definition, is developmental under God's providential care, as the Scriptures show.

4. The Scriptures exemplify God's norms for the basic institutional structures of marriage, the family, the state and the church in a way which establishes their unique 'genetic' structures. Each of them has a special normative structure which it should be free to recognize before God without human dominion.

5. The Scriptures exemplify other norms which act as vectors in terms of which the meaning of other (social) institutions and organizations is to be understood.

6. Human behaviour is to be understood in terms of neither subjective nor objective definitions. Rather, it needs to be recognized that human behaviour (a) is defined by, and subject to, a created law or normative structure; (b) involves the response and action of the human subject; (c) involves the effect of other people's actions on the subject; and (d) involves a whole range of objects which have social significance. No analysis of social behaviour can accurately eliminate man's creatureliness, responsibility, dependence on others and articulations of social meanings.

Sin

1. Man in his sin has withdrawn from his relationship with God, and so has injured the very kernel of his social relationships. Their meanings are awry and without their true foundation.

2. Sin involves a destruction of human understanding of relationships and of norms, so that many different ways of seeing relationships and institutions can develop which are false and exemplify human weakness.

3. Mankind in this situation continually tries to regain some kind of coherence and harmony in social life by creating 'idols' or centres of meaning which give significance to other activities. These 'principalities' further distort the true meaning of people's lives.

4. Sin and human pride lead people to develop justifications of their behaviour which are cultural lies. These can become socially embedded, and mean that many explanations which

are given of social behaviour are potentially false or misleading.

5. The distortion of sin becomes embedded in social development, so that institutions lose coherence, or patterns of domination are established which have a long historical background.

6. In this situation, mankind is not in a position to help himself, because the subjects are themselves a part of what is wrong. Diagnosis of the problems must come from outside the situation, for without the God-given law there is no understanding or diagnosis of sin.

7. The futility and destructiveness of human behaviour and understanding are evidences of God's judgment on it, and bear witness to the created structure of social life.

8. That human behaviour can be false and wrong means that it cannot be taken as the empirical data of sociological knowledge. An empirical, uncritical approach to social life means that true and false, distorted and healthy, are treated as identical, and the deep and real problems in society cannot be identified and understood.

Redemption

1. A restoration of human relationships to their true meaning depends upon people coming to live in peace with God through faith in Jesus Christ.

2. This restoration can take place only when human independence has been exhausted, and God is allowed to demonstrate the meaning of his love, peace, forgiveness, justice, joy and care. Nevertheless, people are continually tempted to put their faith in their own achievements, understanding and power.

3. The new birth of the Christian means a radical re-education in the social norms and institutional structures of life, where they are seen not in egotistical or man-centred terms, but in the context of the rule and love of God.

4. There is no area of social life which is not subject to the rule and law of God, and the Christian is called to realize this and to shake off the sin and old attitudes which compromise his commitment to the kingdom of Christ.

5. The rule of God and validity of his law are of worldwide

significance and are to be exemplified in the lives of Christians. Eventually they will be fully vindicated.

These fundamental Christian points are still a long way from detailed sociological analysis, and we shall now move a stage further by defining different kinds of social relationships and institutions in a way which will introduce the substantive study of later chapters.

Free societal relationships and communities

A Christian perspective is neither collectivist nor individualist in a fundamental sense. Each person is God's creation, is responsible to God and is to be judged only by God, and this means that he or she really is free from any ultimate social control. There are patterns of authority which we shall discuss later, but the example of Jesus Christ shows that people were and are free to live their own lives before God. This means that there is a whole series of relationships which can be characterized as *free societal relationships*; they are ones which do not involve any authority structure or prior shaping of the relationship. In principle, they involve no prior established structure; examples of this kind of relationship would include neighbours, commuters, shoppers, friends, peers and a whole range of other relationships which do not have a communal framework. It is worth noting that many forms of relationship, like those formed with people we read about in magazines or newspapers, see on television or hear on the radio, have this form. The viewer can switch out of the relationship by turning a knob. We also note that they can occur within an institutional context; thus in a public house or restaurant interpersonal relationships are free just as they are among colleagues in an organization whose relationships are not structurally predefined. Free relationships can also exist among groups; the relationships among gangs, rival football supporters, different associations or even different nations are free in this sense.

However, free societal relationships, if they exist at all, must be based upon shared norms. Thus, without linguistic norms, communication would not even be possible. The structure of relationships is therefore to be understood in terms of norms that are or are not shared, and the meaning that these norms have for each subject. For example, in reading this book thus far, even if you disagree with points that have been made, you are likely to be sharing a whole range of norms about the validity of various kinds of discourse and argument and the importance of certain subjects, and we haven't even met yet! In chapter 6 we shall look at the way relationships are constructed and the Christian and non-Christian norms that can shape them.

The next form of social life that we shall examine is that of communal relationships, which exist where norms are established which link members of a group and identify it. The form of the 'community' is relatively meaningless unless the norms that are shared are made explicit. A community may be said to exist, but what that community is can only be clearly seen when the shared norms are identified. It is obvious that there are different levels of community: the European Community, the nation, the region, the city, the East End, the district, the housing estate, the road, the village, the terrace. However, the differences are not only ones of size or complexity, but also of the values and norms that are shared. The variations are much wider than are implied by such terms as 'working class' or 'rural' communities, and in chapter 7 we shall explore more fully what community means.

Basic social institutions

Communities involve no structure of authority; entry and exit from them are free, but society also contains a range of institutions which have a genotypical structure and involve authority relationships. The patterns of authority vary widely and we shall shortly examine the possible range of variations, but first we must define what we mean by 'institution'. To a Christian the word means essentially what it originally stated: it is a unique social structure instituted or established by God for mankind, which is subject to its own specific norms. Derivatively it is used of all kinds of established social structures in our society, but this prior meaning is of crucial importance. People are not arbiters over basic social institutions like marriage, the family, the state, education, the church and work, but rather these institutions define what people are like in fundamental respects which cannot be ignored. The permanent and universal presence of these institutions and/or substitutes in all societies bears witness to this, and we shall be seeking insight from the Scriptures into the genotypical structure of these basic institutions. This will be the subject matter of various chapters, but first we need to look at some general points about them.

The first is that this view of institutions leads to an important conclusion about the prescribed structure of human society. Within the Dutch Kuyperian tradition it is described as the doctrine of sphere sovereignty, and it can be expressed in a variety of ways.[1] However, the basic argument can be stated as follows. In a fundamental sense the ordained structure of society is *pluralist* in that God has instituted a variety of structures which are subject to his law in specific forms, and there is therefore no one human institution or focus which can dominate these structures without usurping God's place and distorting this pluralism. The argument can be represented thus:

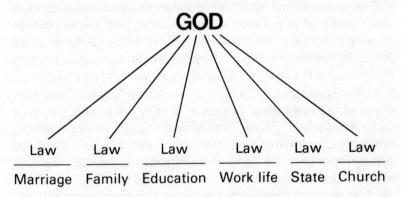

Each institution has its own integrity before God, and its unique position in society needs to be respected and allowed by other institutions.

This Christian perspective therefore offers a critique of totalitarianism on four different levels, if we understand by totalitarianism the situation where one institution, such as the state (or the church or economic institutions) has effective control

[1] The most thorough is H. Dooyeweerd, *A New Critique of Theoretical Thought* (Amsterdam, 1953) Vol. III, pp. 157–626.

or domination over all the other basic institutions in society. The first level is that it is wrong for any institution which is merely human to claim to itself the kind of sovereignty that only belongs to God. The second is that it is wrong for any human institution to have any kind of ultimate authority over the individual, who is responsible to God (although this is often not acknowledged) and is not to be dominated by any institution. Thirdly, for one institution to interfere in, and attempt to control, another basic institution means that it is interfering where it does not have competence, and is therefore obscuring the created diversity of basic institutional genotypes. The fourth argument is that, in interfering and seeking to control other institutions, an institution obscures its own created structure. Thus if the state controls the functioning of other institutions in society, it becomes difficult for it to be impartial in its judgments, since it is often acting as judge in its own case. These arguments are key ones in various structural analyses which are to be found in later chapters.

The grounds on which this basic pluralist perspective is developed need to be explored more fully. In part, this can only be done by showing the *instituted* nature of these basic units. Nevertheless, the argument can perhaps be understood intuitively by looking at the structure of many of Peter's and Paul's letters in the New Testament. They tend to have the following form: after developing some central themes of the Christian faith, they then move into various specific institutional areas of life like marriage, family life, work, political life and church life, and elaborate principles or give advice in these different areas. The teaching assumes that the rule of Christ extends to all these areas, and that the Christian is to live before God in each ot them, because God's sovereignty is over them all. For example, Paul exhorts the Colossians in the following terms:

3:19.   'Husbands, love your wives, and do not be harsh with them.'
3:21.   'Fathers do not provoke your children, lest they become discouraged.'
4:1.   'Masters, treat your slaves justly and fairly, knowing that you also have a Master in heaven.'
4:17.   'And say to Archippus, "See that you fulfil the ministry which you have received in the Lord."'

The pluralism implied by living normatively in these different areas is recognizable and has further implications.

Structures of institutional authority

The perspective on authority relationships is an important part of the view of institutions, and at this stage we can make some general points that will be developed in later chapters.

The first is difficult for some people to accept and concerns the source or basis of authority. The Scriptures teach that sovereign power and authority rest with God (Psalm 2; Daniel 4; Acts 4:23–31), and this means that no human institution can lay claim to absolute authority and that authority can only truly be experienced as service of God. Anybody who is in a position of authority is subject to the law and norms governing that position, and will be judged in his execution of it, as Paul pointed out in Colossians 4:1. Thus power is not the basis of authority, nor is popularity, nor is the use of force, but authority is instituted by God, and is subject to his law and judgment. In Acts 12:21–24 we read:

> 'On an appointed day Herod put on his royal robes, took his seat upon the throne, and made an oration to them. And the people shouted, "The voice of a god, and not of man!" Immediately an angel of the Lord smote him, because he did not give God the glory; and he was eaten by worms and died. But the word of God grew and multiplied.'

It is not difficult to compare Nebuchadnezzar and Herod with Hitler and Nkrumah, nor is it difficult to see the lie at the heart of the doctrine of the divine right of kings. Any autocratic conception of authority ignores the fact that the father, mother, teacher, judge, employer, *etc.*, are *under* norms. A term which describes this position is that of *office*, a Christian concept which emphasizes that the office holder is subject to the norms of his position. Our argument is that power established on any other basis than legitimately holding office and fulfilling its norms is falsely based and is, in the end, likely to be unstable and destructive.

Secondly, institutional authority is limited in scope. This follows from the fact that institutions have their own sphere of competence before God which is circumscribed. Authority in each institution is therefore *sui generis* and is not to be generalized without distortion and a form of institutional domination developing. Thus, if a church leader tries to exercise control within the family or a politician within the church, domination rather than legitimate authority is being practised. Human authority is necessarily finite, specific and limited, but there is continual pressure from various forms of pride for people to claim more general authority than they legitimately ought.

A third point is that a Christian view of authority involves no concept of superiority and inferiority, *i.e.* of elitism. This assumption of superiority is so widespread that it is difficult for many people to question it. For example, husbands assume authority over their wives because they are superior, and parents likewise over their children; elite groups appear in churches, firms and political institutions. However, the teaching of the Bible cuts through this linking of authority with superiority. Firstly, those in authority are sinners like everyone else, and this undercuts their claims to merit. Secondly, since an office is God-given, it follows that the authority is not intrinsic to the person who holds that office, nor is any office inherently superior or inferior to another. The whole issue was settled for ever when Christ declared to his disciples, 'If any one would be first, he must be last of all and servant of all' (Mk. 9:35). A corollary of this, which the Bible often teaches, is that it is not a sign of inferiority to be subject to a person in authority, because the subjection is not subservience to a person, but obedience to God. This principle was stated very graphically by Abraham Kuyper, who said that when you bow your knee to God, you bow your knee to no other man.

Another aspect of the argument concerns the subject's relationship to institutional authority. The 18th century individualist tradition saw this in contractual terms: the individual submitted to the contract as long as it suited him. However, the position as presented in Scripture is much more complex, depending on the basic institution in which the authority relationship is to be found. For example, we voluntarily submit to structures such as marriage, employment and church, but these differ in that marriage is a troth commitment for life while work is a terminable contract. At the same time, a person must necessarily submit to the authority of family and state, but the meaning of authority within these institutions varies widely. Thus the tendency of some sociologists to reduce authority patterns and power relationships to a single form helps to obscure important differences, as later chapters will show.

At this stage we are in a position to meet one of the vexed questions that is often posed in relation to authority. The question is often misstated in the following form: if authority is God-given, can the Christian ever not be subject to it? Sometimes it is set in a political context: is revolution ever justified? We have already looked at the way authority is defined in terms of office, as being subject to God and the norms of office. However, those in authority often ignore the norms which ought to govern their behaviour, so that a clear conflict arises between obedience to God and obedience to them. The Scriptural pattern in this situation seems clear. Obedience to God overrules obedience to wrongly exercised authority, but at the same time the subject remains committed to the God-given office of authority and does not move outside it. For example, when Peter and John were forbidden to preach in the name of Jesus, their reply to those in authority was:

'Whether it is right in the sight of God to listen to you rather than to God, you must judge; for we cannot but speak of what we have seen and heard' (Acts 4:19, 20).

The rulers, scribes, elders and high priests were told, 'You must judge'. This meant of course that Peter and John had to be prepared to answer in their own persons and with their own lives if necessary. Nevertheless, it meant that they did nothing to destroy the authority of the rulers by violence, rebellion or the use of force, but on the contrary they enhanced the authority by the respect they gave the office. Thus the Christian principle, established in Christ's own example, is that wrongly used authority should be opposed in principle and through suffering and even martyrdom, rather than through violence and revolution. This rests on the belief that sovereign power and vindication lies in God's hands not man's. There are complex issues involved in understanding what the proper scope of authority is, and what the correct exercise of authority is in specific institutions, but this preliminary analysis allows us to move beyond the pathetic subservience of some Christians and the total revolutionary identification of others with the underdog.

Seeing institutional authority as service, normative, limited, non-elitist, pluralist, open to criticism and subject to God will be the basis of the analysis in later chapters.

Free institutions

There is in most developed societies a range of institutions which have grown up and become important in our social fabric, but which are not the basic institutions found in most elementary societies. Some examples are newspaper, radio and television companies, health services, transport networks, the post office, art galleries, museums, libraries, social work organizations, hotels, funeral directors, sports centres and football leagues. A perspective on these institutions is an important part of any social analysis, and this must start with a developmental understanding. These institutions, it can be argued, have sprung from the acceptance of various norms, and their meaning must therefore be stated in normative terms. Thus, social work develops from a norm of neighbourly care, and art galleries express certain standards in art. As these examples suggest, some of the institutions are part of secondary sociological analysis in that the guiding norms are extrasocial, while others are within primary sociology. However, we need to look further into this process of development. How has it occurred and how is it to be evaluated? It has occurred when institutions like the state and the church have not exercised the kind of totalitarian and conformist control which prevents these institutions from emerging. Positively, it has occurred when norms have been pursued by certain groups and when technical developments have allowed new possibilities to be realized within the norms. The evaluation of this process is to be done within a Christian normative perspective at at least two levels. Thus a casino might be criticized because it is based on a materialistic norm rather than a Christian one, and a hotel because its practice of the hospitality norm is defective; both norm and performance need to be evaluated.

At this point, it is worth noting the primitivization of much Christian social thought. During the 19th and earlier centuries,

Christians developed a plethora of such institutions as a response to biblical norms: children's homes, court missionaries, temperance societies, hostels, Sunday schools, housing charities, missionary societies, brass bands, *etc.*, many of which were the germs of substantial institutions in contemporary Britain. However, the prevailing attitude today is that these institutions are secular, and that the Bible does not say anything about social work or probation. The Bible in fact constantly reiterates the norms for these two professions, and it is time that Christians generally woke up to understand contemporary institutions in non-simplistic ways.

These institutions are however complex. The guiding norms may well be extra-social, *e.g.* artistic, biological, linguistic, *etc.*, but there will also be social and economic norms. Firstly, all these institutions, whether art gallery or hospital, are under a norm of service, and this must be fully articulated within the institution, otherwise it will easily become self-serving and thus compromise this norm. Secondly, when service is given within this complex division of labour pattern, it is important how each institution should be funded. This raises important issues, for there is a wide variety of ways of funding institutions: by selling goods and services, by subscription, by gift, by subsidy from general taxes, by specific taxes or by various forms of levy and charges, and there is a wide variety of groups which can be considered as the basis for funding these institutions. It can be argued, for example, that the health service, instead of being funded by the state, should be supported by a levy established by a separate communal vote, and such possibilities arise when we consider the complex structure of these free institutions.

Even to call them free is to raise a whole host of questions, for many of the institutions mentioned actually come within the public sector or are profit-making companies, but the fact remains that many questions need to be raised about the institutional structures that at present exist. For example, if the guiding norms for the health service are medical, it is inaccurate to talk of political control and to make a Minister of State the final authority within the institution. The issues are again complex, but the general point is that the institutions are free in the sense that they are normatively defined, and there is no *a priori* reason why they should be controlled by the state or any other institution. It follows from this that their organizational structure should grow out of these norms, rather than being imposed from outside, but that it should reflect the subsidiary norms to which the institution is subject.

In chapter 10 we shall look at free institutions within the mass media in these terms, and clearly the analysis can be extended further.

A critical perspective

The Christian understanding of the norms and institutions which define social life gives us only some of the framework necessary to analyse what is actually going on in society. The physiologist who understands how a healthy body functions cannot necessarily identify symptoms, diagnose or prescribe treatment. A Christian perspective is necessarily critical or diagnostic in its awareness of the fundamental effect sin has had on human life. We begin by looking at the way it has affected understanding.

The Bible teaches that man was created to find his meaning in God and God's creation, but throughout history people have attempted to integrate their lives in other religious perspectives. One obvious possibility has been for man to worship the creation:

'they exchanged the truth about God for a lie and worshipped and served the creature rather than the Creator, who is blessed for ever! Amen' (Rom. 1:25).

Thus sin leads to a basic cultural lie; we have already looked at one example of it in the emergence of man's worship of man in the 18th century and subsequently. The possible false integration points are numerous—some that have dominated our modern era include possessions, pleasure, peace of mind, reason, science, status, race, nationalism, power, happiness, independence, freedom, love and sex. Each has become a frame of reference, a cultural idol, directing people's hearts to put something within the creation in place of God. However, the result is distortion. Happiness, robbed of its proper context of meaning, becomes yearning, power corrupts and enslaves, possessions own people, status isolates, freedom becomes meaningless, love is possessive and sex a lie. In other words, when the cultural perspective contains fundamental falsehoods, they will in time become evident, even though they are difficult to diagnose accurately without guidance from the Word of God.

However, it is not just at this fundamental level of life that the lies of sin operate; they are also to be found in institutional structures. Various common conceptions of marriage, family, economic and political life are fundamental distortions, which again result in serious long-term problems. Moreover, conceptions are historically shaped and often waver from one distortion to another in attempts at correction, so that we have lurched from rational, contractual marriage to romantic love marriage, and from the *laissez-faire* state to a socialist one, and these represent misconceptions of these institutions which have caused or are causing serious problems. Analysis of institutional distortions of marriage, commerce, the state, the church, *etc.*, will be dealt with in subsequent chapters.

Again, the meaning of norms can be fundamentally distorted when they are seen within a non-Christian perspective. It is not just that different perspectives result in different norms, but also that the meaning of norms depends upon the framework in which they are understood. For example, the norm of honesty can mean that you should be honest before God, or that you might get caught if you are not, or that it is the best policy, or that people generally approve. The formal standard means different things depending on the perspective in which they are set. Thus another whole area of problems concerns norms which have become hollow or lost their context and become brittle, and norms based on a false perspective, which people obey faithfully to their cost.

Finally, the attitudes of individuals which are shaped by the faith which governs their lives create many problems in their social lives. This applies not only to private institutions and relationships, like marriage, family and friendships, but also in big institutions, where, for example, the tussle of contradicting attitudes or the domination of one mistaken individual can compromise the best institutional structure. We recognize therefore that personal attitudes and faith have their place within sociological analysis alongside more macrosocial studies, and that the aim is not to go behind people to some impersonal forces which explain away their behaviour.

This becomes even more evident when we look beyond the points that have just been made. It is one thing to say that there is misunderstanding at cultural, institutional, normative and individual levels, but it is another to say that the misunderstanding is culpable. Yet the Scriptures emphasize this point in a wide variety of different contexts. The truth is suppressed by wickedness, or to put it another way, people are continually rationalizing what they know to be wrong. Actions shape beliefs. Again, we can see this process in operation from the macrosocial to the personal levels. We watch nations rationalize wars in which their part is despicable; we watch parties in power justify political actions on spurious grounds; we see murder justified by a new norm of legitimate violence; and we see individuals who do wrong justifying themselves and rationalizing their action. 'The woman whom Thou gavest to be with me, she gave me fruit of the tree, and I ate' (Gn. 3:12). No more needs to be said.

Thus, a Christian sociological critique needs to be multifaceted, and it also shows why sociology must be critical. If human actions are compounded of good and evil, true and false, healthy and distorted, as Scripture suggests, then an uncritical and undiscerning approach, which treats all human actions as data, bypasses most of the important issues. This, it could be argued, is the effect of an empiricist approach to sociology.

From this introduction to a Christian perspective we shall therefore turn to substantive sociological analysis.

Chapter 6

Free relationships

Free societal relationships

We have already established the difference between free societal relationships and communities; the former do not have and the latter do have prior norms which structure the relationships. For example, if a group of people meet in a public house, the relationships are free, but if there is a prior agreement that they should play darts and each should buy a round of drinks, they have formed a certain kind of community. Although we are initially looking at free relationships, it is evident that few contacts have this pure form. Most people in Britain agree to address one another in English; this is a norm in much of the nation, and strangers on meeting one another normally pre-suppose this community of language. Nevertheless there is a vast, undefined area in which people work out relationships, and these will be our concern. When people or groups meet, there are various attitudes or responses or policies which they can adopt in their relationships. The aim of this chapter is to identify some attitudes which are widespread and important, and to analyse their content and effects.

It is worthwhile to relate this analysis briefly to the great amount of work that has been done in recent years on the technicalities of group and interpersonal dynamics. Analyses of non-verbal communication, expectations, linkages, social space, unconscious group processes, roles, transactional patterns, *etc.*, have produced new and exciting views of interaction processes.

At the same time T-group and other forms of group therapy have been carried out in the belief that greater depths of personal insight and awareness are available through group interaction.[1] However, although much of this work is valuable, some of the fundamental religious dimensions of interpersonal relations remain undisclosed. As these provide the necessary basis for more technical analysis, we need to begin by considering what relationships mean to persons.

The chapter will be largely problem orientated. This does not mean that all relationships are problematic, but it provides a framework for defining some of the problems that exist. The basic thesis is that the insoluble humanist dilemma of the conflict between individualist and collectivist views of social relationships has been articulated in a whole range of day to day contacts, and because the perspectives are false, the results are destructive. It is worth noting that evidence to support this approach is not available from research material, simply because it is a radically different perspective, although some material can fairly be used. The substantive test of whether these attitudes are widespread comes as each reader compares them to his own experience. At the end of the chapter we shall look at the alternative perspective for free relationships provided by the various Christian norms.

The individualist pole

Individualism is a deep and pervasive modern, spiritual force. Not only have existentialist philosophers given us the idea of man in the world constructing reality from his own ego, but people are also expected to be at the centre of their universe in everyday affairs, and their independent, self-regarding, self-authenticating egos are nurtured by many aspects of our culture. Many of their deepest thoughts and beliefs validate and support some facet of their ego, and these attitudes are preconscious in that they have been internalized without being consciously considered, because the prior, humanist, religious commitment is so pervasive. We shall now consider a number of distinct responses to free relationships within this overall perspective.

[1] Of special Christian interest is the work of the Grubb Institute of Behavioural Studies, 1 Whitehall Place, London SW1.

The egocentric response   Some people create the impression that they neither know, nor want to know, anything about other people. The focus is on their own activities, life-style, characteristics, problems and wishes; other people are just part of the furniture. Yet while some people obviously have this attitude all the time, most of us at some time or another are gripped by this kind of response. It may find expression in ignoring other people, being preoccupied by our own problems, lost in self-pity, intoxicated with our own success, or being concerned solely about our own pleasure. In this situation another person can only enter into a relationship on the terms of the subject's egocentricity; he can only listen and not be listened to. Clearly this pattern is very unbalanced and is destructive of relationships. The basic desire is to bring more and more of the social environment into the scope and power of the subject, and it reveals the fundamental weakness of the idea of the autonomous ego. It is a failure of true identity, which needs correction, as Peter discovered (Mk. 9:2–8).

The possessive response   One common form of individualism is materialism, where the individual's relationships are dominated by the idea of possession. Goods are seen as a means of security, satisfaction and identity for the individual. The consequence of this attitude, which is the same as the biblical concept of coveting, is that objects and goods are put between one person and another. This is true spatially as more and more detached houses are built and increasing use of the car results in greater insularity. It is also true in temporal terms as the business of making and spending money gives people little time to spend with others. Within relationships, also, possessions act as barriers; if I covet what is my neighbour's, the relationship with him is closed. One classic example is that recorded by Willmott and Young:[1]

'People are not very friendly here. It's the same on all the estates. They've nothing else to do when they've finished work except watch you. It's all jealousy. They're afraid you'll get a penny more than they have. In London people have other things to occupy their minds. Here when they've done their

---

[1] M. Young and P. Willmott, *Family and Kinship in East London* (Pelican, 1962), p. 160.

work they've nothing to do. They're at the window and they notice everything. They say, "Mrs Brown's got a new hat on." They don't miss anything.'

At the same time this attitude, transferred to persons, creates possessive relationships, attempts to own others, to make them securely one's own or sources of one's own satisfaction. Not surprisingly, this provokes fundamental resistance.

The competitive response Another individualist attitude is that of a person seeking to enhance his identity by gaining advantage over another person or persons. Often competition is normatively enclosed within the context of a game, simply to make sure that it is restricted and not taken too seriously. When the communal framework breaks down, games can become dangerous; there may be a punch-up at a football match, or a game of cards may become vicious. When a situation is actually competitive, such as when several people are being interviewed for one job, the relationships can be fairly uneasy. The underlying motive aims at the eclipse of the other person and the enhancement of the subject, and as such it destroys the possibility of balanced relationships. Individual identity is established at the expense of other people. If a person is committed to winning in relationships, it is not surprising that he becomes isolated.

The areas in which this competitive motive can be developed are legion. Dress, conversation, intellectual and physical activities can all be used in this way, but the degree to which competitive relationships are encouraged varies. Middle class families and educational institutions seem to emphasize them more, and the 11 plus and other examinations have provided a convenient focus for these attitudes. The 'successful' and those associated with elitist organizations are more tempted to depend on this kind of prop to their identity, but the ethos is certainly deep in our culture.

Individual pressure Another response which grows out of the individual's desire to control relationships, so that they are conducted on his terms, is the use of various forms of social pressure. These may include physical force, anger, presuming the wishes and intentions of others, ostracism and the verbal put-

154

down. The focus is the will of the individual, and the use of these forms is directed towards the validation of that will. Laing has studied the effects of this kind of behaviour within families and its relationship with schizophrenia.

> 'Maya once said, however, that she could remember the occasion quite clearly. She was dicing some meat. Her mother was standing behind her, telling her how to do things right, and that she was doing things wrong as usual. She felt something was going to snap inside unless she acted. She turned round and brandished the knife at her mother, and then threw it on the floor.'[1]

This more extreme form of pressure through nagging shows something that occurs in more moderate forms in all kinds of relationships. It is not without significance that one of the more successful techniques in group therapy is to withdraw all forms of pressure and see what happens. Nor is it to be overlooked that Christ's dealings with people had the characteristic of not involving any kind of pressure.

The manipulative response Competition and pressure are overt, if often subtle, but manipulation is a covert method of gaining advantage. One form is the manipulation of people's feelings to achieve one's own ends. This can be the 'war wounded person who wants money for a meal', or more seriously the person who plays on another's pride to get what he wants. Flattery is widespread in selling, industry and politics, and is but one form of covert self-interest. 'You owe it to yourself', 'I know you're a fair person' and many other such phrases, by working on the self-image of others, help the subject to achieve what he wants. Another form of manipulation is presenting half-truths or using a person's ignorance. Yet another is to use a person's sense of guilt, of which blackmail is an extreme example.

A characteristic of this response is that it depends on knowing a person's normal behaviour. It is worth noting that the extraordinary expansion in behavioural studies in recent years means that the equipment for manipulation, often on a large scale, is

---

[1] R. D. Laing and A. Esterton, *Sanity, Madness and the Family* (Pelican, 1970), p. 41.

available as never before. The way in which it muddies relationships by interposing a level of secrecy and deceit is soon evident, as is the fact that the end result is distrust.

The self-validating response   The individualist, because he is his own final authority, has a need to be right, and may use other people to validate himself and his opinions. There is some evidence that people even choose the kind of friends who will do this. The friend is used as a means of supporting the subject in his opinions, and if the friend disagrees with the subject, the basis of the friendship is threatened. This contrasts with the teaching in Proverbs, 'Faithful are the wounds of a friend' (27:6), and 'He who heeds admonition gains understanding' (15:32). Within this pattern the important issue in any argument or discussion is not what is correct, but *who* is right; self-validation has priority over understanding.

In fact, a self-validating attitude is unlikely to produce much agreement or understanding, because the subject's attitude will be inherently hostile: he will be unable or unwilling to regard the views and attitudes of others with empathy or understanding, because the validation of his own views is so compelling. Moreover, the emphasis on being right closes the possibility of wider understanding; new knowledge is a shock to the opinion structure which supports his identity. Sometimes it seems that only a thin line separates love of truth from love of *my* truth, but in reality there is a deep chasm, and there are few of us who have not sought self-validation and cannot identify the harm that it has done in relationships. The truth is not subject to a single person's ego.

The comparative response   It is not uncommon for people to relate to one another by comparing themselves with others. Often the comparisons are relatively innocuous, but equally they may contain an element which can be identified as self-glorification at the expense of others or the obverse, envy of others. If I am better than, more beautiful than, more popular than, more balanced than, more mature than, healthier than, humbler than another, it can be a source of self-congratulation, a hook on which I can hang my cap, which cannot but divide me from others. It is dangerous, as well as false, to walk around hugging our own egos. James Baldwin has often argued that the free relationship of whites with blacks has this character, in that the former need and use the latter to bolster their self-respect. Moreover, it is easy to choose a point of comparison that favours oneself.

'Boys and girls from Tops families by the age of ten think Bottoms children their own age are "tough, stink, and dumb"; the latter label upper class children as "sissies, smart-alecks, and stuck up".'[1]

Conversely, if people are induced to think within this perspective and identify themselves by what they lack or how they are inferior, relationships are impaired by the lack of self-respect.

This attitude affects people in complex ways. It is not only that self-glorification creates social distance and that the comparisons are given a false significance, but also that the nexus on which relationships function tends to be the point of comparison. If one person lives in and depends on the assertion that he is 'more intelligent', this will continually overshadow conversation. The fact that many of these attitudes are learned at an early age, and are fairly automatic processes in interpersonal exchanges, makes them especially debilitating.

The self-righteous response Christ told this parable to some who trusted in themselves that they were righteous and despised others: 'Two men went up into the temple to pray, one a Pharisee and the other a tax collector. The Pharisee stood and prayed thus with himself, "God, I thank thee that I am not like other men, extortioners, unjust, adulterers, or even like this tax collector. I fast twice a week, I give tithes of all that I get"' (Lk. 18:9–12). Since he said that, self-righteousness has never really recovered. Nevertheless, there is a tenacity with which many of us believe in our own goodness and make that belief an important part of the construction of our own ego. Moreover, the forms of goodness which we can identify within ourselves give evidence of considerable powers of invention. However, again we find that the attitude gives a certain warped form to relationships. If I am

---

[1] J. Unseem *et al.*, 'Stratification in a Prairie Town' *American Sociological Review*, VII, 1942, p. 339.

good-humoured, then when something goes wrong it must be the other person who is being awkward. So the inevitable concomitant of belief in one's goodness is blame of others, and normally the blame will be strongest in the area where the virtue is thought to be greatest. The thrifty will blame the spendthrift, the tidy the untidy, and the moral the immoral. Again, it is evident that this form of the individualist perspective creates a judgmental barrier between person and person, which is often felt if more rarely spoken.

Paradoxically, however, the supposed source of ego strength is at its most brittle when driven by this individualist motive. The person who considers himself to be thoughtful to others, or competent, loses an ability to be self-critical, and therefore is weak at that very point. 'You hypocrites, you whited sepulchres, which outside are clean but inside are full of dead men's bones.'

The privatized response   Privacy is a complex social concept. There are large areas which are private to the marriage relationship, and a different kind of privacy needs to be respected by the state in relation to individuals. However, there is also a privatized response whereby people are unwilling for self-protective reasons to reveal certain areas of their lives to others. This response is shown by a variety of patterns of behaviour: discussing neutral subjects, evading questions, lying, changing the subject, rudeness, blustering, creating social distance, retreating into roles, presenting a front or seeking anonymous situations. People talk about 'keeping themselves to themselves' and 'minding their own business' and seek privacy by isolation, busyness and high mobility. The pattern is widespread, and it develops not just through fear of gossip, misunderstanding, judgment or abuse, although some people fail to create the trust that dispels privacy.

The attitude of the subject is essentially a self-protective one. By creating barriers he is able to protect some area of his life from external scrutiny, and this creates a security for the person's ego which would not be available in a more transparent set of relationships. It is a process whereby people hope to conceal things that are wrong in their lives. However, this social security is obtained at a cost. Firstly, it involves a fear that contact with other people will be more direct than the subject wants. Secondly, it is a process of covering up wounds or problems without solving them, and inevitably there comes a time when they are revealed and prove to be even more intractable. Thirdly, this attitude prevents the sharing of problems, and it is often only by sharing that the solutions to the problems of life are found. Again, the obvious result of a defensive, individualistic response is to undermine the possibility of full transparent relationships.

The hedonist response It is also possible to see relationships in terms of the pleasure that they give. This has two elements: the subject enters only into those relationships which give him pleasure or satisfaction, and he requires that the relationship should be pleasurable. The effect of the first is that there is a great deal of selectivity in that permanent links are established only with those whom the subject likes. The concept 'liking' implies, it could be argued, that the subject will get pleasure from the relationship; it is egocentrically grounded. Further, because the *sine qua non* of the relationship is that it should give the subject pleasure, its basis is extremely fickle. As soon as the subject is required to give, suffer, *etc.*, there is considerable strain.

That this kind of relationship proliferates can be inferred from the normal pattern of contact with television and other mass media stars. The relationships are nearly always one way, and the nature of most of them is that the comedian or star gives pleasure to the persons with whom he relates through the television set. This archetypal relationship can easily be carried over into a range of other free personal relationships, and the burden that it imposes on the person who is expected to give pleasure is obviously great.

The collectivist pole

Collectivism and individualism are not mere alternatives which can yield a golden mean. They are in dialectical tension as opposites; both are inadequate and each contradicts the other. The individualist perspective cannot provide an adequate basis for human relationships and, as we have seen in our preliminary analysis, warps them in fundamental ways. Sartre's cry, 'Hell is other people', points the whole spiritual direction of this perspective. Nobody can consistently live within this humanist perspective. Its ultimate meaninglessness pushes men to seek part of their identity in relation to other people. Thus collectivism is also a necessary response, and people are inevitably caught in the antinomy between the two poles. They experience both individualist and collectivist responses and the contradictions and problems of both dog their relationships. Again, these are collectivist responses where the person seeks to establish the meaning of his identity in terms of other people, and these we shall now seek to identify.

The image-creating response   When someone becomes dependent on other people for his identity, in whole or in part, there is a tendency for this identity to be what other people ascribe to him. The response within a relationship therefore becomes that of creating an image with others, with the implicit understanding that the image is 'me', or is at least strongly supporting my ego. That this kind of response is widespread is evidenced by the backing given to image-creation, or reputation building, in advertising, in a whole range of 'personal success' literature, in politics, in the mass media, and also by institutions like banks, multinational companies and airlines. The logic of this attitude has been investigated in depth by Erving Goffman[1] in a range of books, in which he analyses the presentation of the 'self' to others in widely differing situations. However, the root philosophy of this attitude is not always critically examined in Goffman's work.

Essentially, either the attitude is hypocritical, that is, the person knows that he is something other than he is presented as being, or the person is the image, that is, other people's views of him are correct. The problems with both these positions are readily apparent. The first means that there is a basic discontinuity between the private and the public self which prevents relationships from being transparent and open. Just as two people wearing make-up never truly meet face to face, so this attitude precludes open relationships. If, however, a person is his image, the

[1] E. Goffman, *The Presentation of the Self in Everyday Life* (Pelican, 1971); *Stigma* (Pelican, 1968); *Relations in Public* (Penguin, 1971).

meaning of his life consists in acting one or many parts. The hollowness of Shakespeare's picture of life in the soliloquy 'All the world's a stage' conveys the personal void that exists when life is mere role playing. There is no hypocrisy, because a person is what he pretends to be. This latter position is too desperate to be the *Weltanschauung* of many, and the more normal pattern is rather for image-creating to be tied in with various forms of egocentricity, so that the person has a strong vested interest in a hypocritical image. Few of us are immune from this humanist dilemma, and yet many of us have probably tasted the pure clear water of unhypocritical relationships.

Extrinsic relationships It is possible for relationships to form around some activity or focus which is external to the people concerned. They may play football, drink, dance or work together, have children at the same school, have similar homes and clothes. Indeed in our society it is interesting how many relationships are limited to these situational factors. The basis of the relationship is the circumstances or activities. What X and Y have *in common* is a relationship with a third element. An identity is established between the two as golfers, cooks, mothers, business men, *etc.*, which provides common meeting points and topics of communication.

It is readily apparent that, if this remains the sole basis of the friendship, problems will appear. Mothers will talk obsessively of children, business men of work or golfers of golf, for when the relationship moves out of these areas it is on shaky ground. Or, to put it another way, if the friendship is to develop, it must do so in a golf or maternal direction. Thus there can also be a tendency to become heavily committed to the context in which the person finds friendship, or at least finds something in common with others. This explains some of the popularity of the public house, the clubhouse, the shops and the church. Many people may feel and regret the closed nature of these kinds of relationships, but they cannot get outside the cultural matrix which makes them so dominant in our society.

The acceptability focus A common drive in all kinds of relationships is the desire to be liked. Many people want to be liked and fear being snubbed, excluded and avoided. Conversely, many people feel and express liking for or dislike of other people. This matrix of attitudes is very strong and bears further analysis. What makes people acceptable or unacceptable to others? One answer is that the acceptable person is or does what the other person approves of or wants. The arbiter behind popularity is always the other person, and the attitude of wanting to be liked is therefore, in Riesman's phrase, 'other directed'. The threat of disliking can become a very powerful weapon and it is one that children experiment with very early. 'Lend me your ball.' 'No, I don't like you.' 'I don't care', is the archetypal interchange which often becomes no less important in later life.

The results of this are all too evident. Riesman[1] describes how the characteristic of the other-directed person is anxiety—a continual fear of other people's disapproval or rejection. This fear can easily, in turn, lead to manipulation. If you want to be liked you can be manipulated into buying rounds at the pub or going to bed with your boyfriend. It may force people into a character mould; they create an acceptable image of the jolly comedian or the easy-going fellow and cannot get outside this acceptable pattern even when they want to. Again, what people like is different, and a person may therefore feel he has to be a tough, shrewd, get-ahead man at work, but feels pressured into behaving very differently with his wife and friends. The other side of this pattern is that those who are rejected or disliked, and who cannot move outside this perspective, feel and become social outcasts, and misery can become a dominant element in their lives. The whole complex of attitudes therefore induces various forms of behavioural and emotional slavery, which is a destructive basis on which to establish any (supposedly) free relationship.

Group identity   A further development of this general perspective is when the subject's identity becomes vested in some social group or another. The stream of teenage identity groups stretching from Teddy Boys to Hell's Angels and beyond suggests that group identity is a common response during the crucial years of young adulthood. However, groups large and small with many

[1] D. Riesman, *The Lonely Crowd* (Yale University Press, 1961).

different kinds of significance intersect in our society and the larger ones of nation, race, region, county and city have considerable subjective importance for many people. There is a considerable industry on television and radio, and in magazines, newspapers, books and education, which promotes a county identity (not only in Yorkshire). Football or cricket teams often have a totemic role in these group identities. At the same time there are the more immediate groups with which a person can identify. Most of them will necessarily be exclusive, in that the group identity will exclude those who do not meet the entrance requirements. This exclusiveness can in turn be the basis of rank. Further, the group will demand conformity to its practices and loyalty. The potential power of these groups can perhaps be grasped from the fact that Chie Nakane makes them the central concept in her interpretation of Japanese society.[1]

The consequences of this kind of concern, of wanting to be 'in' rather than 'out', are again destructive of free relationships. Groups offer the individual an identity which is based upon the group characteristic, but this identity constrains the depth of relationship in the group. The hearty group cannot acknowledge that its members have problems; the Old Boys Union is necessarily retrospective; the ruling clique centres round its power.

The conversation of the cosmopolitans in Banbury can almost be heard from the following description of them:

'Cosmopolitans are a category; although united by the fact that all live in Banbury, they have their frame of reference in a wider society. Their key question is one about achievement—What does he do? What has he done?'[2]

Thus on the one hand the full personhood of people tends to be eclipsed, and on the other the group can induce passivity, dependence, submissiveness, fear of sanctions and a non-critical attitude towards group activity. Teenage vandalism and violence seem to fall predominantly within this group ethos. The problems created for the excluded, or the non-conformist, are too obvious to need further comment.

---

[1] Chie Nakane, *Japanese Society* (Pelican, 1973).
[2] R. Frankenberg, *Communities in Britain* (Pelican, 1966), pp. 163–4.

The other-directed conscience   Free relationships always have a strong normative or moral content, but few have noticed that in our secular society many, if not most, people allow their conscience to be shaped by others. Their prime concern is what other people will say, and in a very powerful way friends, colleagues and neighbours become the moral imperative of their lives. This tendency is reinforced by the strong inclination of some people to pass judgment on the lives, habits and activities of others. There is some evidence that previously religious areas where Christian conviction has been replaced by social conviction tend to be strong in this kind of judgment. The *Under Milk Wood* pattern is one where gossip and tut-tutting are expected to act as moral cement. The pattern can be carried further; in China public shaming is still a widely used form of punishment.

When the moral approval or disapproval of other people are arbiters of right or wrong, the subject often becomes strangely amoral in his attitudes. Goffman describes it thus:

'We now come to the basic dialectic. In their capacity as performers, individuals will be concerned with maintaining the impression that they are living up to the standards by which they and their products are judged. Because these standards are so numerous and so pervasive the individuals who are performers dwell more than we might think in the moral world. But, *qua* performers, individuals are concerned not with the moral issue of realizing these standards, but with the amoral issue of engineering a convincing impression that these standards are being realized. Our activity then, is largely concerned with moral matters, but as performers we do not have a moral concern with them.'[1]

It can be argued that pilfering, fraud, and shoplifting are so common partly because, when people are not being watched, there are no other moral constraints operating. More importantly, when people pass the buck of their conscience to others, their moral education is starved, and they find themselves in situations where they do not know what to do. They become morally passive, capable of being swayed and manipulated by anyone with social standing or charisma. Moreover, when wrong

---

[1] E. Goffman, *The Presentation of Self in Everyday Life* (Pelican, 1971), p. 243.

is done to them they have no rationale for doing anything but wrong in return.

The status response The concept of status has an uneasy position in sociological analysis. Many would like to use it in a neutral sense, denoting position, but most would agree that status denotes the conferring of honour, prestige and superiority. However, this immediately raises some of the problems associated with the concept. Who confers honour? On what grounds or criteria is it conferred? Do others agree? Does the subject fit in with this schema? These questions introduce issues which can be partially answered within the collectivist paradigm. Status can be defined as the result of collective self-glorification, and it involves using some criterion which is seen as significant to create an exclusive group which confers honour on itself and hopes that others will too. Most status systems start from the top; that is, they are generated by those to whom they think honour is due. The Hindu caste system can thus be seen as the result of Brahmanic special pleading in the Vedic period.[1] They then become vehicles of social power, especially if they become widely accepted, although it is likely that competing status systems, based upon different patterns of self-glorification, will exist in any society. The actual pattern in British society is complex and socially destructive. Self-glorification is vested in occupation, wealth, race, standard of housing, type of car, lifestyle, patterns of consumption, education, dress, trendiness or importance, and it often takes quite a while to discover what are the status criteria in any particular group. For the subject the key issue then becomes whether he should bid for honour or prestige on the terms laid down by others. When he does so (and the social tools used to put pressure on the subject can be subtle and varied), the status system becomes more extensive.

The divisive power of this collective self-glorification has been evidenced many times. Its power can be felt from the following comment on the Willmott-Young study of Woodford:

'Inside people's minds, as we have shown in this chapter, the boundaries of class are still closely drawn. Classlessness is not

[1] See R. Thapar, *A History of India* (Penguin, 1966), pp. 39, 40.

emerging there. On the contrary, the nearer the classes are drawn by the objective facts of income, styles of life and housing, the more are middle class people liable to pull them apart by exaggerating the differences subjectively regarded. In Woodford this has been done with such success that to a very large extent social relationships are confined to one side or another of the dividing line in the mind.'[1]

The reader can probably detail the divisions that collective self-glorification causes in his social environment, and can also recognize the drive of this humanist attitude in the construction of his and other people's identity.

The dilemma

Even without taking into account the macrosocial pressures on free relationships there is, therefore, likely to be a range of attitudes which destroys and perverts free relationships. The humanism, expressed concurrently in individualist and collectivist forms, is so widespread in our culture that most readers have probably experienced at least some of the responses sketched here, and also know the result of these attitudes on their relationships. However, there is no mean between the two poles, because they are both necessary developments of the humanist religious perspective. The only alternative is one which moves outside humanism to find another religious root, and which radically undercuts this whole complex of problems. To that alternative we now turn.

The Christian perspective

There is a whole range of norms which define a Christian understanding of free relationships, but before we examine them, it is important to explain the rationale for a different perspective. For the individualist and collectivist views are not just problematic, but also fundamentally wrong from a biblical viewpoint. The crucial issue is that persons can only find their true identity in

---

[1] P. Willmott and M. Young, *Family and Class in a London Suburb* (Mentor, 1967), p. 107.

relation to God, their Creator, and not in their own autonomy or in other people. A denial of the true source of meaning of a person's life necessarily involves some denial and/or perversion of his created personality. As Augustine put it, 'Thou hast made us for Thyself alone and our hearts are restless till they find their rest in Thee.' When a person is committed to love the Lord his God with all his heart and with all his soul and with all his mind, the solutions to the relational problems appear as compelling arguments. They all follow from the break from a man-centred faith. It is interesting at this stage to show how John Calvin analysed similar problems in *The Institutes*, changing the basis of the argument from a man-centred to a Christian one. We are doing no new thing.

'For so blindly do we all rush in the direction of self-love, that everyone thinks he has a good reason for exalting himself and despising all others in comparison. If God has bestowed on us something not to be repented of, trusting to it, we immediately become elated, and not only swell, but almost burst with pride. The vices with which we abound we carefully conceal from others, and flatteringly represent to ourselves as minute and trivial, nay, sometimes hug them as virtues. When the same qualities which we admire in ourselves are seen in others, even though they should be superior, we, in order that we may not be forced to yield to them, maliciously lower and carp at them; in like manner, in the case of vices, not contented with severe and keen animadversion, we studiously exaggerate them. Hence the insolence with which each, as if exempted from the common lot, seeks to exalt himself above his neighbour, confidently and proudly despising others or at least looking down upon them as his inferiors. The poor man yields to the rich, the plebeian to the noble, the servant to the master, the unlearned to the learned, and yet everyone inwardly cherishes some idea of his own superiority. Thus each flattering himself, sets up a kind of kingdom in his breast; the arrogant, to satisfy themselves, pass censure on the minds and manners of other men, and when contention arises, the full venom is displayed. Many bear about with them some measure of mildness so long as all things go smoothly and lovingly with them, but how few are there who, when stung and irritated, preserve the same tenet of moderation? For this there is no other remedy than to pluck up by the roots those most noxious parts, self-love and love of victory. This the doctrine of Scripture does. For it teaches us to remember that the endowments which God has bestowed upon us are not our own, but His free gifts and that those who plume themselves upon them, betray their ingratitude. "Who maketh thee to differ," saith Paul, "and what hast thou then that thou didst not receive? now if thou didst receive it, why dost thou glory as if thou hadst not received it?" (1 Cor. iv, 7).'[1]

Thus the argument is that all the immediate problems of manipulation, social distance, egocentricity, self-justification, privatization, superficiality, social pretence, dominance, status, passivity, conformity, *etc.*, have their roots in the false humanist answers to the issue of who a person is. Conversely the Christian answer is the root answer from which all the proximate answers come.

Various individualist responses are wrong because your neighbour is also created and loved by God, and you therefore have no central place in the universe. You cannot love God (and your neighbour) if you also love mammon. You cannot seek to glorify yourself in competition with others when God knows the sordid basis of that self-glorification, and when it obviously reflects an inadequate relationship with your creator. Manipulating others is ruled out, because although you can fool some people some of the time you cannot fool God at all and his judgment is uncannily precise. Why do I need to be right when God is my judge, and why do I need to compare myself with others when my relationship with God is unique? Why the pretence of self-righteousness when God knows my sin? Why retreat into privacy when, O Lord, you have searched me and known me? Why search for my pleasure when joy is a gift from God? The underlying rationale of these individualistic responses crumbles under these arguments.

Similarly, collectivist responses become hollow. Why do you try to create an image when you are the image of God, and he penetrates every aspect of you like a laser beam? Extrinsic

[1] J. Calvin, *Institutes*, III. vii. **4**.

relationships become meaningless with a full understanding of what two people have in common. When accepted by God, why do we need to be accepted by one group or another? One by one the responses disintegrate and become meaningless, and new norms of relatedness grow up out of Christian doctrine and teaching.

These can be expressed prohibitively as a warning. Thus, no one should withhold food, drink, clothing and shelter from his fellow who is in need, even if that person is an enemy (Dt. 15:11; Pr. 25:21). There is to be no stealing from, or robbing, or oppressing the neighbour in any way, especially if there is economic advantage (Ex. 20:15; 22:22–27; Lv. 19:9–13). One is to lend to a poor person and not necessarily expect repayment (Dt. 15:1–11; Mt. 5:40–42). A man must not be unjust to, bear false witness against or slander his fellow man (Lv. 19:15, 16; Pr. 11:9–13), nor must he hate his neighbour in his heart, be rude to him or seek his harm (Lv. 19:17, 18; Dt. 19:11–13). Moreover, these norms are not discretionary, for it is clear both from the Old Testament and the parable of the good Samaritan that anybody with whom we have contact is to be regarded as our neighbour and loved.

The positive content of these personal norms is, however, far deeper. Consider, for example, the free relationships which are closed up by feelings of resentment, of being wronged or offended, of being annoyed or hurt. Pride makes a renewal of the relationship seem impossible. But the biblical norms transcend this impasse. It is a man's glory to overlook an offence (Pr. 19:11) and to *forgive* one another is necessary because God in Christ forgave us. There is a basis for treating the issue that has arisen, and it involves recognition of the sin and forgiveness. The power of renewal that results when old, tired relationships are washed by repentance and forgiveness is tremendous. It has been felt by countless Christians, and in the Civil Rights Movement under the leadership of Martin Luther King it possibly prevented serious breakdown in many communities throughout the USA. The same may yet be true in Northern Ireland.

Thus the norms of love, peace, patience, kindness, meekness, compassion and forgiveness, in their biblical meaning, dwell at the centre of all free relationships. They are, of course, not measurable sociological variables; they are not impersonal causal factors which allow explanations of behaviour patterns. It is, however, impossible to continue the pretence that they are sociologically peripheral. They are, and always have been, the key elements in free social relationships.

With this introductory analysis we can now approach the more complex issue of defining communities and identifying some of the problems involved in their existence in modern urban society.

Chapter 7

Community and class

One of the most elusive and yet important concepts in sociology and in most people's lives is that of community. A community may vary in size from the EEC with its many millions to a small group living as a commune. When people live together in relationships such as these, many issues arise, and we shall now discuss some of them.

Definition

The definition of 'community' is quite a complex issue. We could say that a community exists when a number of people share *norms*, whether they have actually met or not. This immediately forces us to recognize that the concept of community does not necessarily depend on geographical location; we would not call a crowd in a street a community unless there were deeper links that united them. It also brings out the point that the idea of community involves some degree of *permanence*; an academic community is one where the pursuit of knowledge is upheld and valued, and there is a stable understanding that this is the case. Communities may change, disintegrate or form, but there is normally some degree of continuity in the norms that are established.

We also note that a distinction may be made between *passive communities*, which are not organized, and which may not have articulated norms, and *organized* communities, where the norms are stated and developed into aims, and where the members voluntarily subscribe to an organization. Thus, the Welsh people are, in part, a passive linguistic community, while the Welsh Language Society is obviously an organized community. There is a similar difference between a neighbourhood and a commune or a kibbutz. It is apparent that what people normally mean by community is an unorganized or passive one.

Another important characteristic of the idea of community is that membership is *voluntary*. There is freedom to accept or dissociate oneself from the norms of a community. A person of Sikh origins who ceases to wear a turban, and to conform to the other practices of that group, withdraws from the community. Moreover, although there may be institutional forms and authority relationships within a community, the actual communal relations are free; they do not involve coercion or power. Thus it would not normally be meaningful to talk of a prison community. This point is of some importance because we shall later consider cases where the encroachment of pressures and coercion has had the effect of weakening communities.

A further point is that we need to distinguish communities which are primarily social from those which form around another aspect of life. A youth club is obviously primarily social, but there are various other kinds of community which correspond to the different aspects of life in which their key norms are to be found. It is worth spending some time identifying these different types, which are only secondarily social. Some are religious communities, like the Community of the Resurrection, Trappist Monasteries and the Taizé Community, for example. The agreed norms are extrasocial, and the social life is largely shaped by religious and ecclesiastical norms.[1] Similarly there are ethical communities, which range from groups where people can agree not to smoke to others with a better developed ethical perspective such as the Friends of the Earth, the Northern Ireland Peace Movement and the National Association for the Advancement of Coloured People. There are also political or juridical communities: the nation, characterized by the membership criterion of citizenship and more local political communities such as

[1] See G. Moorhouse, *Against All Reason* (Penguin, 1972) for a review of religious community life.

metropolitan areas, counties and districts. Aesthetic ones could range from the Pre-Raphaelite Brotherhood or the Royal Academy to a jazz or folk club. Economic communities exist at the level of the EEC or at a more immediate level. A very important issue is whether trades unions and companies should be regarded as organized economic communities or seen in some other way, since this very much affects the kind of authority which is exercised. The pattern continues with linguistic sharing and norms which not only operate at the level of complete languages, but also through dialects, patterns and conventions of speech, and traditions in literature. Educational communities exist in the form of universities, colleges and schools. There are also important communities of thought: they may be organized like the Vienna Circle, or passive, in that members of the group will accept a certain kind of argument. Whatever aspect directs the community and gives it its characteristic norms, it will also be social, although the social aspect will be shaped by the dominant aspect. There is clearly a difference between a religious, philosophical and musical community in that they will worship, argue or sing together. Given this pluriformity of communal patterns, we must beware of a unidimensional view which would ignore these differences.

We therefore see that the crucial issue for any community concerns the content of the norms about which people agree or disagree. There are several points that can be made at a general level. The first is that the depth of community largely depends upon the degree to which values and norms are shared. Togetherness cannot be simulated or organized or manipulated or assumed; it depends upon the freely given and actually experienced agreement among the members. Secondly, the end of the agreement, temporarily or numerically, marks the boundary of the community. Again we note that as well as the norms of the dominant aspect, the definitive ones, communities also have norms in all the other aspects. Thus a Choral Society aims to make music of a certain standard and kind, but it also has ethical, economic, social, pedagogic, linguistic and even emotional norms. A Welsh Choral Society allows itself a different range of emotions from a Red Army Choir or a Madrigal Society. It follows that it is possible for a community to be disrupted through failure in any of these secondary aspects of its existence.

This brings us to the last general point of definition. The norms which a community shares will normally have some pattern of coherence. Each community has its own ethos or basic faith, and it is often helpful to discover what these are. However, in analysing the norms the sociologist cannot adopt a neutral position, he must either agree or disagree with them, and must make clear the grounds on which he does so. The issues are important. For example, the view of a racial community associated with the NAACP, the Black Power Movement, the Ku-Klux Klan, the Jews, the Pakistani Community, the Sikhs, the National Front, *etc.*, all need to be critically analysed. In many respects they are incompatible; there will often be much to learn from the normative insights of a particular group, but they cannot be viewed neutrally.

Economic community in Britain: Class

We shall begin by looking at the national unorganized or passive community to consider some of the aspects which are most important in the life of the nation. It would be generally agreed that the degree to which the nation is an economic community is decisive. This immediately raises the issues of whether classes exist in Britain, what they are, and what their meaning might be for communal relationships. To approach this subject properly we need first to consider some theoretical issues, and then to undertake an historical analysis of class patterns. We shall then be in a position to develop some conclusions about this aspect of our national life.

'Class' is one of the most overworked concepts in sociology, but it is mostly used as a 'flat' concept which distinguishes occupational and income differences among the British population. These in turn are seen as indicators of various kinds of social behaviour and attitude. Whether the Registrar-General's five point scale or the Hall-Jones seven point scale is used, not much is implied about the significance of the differences. However, certain deeper issues have emerged. One of them is a difference of view between those sociologists who see class as primarily subjective in the sense that a person's self-assigned class, or where a person puts himself in the social order, is what is significant in the concept, and another group of sociologists who see class as an objective phenomenon, which exists independently of people's self awareness, and can be analysed as such. A second area of debate is whether the Marxist two-class model is still, or ever was, a reasonable approximation of what exists in British society. It has been suggested that the working class is being slowly absorbed into the middle class, the embourgeoisement thesis, but this is disputed in a number of studies which identify continuing differences.[1] Another area of debate concerns the nexus around which classes divide. Is it property, power, the means of production, authority or education; and if it is a combination of these, which has priority? Much of the analysis in this area covers important issues, is thorough and helpful, but it has one weakness.

In trying to establish their own conclusions about class many sociologists have tended towards a neutral or acceptable definition of the term, so as to give their findings the status of objectivity. Many empirical studies have assumed that the meaning of the term is self-evident, as, for example, does that of Westergaard and Resler.

'We shall not tie ourselves to rigid definitions of class groupings and their boundaries, fixed in advance. To recognise the force of class division implies no commitment to an arbitrary assertion of particular lines of division from the outset. We start with the view that class "in itself" is manifest as a set of closely related inequalities of economic condition, power and opportunity. The more closely related those inequalities, and the sharper the divisions in life circumstances which they entail, the more firm then is the structure of class "in itself"[2]

Although this might be adequate for the presentation of the evidence collected, it will not do, for unless there is a commitment

---

[1] See J. Westergaard and H. Resler, *Class in a Capitalist Society* (Pelican, 1976) for a study of 'objective' class; A. Giddens, *The Class Structure of the Advanced Societies* (Hutchinson, 1973) for a thorough conceptual study; and the three studies of *The Affluent Worker* (Cambridge Univ. Press, 1968–9) by J. H. Goldthorpe, D. Lockwood, F. Bechhofer and J. Platt for the nub of the embourgeoisement thesis.

[2] J. Westergaard and H. Resler, *Class in a Capitalist Society* (Pelican, 1976).

in definition, the crucial value issues do not emerge. In fact Westergaard and Resler do put forward a definition, and presumably they do regard inequalities as wrong, and their aim would be the eradication of inequalities of economic condition, power and opportunity. The philosophy and the meaning in the concept are the key to uncovering what, if anything, is wrong with class, and how it can be put right. There are two opposing answers to these questions, which we shall now consider, divested of all the neutrality in which sociologists often clothe them.

A capitalist perspective is composed of a number of justificatory arguments, which may be given different ideological weight One is rooted in the concept of natural order, and rests on the idea that wherever markets exist, there will necessarily be some who profit and some who suffer; since it is naturally so, it is useless to quibble at the fact. Another argument which carries rather more weight today is the belief that variations in reward reflect variations in economic worth, responsibility, effort and moral standing, and that to attack these variations is to subvert the moral order of society. Class therefore largely reflects the value of different groups to society. A different view is more individualist. The individual has an absolute right to economic freedom and personal property rights, and any infringement of these is a denial of basic personal rights. Another common argument, the crucial one in South Africa, is that classes are identified by basic cultural and behavioural differences which inevitably give rise to economic inequalities. Again, it is sometimes suggested that the wealth of the masses is largely dependent on the wealth-creating abilities of an economic elite, and that the greater wealth of the latter is therefore justified by their ability to create wealth and by their need of the resources to do so. Finally, there is the classical capitalist view that an individual has the right to use his capital and to receive the rewards of its use. These various views have been diluted with doses of tax transfers and other forms of redistribution, but they remain the underlying ethos of most conservative views of class. Conservative sociologists have re-expressed these positions in the idea that class variations are necessary and functional to society as a whole. But this formulation misses the main point.

However much they are disguised, the origin of those views

which justify existing class divisions is to be found in the Enlightenment. The arguments depend upon the concepts of natural order, individual freedom, the right of property and the enlightened leader which developed in the 18th century among the landed and educational aristocracy. The arguments themselves are not strong when subjected to detailed examination, but what gives them their tenacity is the Enlightenment faith that undergirds them. There may also be a subtle change in the status of argument among the upper classes; rather than an argument being that which carries conviction and demands obedience, there is a feeling that what really counts in life is wealth, and argument is merely what backs up an established position. Thus there may be a sense in which the upper classes are anti-intellectual, insofar as their wealth carries more weight than argument. The strength of this position is on the whole practical in that what is is what obtains, and people have to live with it, even if it divides the community in some respects.

The other opposing form is Marxism, which has proved to be both a very strong international faith with political, educational, economic and social implications, which act as the ideological rationale for many countries in the world, and also the intellectual starting point for most of the critical analyses of class that have been developed in sociology. The argument of this section will be that many of these analyses suffer from the original weaknesses of the Marxist perspective, which again are very much related to the dominant, secular, intellectual trends of the mid-19th century. The first criticism is that the perspective was anormative in the sense that it was rooted in a belief in the ongoing progress of man in an historicist and evolutionary (or revolutionary) sense. It was not a question of man's obedience to standards, but of what man made of himself. Thus at this deepest level the approach was amoral. This led Marx into several major errors. One was that he had to put his faith in one particular class as the means of historical salvation, and his espousal of the working class has a number of implications. One was the assumption that the motives which operated among the capitalist class to make them exploit others would not also operate among the working class; the new society hinged on an idealistic view of the working class. Another was that Marx was led to assume that the working class could be independent and self-subsistent, or to put it in other terms, that the proletariat could be a community in itself not dependent on other groups in society. In a sense there was an assumption that the proletariat embodied what was right, and they were therefore above criticism and limitations. Later we shall consider whether a more critical approach to working class attitudes and responses is needed, especially in view of this idealistic Marxist slant.

The anormative perspective also led Marx to espouse a means of change which was itself amoral. Power, revolution, the overthrow of the means of production were all methods which were not seen morally, in that history was deemed to require such methods. Class antagonism was seen as inevitable rather than as wrong. Yet we have already established that community requires free relationships among people, and that coercion and the use of power cannot be a basis for building this kind of relational pattern. Thus, if community, a permanent normative community, is one of the aims, this is a strange way of achieving it.

Another critical limitation was that the amoral approach placed a kind of mechanistic limitation on Marx's conception of what was wrong. Exploitation was *only* the appropriation of surplus value by the capitalists; it was not recognized that when the motive was present, all kinds of systems and organizations presented opportunities for exploitation in a variety of different ways. At the same time momentous historical weight was attached to the particular form of economic relationships with which Marx was concerned, while in fact, as we shall suggest soon, the structure of economic relationships has gone through a number of revolutions since that time which are just as significant. Another conclusion from this approach was that it was the technical structure of capitalism which would collapse, when in fact technically the market system has far outlasted the criticisms which were aimed at it by Marx. The 19th century tendency to see mankind operating within natural systems denies and limits a Christian perspective which recognizes that all systems grow out of the motives and actions of men, and that the root issue is therefore always normative, concerned with addressing man's responsibility before God.

In view of these general criticisms of the Marxist perspective, what is involved in a normative perspective on class, that does not idealize the working class, or give it a false identity, or limit itself to one technical framework?[1]

The historical background

Much class analysis, as we have seen, focuses on inequality, but inequality *per se* is not an adequate basis for divisions and antagonisms among people. It is when the inequalities are the result of exploitation, or lack of proper care, that the divisions deepen. Moreover, history does not die; lack of trust may be conveyed from one generation to another in a way which places history in the present, and so we need to look at some of the ways in which groups have related to one another in the past.

The basic religious attitudes are crucial. We have already noted that coveting, forbidden in the Ten Commandments, has the effect of making possessions dominant in relationships. If I want what is my neighbour's, I do not regard him in a fully personal sense. Instead of the relationship being shaped by the norms of fairness, love and trust, it is obscured and dominated by the hope of material gain, for the ideas of loving mammon and loving God and other people are mutually exclusive. This is not something that affects only one group, and insofar as there is a general movement towards a materialistic order, it will tend to affect many. However, there are some groups which can be identified as opinion leaders and formers, and we can therefore begin by looking at the landed class in the 18th century, who brought about some important changes.

As a result of earlier enclosure, and the wealth that land brought, there was by 1700 an established group of landowners who had a coherent economic and social position. Moreover they succeeded in establishing a set of views which was very much in tune with their position. The philosophers, clergymen and economists of the English Enlightenment, who often depended on the landowners for their patronage, preached that self-interest was the ideal basis for economic and social life, and on this basis the landed gentry were able to entrench their position by enclosing more land, improving its quality and the level of rents,

---

[1] Most of Marx's writing is now available in the Pelican Marx Library.

making sure that they were protected against damaging foreign food imports, maintaining control over Parliament and finding other advantageous uses for their wealth. Trade, including the slave trade, commerce, banking, mining and other enterprises extended the scope of their activities. In this way the earlier wrath of Christian teaching against selfishness was turned and disarmed; it became the virtue of self-interest. Especially with the high food prices of the era of the Napoleonic Wars, this class flourished and the kind of social life which it represented is written in Bath, Brighton, London and countless country seats which still dominate the rural landscape of the country.

The landed class was open in the sense that those with money could easily buy or marry into it. When, therefore, the early industrialists began to emerge, often after having to strive to organize a workforce and market their goods, they tended to adopt the ethos of the landed class. There was often considerable antagonism between the old landed class and the new capitalist class, but the ethos of self-interest, backed by the undoubted achievement of early industrial progress, was taken up, and many of the new class found themselves in the houses, schools and families of the landed gentry. All of this is standard, 19th century social history.

However, our interest is with the inter-class attitudes which resulted from these developments, for the argument of this section is that these inter-group attitudes are an important key to understanding class in Britain. Both the landed and the capitalist classes were involved in large-scale exploitation, even though it was often done very politely and through a whole range of less scrupulous intermediaries, and this exploitation led to several class attitudes. The first was *fear* of those exploited, both because they might attempt to retaliate and because the exploited group remains a potential judge of the acquisitive one. The Luddites, Captain Swing, the Corresponding Societies, the Reform riots, the Chartists and various radical groups all fuelled the kind of fear which was expressed in the treatment of the crowd at the Peterloo Massacre and in the punishment of the Tolpuddle martyrs.

A second important attitude was the development of *social distance*. This was already evident in the kind of isolation established by the country house set in the landscaped park. It became evident in the way workhouses were built to remove the problem of the poor from the arena of normal life. It was also established in the structures of normal economic life. Just as slavery was maintained at this time by a structure of command which kept those responsible at a distance from the evils they were committing, so a managerial hierarchy administered harsh systems on behalf of others. Contact with those who were an implicit judgment on their masters was closed, except when reports on factories, poor relief and public health opened the door very slightly. At the same time work relationships were narrowed to a nexus of material incentives and disincentives, so that personal and moral issues could be excluded from the strict cash nexus. Cities were beginning to be shaped by the class zoning of houses, and the stiffness with which the British middle class repel the unwanted was being carefully developed to plug any gaps in the pattern of social distance. The question 'Who then is my neighbour?', was being studiously ignored through a careful process of withdrawal.

A third important attitude was that of guilt. When wrong is done and the guilt is not squarely faced, it does not disappear. It can be rationalized away by various justifications of the situation, or it can be modified by attaching blame to the other party involved, or it can be explained as being the result of some inexorable process which the subject could not affect. There were many groups in Victorian society who faced what was wrong, and accepted their own responsibility for the suffering of others, but there was also a lot of guilt sublimation.

These attitudes were not just subjective, but were developed into various structural forms. One way of eliminating fear of a particular group is to *control* them, since a group which is controlled is unable to take any independent action which would threaten the controller. Not only in the early 19th century did the police, the troops, prison hulks and deportation provide a system of control over a population which showed some signs of political instability. More important is the way in which economic control was exercised. Not surprisingly, one of the common weapons was to create fear by fines, punishment and the threat of dismissal. Sometimes the churches were also used to provide moral backing to ensure obedience. There tended, therefore, to be a continual drive to eliminate responsibility, and thus independent power, from the workforce and keep it in the hands of the controlling group. This had the effect, firstly, of creating patterns of centralized, autocratic decision-making and, secondly, of alienating the workers who, through fear, were removed as far as possible from responsibility in their jobs into routine work patterns. Employers learned that the best way of maintaining control and domination was to centralize responsibility and keep the workforce dependent.

At the same time, as well as rationalizing their guilt or meeting it fully by recompense, the dominant classes also gave expression to various other guilt responses. Help or charity tended to be paternalistic and dependence-inducing, although the cost of relief to the poor was kept to a minimum. Charity was often a zealous occupation of those with more sensitive consciences among the middle classes. Also, as the amount of wealth grew, more and more people were introduced to it and allowed to partake of its benefits. This was not, except perhaps at the higher levels, a conscious process of seducing the workers into capitalism; rather, this was the way the market in labour operated at a time when specialization made certain skills scarce.

The response of the working classes was more ambivalent. Although the possession of property and control were beyond the reach of most of them, nevertheless it was possible for the more skilled workers to establish their position within the industrial structure in a way which gave them some independence. Others maintained a position of more or less complete independence, but some, like the million or so servants were very dependent on the wealthy. The general direction, however, could be summarized by saying that there was a general desire to improve living standards, and that the workers sought this end within the structures that made them dependent. Thus the goal was material gain, but the means was by working for improvements within the capitalist, industrial structure.

Occasionally the middle class ethos of control was met by a similar doctrine of countervailing control and the exploitation of fear, as in the writings of Marx. Other attempts at more complete independence, like those associated with Robert Owen and the

Co-operative Movement, were significant, but only as a minority development. When the trades unions became more effectively organized their aims and methods reflected this ambivalence in the working class response. On the one hand they worked within capitalist organizational structures, not really challenging their centralized control, the power of capital and direction of the workforce, but at the same time they were learning what monopoly power and organization could achieve, and began to use the power they had to obtain higher wages. But the techniques developed were largely negative; they centred around non-cooperation, strikes, *etc.* In other words there was a tendency to exploit dependence and towards deferential manipulation. Thus although there was not the class polarization that Marx predicted, the attitudes of fear, guilt, social distance, control, paternalism and dependence were thoroughly disseminated among the various class groups.

Conventional history sees the antagonism of class relationships weakening as a result of the general rise in living standards, the establishment of the welfare state and the impact of the Labour Party. Although there is evidently some truth in this, there is another aspect to these developments which needs to be mentioned. To some extent, it could be argued, the middle class attitudes which we have examined were transmitted to the state, so that it became an agency of middle class paternalism and dependence-induction. Perhaps the position of the Fabians was crucial here in that they were very much influenced by statist political philosophy in the German tradition in their early years. As the administrative organs of the state developed, they were manned by middle class civil servants who set out to provide efficient administrative solutions to social problems. At the same time educated socialists began to develop centralized plans for different areas of social life. The effect of this process was that a vast range of dependence-inducing systems was developed which would bring the working classes to a painless acceptance of the existing order. Thus estates, houses, flats and even external and internal decorations were delivered in a totally planned form to the passive and grateful tenants. The design of estates reflected the middle class view of the working class tenants. At the same time education was planned for the workers as a process of enlightenment which, if it was possible, the educated would pass on to working class children. It was imparted in a great maternalist system right down to the last piece of chalk, with no question of parental or communal participation. The health service, the legal system and the social services all reflected this class paternalism. Millions of people found themselves dependent on payments by the authorities, and the working classes were thus perpetually in debt to the middle class socialist state. And so we find the paradox that even as the state intrudes into social areas to eliminate class differences, it brings these attitudes of fear, control, social distance, dependence and paternalism with it, and sets up a new form of *public sector class*. These are not free relationships, because they are shaped by a system of political and public administration, but the relationships reflect prescribed class definitions and control.

This situation is not evidence of a conspiracy; it is rather that the old reflexes of fear and control work just as well within a centralized system of state socialism as within a capitalist framework. Indeed, it would appear that the system of centralized state control is designed to perpetuate that which it aims to eradicate by requiring a highly trained, directing establishment and passive, obedient masses. It is noticeable that Conservative governments have usually been able to work quite well with the centralized systems created by previous Socialist governments. Clearly the nexus of this system of class relationships was not capitalist in any sense at all, but related to administration, planning, political power and access to public funds. In a slightly different form it is a system which operates as well in Russia as anywhere else.

However, this public sector system of relationships is not the only one which has come to prominence. The old class divisions based on property and ownership of capital are still of considerable significance, but they have largely been eclipsed by the growth of the great organizational systems associated with production, information, communication, administration and the provision of services. In these areas, which dominate the modern British economy, the key to control has become organizational and technical expertise. Self-interest is best served not by control of but by control *within* these systems, which are normally too big and complex for autocratic control from outside. Most of these institutions in Britain are characterized by strong, centralized, hierarchial systems populated by the middle class, and to which access is gained by a careful process of screening and performance assessment. Within this system, where the attitudes have not been faced and eradicated, they still exist as a diffused calculus which can operate at all levels of an organization. Fear, dependence, deferential manipulation, social distance, guilt, control and paternalism are all present, still fed by self-interest and coveting, and still creating a strong set of class relationships within institutions where they are present.

At the same time there is a change in the power of the working class as the unions, developing their own power and organizational ability, are able to bargain more strongly. They go through the endless process of expressing their anxiety on behalf of their members and being appeased; thus compliance with middle class control is bought and the living standards of the working classes rise. The pattern of industrial dependence, initially imposed, is accepted and used. If the power base of the working class is used properly, then problems are solved by others, and passivity has its rewards. Jobs, education, housing and entertainment are provided, and the individual can make the most of his passive situation. Some face more severe problems when they are in acute need and are also powerless, but most get the recompense due to the passive for staying that way.

Modern social class relationships

The problems associated with modern class relationships are therefore multiple. There is still a need to reform the law and structure of companies so that they are not identified with the shareholders; we shall consider this issue in depth in the economics chapters. Further, there are still large inequalities of wealth and property, largely based on patterns of exploitation (although the historical effect of these cannot be accurately established), which require, if property relations are to be put right, a system of wealth distribution. It is more than a little strange that, despite a series of Socialist governments, neither of these basic reforms to the capitalist system has been undertaken.

However, the full range of social class problems is far wider than these two issues.

One is the set of tensions in which the middle class is involved. The commitment to materialism is one of faith, and the search for satisfaction and pleasure is therefore often quite relentless and demanding. The 'good life' must yield its rewards, and the process is continually pushed to new levels of consumption. At the same time consumption is relief from the pressures required to obtain higher levels of income. Middle class control is often very demanding, involving expertise, long hours and stress, and an absence of the security which it used to provide. Insecurity, self-interest, organizational control and the use of power affect people to varying degrees, and create interpersonal and group barriers which are often quite tenacious. In particular, there are aspects of the normal middle class response which systematically disrupt relationships. The attempt to control the shape of a relationship with other people, which means that the relationship is not free, is a common temptation to those who are trained in the ethos of control. Fear and distrust make themselves evident very readily. People are actually prisoners of the social distance which they have been taught to practise for most of their lives. Forms of self-justification are built into the forms of speech habitually used, and the tendency to organize others asserts itself in free situations.

It is not without significance that most sociologists have looked to the working class for the delineation of community. The studies carried out by Willmott and Young have carefully conveyed the way in which these middle class attitudes create a kind of distance and isolation which is not found so much in undisturbed working class areas.[1] It is not that the people are intrinsically different, but that the attitudes have permeated and had their effect.

Another aspect of the middle class—a term used as a shorthand for the group which is affected by this material commitment and the attitudes which grow from it—is the morality which it implies. On the one hand certain kinds of discipline and standards are very

[1] See P. Willmott and M. Young, *Family and Kinship in East London* (Routledge and Kegan Paul, 1957); *Family and Class in a London Suburb* (Routledge and Kegan Paul, 1960); and P. Willmott, *The Evolution of a Community* (Routledge and Kegan Paul, 1963).

highly developed, but not so much on principle as because they are necessary to the right kind of advancement; on the other hand self-interest and the search for the good life make fixed principles wobble. Thus rather than living in a firm moral universe, the middle class is fed on pragmatic expedience, and the kind of organizational framework which makes independent opinions and principles a luxury.

Yet, because they have the ability for independent action and initiative, it is among the middle class that social organization tends to take place. A plethora of well-organized charities and organized communities or associations develops, which often give the appearance of a flourishing social and community life. Many of these are activity orientated or directed at some extrasocial goal, but they are scarcely able to overcome the social distance against which the middle class community has to fight.

In the working class communities the opposite is the case. The dependence and passivity that we have already described mean that it is very difficult for communal action and organization to take place, as many social workers in community work would confirm. At the same time the experience of being directed and organized means that, when that direction is no longer available, social contact tends to be characterized by drift or at least becomes less active. There tends to be dependence on middle-class inspired forms of leisure activity or on passive, consumer forms of leisure.

The change in working class moral consciousness also follows this general pattern. The key value is solidarity, because support for the group becomes the route to an improved way of life. However, the long-term minimizing of responsibility in the life of the working class also affects their moral perception. A substantially controlled life does not seethe with moral issues, and if the middle class has aimed to eliminate the ability of the workers to make independent decisions, it may have succeeded in part. Extreme examples of an amoral response to a controlled, dependent, non-responsible class situation may occasionally surface in the form of vandalism or football hooliganism, but in general the passivity of the working class population is accepted. Some who cling to the notion of an independent working class capable of revolutionary action try to change things, but their strongholds are the areas of urban decay, and the other workers are already moving out to the suburbs.

Finally, we find that relations between various class groups are more ambiguous. In part they are planned and defined by the public sector, and so we find zoning of estates, schools, *etc.* Sometimes the organizational attitudes of the middle class are prominent, so that acute differences appear among various groups. At other times because the material aims of all the classes are similar, these differences become minimal. Thus, crude differentiations on the basis of income, occupation, inequality or economic position that we looked at earlier, do not begin to get near the actual situation. It is not that we are looking at 'subjective' perceptions, to go back to that particular debate, but that religious motives and attitudes have shaped institutions, structures and group relationships 'objectively', and that people's current attitudes are also feeding into the situation. Although we have presented a general sketch of the development of these attitudes, it is obvious that the extent to which they apply in any specific situation is open to question and examination. We hope that the reader will be able to do this for himself.

This analysis is not just critical. It asserts the value of free relationships among people, which are not controlled or obscured by material possessions, and it points us to the strength of the life of Jesus Christ. He constantly refused to control people or by-pass their responsibility. He was acutely aware of the knife-edge between serving God and serving mammon. He never allowed self-justification to obscure true guilt and showed that wrong required repentance and recompense. He cast out fear with love. He never allowed the threat of power to compromise his complete security in God. When, in obedience to him, people are freed from these binding attitudes and change their relationships and the structures in which they live so that they turn away from this kind of slavery, economic community will become more meaningful.

Social communication

Basic to any social community is the nature of its communication. In the 1950s Richard Hoggart became aware that the forms of communication which he had grown up with were becoming impoverished to such an extent that the communal way of life he had known was disappearing.[1] This disturbing discovery is, however, not limited to any one locality, and in this section we shall try to isolate some of the factors which are operating to bring about this result. Communication, like other aspects of social life, is governed by norms; these will include standards like truthfulness, respect, openness, sharing, the freedom to disagree, providing accurate information and finding people's needs. The role that communication plays in a community, and the standards which it represents, are thus of central importance.

The first point is that much communication is directly or indirectly bought, in the form of television, radio, newspapers, books, magazines and films.[2] This places one vital constraint on communication; it can only be one way. It also has the effect of standardizing it. Most important, however, is the fact that it induces (not necessarily, but often) the practice of *entertainment* communication. This is a contradiction in terms, for the key idea behind entertainment is that the consumers' wants should be met and satisfied. The subject therefore *performs* rather than communicates to the consumer. The degree to which the average citizen is subjected to this form of communication is substantial, if not overwhelming, and it can have a dominant effect on interpersonal communication. It is not unknown for people to perform to one another, or for them to expect to be entertained by those they relate to.

Secondly, communication has been professionalized. It has been taken over by the teachers, the communications industry, the public figures, the experts and the many occupations which border on this area. They polish, present, organize, and complicate language; it is invested with status, authority and impact, and the whole weight of this industry is regularly brought to bear on the rather inarticulate, average British citizen. The effect of this is that the average person tends to retire in the face of this competition, and does not develop his own forms of expression. The ratio of people talking to people listening is lower than it has ever been. Responding to communication is much

[1] See R. Hoggart, *The Uses of Literacy* (Pelican, 1958).
[2] See chapter 10 for a fuller analysis.

more common than initiating it. Obviously we can all think of exceptions to this general pattern, but the confidence that many have in their own communication must be affected by the professional patterns they hear every day, but do not share in.

Another development is the growth of propagandist communication. We define this emotive word as that which primarily furthers a particular interest rather than that which states what is true. The interests involved in communication are innumerable, and each has its public relations staff. The complexity of the situation arises from the fact that, because the aim of the communication is to further the interest, the 'actual' content is shaped to that end. Because what is actually said cannot be taken at its face value, the language becomes debased, impoverished and suspect. This kind of communication introduces mistrust, which is probably quite widespread in our communities. What is your reaction when somebody knocks on your door and tries to sell something?

A further characteristic is the *anonymity* of much communication, in the sense that it is not based upon any prior knowledge of the person being addressed. This is a considerable problem, even in a book, and in the attempt to jump the anonymity barrier certain audience catching techniques are used. These include familiar ones like the use of noise, colour, light, emotive subjects, *etc.,* and more sophisticated ones that the media men continually devise. However, when common forms of language are not shared and developed, communication loses its depth and is reduced to the lowest common denominator which is generally available.

Also, much communication now takes place within tight organizational frameworks which limit it to technical, role-defined forms. These are often tied to written bureaucratic practices, and are therefore not free expression; they are also required to be apersonal. Because many people use language extensively in this context, it is often difficult for them to move out of this framework into wider social intercourse.

If we add to these factors the noise and confusion that mark our social environment, the cost of more personal forms of communication like travel and letters, the saturation levels of intake and the high demands of other areas of life, especially among the middle classes, it is easy to see how communication can become impoverished and impersonal. The commonplace that the Englishman discusses only the weather is a symptom of the way in which intercourse can be narrowed by trends we take for granted.

Status and social Balkanization

In chapter 6 we suggested that the main religious root in status formation was collective self-glorification. In Christ's immortal parable the Pharisee is made to say, 'I thank thee that I am not like other men . . . or even like this tax collector,' and this is the essence of status. It is obvious that any pattern of self-glorification excludes and alienates those who do not receive status, and that this division is antagonistic or at least implies tension.

We can now move a step further and note that there can be a variety of subsidiary motives in the formation of status-based attitudes. Thus, for example, groups could consolidate around competitive or achievement criteria. They could be, and often are, formed around moral criteria. We also note that racialism often contains an element of supposed moral superiority: Jews have been typified as evil and blacks as immoral, and this is based on a status notion of inherent racial superiority. Groups also identify around material possessions, around a particular image or lifestyle or with even the most insubstantial characteristic. As C. S. Lewis explained, the 'inner ring' can be formed in the heart of anyone who wants entry. We conclude, therefore, that apart from self-glorification, a variety of motives can enter into and shape status groups, and that the various forms may tend to be individualistic or collectivistic (depending on the form of superiority), and the groups either loosely or tightly knit.

It would be impossible to attempt to analyse the way in which the formation of these groups, reflecting various degrees of self-congratulation, breaks up the community in Britain into groups which are exclusive and have little contact with outsiders. Most people, if they are prepared to take their own forms of self-glorification into consideration, can recognize the status circles in which they move, but there is one which involves Christians closely and seems to be a potential danger in traditional Protestantism, and this we must examine closely.

We note that biblical Christianity totally undercuts all self-glorifying status distinctions in at least three ways. Firstly, created differences among people in no way constitute intrinsic worth, but merely represent the talents and abilities that God has given them to be used. Secondly, in the face of his sin no man has anything that he can boast of or glory in; sin is the absolute leveller. Finally, God's grace is an absolute gift to totally dependent sinners and no-one can claim any justification or glory to himself. Thus no Christian who looks at the life of Christ and the teaching of Paul can accept any status-bound attitudes (e.g. Rom. 3:19–30). However, there is a form of Protestantism in which doctrine (that which you learn and sit under) hardens into a set of ideas on which people congratulate themselves. Subtly, man becomes the master and uses the doctrine to glorify himself and support his position and status. It is a form of humanism close to the very heart of the Christian faith which really denies the power of the faith and evidences a morbid condition in the people who hold it. This pattern, we would argue, is present in both South Africa and Northern Ireland. In both cases, of course, class relations and privilege compound the antagonisms between the groups, but the Christian status barriers are of crucial importance.

In South Africa apartheid could be described as a system of legitimization for a total, racial, status system, and the legitimization has been formulated in Christian cultural terms. The weight of the argument needs to be appreciated, because it cannot be answered in its own terms. It is that all that is valuable in South African culture has been brought to that country by the whites (the Afrikaaners) through their traditions and ways of life, especially as embodied in the Christianity of the Dutch Reformed Church. Although material wellbeing is often also a strong element in this 'cultural Christianity', the stark cultural differences are easily evidenced and are seen to justify this cultural racialism. However, the justification is not Christian, for the key point about the gospel of grace is that because God's grace is free and cannot be earned, it can be freely spread and knows no cultural boundaries. Thus, the Christian faith is being used, but the crucial contradiction and area of hypocrisy is slowly being revealed. Myths like those which equate the trek of the Boers with the journeyings of the children of Israel can no longer carry conviction. More recently an alternative racialist perspective represented by the Nationalist Party, which is rooted in social Darwinism and elements of the Nazi philosophy, has led to a hardening of this culturally based status perspective into a much cruder theory of the survival of the fittest, where political control is part of the survival kit. Nevertheless the initial 'Christian' contribution to this pattern needs to be recognized.

In Northern Ireland, the cultural superiority is of Protestants over Roman Catholics. The other elements in the situation—unification, political rights, the IRA, economic equality between Protestants and Roman Catholics—are important, but a key social issue is Christian cultural status differences. The traditional Protestant criticisms of Catholic dogma have been reinforced by the economic success associated with the Protestant ethic, with the result that in a country where the word 'community' is frequently used, it normally applies to either the Protestant or the Catholic community. Again we see a situation where the form of religion is held, but the power of it is denied because of self-glorification.

The norms of community

We have considered ways in which the national community is being undermined, by both intrinsic and extrinsic factors, but what is the set of norms implicit in this judgment? These are derived indirectly from the establishment of the children of Israel as God's community under his normative direction. They were a poor and mobile nation but the principles underlying the laws given to them are still relevant to our own communal relationships. We note that the economic relationships in Israelite society were very carefully defined so that they did not dominate the social. Alongside the commandments not to steal and not to covet there was an absolute prohibition of materialism. More than this, there was a complex and comprehensive system of economic care, but unlike ours it did not focus paternalistically on meeting immediate need and income deficiencies, but rather concentrated on establishing the economic independence and viability of families who had fallen from this state. A crude comparison would contrast our emphasis on income redistribution with the Mosaic emphasis on long-term need and the redistribution of wealth. The normal economic situation in Britain is that of an employee while in Israel the position of the hired servant was seen as an abnormal one, to be eliminated by the provision of property at the year of restoration (Lv. 25:39–41). In Deuteronomy 15 the seventh year is laid down as a year of release, when all indebtedness is cancelled and when general financial aid to the previously dependent is required. Then in the year of jubilee, a full restitution of economic independence is granted to all the children of Israel who have become estranged from their means of livelihood (Leviticus 25). There were, of course, various means of immediate aid, but it is notable that the structure of Israelite society worked against control and dependence in principle. This was completely contrary to the prevailing pattern in all the surrounding cultures.

We, of course, live in an era when large-scale enterprise makes it less straightforward for men to control their own means of livelihood. Nevertheless, this perspective does suggest that the only long-term way of eradicating economic class divisions is through helping people to attain economic independence. We also note that the encroachment of other areas of life on free interpersonal relationships was normatively limited. Thus, the command in Deuteronomy 24:10, 11 reads,

'When you make your neighbour a loan of any sort, you shall not go into his house to fetch his pledge. You shall stand outside, and the man to whom you make the loan shall bring the pledge out to you.'

Any form of oppression which might undermine the respectful relationship of one man to another is ruled out. Israelite society was to be free of oppressive power and pressure.

At another level, because all the children of Israel confessed their sins, and atonement was made for them annually, self-glorification and status were in principle ruled out of their mutual relationships. None of them could honestly claim to be better than his neighbour when the Day of Atonement was a constant reminder of his sins and weaknesses. Also, because the sins of the people were confessed before God publicly, the meaning of eradicating evil from the community by repentance was a living reality. In this, and a variety of other ways, the meaning of status was principally undermined by the Mosaic law.

There was a variety of other norms which governed social relationships and these together created a pattern for a respectful and loving community. When wrongs were committed they were to be repented of, so that the pride and egocentricity which generated divisions in the community were broken. Without the recognition of the religious roots of our own divisions, there is little hope that we ourselves will grow towards these community norms.

Chapter 8
Marriage

The sociological study of marriage is often crippled by the neutral, value-free and anormative approach which sociologists have pretended to adopt. In fact marriage involves people so closely that it is essentially bound up with their faith, the deepest values in their lives and basic relational norms. The sociologist who does not recognize the need to explicate his own faith, values and norms in his analysis, will therefore trivialize this crucial relationship. Functional, role-defining and other frameworks of analysis largely miss the basic issues which every husband and wife have to consider and reconsider. What is marriage? What is my relationship to my spouse? Most sociologists miss the point that there are many different answers to these questions, and that these ideologies or faith perspectives on marriage are crucial to the development of relationships which, despite all the macro-social pressures, are moulded predominantly by the couple themselves. Not all of these views can be correct, and if a Christian perspective on marriage is true and these others are false, an analysis of the latter will open up important areas of false marital and sexual consciousness in our society.

Marriage is in crisis. This is the obvious conclusion to be drawn from the divorce waves lapping across Europe. If it is becoming normal in Communist and Western countries, other than those where the Roman Catholic faith is strong, for a fifth, a quarter and even a third of marriages to end in divorce, then a very high proportion of marriages are 'unstable' and the institution is in crisis. Our analysis here will suggest that it is marriage based on various forms of humanist faith that is in crisis and that, despite the charade of church weddings, it is this type of marriage that is characteristic of British and most industrialized societies. Christian marriage is not in crisis; it has almost disappeared. The social echoes of a Christian view are important, but often they are the shell of an addled egg.

Later in the chapter we shall explore some of the implications of a Christian sociology of marriage and look at crucial arguments in a Christian philosophy of sex. These will open the way to a whole range of issues of concern in contemporary marriage and sexual relationships.

Different views of sex and marriage

Faith and marriage go together like a horse and carriage, because marriage involves the person so completely that he or she must have a religious outlook on marriage. Thus the dominant faiths of modern society are transcribed into personal and intimate forms within which countless husbands and wives think.

Individualism and contract marriage The strength of individualism in our culture is deeply reflected in people's views of marriage. The result is that one or other partner is the ultimate reference point, so that marriage is characterized by an inherent bipolarity or tension. The contrast with the Christian doctrine that marriage is a union of all aspects of the lives of husband and wife is clear. The logic of this viewpoint develops somewhat as follows. Two individuals approach marriage, and the question arises, 'What holds them together?'. The answer is to be given in terms of the two autonomous individuals, because there is no intrinsic link or union. Marriage from this viewpoint is therefore a *contract* which is dependent on each partner's willingness to continue and uphold the contract. If it is a success, well and good, but if either partner considers it to be a failure, then the contract can be ended; the individual is sovereign. The implications of this view include the following. Each partner carefully weighs what he contributes to the marriage and expects to get back what he puts in; thinking on a day-to-day basis is contractual. Secondly, since within this perspective the ultimate meaning of love is self-love, the idea of a team dissolves into a calculation of self-interest. Thirdly, faithfulness is *conditional* upon the continued success of the marriage and the absence of stronger attraction elsewhere. Fourthly, sex can come to mean a process of self-gratification; each partner is giving the other what he or she wants. Finally we note that in this view each person becomes the arbiter of the norms of marriage; if in the end care, tenderness, openness do not seem to pay, then the individual can turn his or her back on them and create new norms. Further, the norms that do exist tend to be the obligations to which each partner can hold the other; they obviously become divisive and create the feeling of limiting the individual freedom of each partner. Many, if not most, couples think, feel, respond, react, argue, quarrel, behave, talk, make love, relax and live in ways which incorporate the logic of this individualistic perspective. Some of the ways in which it has become manifest bear further examination.

An obvious one is the development of serial marriage. When the individualist philosopher, John Locke, suggested that there was no reason why husband and wife should not dissolve their marriage contract after the children had grown up, if they so wished, he was developing the rationale for serial marriage. A high proportion of those who obtain divorces wish to remarry and do remarry. The concept of a 'breakdown' in marriage often means that one partner seeks a breakdown or divorce in order to move on to another, *more satisfying*, marriage. The justification in these situations tends often to be in terms of individual dissatisfaction or unhappiness and, not surprisingly, later marriages are more at risk. This is essentially a self-defeating ethos for the reasons which we now consider.

'And they lived happily ever after' hints at the power of the idea of individual happiness in relation to marriage in our culture. However, the logic of this position suggests that in reality a different outcome is likely. If subjective happiness is the dominant goal in marriage through having a beautiful wife, a close companion, security, sexual access or even a good cook, then several developments are likely to take place. Firstly, a concern with subjective happiness prevents a full appreciation and enjoyment of one's marriage partner, because enjoyment is a by-product of who one's partner is, and self-preoccupation prevents a person realizing how wonderful their partner is and can be. Secondly, and not surprisingly, the partner comes to resent being the tool used for the other's self-gratification, and the result is withdrawal and resistance in the area where self-gratification is sought. A further obvious problem is that it is extremely unlikely that the goals of the individual happiness of each partner will coincide; their search will therefore create the possibility of a divergent relationship. Nevertheless, when disillusion and sadness result from the search for happiness it is easy for the other partner to be blamed rather than the illusory individualist perspective.

Another way in which this individualism has developed is through existentialism, and especially Simone de Beauvoir, into one strand of the women's liberation movement. 'Hell is other people' becomes 'marriage is hell'.[1] To make the absolute reference point of the individual in himself is an ultimate threat to the identity of the wife. De Beauvoir expresses it thus:

'For him she is sex—absolute sex, no less. She is defined and differentiated with reference to man and not he with reference to her; she is the incidental, the inessential, as opposed to the essential. He is the Subject, he is the Absolute—she is the Other.'[2]

The humanist autonomy, the self-created god that the male has made of himself, requiring praise, service, homage, reverence, glory, obedience and sacrifice, has produced its reaction. The tension is similar to that expressed in the scene in *Women in Love* where Birkin, after a row with Ursula, pelts the reflection of the moon in the water to annihilate it. The autonomous identity of man and woman is threatened by the other. But the feminist reaction has tended to be in similar terms, asserting the absolute right of the wife or woman to her own freedom, independence and life. Thus the cultural result is that both sexes are guarding their own individual freedom, while each is also threatened and constrained by the other. In more muted terms this is a common pattern of response within (and before) many marriages.

A recent variation of the same motive is the idea of

---

[1] Kathrin Perutz, *Marriage is Hell* (William Morrow, N.Y., 1973).
[2] S. de Beauvoir, *The Second Sex* (Cape, 1968).

compatibility. The rationale behind this view is that a successful marriage will be based upon the fact that the individual characteristics of husband and wife fit closely. Computer dating is an extension of this idea across the anonymity of urban life. If the characteristics do not fit, the implication is that the marriage is likely to break down. In forming their conception of their partner-to-be, many people tend to develop a 'shopping-list' of characteristics, and the powerful pattern of thought behind this approach is that the requirements which the other partner must fulfil are articulated in selfish forms. This attitude will inevitably lead to disillusionment, because its structure is egocentric and divisive.

Authority relationships also present a problem within this perspective. Either authority is autocratic, or else there is some form of power struggle as to which partner shall have the say. When husband or wife is able to impose himself or herself on the other, it is to carry out the wishes of that individual, and it is not unknown for economic resources, physical strength, control of the home, children, nagging and token strikes to be used in the competitive battles for power that develop in the home.

There are many more elaborations of this basic religious perspective in marriage, but the general point is that any event, attitude, or aspect of marriage, when interpreted in individualistic terms, becomes devisive. The husband becomes possessive and does not share 'his' car, leisure and money with his wife. The concern of husband or wife with sexual self-gratification removes the joy from love-making. The concern of one partner with his or her own problems cuts off the possibility of understanding the other's and ideas of individual superiority begin to develop. The examples are numerous, but the central issue is that when the individual becomes the god, marriage is defined in a way which invites disaster. Of course the actual part played by this perspective in a marriage will be limited, and the inherent logic may be countered by all kinds of other views, but there is plenty of evidence that this perspective shapes many people's view of marriage in Western societies, and the perspective is bearing its bitter fruit.

Other-directed marriage Marriage is so important that it is perhaps not surprising that one form of humanism is to vest the *relationship* with ultimate meaning. The meaning of my life is my husband or wife. In an era when the great relationship with God is often ignored, there is a tendency for the partner to be worshipped. The sexual relationship comes to have a religious intensity which was not so evident in previous eras. The growth of this attitude is historically associated with the growth of humanism. During the Renaissance a new human Venus appeared in art and Italian life. She had a Platonic and a more sensuous variant, the former having something in common with the tradition of courtly love of the Middle Ages.[1] The development of idolized women plays an important part in the shaping of the Western culture of marriage. The tradition continues in the great idea of romantic love, which is often not recognized as a religious attitude. Romantic love is where the partner is the inspiration of love and the object of worship. The union is total in its significance. It has been a strong theme throughout the 19th and 20th centuries, and has repeatedly entered every home through the Hollywood transmission of the idea.

However, a closer examination of this tradition shows how it is associated with disaster. It is not just that the great love relationships of Renaissance literature, like those of Romeo and Juliet and Antony and Cleopatra, are tragic, as Denis de Rougement points out in his analysis of this theme,[2] but also that the development of romanticism is agonizing and pathological. The relationship is ultimate and therefore obsessive and those who followed through the logic of the romantic obsession were people like Swinburne. The reason why this perversion and obscenity grew out of romanticism is not difficult to see when the perspective is understood.[3] Within this perspective the person is dependent on the relationship, the other. He, therefore, is parasitic on the other person and the sexual activity. In this situation sex, rather than conveying interpersonal meaning, is

[1] See C. S. Lewis, *The Allegory of Love* (Galaxy, 1958); J. Burckhardt, *The Civilization of the Renaissance in Italy* (Phaidon, 1965), pp. 240–3, 272–3; K. Clark, *The Nude* (Pelican, 1960), pp. 64–161.

[2] D. de Rougement, *Passion and Society* (Faber, 1940).

[3] See M. Praz, *The Romantic Agony* (Oxford Univ. Press, 1920).

seen as the source of meaning, as totemic or iconic. In order to feed the identity of the romantic it is obsessively manipulated and perverted. Similarly the other person is required to be the source of love, inspiration and meaning; the romantic thereby becomes intensely demanding and possessive. Again, the way in which this kind of other-directed relationship leads to one person feeding off the other is best illustrated by D. H. Lawrence in *Women in Love* where Gerald and Gudrun's relationship implodes on this perspective. Another example is Anna Karenina's tragic relationship with Vronsky.

From a Christian viewpoint the weaknesses of this perspective are easily evident. A human love relationship cannot bear the full religious weight that a person's relationship with God should carry. It leads to that relationship becoming exclusive and unbalancing other relationships. It leads also from illusion to disillusion, and perhaps to cynicism and despair, because no person or relationship can carry this kind of ultimate significance, and close acquaintance sooner or later makes this evident. All men and women are sinners, and the time must inevitably come when they cannot inspire love and adoration, but only some less noble kind of reaction.

Thus far we have discussed other-directed love at a rather heroic level, but the implications in modern Britain for marriage at the day-to-day level are no different. The romantic or other-directed faith, not satisfied in marriage, can be directed outside marriage, and often is. At the same time the basic dependence of one partner on the other means that there are no resources outside the marriage; it is the total reference point for their lives, and when something goes wrong in the marriage, there is no other recourse. What can the wife who is hurt do, but strike back? Thus we can see the way in which the relationship can close in upon itself, and each partner put tremendous strain upon the other. Similarly, within this framework, where each partner depends totally upon the other, some form of rejection, withdrawal or disapproval leaves the husband or wife totally unsupported; it inspires fear and a person will do anything to avoid it. This situation of weakness opens up the way for various kinds of manipulation.[1] Perhaps the biggest

[1] See P. Tournier, *The Strong and the Weak* (SCM Press, 1963).

and most common danger is that the first flush of the romantic, total, exclusive relationship will cool into disillusion and relative indifference.

Naturalism and marriage A third perspective which has affected modern attitudes to sex and marriage is naturalism. This religious perspective has been very powerful; it is not only present in ancient Greek thought and continued through the Dionysian cults, but also in the Old Testament Baal worshippers. It continues in the Roman period, typically in the work of Lucretius,[1] but it also has a long pre-history in the nature religions of Northern Europe and Africa. The strong undercurrent against Christian influence that existed for centuries was given a rationale in the 18th century, as we saw in chapter 1. Since that time it has become fully established in British culture.

The key to this perspective is that the meaning of a person's life is to be found in nature. This process of identification with, or worship of, nature leads to a reinterpretation of sexuality and marriage in that sexual experience becomes either just biological or a means of identification with nature. Thus it becomes detached from the interpersonal relationship and becomes a naturalistic ritual, as for example in the orgiastic rites of the Dionysian cults and the Baal worshippers; a similar emphasis is present in fertility rites which interpret childbirth within a similar perspective. This impersonal, religious interpretation of sex has become extremely important in the 20th century. Gauguin made his pilgrimage to Tahiti, D. H. Lawrence turned to this kind of naturalism towards the end of his life, and Freud defined sex as the basic natural dynamic of life especially in his definition of the libido. From this background has emerged a whole range of views which see sex as authenticating man's relationship with nature, and as therefore 'true'. The serious pornography of the last decade or two presumably has this naturalistic faith behind it.

An important aspect of this perspective is that, because there is no marital doctrine of sex, both heterosexual and homosexual relations are seen as legitimate. Indeed the periods when

---

[1] See Lucretius, *On the Nature of Things* (Centaur Press, 1963), pp. 148–155, for a naturalistic interpretation of love.

homosexual relations seem to have been most common are those when naturalism has flourished. Sex is identification with nature and not the expression of love between man and woman. This point is not new, since Paul makes it in Romans 1. He points out how people have moved from honouring God to worshipping various natural forms (verse 23) and that God gave them up in this worship to perversions like homosexuality. Whatever the personal and psychological aspects of homosexuality, it is evident that it is culturally mediated and based upon a naturalistic religious perspective.

The most important point, however, is that naturalism provides a rationale for premarital, extramarital and promiscuous sex. The argument is that, since sex is natural, it is wrong to confine it to any limiting pattern like marriage. The extent to which this argument is presented day in and day out by the media and countless cultural forms means that the context is often set for 'permissiveness'. That this is at present a dominant ethos is readily apparent. The backlash against impersonal sex and perversions that is now gathering momentum often fails to recognize the deep religious roots of this perspective.

Asceticism It is interesting that naturalism, perhaps because it leaves unanswered the question of why man is different from the natural world, has tended to be accompanied by an antithetical religious reaction. It has normally taken the form of stressing what is 'higher' or 'non-natural' about man. The dualism that results means that man's 'mind' or 'spirit' is idealized and identified with his humanity, while what is natural, including man's sexuality, becomes inferior or evil. This dualism, present in much of Greek culture, strongly influenced the Roman Catholic Church, especially through Plato's teaching, and celibacy and asceticism came to be accepted as more holy and spiritual. Thus priests, unlike the apostle Peter, could not be married, and all kinds of celibate orders flourished. This ascetic attitude towards marriage was still evident in the Church of England marriage service until recently; the first reason for marriage was seen as the raising of children, the second that of preventing fornication, and only then is it recognized that marriage is a union of mutual help and comfort. However, it is now widely recognized that this has wrongly affected Christian attitudes to marriage and it has to some extent been corrected.

The form in which our generations have experienced asceticism is in the idealized romanticism of the Victorian era. During this period the bourgeois classes tended to make love a sublime, subjective feeling, and under the influence of a misguided pietism tried to make it as asexual as possible. This other-worldly view of love inevitably provoked a reaction in the undercurrent of prostitution that spread from the Strand and Hyde Park throughout the kingdom; the attitudes of the period seemed very hypocritical and a reaction set in. The spiritual ideals and sentiments of the period also ceased to have the same meaning in the post-Gladstonian era, and ascetic romanticism weakened. Now it is chiefly experienced as that condition which, by comparison, is evidence of our present state of enlightenment.

The ways in which these various perspectives affect people's marriages are very subtle and deep, often because they are not expressed and cannot be examined critically, but also because they involve a commitment of heart and faith. Husbands and wives are individualists, other-directed, ascetic and naturalistic, and these attitudes work themselves out in all kinds of odd corners of their lives, and because each perspective is defective, both contradictory elements are often present at the same time. One element in the crisis of marriage is undoubtedly rooted in these humanist expressions of the institution.

Sexual truth

The Christian norm of sexual faithfulness is so often dismissed, that it is worth pausing to consider an argument with which few people who face it disagree.

Sexual intercourse is commonly described as making love, and there can be little doubt that the act means 'I love you', 'I give myself to you'. The statement in physical terms is as clear and plain as any in the English language. But it is either true or it is false.

If it is true, then each person gives himself or herself to the other and the union means marriage. If, however, the meaning behind the physical act is false, a range of problems arise. Since the physical and sexual commitment is so basic to a person's identity, it is evident that falsehood or hypocrisy is buried deep into that person's life. More than this, because the act and the sexual statement are so intimate, it is inevitable that the falsehood will become evident; also, to break off a union later is to discredit the meaning of the initial physical statement. However hard we try, therefore, we cannot maintain that we can love physically while denying subjectively that it means an unconditional commitment to another. The sexual lie becomes evident in the end both to the subject and to the partner. Thus there is an antithesis between true sexual union and the sexual lie; the latter fundamentally undermines the identity and the relationships of the liar.

Of course it is possible for one or both partners to deny the meaning of the explicit bodily statement involved in making love. The process is then one of self-gratification for one or both partners. But if this most intimate of interpersonal acts in the whole world is self-centred and involves using another person for one's own ends, is there any escape from loneliness? The saddest aspect of the pornography trade, apart from the way in which the subjects are lovelessly used, is the loneliness and isolation it represents. A similar isolation has been observed among prostitutes, as the paintings of Rouault show precisely. This attempt at defusing the lie does not work because the commitment is so tragic.

Thus the conclusion is that sexual joy that lasts is only to be found when the act of sexual union tells the truth, and that means when it is a statement of a full, unconditional union of man and woman. Conversely, it can be argued that the industry devoted to providing sexual satisfaction in a variety of forms continually misses the point. The key issue is sexual truth and the symptoms which preoccupy the therapists, like impotence, merely mask the key issue. When you make love to me, do you really mean it? Within this perspective the view of marriage which is presented below makes sense in a way that no other one can.

A biblical view of sex and marriage

Priority must be given to the biblical teaching about the created complementarity of man and woman. 'When God created man, he made him in the likeness of God. Male and female he created them, and he blessed them and named them Man when they were created' (Gn. 5:1, 2). Thus the male does not equal man, nor does the female; both are needed for the completeness of humankind. This complementarity is not narrowly sexual, but enters into all the groups and activities in which men and women participate. Father and mother, man and woman worker give differently of themselves. There is a mutuality in doctor and nurse, secretary and manager, gardener and cook, which grows out of the different gifts that male and female bring to a situation. This does not mean that the roles can be prejudged; it may be that the nurse is male and the doctor female. Rather it means that the created complementarity of the sexes needs to be recognized, respected and allowed to come to fruition.

This basic doctrine denies at one stroke three important social ideologies. Firstly, the autonomy of a person or of one sex, although it is one response to male/female tension, is obviously a false answer, since each sex so evidently depends on the other. There is a large number of social groups which, with their one-sex membership, actively attempt to establish independence from the other sex. Paul stated the argument in these terms: 'Nevertheless, in the Lord woman is not independent of man nor man of woman; for as woman was made from man, so man is now born of woman. And all things are from God' (1 Cor. 11:11, 12). Secondly, the superiority of either sex is ruled out. The concept of superiority or status is undermined by the biblical doctrines of creation, sin and grace, and in Galatians 3:28 Paul rules out cultural, economic and sexual superiority. When male or female tries to lord itself over the other sex, it is living a lie. Thirdly, the male/female division prevents all ideologies which regard man merely as the 'masses'. Male and female are created different, complementary and unique; mankind cannot be reduced to a common denominator.

The next point is that marriage is not seen as an automatic development, but as a possible, conscious choice, which may be right for some but not necessarily for all. The commitment to husband or wife excludes other possible life commitments, and the choice is one which needs to be carefully weighed. Paul identifies a range of practical reasons why the single life might be better, but also recognizes the power of desire and the need for marriage. Thus, within the biblical perspective, the single life has a meaning which our conformist, married society often does not recognize.

The basic element in a Christian understanding of marriage is that it is a created structure. 'Therefore a man leaves his father and his mother and cleaves to his wife, and they become one flesh' (Gn. 2:24). Thus there is a structural union, a holy estate, into which the partners enter. A man and a woman recognize that God has made them for each other, and they enter the union, the norms of which they must respect. 'For the wife does not rule over her own body, but the husband does; likewise the husband does not rule over his own body, but the wife does' (1 Cor. 7:4). There are other crucial norms for marriage like faithfulness, respect and love, and those who enter the institution must obey them, or else they do violence to their new married identity. Thus marriage is not a negotiated relationship, but has a prior normative character which cannot be ignored.

The first characteristic of this union is that it is between one man and one woman. This norm has often been countered by examples of polygyny and polyandry. However, these examples usually relate to situations in which certain men or women have power over the opposite sex, or one sex is seen primarily as an economic asset. The most common pattern is for a few rich, older men to use their influence to obtain two or more wives. From a biblical perspective these are to be seen as defective patterns. This is not as outrageous an assumption as it seems to some, for from China and Japan to the Old Testament, South Africa and to Hollywood there is an abundant literature of the quarrels, jealousies, bitchiness and trouble that polygamy causes.[1] The problem is insoluble because it is not possible for one person to give himself or herself fully in a marital sense to more than one person. The marriage relationship is necessarily exclusive and jealous, as the Song of Solomon shows, and departure from monogamy compromises the union at the centre of marriage and this creates inevitable problems.

Secondly, the marriage union of love and faithfulness operates

[1] See Genesis 21 and 30, and I. Schapera, *Married Life in an African Tribe* (Pelican, 1971), *e.g.* p. 251.

in all aspects of the lives of husband and wife. Thus marriage is not *primarily* a legal, economic or sexual relationship, definitions which have often been accepted. Nor is it a partial relationship, *i.e.* one in which the legal, economic or sexual aspect can be ignored (*e.g.* 1 Cor. 7:1–5). The mistress who is not legally recognized, and who is kept for sexual reasons, is experiencing a perversion of marriage. It is perhaps worth enumerating some of the aspects of life where union may be strong or defective. Is there full sharing of faith, commitment, legal rights, parents, friends, freedom, financial resources and work, social life, a sense of beauty and order, communication, day-to-day experience and development? Does a couple share ways of thinking and emotions as well as each other's body? Many problems, it can be argued, arise from the partial view of the union which is implicit in the marriage, and which constantly distorts the true normative pattern. It is surprising how an aspect of the life of husband or wife can remain closed to the other partner for years, and shrivel by neglect, and how many husbands and wives feel they do not know their spouses fully.

Further, we need to recognize that, because marriage is a union in which there is no privacy, in which all of one person is open to all of the other sexually and in every other way, all the deepest issues of personhood are relevant. Marriage does not provide automatic solutions. The issues of identity, human pride, inadequacy, sin, forgiveness, peace, self-control, faithfulness and honesty lie close to the centre of most marriages. Marriage will not of itself help a person to find his identity or that of his partner; it will just give the problem a new form.

Another point about the structure of the marriage union is that it has a form of authority between husband and wife. The offence that the idea of a husband's authority creates today arises from the fact that it is seen in humanist terms of assertiveness, dominance and arbitrary power. The Christian view of marital authority is complex and, as with all offices or responsibilities, implies no superiority. The first element is at the level of the created difference of the sexes. The wife is physically in need of care and protection. More than this, because her most immediate involvement is for a while with the young children, it is natural that the husband should have authority in external transactions.

He provides a shelter for his bride. Essentially, therefore, the authority of the husband here is to care for or to cherish his wife. However, authority also rests with the husband because of sin. Sin means quarrels, disagreements, *etc.*, and the providential solution is that where there is continuing disagreement the husband shall make the decisions rather than that the marriage should disintegrate. Husbands, including this one, still make wrong decisions, but they are accountable for them and with patient education they may improve. This second element is therefore a providential response to sin in marriage which safeguards the union. It is instituted in Genesis 3:16. The third form of authority is very beautiful. It is that the wife should submit herself to her husband, so that he might love her and help her to grow in purity and grace (Eph. 5:24–33). The wife is agreeing to let the husband make her more wonderful before the Lord. This is only meaningful within a Christian marriage, but a visual analogy is that of a wife who allows her husband to brush out her hair or dress her in fine clothes. She is his glory.[1]

There is one more element in the intrinsic structure of the marriage union that should be mentioned. Marriage is shaped by the *norm* of love, not by romantic love, feelings of love, adoration, obsession or love at first sight, but by faithful, for better or worse, sacrificial love of the kind that Christ has for his church and of the kind defined by Paul in Ephesians 5, and 1 Corinthians 13. For this kind of love permanence is no problem; indeed it will outlast everything else. The key issue is that it is given by God and all our human inspired substitutes tend to show severe limitations. There cannot be many husbands and wives who have not experienced the inadequacy of their own love before the true norm of love. Sadly, fewer have actually shared that inadequacy with God.

If we move on now from the intrinsic nature of the marriage relationship to its extrinsic relationships with other institutions, we face an important misconception current in society and sociology. Fletcher states it thus:

'Another point of great importance is that the family is not

---

[1] D. M. Lloyd-Jones, *Life in the Spirit in Marriage, Home and Work* (Banner of Truth Trust, 1973), pp. 85–236.

rooted in marriage, but marriage is an institution rooted in the family. This is the conclusion of Edward Westermarck in his book *The History of Human Marriage* (1921) ... All that needs to be said here is that—whatever the validity of Christian theology for committed Christians—on the grounds of comparative sociology Westermark's statement holds good. Marriage does not exist in and for itself, but is an institution whose raison d'être is the foundation and maintenance of the family.'[1]

This perspective arises from seeing marriage as a mating relationship which is instinctive and casual and which derives its meaning and purpose from the care of children. A Christian perspective contradicts this view; the marriage relationship has intrinsic meaning and its own institutional structure, and the relationship of this institution to the family and to other institutions requires careful definition. Later we shall argue that marriage is a necessary proper foundation for the life and development of children. At this stage we may note that many newly-weds and childless couples would question that their relationship was meaningless because it was not a family one.

The distinction of marriage from the family is an important one. In the first place marriage involves a definite break with father and mother (Gn. 2:24). Obviously, if parents in any way intrude into the relationship, the union is hampered. In marriages throughout the world mother-in-law jokes are not a joke and in parts of the Far East it has often seemed that the bride is marrying the mother.[2] At the same time when children arrive, although the two institutions are intertwined, they are also distinct. Thus, for example, the purpose of the incest taboo (see Lv. 18:6–18), which is more or less universal, is to keep the institutions of marriage and family separate. Jesus, Peter and Paul repeatedly treat the two separately in their doctrinal teaching. The two propositions that we shall consider later are, firstly, that sometimes the marriage relationship gets wrongly submerged into family life, and, secondly, that most family problems can be traced to weaknesses in the marriage relationship.

[1] R. Fletcher, *The Family and Marriage in Britain* (Pelican, 1966), pp. 22, 25.
[2] See A. Waley, *Chinese Poems* (Allen and Unwin, 1961).

Marriage is similarly distinct from economic activity. 'If a man offered for love all the wealth of his house, it would be utterly scorned' (Ct. 8:7). Thus economic transactions do not occur within the marriage union; they cannot without undermining the love basis of the union. Unconditional giving and receiving is the norm within marriage. At the same time financial issues should not cause divisions or strain to the union. Nehemiah took firm steps to prevent this in the name of God as Jerusalem was being rebuilt (Nehemiah 5). It seems that we are moving into a situation where economic penetration into marriage is increasing and creating new tensions.

However, although the relationship of marriage to these and other areas of life is significant, the intrinsic nature of the tie between husband and wife is the crucial issue. In this intimate area of life, where the relationship is not (unless it is allowed to be) predetermined by external pressures, the view of marriage is crucial. Thus, although the inter-institutional issues are important, the key point is whether marriage is Christian or secular.

Crisis or not?

One common sociological view is that marriage is far from being in crisis. On the contrary, it is more popular now than ever before. Even divorcees remarry to an extraordinary extent. Moreover the length of marriage is now very much greater, with couples marrying earlier and having a longer period together after the children have left home. Marriage has also changed from a pattern of segregated roles, friendships, leisure patterns, spheres of authority, etc., in the classic, working-class family of the Bethnal Green type to the more nuclear, symmetrical family where each partner's contribution is more balanced and where the home is the focus of life when work is over. With smaller families, it would seem that marriage is a much stronger institution with companionship and a close union the norm.[1] There is undoubtedly a strong element of truth in this. The extent to which couples have concentrated their investment in their homes is to some

---

[1] P. Willmott and M. Young, *The Symmetrical Family* (Routledge and Kegan Paul, 1973; Penguin, 1975).

extent a reflection of an 'investment' in marriage. Nevertheless, this new symmetrical marriage also carries far greater expectations. Both husband and wife, especially if they are isolated from friends, relatives and workmates, look to each other to be friend and colleague. The bridge that carries extra weight has to be a strong one. We shall, therefore, continue our analysis by looking at ways in which the marriage relationship, although symmetrical, is under internal stress.

The breakdown of love

It is a commonplace to say that love can disappear from a marriage relationship, so that a couple become disillusioned, hard, uncommunicative and judging towards one another. The norm of love is not fulfilled. What has gone wrong?

In the first place, it is necessary to realize that love has a strong social context. A person learns how to express love from parents and friends, and also circumscribes that love by all kinds of conventions and inhibitions. It may be expressed by a gruff compliment, hard work, a warm expansive hug, silence, talking or in a hundred other different ways. More specifically a person learns many forms of married love from his or her parents. Thus when two people come together in marriage each needs to learn and respect the way in which the other expresses love. If a child is unloved or is unable to express love in relation to the parents, the problem will be reflected within the marriage in one way or another. Again, if the parents' marital relationship is cold, distant or broken, the children, when they mature, will find it difficult to give or receive love, and even to face marriage. Thus there is a culture of love specific not only to certain countries, areas and classes, but also to families. It is possible to assume that love is absent when it has merely gone unrecognized.

Secondly, it is important to define what kind of love it is that has grown cold. There are many kinds of love which do not stand the test, which are not permanent and stable. When a couple come to feel that love has a hollow ring, the question is *what* love is hollow? Individualist love does not succeed in being love *for* another, because in the end it demands some kind of reward or self-gratification. It is contractual love in which each partner weighs what is done for the other. It is love which necessarily tends to degenerate into self-interest and pleasure-seeking. A marriage may keep going on this form of love with some stability, but equally it may lead the couple to grow apart, for when what was originally seen as love is shown to be only self-interest or self-gratification, the union is seen to be undermined. Similarly, other-directed love is dependent upon the other partner for its inspiration. Loss of beauty, strength, health, status or wealth can eclipse the glow of love so that it becomes lost in vicious circles of disappointment, blame and disillusion. We also recognize that love which has its roots in sexual desire tends to be unstable and even promiscuous. Perhaps an even more widely held view of love is to see it as *subjective feeling*. Thus it is rooted in the emotions of the individual. Love is outside rational discussion, which means that when it is no longer felt, there is nothing more to be said about it. This does not mean that many marriages do not know love, but rather that much of what some couples describe and think of as love is inherently weak and is an essentially fallible conception. The disillusion that follows from the discovery of the weaknesses of these kinds of love may break marriages, although the reality of the relationship is so strong that other norms like loyalty and faithfulness can keep it intact.

The contrast between these other kinds of love and Christian love is a radical one. The Christian love which Paul defines 'never ends'. Why is this the case? This love does not originate with man and is not subject to his inspiration. Indeed, it recognizes the weakness and sinfulness of man and woman. Love is God's care, steadfastness, patience and sacrifice for mankind, and His mercy and endurance of each person. Human love is essentially dependent upon and responsive to God's love; we love because he first loved us. It is only when the pride that men and women have in their own love is fully exposed for the weak and totally inadequate thing that it is, that the possibility of spiritual, God-dependent love is fully realized. The actual characteristics of this kind of love are described thus:

1. Patient.
2. Kind.
3. Not jealous of others.
4. Not boastful.

5. Not arrogant.
6. Does not insist on its own way.
7. Does not lead to irritation.
8. Is not resentful.
9. Is not glad when others go wrong.
10. Is joyful at what is right.
11. Carries, sustains everything.
12. Is never cynical.
13. Involves assurance in all circumstances.
14. Lasts through everything.
15. Eliminates fear.
16. Establishes discipline and self control.
17. Covers a lot of sins.
18. Eliminates selfishness.
19. Replaces conceit with humility.
20. Involves sympathy with others.

By these criteria we see that much of what we call love is *ersatz*. When the dross is cleared away, we learn from the Scriptures that there is a surer foundation for marital love. This is a response to God's love for us, and an obedience to the norms of love which we cannot achieve by ourselves, but only through the Holy Spirit. The breakdown of marital love is therefore often inevitable; the pity is that more marriages are not based on the true foundation.

The breakdown in communication

Marriage is a union between two complete personalities; it is a community. This structural reality is often a shock to newly-weds; a romantic relationship, a pattern of going out together, making love, or a process of mutual attraction suddenly becomes a full-blown relationship where everything is shared. There can be all kinds of response to this situation. A traditional one, associated with large families, small houses and long working hours, was for the husband and wife to live separate and largely non-communicative lives. The stereotype is that his time was absorbed by work and pub, hers by children and relatives. Communication was little, limited and unexpected. This pattern is neither possible nor relevant today in most marriages for several reasons. Firstly, shorter working hours, longer lives, smaller families, the decline of the old 'extended family', better homes and television have resulted in couples spending far more time with each other. Secondly, geographical mobility, the distance between work and home, low-density housing and an allocative educational system have made husband and wife more dependent on each other's company. Thirdly, it is now clear that companionship is an accepted norm of marriage in a way that it used not to be; couples expect to share chores, leisure, friends, bank accounts, looking after the children and so on, far more than used to be the case. Thus communication in marriage is now at the centre of the stage; it is a crucial issue.

There are various factors which affect communication like routines, timetables, hyperactivity, television, lack of privacy, shiftwork, noise and physical distance. It is also obvious that differences in background, education, age, class, temperament and geographical origins can profoundly influence communication. However, there are deeper issues involved. One is that in a culture dominated by visual and therefore, in McLuhan's terms, relatively contentless communication, couples can easily assume that communication has been effected, when it has not actually been spoken. Further, it is easy for the norms of communication to be ignored. Time, care for the views of others, respect, honesty, full sharing, not misrepresenting, not opting out, expressing views within the firm context of a loving relationship—all of these can be and are easily ignored, especially when this aspect of life is given such low priority. Communication is an active process; there is a sense in which husband and wife give themselves to each other verbally, and unless this is recognized communication can easily break down.

The breakdown always involves a crucial step. Either anything can be discussed within the framework of trust, sharing and communion, or there can be a movement to the individualist 'I', where hostility, argument, withdrawal, silence and recrimination characterize the responses. The breakdown involves introducing an inherent subjectivity to the union. Each partner rightly feels that he or she is not understood, because the perspective of the other is firmly egocentric and perhaps defensive. The result is that each partner is prevented from developing a clear understanding of the other's point of view, for it is surprising how difficult it is for a person to quarrel with a spouse whose views are fully understood. So either areas of communication become closed, an obvious defeat for the marriage union, or else egocentric attitudes like self-justification, blame, pride, self-pity and cynicism tend to hold sway.

How can this kind of radical, or less serious, break in communication be healed? It is no easy task, but the Bible teaches that it is not the created union or communion which is at fault, but the couple who stand over against one another, ignoring their own sins and the fact of their togetherness in marriage. As long as they stand on their autonomy the deadlock cannot be broken, but when each partner becomes self-critically aware of what is wrong, and repents before God, the possibility of blessing in a newer and deeper sharing opens up.

How rich is the communication? Is it limited to certain areas? Does it include the jobs of husband and perhaps wife? Are emotional, social, economic, and other aspects all open to discussion? Are there areas in which one partner switches off? Is communication often a tacit way of saying something else? Is there a fear of not being listened to and taken seriously? Is superiority or pompousness expressed in communication? Is there a refusal to consider alternative points of view? All these questions and many others will be answered in different ways within each marriage, because the shape of the union between couples is largely private. The answers, although different, are all very important.

The breakdown of authority

Many people would see the breakdown of the husband's authority as no problem. However, this is because authority is understood in terms of autocratic rule. There is little doubt that in the 19th century most wives had very little power, while most husbands had a lot of economic, legal and physical power, although the stereotype of the Victorian husband is far from accurate in many respects. Autocracy could lead to treating the wife as a servant, to cruelty and to a hypocritical set of double standards in sexual morality and other areas. Perhaps the most forceful motive in this pattern was the idea that the husband earned the money which made the home life possible, and therefore the wife had better toe the line. Whatever the degree of reality or myth in this pattern, there is no doubt that we are now in reaction to it; the husband has come down from his autocratic pedestal.

There is no doubt that all members of the women's liberation movement would be extremely angry at the idea that the husband has authority in a marriage. In fact, the only resting place for a humanist perspective other than autocratic authority is the denial that there is any authority structure at all to the union. This would seem to be the most widespread present view; however, it is untenable. Women's lib. is a movement which meets the existence of male power with female power. Quite rightly it realizes that an absence of power is not possible in marriage, because every decision that either partner takes necessarily affects the other.[1] However, we can now see some of the weaknesses of this position. Marriage becomes a confrontation between two authorities; issues are settled as a result of the relative power or assertiveness of each partner. Couples can compete with or bargain with each other, and the exercise of power becomes tyrannical because there is no overarching authority structure in which each can submit to the other.

We have already looked at the different levels of meaning in the biblical view of marital authority. The problem of autocracy disappears; the husband has a responsibility before God for the marriage and his wife which makes him subject to norms of love, care and service of his wife. Exercising authority is a matter of obedience and responsiveness to God and, as Christ taught, the person under authority is greater than the one with authority (Lk. 22:24–27). The common acceptance of a marital authority structure can and should take away the element of self-created power. What has often become a tense contest can be moved onto a completely different footing.

[1] See Ann Oakley, *Housewife* (Pelican, 1976); Juliet Mitchell, *Woman's Estate* (Pelican, 1971); and Juliet Mitchell and Ann Oakley (Eds.), *The Rights and Wrongs of Women* (Penguin, 1976) for a fuller analysis of male power and its effects.

The breakdown of faithfulness

It is sometimes suggested that divorce merely reflects the situation where a number of marriages happen not to work out, or a couple is incompatible. Divorce is irretrievable breakdown. This view misses the point that the increases in divorce in both West and East are a cultural tide. The level is steadily increasing from year to year, and it is still much lower in predominantly Roman Catholic countries, but Britain, still way behind the USA, is approaching the situation where one-third of marriages will end in divorce. This trend clearly represents a change in attitude to the norm of faithfulness. Different views are slowly fermenting; one person puts his individual happiness before faithfulness to his wife, another is infatuated with a woman and leaves his wife, a third sees adultery as natural. The perspectives of individualism, romanticism and naturalism are slowly working out in people's lives.

The consequences are more serious even than the tragedy it means for the partner(s) and the children. A most insidious one is that the fear of unfaithfulness enters into marriages that are part of this culture. Since advertisements have begun to play on it, we can only assume that it is a fear which quite a few people already know consciously or unconsciously. Conditional marriage fundamentally undermines the security and peace of the relationship. Further, as the divorce rates for remarriages suggest, divorce is a way of running away from a lot of problems which then recur in the second marriage. The premise of the active divorcee is that what is wrong with the marriage is the other partner; usually this is less than the whole truth.

Another serious consequence is that this pattern allows the strong to exploit the weak. The wife who has committed herself to husband and family, possibly without much help from the husband, finds herself left after years of struggle. The husband who works hard to give his wife all he can, finds that she has found another partner. The law does not now protect the woman *qua* wife and the man *qua* husband. It has condoned continual exploitation and desertion.

A final aspect of this cultural trend is that it is part of the tendency evident in many areas of life for people to run away from the consequences of their actions. Abortion, views on punishment, political responses, and economic make-believe all reveal this same attitude. The cry to the universe is, 'Why should not everything work out right for me?' 'The universe is letting me down.' The humanist arrogance of this attitude is pathetic. 'Woe to him who strives with his Maker, an earthen vessel with the potter!' (Is. 45:9). To enter into marriage is an historical act, a choice, with profound consequences which have to be faced and understood, not run away from.

Marriage and other institutions

Family   Is the two parent family just a convention? The question posits the meaning of the relationship between marriage and the family. The Christian would argue that the former is the necessary prerequisite for the latter in a far fuller sense than is normally recognized. That more than ¾ million children experienced their parents' divorce during the first half of the 1970s, and that children born outside marriage number about 60,000 a year, are crucial failures which will in the future be recognized as far more serious than they are now. Marriage should obviously provide a secure, permanent and stable shelter in which children can grow up; it is a caring team which provides great strength for each child. Moreover, because a couple can find in their union the companionship, sexual fulfilment and love which each seeks, their attitude to the children should not be one of demanding affection, but can be a giving of love in the way God loves his children. When the parents' marital relationship is unsatisfactory and they seek fulfilment in their relationship to their children, this all too often results in possessiveness, domination and a failure to respect the children's marriages later. Unmarried and widowed mothers face this as a strong immediate problem, but the situation is no less serious when a mother refuses to sort out her marital relationship and loses herself in her children; men more frequently find escape in their work. The need for a properly based marital relationship is fundamental to the growth of a family. Indeed, it is not difficult to trace how so-called problems with children often originate in the marital relationship of the parents.

More generally, however, the presence of two parents provides the child with close, continual contact with both sexes; the relationship between the parents is one which does not directly involve the child, but which the child must observe and respect; it is crucial in helping the child to move away from egocentric relationships to communal living. Moreover, each parent is not totally tied to the children in a way which limits the full development of his or her life. Thus if the basic nature of the marriage relationship is recognized, with its norms of love, help and faithfulness, the family has a sound basis. However, not only are these points being ignored by those who wish to rationalize patterns of non-marriage and divorce, but the principle is also being ignored within many homes. The marriage relationship is often swamped by the growing family. This is especially a problem if the wife is left to cope with family work unaided, and the husband often resents the reduced relationship which he then experiences. Another problem is that one parent, usually the mother, finds herself tied to the children by the various factors like transport and working hours, and the family structure becomes unbalanced. However, the basic issue is that if the marriage is a full union, *both* parents will bring up the family.

The economy In general the hours of work and the remuneration of the average worker now put less pressure on marriage than formerly. This is obviously true in many 'symmetrical' families, but there are some factors which pull the other way.[1] Firstly, although there has been a fall in hours worked per week, the pattern is by no means uniform, and many occupational groups, both highly and lowly paid, still experience very long hours of work. Then again the increased number of working wives can mean that more of the time spent together is consumed in necessary housework. The steady climb to over one million in the numbers of those on shift working has also eroded the time many couples can spend together, as has the fact that many men, especially commercial travellers and lorry drivers, have to spend much time away from home. Thus recognition needs to be given to the fact that many occupations, like that of the police, assume a

[1] P. Willmott and M. Young, *The Symmetrical Family* (Penguin, 1975).

priority over marriage and family commitments which is a dubious right.

The second way in which the economy can intrude into marriage is through consumption. The pressure to consume, the time taken to earn and buy the commodities, and the extent to which consumption predominates in leisure activities means that it is easy for a relationship to become increasingly object centred. The middle class 'ideal home' mentality and the coveting engendered by the media can dominate the marriage relationship in a way which does obvious harm.

The state The state as an institution is concerned with justice within marriage and justice for marriage. However, we note briefly that the new 1971 Divorce Act, which is strongly related to the rapid increase in divorces, is individualist in philosophy. It takes as its starting point the *individual* happiness or otherwise of each partner, and not the rights of each partner as husband and wife, and technically allows for a spouse to be divorced against his or her will after five years desertion. Because each partner appears in divorce proceedings as husband and wife, this would seem to be weak legal thinking, but nevertheless it needs to be recognized that the present legal concept of marriage is that of a terminable contract based upon an individualist conception of marriage. This departure from a Christian legal basis for marriage has already led to innumerable women and men being wronged and left unprotected by the law in a way which has seared their hearts. Eventually, when the legal security which has existed hitherto has given way to mistrust and hardness, it will be realized that this legal change was a major disaster.

The churches The churches have obviously defended the Christian view of a faithful lifelong union, but recently problems have arisen. The first is that the established church has found it difficult to recognize that the legal and ecclesiastical aspects of marriage are different; as a result there has been a slowness to recognize the difference between the legal contract, now based on humanist individualism, and the church wedding with its much fuller commitment to union. The Report *Putting Asunder* fell into this confusion and, as a result of following the legal pattern, was led to consider the possibility of the remarriage of divorcees in church, even if the divorcee was responsible for the end of the first marriage.[1] To have marriage vows made in church which effectively break previous marriage vows made in church is totally to devalue a very precious trust. Thus far the Church of England has to its credit resisted this step.

However, there is another way in which Christian marriage has been less clearly defended. The meaning of Christian marriage lies not just in a set of narrow moral rules, but in the great Christian doctrines of creation, faith, grace, love and providence. Yet the practice whereby anybody, irrespective of their faith commitment, can go through the social convention of a church wedding, introduces a lack of clarity to the distinctive nature of Christian marriage.

Our analysis shows the uniqueness of a Christian perspective on marriage; the norms of this institution are not cultural conventions, but are rooted in the creation, fall and redemption of mankind, and to ignore them is to pervert the true structure of this relationship. A marriage between Christians which does not grow in obedience to these norms can fail to be a Christian marriage, and conversely non-Christians may come closer to these norms. However, this kind of marriage is not likely in a non-Christian culture: the norms become brittle and are eroded when they are not rooted in a Christian faith. The humanist perspectives of individualism, other-direction, romanticism and naturalism are producing a long, tragic crisis in this basic social institution, and the only way out of this dilemma is to question the fundamental religious attitudes which they represent.

[1] *Putting Asunder* (SPCK, 1966).

Chapter 9

The family

The family is an institution which is given great weight in the Scriptures, and it is not difficult to see why, for it is rooted in the creation (unlike the state which is a consequence of human sin), and the office of parents is procreational, not only in the obvious sense, but also in the sense that the parents play a secondary role in the creation of each human being. They are God's stewards in helping the development of people made in God's image. Another basic point about the family is that the relationships within it are not free. None of us has yet been able to choose our parents nor could we exist without them. To some extent parents are free to choose whether or not to have children, but it is meaningless to think of them choosing which child to have (except through the process of adoption). Thus, we are loved because we are born into a family, and not because we have certain characteristics, and this is a very important shadow of God's relationship with all people. Structurally the family is a community of love which is an important part of the creation order, but it is easy for its deepest meanings to be lost.

The office of parenthood is normative. Parents are entrusted by God with the responsibility of leading children into life, and they are to do it in his way. When God ordains parental assistants to help in this process of life-bringing, they are given guidance. The normative example is God himself. The cosmic care, love and patience with which God treats mankind is the basis on which the family is constructed. It is the Father from whom every family in heaven and on earth is named. (Eph. 3:14, 15). This means that the parents' job is as big as life itself. It is not something that can be limited to the fulfilment of certain social functions which may or may not be done by the parents, but is instituted by God as a basic part of the creation order.

Marriage and the family

We have already looked at the way in which marriage is the grounding for family life. Children are intended to be a product of, and a blessing on, the permanent union of marriage which is the cradle into which the child is born and the necessary prerequisite for its upbringing. However, at the same time, the two institutions are distinct, and must be carefully recognized as such. Thus, for example, the purpose of the incest taboo (see Lv. 18:6–18), which is found more or less universally in human societies, is to separate firmly the sexual relationship of marriage from those of the family. There are various pathological patterns, including Freud's Oedipus complex, which develop when pseudo-marital relationships appear in the family. We conclude, therefore, that a family is founded on the union of husband and wife, and is a result of their sexual union, but is not to be identified with marriage.

Because the two institutions are so intimately related, we need to look again at the effects which the marriage relationships can have on family life. It is possible to argue that most family problems have actually been transposed from the marriage. If there is no real community of attitudes between husband and wife, parental discipline is likely to be inconsistent and confusing. If the partners quarrel, the children will probably do so too. If the parents do not communicate properly with one another, they will tend not to do so with their children. If resentment is felt by one partner against the other, it may well be expressed against the children. If the marriage relationship is insecure and lacking in trust, the childrens' experience is likely to mirror it. So there is a constant pattern in many familial problems. The origin is in the marriage, but because husband and wife are too proud to face what is wrong with them, or are unable to recognize the problem, the symptoms repeat themselves in the children, where their ugliness is probably very apparent.

225

Thus the hope of being able to escape from marital problems into the family is a false one. The marriage union is the foundation of the family, and if it is not a proper union, it is not a proper foundation. As we noted in the last chapter, this may be especially a problem for mothers, and is the origin of the so-called mother-in-law problem. A mother who cannot trust or depend on her own husband is not likely to be well-disposed to her daughter's.

A key element in this situation is therefore the kind of love which exists between husband and wife. Marriage is such that each expects a mutual giving and receiving of love and depends on it. When the love is present each partner feels whole in the union, and there is a completeness which leaves the couple free from dependence on the love of others; the parents are free to love their children without needing to be loved in return. This is one of the great characteristics of God's love for his children; it is not a dependent love, but one which is steady and enduring whether requited or not, as the parable of the good Samaritan clearly shows. When, therefore, parents are secure in each other's love, they can in a pale way mirror one of the characteristics of God's love. This means that the children can grow from dependence into the free power to love without being subject to psychological pressure and having emotional demands made on them. Thus marital love plays a key part in the development of patient, sacrificial and forgiving parental love and gives it greater strength.

More acute problems are raised by families which are not based on the marriage union. The point was initially established by Bowlby's analysis, and has been frequently confirmed since. A study of 530 prostitutes in Copenhagen showed that one-third of them had not been brought up at home. Another study of 255 promiscuous men showed that 60 per cent came from homes which had been broken up by death, separation or divorce, and a study of 100 unmarried mothers revealed that 43 had a background of broken homes.[1] The current fashion of regarding marriage as an optional extra for family life is so shallowly

---

[1] J. Bowlby, *Child Care and the Growth of Love* (Pelican, 1965), pp. 42, 113, 115.

misconceived that only a liberal dose of optimistic, human faith in freedom could keep it alive. In reality one-parent families face problems deeper than can easily be understood. The single parent who gives everything for the children, knowing that he or she cannot ask in return, and who has neither companionship nor help in the process, is in a very lonely position.

Much is made of the stigma attached to 'illegitimate' children or 'bastards'; obviously this is wrong and any stigma that exists should disappear. However, moral indignation on this point tends to draw attention away from the main issue, which is that children without two responsible parents are seriously deprived *by the parent(s)* who fail(s) to take up their role. The stigma is secondary to the real parental deprivation. A subsidiary problem that arises in this situation is that a one-parent family, especially in pre-school years, can hardly be economically independent, and the parent is therefore under additional strain. Yet we see that the number of births outside marriage has been slowly rising to a level of about 9 per cent of total live births. Liberal humanists usually hold that the 'technical' answer to this problem is free contraception and comprehensive sex education, without considering the possibility that a technical let-out is no substitute for an understanding of what marital and family love really involves.

Another aspect of the same issue is where conception pushes a couple into marriage. The high proportion of legitimate births among newly married mothers, especially those under twenty, suggests that 'shot-gun marriages' are common. The coercion involved in this process, and the lack of marriage experience before the family arrives, means an obvious encroachment of family on the marriage relationship. It is small wonder, therefore, that such marriages are more at risk.

The major problem in this area is, however, that created by divorce. There are about one million children in Britain with divorced parents, and the number is increasing each year. A liberal, permissive view of this situation is that it is better for the parents to get divorced than for the children to suffer constant quarrelling. There is a sociological shrug of the shoulders while the numbers continue to grow. However, the fallacy of this argument is that it assumes that parents cannot stay together without constantly quarrelling. Many couples who do not consider divorce as an everyday option, and who marry for better or for worse, manage this quite easily, and a commitment to marriage *and* solving differences is not an option which can be ruled out so easily. On the other hand the logic of divorce means that one parent, at least, puts personal happiness before that of their children, and that one parent will have to be chosen and the other rejected. It may also mean that the childrens' own faith in marriage will be seriously shaken, and even that the children will be in the position of having to protect their parent, a sad reversal of the family roles. The incredible scale of divorces involving children, and the depth of the damage that it can do to them, suggest that this is one of the great tragedies of our society, although the dominant culture means that it cannot be recognized as such.

Abortion

Much has been written about the medical and ethical aspects of abortion,[1] but our concern will be with the concept of parenthood which is normally the basis for supporting abortion on non-medical grounds. It will be generally agreed that, compared with any other period in our history, the social and economic pressures on mothers have never been less than they are today, when small families and much higher incomes are the norm. Whatever the reason for the acceptance of large-scale abortion, it is not that conditions are more difficult or hardship greater. The change is primarily one of attitudes. The main argument or assumption is that the parents (or more usually the mother) have the right to decide whether a child will be born or the pregnancy terminated. What is the nature of this right? It is often seen as a right of freedom from interference by the law and medical profession, but basically it is seen as an absolute right over the fetus. Nothing less than an absolute right would be a sufficient justification for killing the fetus. Thus it becomes evident that the underlying philosophy of this attitude is the assumption that the individual is autonomous and is free to do whatever he or she wants. This autonomous, humanist freedom does not, and cannot, make

[1] See R. F. R. Gardner, *Abortion: The Personal Dilemma* (Paternoster Press, 1972) for a good analysis.

much sense of a marriage union, and so the right to bear or not to bear lies mainly with the woman, and the father retreats into a rather shadowy role. Not unnaturally, this kind of absolute assertion of freedom is also accompanied by the idea that children are a threat to the freedom of the parents. In this man- and woman-centred cultural whirl the fetus is merely a possession.

The underlying Christian view is radically different. The process of conception, pregnancy and childbirth is an almost incredible process of God creating a human being within the mother. Few who are aware of the breathtaking process of development, and the changes that take place in the mother, can do anything but marvel at the way we are all created. The mother is, therefore, used by God for the creation of a new human being, and the parents are responsible before God for the nurture of that which results from their union. They are the servants of the child, day and night. The idea of the mother, or parents, interfering with the process of God's creation in an arbitrary way is thus completely alien to this perspective. Mankind, including parents, does not have that kind of autonomy.

Discussions of the legal and medical technicalities of abortion always tend to be obscured because these two underlying concepts of the meaning of parenthood always shape the discussion into deadlock. However, this has not been the only influence on the debate. There have been plenty of people on both sides of the debate who have spoken and acted with conviction, but on the pro-abortion side there has also been a powerful material interest. Abortion Clinics outside the National Health Service have been carrying out more than 50,000 abortions a year for the last few years. At an average cost of £100, which is probably an underestimate, this means that these relatively few clinics have an income in excess of five million pounds. The keenness which many of these clinics showed in attracting girls from abroad, until it was curtailed by law, suggests that money has been a strong motive. Moreover, the fact that discharge from the clinics after abortion is often within twenty-four hours means that there are relatively low overheads. Thus, irrespective of the intentions of well-meaning people, financial motives may well be shaping actual practice in this area to a considerable degree. What is the normal rate of pay of a private abortion clinic doctor?

Parenthood

There is a strong tendency in some cultures towards intense family loyalty. One of the highest virtues is an unquestioning attachment to the family, and in Japan, China and some other areas this even extends to worship and veneration of the family ancestors. Especially in earlier periods of history, family, clan and tribal loyalties tended to be the main dynamic of much social interaction, and in some areas of Africa tribal loyalties still dominate politics. There is not much difference in principle between family loyalties and racial ones, since they are all rooted in the idea of the primacy of the blood relationship. It is not difficult to see how the Christian faith transcends this perspective. In Old Testament times relationships among the children and the tribes of Israel were not allowed to be of this particularistic nature, but all were made to recognize their equality before God. This can be seen, for example, in the way the promised land was divided. This same point is evident in Christ's own teaching.

'While he was still speaking to the people, behold, his mother and his brothers stood outside, asking to speak to him. But he replied to the man who told him, "Who is my mother, and who are my brothers?" And stretching out his hand toward his disciples, he said, "Here are my mother and my brothers! For whoever does the will of my Father in heaven is my brother, and sister, and mother"' (Mt. 12:46–50).

Thus the natural blood relationship is by no means idolized. The Christian faith does not allow the family to be self-centred, self-regarding or self-glorifying.

Perhaps this kind of particularism is one of the marks of our own culture. In nuclear families throughout the nation there is consuming concern for the family's standard of living, comfort, holidays, education and entertainment, which pushes the units into greater and greater isolation from neighbours and other forms of relationship. Status can have just as much meaning in a family context as in an individual one. It is even possible in our largely mass culture that the home and family become a retreat and a bastion against the anonymous world in a way which is contrary to the spirit of Christ's teaching. To what extent are homes limited to infrequent patterns of visiting and characterized by isolation, and why is this the case? The reader can supply his own answers.

The underlying faith of a family is therefore of crucial importance, and here again we need to make use of the distinction between an immanent faith and a faith in God. An immanent faith involves believing in some aspect of society, and it has two important manifestations in the context of the family: it may be child-centred or parent-centred. These alternatives to a commitment to fear and serve God are not mutually exclusive, but in a strange way tend to lead to one another. Thus it is possible in practice for families to be both parent and child-centred, and to experience the tensions of both. Indeed, in our humanist culture family life is constantly being pushed in this direction. For the purposes of analysis, however, we shall look at each type in turn.

Child-centred parenthood. Dr. Benjamin Spock says of the American family:

> '*Child-centred America.* In America very few children are raised to believe that their principal destiny is to serve their family, their country or God. Generally we've given them the feeling that they are free to set their own aims and occupations in life according to their inclinations. In a majority of cases these are visualized mainly in material terms.
>
> The tendency is for American parents to consider the child at least as important as themselves—perhaps potentially more important.'[1]

This pattern at its most extreme is easy to parody. The children are smothered in toys and all their wishes are taken as authoritative; they are rarely disciplined or contradicted; they develop a powerful and noisy system of threats; they are the focus of all around them, and their conversation overrules any other that is going on. Inevitably the children become selfish and spoilt as a result of the lack of respect that they show to others. Normally, of course, child-centredness is not present in this extreme form, yet the spirit which directs these attitudes is quite strong, and it could be claimed that the pattern is quite common. In fact the danger is almost naturally present in a one-child

---

[1] B. Spock, *Baby and Child Care* (New English Library, 1969), p. 24.

family, where two parents can focus on one child in a way which is physically impossible in bigger families. Moreover, with the modern relativization of morality in so many areas there are often no firmly held convictions with which parents can meet their children's wants and demands.

The results of this pattern are disastrous. Because self-centredness is encouraged in the children, by a strange process the children tend to grow up dependent on their parents, because they need people who will indulge their wishes, and they feel lost and hurt when they are not at the centre of things. They find it difficult to cope when everything is not provided for them. What begins by being total freedom for the child ends by being binding dependence. At the same time the fact that the child has such power over his parents is obviously disturbing. Sometimes, even, a child will provoke a situation demanding punishment in order to resolve the unnatural state of affairs where he is the boss. Thus, while the parents may feel that they are loving their children to the limit, they may in fact be doing damage because they are merely encouraging a humanist, egocentric faith.

What are the underlying philosophical attitudes of this view? One is probably a Rousseauist belief in the goodness of children, and especially of one's own children. This is especially likely to occur when parents are aware of their own evil and guilt but, instead of facing it directly before God, seek to keep their children in a cocoon of goodness. Historically, it has been important to many postwar parents that their children should not have to go through what they experienced during the Depression and World War II. The emphasis placed on freedom, self-expression, creativity, anti-authoritarianism, and the magic powers of education by our optimistic, humanist culture have all contributed to this general ethos. However, there is one other factor which is of overriding importance, and that is the guilt of the parents. Most parents feel guilty because of one aspect or another of the way in which they bring up their children. If they cannot face what is wrong, repent and receive God's forgiveness, they are left in a position where they continually live with that guilt. Then it is not difficult to rationalize this position by saying, 'The children are not really to blame, but we are'. Or the argument can be put another way. Is it possible for the parents to discipline or punish their children when they themselves are guilty of all that they are seeking to correct. There is a fear of the parental hypocrisy which says, 'Don't do what I do, but do what I say'. The thesis therefore is that unresolved parental guilt is one of the mainsprings of a child-centred orientation.

Parent-centred families There is a certain element of repetition in basic social sins. The 19th century form of the parent-centred family was one where the 'children were to be seen and not heard', and where a nanny and a boarding school system effectively kept the children at bay until they were of an age to be tolerable. There were one or two occasions during the week, like going to church on Sundays, where the children were to be paraded, but generally the organization of this kind of middle-class household was such that the children would not be under the feet of the parents. In working-class homes, as well, there were plenty of time-consuming occupations that children could be pushed into at the earliest possible age, and not always just to boost the family income. This stereotype is only part of the picture but it was a real part, as Shaftesbury (who suffered just such an unhappy childhood) and many others would testify. This is not the place to discuss the fight that was waged by many good Victorians for children against their parents; it was a tough one and there are still many evidences of their victories around us. However, parent-centredness has found modern forms in which to appear.

It is not uncommon for discipline to be an expression of resentment at the way in which children interfere in the parents' life. Further, it is easy for children to be seen primarily as reflecting shame or glory on the parents, so that in a subtle, or even fairly obvious, way the lives of the children revolve around the egos of the parents. It is also possible for the lives of the children to be organized to suit Mum and Dad, so that the parents rarely think of undertaking leisure activities with their children rather than with their own friends. The form of contact with the children can be predominantly mechanical, in that food, shelter and clothes are provided, but open personal contact is kept to a minimum. The television is especially useful here in that it keeps the children occupied for crucial periods each day, and also obviates the need for contact. The pressures which produce these attitudes are strong, especially in certain social groups. Many jobs demand a level of commitment which effectively rules out family life, and the search for material comfort for the family is often only attainable at the expense of family life.

When parents effectively withdraw from their children in these ways, it is not surprising that, when the children come of age, they in turn withdraw from their parents. Nor is it surprising when lack of communication and interest leads to parents missing important stages in the development of their children, and to failure to respond to their needs until they have become acute. Further, if parents put themselves first, and know that they do, their guilt feelings are likely to lead them to indulge their children in those areas where they can most easily do so. Again, if parents are self-centred, their children will learn that pattern of behaviour from them, and it is more than likely that the family will be characterized by a lack of co-operation and empathy which will cause the parents many problems. Thus these two perspectives are locked in continual tension, that cannot really be resolved as long as the family is self-centred, rather than God-centred. Faith is as crucial to this institution as to all of the others.

Family structure

The relationships of the immediate family include those between parents, the variety of parent-child relationships, and the relationships among brothers and sisters. All of these are important and worth exploring, but the structure given to them depends on the fact that the family is a community of love under the authority of the parents. Thus, the parents can be willing to receive into that community an adopted child who thereupon becomes a member of it. The New Testament teaching that those who repent and seek God's forgiveness are adopted as children of God establishes the point that it is not the blood relationship which is authoritative in the family, but the love of the Father and hence of parents. The biological relationship is the origin of the family, but it is defined by love.

Between parents The relationship between parents is interesting. Although it is clear, as we saw in the last chapter, that the marriage relationship has an authority structure, there is every indication in the Scriptures that there is no difference in the authority attached to either father or mother. In other words, the onus of developing a unity of purpose and attitudes lies in the marriage, and it is assumed that the parents' relationship with their children is one of unison, where neither parent needs to overrule the other. Or, to put it another way, if one parent is countermanding what the other one says, there is a need for them to get together as husband and wife and sort a few things out. This principle of the equality of parents, present in the Ten Commandments, is departed from in a variety of cultures.

The two major variations are normally described as matriarchal and patriarchal family types, but this covers many variations in meaning. One matriarchal form is associated with the West Indies and with the black families of the USA. It is often argued that the effect of slavery was so to reduce the authority and standing of the father that he became a secondary parent. The mother became the lynchpin and the father, because he had no authority or responsibility at work, exercised none in the home. Moreover, a pattern of temporary cohabitation became a normal pattern for marriage, and fathers, therefore, tended to move on. The way in which this pattern has been repeated in generation after generation evidences the tenacity of these family forms. Another matriarchal form is associated with a home close to the mother's relatives, whose influence tends to be exercised on behalf of the mother and to enhance her position. Yet another form occurs when the father, through his work, is absent for long periods of time, so that the mother has to assume overall authority for the family. Another occurs in some parts of Roman Catholic Europe where the mother combines with the church to assume a more total responsibility for the upbringing of the children. Again, where elements of power enter into the male-female relationship it is easy for circumstances to affect the relative influence of the spouses and, where the father is unemployed, he may find his authority within the family weakened.

The more typical form in Britain which exists in all classes is for a division of labour to be observed whereby the father provides for the family through his income, and the mother is seen as being primarily responsible for bringing up the children and looking after the home. It becomes in effect her domain. The father in a complementary way agrees to be passive in the home, perhaps occasionally backing up his wife's authority, provided there is no interference with his life outside the home. In these circumstances the mother battles through on her own, possibly becoming quite an autocrat in her domain. When the husband retires, it is not unknown for the wife to transfer her matriarchal attitudes to her husband and to find it very difficult to have him around in her domain!

Patriarchal patterns also vary but they tend to revolve around the power of the father. It may be merely the physical power he has, which, if there is any fear that he will use it, will tend to make him the dominant partner. A more common pattern is where the father's economic power affects the structure of the family, which will then be very much dependent on the income which he brings home, and this power can be used to establish his position in the family. This pattern is found especially when the father is absorbed in his job and among middle-class groups. Another form occurs when the mother is associated with all the routine elements of family life and work, while father is at the centre of all the exciting things that happen, and thereby gets the aura of popularity which establishes his position.

These deviations are unlikely to happen, however, when there is a close living relationship between husband and wife, and they also involve a denial of the biblical meaning of the parental office. The position of parent is not based upon power, popularity, influence within the home or any other social factor, but upon the responsibility which God has laid upon the parent. If, therefore, either parent is using any such factor to gain a dominant position within the home, this is a denial of the joint office they hold as well as being evidence of the weakness of the marriage relationship.

Parents and children The relationship between parents and children will be affected by these foregoing issues, but it is also an area with its own specific normative structure. One of the commandments is to 'Honour your father and your mother, that your days may be long in the land which the Lord your God gives you' (Ex. 20:12). The respect due to the parents and the love and care due to the children thus constitute a unique relationship. The authority which parents have because they are given stewardship over dependent children is different from any other kind of authority relationship, and its inner structure needs to be opened up, for there is no doubt that this particular relationship is subject to attack in our culture.

A century ago the dominant conception of bringing up children was moralistic. They were brought up to do what was right and to avoid what was wrong. After a while, however, the situation arose where predominantly non-Christian parents had no grounds for appealing to a higher moral authority. Sometimes they called in 'God', or the authority of the church, to back up their point of view, but in effect there was no higher authority than the parents. 'Do this because I say so' was the structure of the ethos, because humanism decreed that there was no higher authority and the father had authority in the absolute sense of being able to decide what was right and wrong. This autocratic position still lingers on. It is possible for authority in the home to be an assertion that father is always right, an expression of his whims, a buttress to his ego or a cover for his weaknesses, but on the whole there has been a reaction against autocratic parenthood, and it is worth asking why.

There are several possible reasons for its decline. The first is that the higher level of education of most children has made the statement, 'Do this because I say so', an inadequate reason for obedience. The answer persistently comes back, 'Why should I?' A second reason is that the humanist idea that man is his own master has filtered down beyond the autocratic parent to the teenage generation. If the parents were arbiters of what they thought was right, there was no adequate reason why the next generation should be held to any higher authority, even that of their parents. For some children this was a 'discovery', but for others the change was purveyed by their parents. For generations non-Christian parents had lived on the capital of Christianly-based standards; they had accepted the conventions without their basis. As a result the morality had become brittle, and parents felt that they could not really pass on what they themselves did not believe. Thus parental upbringing tended to become permissive in the sense that children were left to discover their own moral guidelines. Another possible reason was that the autocratic view of authority outlined above left parents in an intolerable dilemma. Any authority which they exercise will, on this view, be autocratic, since there is no higher authority to whom they are subject. Less authority is therefore present and less expected. Thus the polar views of authority, the autocratic and the permissive, wage war on one another with tedious regularity.

These two views of authority can to some extent be expressed in terms of the class differences discussed earlier. In simplified terms the pattern is as follows. The middle-class ethos of control through expertise means that there tends to be an emphasis on developing skills to a high level, and parents therefore have a variety of ways of putting pressure on their children to develop higher levels of performance. It is usually argued that this is done through various forms of emotional and verbal coercion. The working-class ethos is one which involves dependence, and it is therefore morally passive and tends to permissiveness. However, the form of control exercised over many working-class employees tends to give them a more autocratic view of authority. Thus both groups have a rather ambiguous attitude to parental authority, and a number of problems result from these patterns.

If these are some of the problems that surround the parent-child relationship, what is a more biblical definition of the relationship? A Christian view involves a recognition that the parents are under the authority of God and are bound to obey him in what they do. The parents must therefore obey the rules which they teach their children, and to more exacting standards. Rather than being a law unto themselves, they are merely teaching a set of norms which are independent of them and to which they are subject. Moreover, because the parents will necessarily be aware of their own sinfulness, their authority carries no pedestal with it. Rather, they will make clear to their children that they, too, do things that are wrong and need correction. At the same time there is no optimistic pressure leading them to assume that their children will not sin, or that they are ultimately responsible for their children's wrongdoings. Corrective discipline will be a normal part of loving upbringing.[1]

---

[1] See L. Christenson, *The Christian Family* (Fountain Trust, 1971), chapter 4, for a good straightforward North American interpretation of this.

This is nowhere better explained than in Hebrews 12:5-13:
"'My son, do not regard lightly the discipline of the Lord,
nor lose courage when you are punished by him.
For the Lord disciplines him whom he loves,
and chastises every son whom he receives."
It is for discipline that you have to endure. God is treating you
as sons; for what son is there whom his father does not
discipline? If you are left without discipline, in which all have
participated, then you are illegitimate children and not sons.
Besides this, we have had earthly fathers to discipline us and we
respected them. Shall we not much more be subject to the
Father of spirits and live? For they disciplined us for a short
time at their pleasure, but he disciplines us for our good, that
we may share his holiness. For the moment all discipline seems
painful rather than pleasant; later it yields the peaceful fruit of
righteousness to those who have been trained by it. Therefore
lift your drooping hands and strengthen your weak knees, and
make straight paths for your feet, so that what is lame may not
be put out of joint, but rather be healed.'
It is sad in this context that the meaning of discipline has been so
narrowed. Discipline, or subjection to rules, norms and practices,
is the key to any kind of learning, and it therefore has a natural
and important place in the family. It would be interesting to
know, for example, why such a high proportion of the world's
finest violin players grow up in Jewish families. At the same time
it is important to recognize another aspect of the meaning of
discipline. Children grow into responsibility before God, not into
responsibility to their parents, and it is not therefore the parents'
task to make the children do what is right or to demand obedience
to themselves, but merely to teach them what is right and to
discipline their learning. It is easy for parents to assume too
complete a role in their children's lives, and to forget that they are
merely stewards.

Among children Relations among children are wonderfully
straightforward and open, yet there are external pressures which
can easily pervert them. An obvious one is where the parents show
some kind of favouritism, or adopt a judgmental attitude to one
child. A similar effect can result when the family values

achievement highly, and some children achieve while others do not. Another factor is that our society is highly regimented into age cohorts at nursery, school, church and in many other areas. This can effectively compartmentalize a family through much of its development, and impoverish the relationship of one sibling with another.

Thus we see something of the importance of the internal relationships of the family and the structure of this basic creational unit. Now we need to consider some of the external pressures operating on it.

The family and society

When we turn from the internal relationships of the family to look at its broader place in society, we face a chorus of sociological comment that the institution is being stripped of its social functions and is becoming far less important. Before these arguments can be assessed, we need to correct the fallacy that the family is a *functional* institution. The loving community of the family does not exist *for* society, but has its own integrity before God. Bearing this in mind, what changes are affecting the family?

An important one is the development of a professional child-minding ethos. In our mass-production society it is easy for the conventional form of parental care to seem inefficient and dated. Is it not better for both parents to work and for the children to be catered for by professional child-minders in nurseries, play-groups, *etc.*? It saves the inefficient use of labour in the home and allows the labour force to be expanded. Gradually, and by a lot of indirect pressures, there has been a substantial transfer of emphasis in postwar Britain to the pattern of both parents working with some form of professional child care. The proportion of married women who work for pay rose from 26 per cent in 1951 to 49 per cent in 1974 (*Social Trends*, 1973, 1976), and the latter figure probably understates the increase of those in the age groups with young families who are rapidly returning to paid employment. Smaller families, higher educational levels among women and more efficient homes have all contributed to this trend, but one feels that the main rationale is the idea of professional large-scale units with their notional advantages.[1]

The economic aspects of this change are interesting. The lure of a two-income family has obviously encouraged the trend, especially when there are two professional incomes, but the calculations on which the comparisons are made are not strictly comparable. The money income of the family may rise (and a considerable part of the recent increases in the level of real national income must have resulted from the incorporation of more women into the labour force), but at the same time the family has to purchase more goods and services because the work available in the home has fallen. Expensive, highly prepared and packaged foods, labour-saving devices, home and educational help and other costs are all incurred. Some families even finish up in the situation where they 'need' two cars. Thus, although they have a higher level of income, this has to be weighed against the higher level of expenses. Although for some people these calculations might seem relatively straightforward, it is possible that what we mistake for a higher standard of living may really be merely an increase in social organization.

Related to this is the development of the women's liberation movement. The widespread attitude which identifies parenthood with the mother and sees her as naturally tied to the home has deservedly provoked a backlash. Although many women still find their work in the home, and the immediate care of the children, a complex and fulfilling vocation, some have seen the home as a constraint on their right to their own career and to the development of their interests. Sometimes this reaction is marked by male/female antagonism, and wives have often felt that they need to fight for their freedom so that there has been something of a crusade out of the home. At the same time many parents have worked out their own division of labour between home and paid labour with little trouble. However, there is one element in this developing pattern which is rather disturbing. The impression is often conveyed that one reason why a woman works is that it gives her some financial independence of her husband in a society where divorce is all too common. Thus the movement towards

[1] See R. and R. Rapoport, *Dual Career Families* (Pelican, 1971) for examples of this pattern.

this kind of independence is a symptom that trust between parents has weakened. Insofar as this independence motive is present, the structure of the family is seriously weakened.

It is also worth noting that there is a strong political motivation for professional child care in the socialist countries of Eastern Europe. In these countries children are often looked after by the state from the age of one onwards. Apart from the economic motives of freeing the female workforce to do paid labour, there is also the feeling that the family still remains an institutional area which is independent of the state, and therefore a potential threat to state socialism. By reducing the teaching role of the family to an absolute minimum, the state (or the party) can reduce this independence. Nevertheless, given the closeness of the ties in Russian and other families the state will find that even this policy will not destroy the independence of these basic units. Although the political motivation of democratic socialists is entirely different, it has been noted that the problems created for the equal opportunity ideal by different family backgrounds might be lessened if the same socialization process was available for all at an earlier age than five—equal oportunity from the cradle to the grave.

Overall, we see that economic pressures tend to lead to both parents being much more fully involved in paid work, especially since it is normally out of the question for the father to work part-time. The ethos of efficiency on a mass-production model, and the drive to gain more freedom and independence for the housewife, similarly point in the same direction, and there is even the same political direction. The net effect is that there is a lower commitment to home, and possibly to parental care. Yet few would argue that children do not need close, personal, time-consuming, immediate attention, especially during their most intense period of learning before they start school. The pupil-teacher ratio is always too high in schools; in the home it is normally about right. It is not that the family's functions are disappearing as the result of a neutral pattern of social progress; it is rather that the low priority for family care is the outcome of materialist, mass production and professional ideologies. As we now look at the family in relation to other institutions, we can focus on the way education has also been isolated from the family in Britain.

The family and education

The Scriptures tend to identify the responsibility for educating children with the parents, but they see education in a wider sense than is usual today. It includes teaching the child about the creation order, teaching him wisdom and discernment, teaching him to fear and love God, and to be obedient to his laws and norms. Thus education is, and must necessarily be, grounded in a religious perspective, and it is the responsibility of the parents to give due honour in their children's education to what they themselves believe. A statement of this is found in Deuteronomy 6:4–7.

'Hear O Israel: The Lord our God is one Lord; and you shall love the Lord your God with all your heart, and with all your soul, and with all your might. And these words which I command you this day shall be upon your heart; and you shall teach them diligently to your children, and shall talk of them when you sit in your house, and when you walk by the way, and when you lie down, and when you rise.'

This perspective on education is religious, not in a narrow sense, but as a total world and life view, and it is from this deeper meaning of education that we consider this parental responsibility.

The trouble, as usual, began with the churches. They obtained a near monopoly of education between the Restoration and the early 19th century. The established church succeeded in excluding Nonconformists from the universities and many other educational institutions. At the same time the concept of education was theologized and moulded by the Anglican church. The impoverishment of Christian education was considerable throughout the 18th century and in the early 19th century the squabbling of Anglicans and Nonconformists further retarded the expansion of the educational system. By 1870, when the state began to intervene decisively in the system, the concept of Christian education had become very weak. A form of Christian moralism existed in public schools, but by this time the main leaders of opinion were firmly secular. It is interesting that Shaftesbury, who was involved up to the hilt in education through the ragged schools, opposed the development of state education because he thought it would effectively wipe out Christian education. This has actually happened both in principle and institutionally, and people do not realize how quickly and completely it has come about. Even in 1944 half of the schools in the country were still church schools. Moreover, the idea of Christian education has been narrowed to one or two lessons of religious education which soon tended to be seen in comparative religious terms, and by 1977 some syllabuses even required that parts of the Bible be taught as myth.[1] Thus the idea of Christian education has been pared to a minimum in most of the British educational system.

A contrast which is worth noting is the situation in the Netherlands, where far-sighted Christians succeeded in obtaining parity of treatment for independent state-funded schools; there 70 per cent of the secondary schools are independent, and are allowed to have a Christian foundation and curriculum if they wish.

At the same time as the secularization of education was taking place, parents were being excluded from the educational process. A major step in this direction was the abolition of school boards by the Education Act of 1902, but this was just part of a continual development of state paternalism in education. Control of schools has been firmly in the hands of the Board/Department of Education and the Local Authorities, and directives have gradually assumed greater and greater authority. Parents are almost considered to be intruders in the child's educational process. Indeed, the idea that the state should eliminate differences in educational opportunity (which parents obviously affect) has meant that the parents *should* be eliminated as much as possible from the process of schooling, which, as Illich points out, is often wrongly identified with education. Most administrators, and even most teachers, see parents merely as a nuisance or as a challenge to their professional expertise.

The situation for Christians is extremely serious. Most schools are teaching the orthodox, examination-orientated, secular

---

[1] David C. C. Watson, Head of R.E. at Rickmansworth School, was dismissed in January, 1977, for supporting a non-mythical interpretation of the early chapters of Genesis.

patterns of thought, but increasingly it is being realized that this orthodoxy is not only false to many standards of Christian truth, but that it also has the weight of an established monopoly, with many vested interests at all levels, political and educational, which work against any independent view of education. The problem is made worse by the fact that the only kind of independence available is in the form of elitist, fee-paying public schools. Thus the parent who recognizes this basic responsibility before God for the full education of his child finds that structurally it is almost impossible to exercise it. For the British state educational system, with the exception of Roman Catholic Schools, does not allow different *kinds* of education; it does not seem to be realized that this is a major infringement of the rights and responsibilities of parents. The idea that there is one single kind of education is being pushed even harder in the form of compulsory, common or core curricula. The political pressure for a uniform educational system has also been very great under recent Labour governments.[1] Thus the Christian parent is caught in a system which does not allow him to fulfil his God-given task.

There are, however, more immediate problems for parents. One is the way in which teachers exclude them from their professional domain by surrounding the teaching process with all kinds of technological and liturgical mystique. So parents cannot teach a child to read, it is argued, because they might use the wrong methods, although most parents are able to read and are ideally situated to impart their knowledge. Further, they are not expected to have opinions about what their child is taught. In only a few schools is it recognized that parents are often very competent teachers, who know their children well and can give them far more attention than the average teacher. As a result there tends to be a gigantic, professional, protective reflex which operates against the parent. The paternalist assumption that the teachers or the State know best is firmly entrenched, especially in working-class areas.

[1] See A. Storkey, *Politics and Education* (Nottingham University Library, 1976).

The family and the economy

There are two aspects of this subject, internal and external. On the one hand the family is an economic unit within which there is dependence and support. A mother of young children, and the children themselves, are necessarily dependent. On the other hand the family as an institution has a certain relationship with other economic institutions, and this raises several issues.

The economic integrity of the family is under stress in many cases because of the growing scale of divorce and of one-parent families. This is a problem which requires the kind of compassion shown to the widow and orphan throughout the Bible, and the argument that welfare provision for one-parent families acts as an incentive to this pattern wrongly identifies the problem; most people do not organize their social lives around economic incentives and disincentives. At the same time the economic responsibility of the father who is not married is an important legal right of the relatively helpless child and should be recognized in law much more fully than it is. Perhaps maintenance payments should also be deducted with income tax, so as to counter the widespread avoidance of payment.

There is another set of issues which is concerned not so much with the incomplete family as with the normal family unit. If, as Scripture seems to suggest, the economic independence of the family is a principle (see Jos. 13:15–32), in a country where housing is especially important because of the weather it is a priority that each family should have and own a home of their own, even if this involves a substantial redistribution of wealth. Our present tax system minimizes the redistribution of wealth, and by absorbing all taxes into the Consolidated Fund also obscures the idea of communal giving and receiving. It would be possible, for example, to direct the revenue received from a wealth tax into the hands of young people coming into the housing market. When young people come of age they could be given a lump sum payment which represented their share of the redistributed wealth. Such a scheme, provided that it was not introduced in a period when it fuelled a speculative boom, would help to reinforce the economic independence of the family unit.

There are many other pressures on the economic independence

of the family. The level of hire purchase repayments works out at an average of £50 per head each year, and so some families are obviously very heavily committed. The effect of inflation is to convince people that it is better to borrow and spend rather than to save, and consumer spending is further encouraged. Thus, even when economic pressures should be light with small families, there are still many families which are pressurized into overspending. Fluctuations in the housing market and the mortgage rate add to the situation, but the root issue is that few take the economic independence of the family seriously as a principle for personal and national life.

The external aspect of the subject mainly involves the direct interference of economic institutions in family life. Jobs dominate families. This is not only true of many in the managerial class, but also of those on shifts and those who are compelled to travel. This is partly because companies may demand such a high level of commitment to the job from their employees that their home life must be compromised; and also because the pattern of union bargaining and the costs to firms of the pension and National Insurance contributions make it necessary to employ fewer people at longer hours than would be necessary with a different approach. Sometimes the reason is just that the ego of the father is so bound up with his job that the family is automatically secondary. Many self-employed people also work very long hours. Mothers also may go out to 'work' as a way of avoiding and escaping the more demanding work at home. The incentives to earn overtime payments and many other factors like continuous process production all conspire to make sure that some families are economically dominated.

The pressures on this institution, where giving and receiving rather than exchange are the norm, are therefore considerable. The family does not have great power in a society of large organized corporate bodies, but it is also weak because its internal structure and foundations are weak. That it is expendable is a foolish idea. Its weakness means the weakness of society as a whole in one of its most personal and creative areas.

Chapter 10

The mass media

Those who take a literalistic view of the Scriptures sometimes argue that they cannot be relevant to our own social situation because so much that is central to our lives to-day has no place in their pages, and this, of course, is literally true of radio, television and newspapers. However, it is not very difficult to penetrate beyond this simplistic concept of relevance by considering what the mass media are. Principally they are a means of social communication, and it is evident that there is continuity in the principles and norms that govern communication even when it changes its forms. There is, for example, a great deal in the first four verses of Luke's Gospel which a modern reporter would have no difficulty in transposing into his own situation. Thus the perspective from which we approach the mass media grows out of an understanding of the biblical perspective on communication, and the norms and principles which apply in this area.

At one level the Bible is literature, a form of communication, but any reader is very quickly forced to recognize that it is also a record of an incredible range of different forms of communication. Poem, taunt, song, letter, history, proclamation, prophecy, prayer, lament, hymn, proverb, dream, symbolic and acted communication all jostle closely with one another in a tapestry which is richer than any other book. Nevertheless communication has a particular direction in the Scriptures; the various forms are all under the guiding principle that the truth must be communicated in a society where self-deception, hypocrisy, lies, half-truths, propaganda and other attitudes are normal. At the same time there is a recognition of the weaknesses of man's views which take no account of the revelation by God of his truth. Norms of honesty, self-criticism, obedience to God and his law, purity and humility are woven into the message of the Scriptures. Communication, we quickly discover, depends on truth, God's truth about ourselves and about others.

At the same time the Scriptures show that, because we are created by a personal God and are created in community with one another, communication is meaningful, of central importance and is free. Although there is communication which takes place within institutional structures (the witness swears that the evidence he gives will be the truth, the whole truth and nothing but the truth), most communication is free. Just as we are not compelled to pray to God, so we are not under compulsion to talk to others, or to talk in a certain way; there were occasions when Christ answered not a word. Although there is a multitude of powers at work processing our communication, we are each responsible for what we say and what we choose to hear. Communication is not, and should not be, controlled. More than this is not needed for the immediate task of looking at some of the problems in the mass media.

The free media

The *free media* are a rather loosely defined category including all the forms of communication which do not have a mass institutional framework. Some of them, like letterwriting, are far from 'free' and others like the theatre have obvious institutional forms, but they are not 'mass' in that there is no technical transmission to very large audiences. It is in the free media, which includes what is generally called the arts—painting, poetry, sculpture, singing, the writing of novels, architecture, music and theatre—that we can observe most closely what the free communal patterns of communication are, without any strong external pressures being present. The variations among the different media forms are a very fertile area of study, but we shall consider just one simple point: that in the free media there is widespread evidence that the audiences are highly fragmented. It is possible to seek an explanation for this, as has been done, especially by Drs. Schaeffer and Rookmaaker,[1] but we are not going to evaluate the point; we shall merely use it by way of contrast with the mass media.

If we consider the pattern of the visual arts, painting has, since the beginning of the century, moved into the position where there are endless different schools, each of which is appreciated by only a relatively small proportion of the population. There is no obvious, shared culture in which paintings can form a single tradition, but a number of different traditions which are developing alongside one another. It is unlikely that two people sitting side by side in an Underground train would like the same paintings; similarly, not everybody likes the same music. Soul, classical, pop, rock, contrapuntal, organ, band, traditional jazz, spirituals, country and western, ragtime, punk rock, *etc*, all suggest that there is a wide variety of musical traditions in our culture, each with its specific audience. Significantly, it is only on the radio that an attempt can be made to bring together a homogeneous core of all-time musical favourites in programmes like 'Your Hundred Best Tunes.' Thus, although the fact tends to be ignored, because it concerns aspects of people's lives which are normally excluded from the professionalized mass media there is an incredible heterogeneity in the free media. The contrast is obvious. If people are so different in their tastes, attitudes and preferences in these free media areas of communication how is it that 10, 15, or 20 million people can be persuaded each night to watch the same television programme? That people do is well-known, but the question is rarely asked, although it is so important.

The television audience

Almost all households in Britain own a television set, and the average viewing hours per week in 1976 for persons aged over 5 were 19.9 in winter and 14.7 in summer. Or to put the figures in a different form, the average person spends the equivalent of seven whole years of his life, twenty-four hours a day, watching

[1] See F. Schaeffer, *The God Who is There* (Hodder and Stoughton, 1968) and *Escape from Reason* (IVP, 1968); H. Rookmaaker, *Modern Art and the Death of a Culture* (IVP, 1970).

television.[1] The power of television to gather audiences to watch a single programme is staggering; it is known that 15 million people regularly watch the same programme. Moreover, with the introduction of BBC 2 in 1967 and the ending of restrictions on the hours of broadcasting in 1972, audiences now have more programmes available for longer viewing periods. So there has been a threefold increase in the output of television since the early 1960s. What are television audiences looking at and why do they watch the same programmes in such large numbers? Undoubtedly, one reason why the audiences are so large is that many programmes are of high quality. Compared with those of other countries, British programmes are very highly rated by many. There are high standards of fairness and accuracy in reporting, issues are covered thoroughly and from different angles, the technical standards are exacting, the range of programmes is considerable, and there are many that evoke praise. Nevertheless there are some disturbing aspects of what the television audience sees, and we shall now concentrate on these.

The fictional content of television

Television audiences are looking at *fiction*. In a recent copy of the *TV Times* an estimated 56 per cent of television time during the week was taken up by films, serials and plays which were fictional. This compares with the 52 per cent found by Raymond Williams a few years earlier.[2] The percentage on BBC is lower, but still of major significance. The reasons for this pattern are various. Firstly, these programmes are often the most successful, measured in terms of viewing audiences. Secondly, they are also able, in serial form, to provide viewing continuity and, not surprisingly, familiarity is important to family viewing. Thirdly, buying old films is often cheap, compared with the cost of live productions. The pattern is understandable, but what does it mean?

The fiction is the fruit of an industry, producing for cinema and

[1] *Social Trends, 1976* (HMSO), p. 183.
[2] R. Williams, *Communications* (Chatto and Windus, 1966), p. 72.

television, independently and within the television companies. The product needs to be successful, and the measure of success is whether the film, serial or play commands and holds an audience. One answer to our initial question about the size of television audiences is therefore that the audiences are so big because the producers aim to have big audiences. This is not a trivial conclusion. The method by which the audience's interest is captured and held by fictional material is fairly obvious, one being that most programmes operate on a *suspense formula*. The programme sets up a situation of suspense which is resolved at the end of the programme, or in the next episode.

The viewers' response is programmed; he is required to be hooked by the formula. The variations are innumerable: will she marry him? will the spacecraft get lost in outer space? Will he get caught, die, suffocate, fall, win, drown, succeed, solve it, vindicate himself, stay honest, crack up, escape, win the war or get his trousers on in time? It is of course obvious that physical situations and violence are most useful in building suspense. Most viewers are concerned that an actor should not get killed or that an attacker should get caught. It is likely that the formula will become more sophisticated in the future as the industry's technical expertise increases, but more important is the meaning of the communication. One characteristic, it could be argued, is that the suspense is the meaning to the exclusion of content. That is, the viewer is being manipulated into the suspense formula, and other issues of meaning and content are subordinated to this non-communicating end. Incidental messages get through, but there is a subtle difference between communication to which you respond and a presentation which you are merely required to watch. Much television fiction does not require a personal response. At the same time its content because it is produced by a centralized entertainment industry, is remarkably different from the way people actually live. You are a million or more times more likely to encounter violence on television than you are in real life. You probably have never met a detective, an astronaut, a cowboy, a murderer or a hero. You probably face decisions which are more complex and less dramatic than those you watch, and your normal day is probably much longer than that of your television characters.

Non-dogmatic television

We have already suggested that there are wide differences of attitude, language and message in the free media, and we recognize that in Britain there are all kinds of people with differing views. We are a nation of Muslims, Communists, hippies, Liberals, moralists, Tories, hedonists, anarchists, Hindus, Socialists, Roman Catholics, loyalists, *etc*; and are, we are told, divided by race, politics, religion, sex, age, education and class. Given this lack of homogeneity in British culture and attitudes, it would seem that communication among people of different views is a serious matter for the media. This, of course, is realized by the broadcasting companies and a lot of time is devoted on television to the presentation, discussion and intermingling of different views which make television in effect *the* national forum. The standards and aims of many of the people involved in this process are very high.

Yet it could be claimed that television partly fails in this aim because the result is a neutralization of different views. Paradoxically, one of the ways in which this happens is by discussion. It takes time and care to express views, and people do not normally change their opinions rapidly. However, the pattern on television and radio tends to be rapidly moving, cross-firing discussion in which a clever phrase or a quick reply comes out best. The programme is set up in terms of a contrast of views, and the content is quickly varied and tightly controlled by the producer. Often the primary requirement is that the programme should be interesting and entertaining, and the ideas and views are either subordinated to that end or are monitored within that framework. That views should tend to be neutralized in this and other ways is understandable for two reasons. Firstly, any strong opinions, expressed at length, are bound to alienate some of the audience, even to the extent that they might turn the set off. The commitment to a majority audience means that it is out of the question for a communist, a member of the National Front, an art student, a clergyman or a vegetarian to spend an hour explaining his views. The requirement of entertaining viewing always gets priority over a full acceptance of pluralism. Secondly, truly independent opinions remove control of the programme content from the television company, since it no longer has the power of editing, asking certain kinds of questions and structuring the development of a programme in the way that it wishes. Thus the tendency is for discussion to be entertaining and channelled. The assumption is often that people should enjoy the views rather than take them seriously. As a result, there is a subtle processing of ideas and views, so that content becomes the handmaiden of the medium.

It could be argued that the introduction of access programmes is an attempt to break out of this framework. Clearly many are interested in participating and audiences are reasonably high, but there is a fundamental difference of perspective between programmes which are independently directed, and those which are directed by network staff. The Annan Report says of access programmes,

'The enthusiasm of the BBC and of the IBA for these programmes was somewhat more muffled. They inclined to see them as adjuncts to the professionally produced output.'[1]

It does seem, therefore, that there is a fundamentally anti-dogmatic commitment to television. It is not that different views are not discussed; on the contrary discussion is an industry. Rather, the emphasis on entertainment, balance, momentum and the control by the network of the programme's flow all tend to process and neutralize views. Criteria like interest, topicality, variation, continuity, *etc*, all shape the way in which views are presented and packaged in a manner too subtle for most of us to notice most of the time.

One area of special interest to Christians is religious broadcasting. The sight of a clergyman preaching from the screen is an incongruous one, because of the ethos that we have already analysed. A medium which rules out dogmatism and puts the emphasis on entertainment and pleasing most of the audience will not easily allow for a presentation of the Christian gospel. The Christian message cuts across the ethos of the medium, and something has to give. What then is happening? The *BBC Handbook* suggests an important trend.

[1] Report of the Committee on the Future of Broadcasting. (HMSO, 1977, Cmnd. 6753), p. 292.

'A decade ago almost all producers were clergy of the Church of England and other main churches in the country. Though they were talented people many of them suffered the disadvantage of coming into a profession late in life. In 1975 about half are laymen and the proportion is still rising. What is more, many of them are appointed at or near the beginning of their working lives so that they learn the craft of programme production from the bottom up. This has already had a marked effect on programmes and should in due course raise professional standards to a very high level'.[1]

Perhaps this extension of network professionalism marks the full takeover of popular, bland, interesting and undogmatic religious entertainment. The test lies, of course, in the programmes themselves, but it may be that they are so well produced that nobody notices what has been lost.

News

Another of the ways in which a television audience is maintained is through the news service. This service is a success in that the electrical transmission of news is immediate, allows more direct forms of contact with events than printed news and is cheaper and less wasteful. BBC 1 devotes more than one fifth of its time to news and current affairs and the programmes are broadcast at peak viewing times. Here is one of the keys to the large audiences.

However, again, we have to ask what it is that is transmitted in order to hold these large audiences? What kind of news do we get? There are all kinds of criticisms of television news. One is that television is likely to deal with what is sensational, visually exciting and immediately interesting to the viewer. It is not insignificant that a lot of effort is expended in persuading the viewer to watch the news. This may be because the over-dramatized, essential daily news is not in fact really necessary, as some people discover on holiday. It will generally be conceded therefore, that there is a tendency towards the audience-gathering news. This means that personalities tend to feature strongly and that action and violence and tragedy, because they offer chances

[1] *BBC Handbook, 1976* (BBC, 1975), pp. 35–36.

of visual drama, are quite dominant. Another criticism is that television news creates itself, in that all kinds of groups seek the publicity that the newsmen give them when they do the right kind of newsworthy actions. The television companies are aware of these issues and have gone some way to avoid these weaknesses. However, a more serious criticism is the source of news. The fact that all news comes through a few news agencies, and the BBC and IBA news services, means that it is gathered on a very narrow front. The process of selectivity is very great; the slant is London-centred, political, dependent on articulate and easily available sources; it stresses obvious, accessible changes and focuses on news that can be most economically obtained. To some extent there has been a realization that news is more complex; there is a differentiation between local and national, and different correspondents cover economic, scientific, social, international, industrial and other aspects. Nevertheless, the source of the reports, their transmission through the normal channels, the patterns of reporting and the use of cameras limit the kind of news gathered. Perhaps it is too exclusively dependent on professional reporters and correspondents. It might be of great value if managers, dockers, policemen, politicians, farmers, doctors and others conveyed their views of events more fully. This would reveal more of the complexity, would tap a wider range of sources and expertise, and would also convey that each day's news is in effect contemporary history which is less well understood than the authority of news reports sometimes implies.

Another problem with regular news bulletins is the view of time which they imply. The instantaneous nature of television news leads to an emphasis on the immediate happening: 'at a meeting this afternoon', or 'a spokesman said this evening'. Time scales are much more complex—a lifetime, a generation, an economic cycle, a parliamentary session, a season, a working week, a planning period, *etc*. Because television focuses on its saleable, instantaneous quality, the other time scales, which are both more relevant to the public's own lifestyles and also more significantly long-term, are occluded. We are, for example, more likely to hear of a British Leyland strike than a six-monthly report on the company. One thing that is especially worrying is that the insatiable demand of television for comments and statements puts great pressure on politicians for immediate solutions and short-term initiatives. They are constantly encouraged to be superficial and short-sighted, and it could be that the shape of television news is affecting the political platform of decision-making and policy formation.

Thus, the appeal of the television news service raises many more problems than is often realized, and the very ethos that is found to make the most appeal has dangers that are quite significant.

See-through characters

People are very complex and difficult to get to know. A friendship takes time to form; a psychoanalyst spends many hours with a client; relationships change over a period of time, and it is not possible to know exhaustively even somebody whom you meet each day. This real life world of relationships, which is costly, demanding, unpredictable and full of direct emotion, contrasts absolutely with life as we see it on television. The creation of characters on television is an industry; personalities are created for the enjoyment of the public with great technical expertise. They are normally very easy to get to know; it rarely takes more than half-an-hour. They create no problems for the viewers and the audience is never directly disturbed by them; an interesting convention has developed that the viewer is never directly asked a question. Television personalities are easier to get to know than the neighbours, and the viewer is allowed to enter into a relationship which is completely undemanding and passive.

How easy, therefore, it becomes to watch television. Normal people are so inconsistent compared with Kojak. The visual escape route is offered. Why are real relationships so demanding and unexciting? Why are real life problems so complicated and insoluble compared with those acted out on the screen? Why cannot X be like that character? That's exactly my situation— taken advantage of. Why are real people so complicated? Every night all over the country television characters are chosen in preference to other members of the family, and in millions of heads a private thought-world conceives actual social relationships in terms of the characters created by scriptwriters and actors. Much of the time, people base their thinking on myths associated with the industry and the cult of personality—one that offers higher monetary returns than any other in the Western world—and it is sad that the popularity of television is again rooted in an ethos which is both highly materialistic and often also a denial of true communication in this fundamental sense.

Continuity

The continuity of television programmes is now taken for granted. Since 1972, they have been allowed to be broadcast at most times of the day or night. However, nobody would think of going to the cinema or theatre four times in an evening, or reading a chapter from four different novels at a stretch, yet millions watch for an equivalent amount of time during a single evening without questioning it. Continuity or flow has become a vital part of normal presentation.[1] There are various techniques which obviously contribute to this process, like serials, programme information, the trailer before the advertisement and the absence of breaks. It is well known that there is especially intense competition for viewers in the early evening, because once a viewer is tuned to a certain channel he is likely to stay there for the rest of the evening. The expertise involved in this inducement to continuous watching is very great, as is evident to anyone who watches through an evening carefully. Another important element in continuity is the low cost of television viewing, which we shall consider later.

The assumption involved in this practice of continuous broadcasting is very important. People are expected and encouraged to view all the time, and the aim of the broadcasters is to maximize audiences. The choice of switching off or changing programmes is therefore not fairly and openly given to the viewer, and television watching is seen as, and becomes, a process rather than a choice of discrete programmes. Nobody seems to consider that the idea of continuous viewing might be as misconceived as the idea of continuous education or drinking, and that the

[1] See R. Williams, *Television—Technology and Cultural Form* (Fontana, 1974), pp. 78–118, for a good analysis.

broadcasting companies have a duty not to establish endless viewing and not to pressurize people into this pattern.

Variation and change

It would seem to be no easy task to hold an audience throughout an evening, but there is a range of techniques through which this is achieved. The first is through the variety of programmes planned for an evening; they must be short enough, especially at key times, to allow people who are not strongly committed to that programme to sit through to the next. They must switch interest, location and emphasis; each evening is a carefully planned mosaic. For example, one typical evening's broadcasting on BBC 1 from 6 o'clock onwards is: news and sport, cartoon, detective film, comedy show, news, serial, chat-show, pop concert, film; another is: chat-show, science fiction serial, feature film, comedy show, film series, news, sport, chat-show. However, this principle does not just occur within an evening, but also within programmes. Variety programmes are an obvious example of this principle of variation and change, but there are other ways in which it is done. Every programme is normally a careful orchestration of location, emotional level, lighting, topic and personalities, which is frequently varied to hold the viewers. There are many technical Mozarts in television who learn that there are well known patterns, the sonata forms of films and drama, in which tension is repeatedly raised and lowered according to the preordained pattern. At another technical level the camera constantly changes focus, angle, background, lighting, so that one person's face becomes a kaleidoscope of visual experiences. The viewer's eye is never, and must never become bored. There is always some visual or aural stimulus, and it is very easy to understand why people are held by this change at an almost mechanical level.

However, again, we see that a lot of this technical expertise can be directed merely at holding the audience, it is not integrated with the content of the programmes in an authentic way, so that the programme is what it is, but is also a manipulation of the viewer into mechanical, visual, emotional or quizzical participation. This kind of programme production now *has* to be

259

adopted. There is little outside this highly sophisticated frame-work, and it is clear that if one camera were used statically in a large number of programmes the audiences would rapidly fall, and the people left viewing the programme would be those who were actually interested in its subject matter. Again, we see that the result is not unexpected, given that the present networks are systems controlled by producers. The institutional framework, largely unquestioned, produces what grows from the basic rationale of maximizing audiences. Thus we see that there is an explanation of the way in which the television network maintains these massive audiences of 10–20 million viewers. The result is a carefully calculated organization of effects which achieve the ends of the organizers, but which can have serious effects on the viewers' attitudes and relationships in the long term. However, we need to define more carefully what is meant by the effects of television and investigate them further.

The effects of television

There now exists a small industry which is concerned with developing a thorough, sociological analysis of the effects of television on viewers. Its general aim is to discover whether there is any quantifiable change which can be ascribed to the effect of violence, advertising, political coverage, *etc.*, on television. However, researchers face the problem that the audience is so heterogeneous that any logical findings are going to be very difficult to establish; clear answers cannot be forthcoming on most of these issues. Yet at the same time there is a range of possible effects that needs to be carefully considered.[1] The social effects of substantial television viewing on communal and family life have often been noted. There has been a switch from draught to bottled and canned beer, cinema attendances are down, the use of public transport in the evening has declined, and meals have become more informal. The main argument is that the twenty hours a week committed to television are at the expense of communal and family intercourse. Even this is very difficult to

[1] See J. D. Halloran (Ed.), *The Effects of Television* (Panther, 1970); J. D. Halloran, *The Effects of Mass Communication* (Leicester Univ. Press, 1968).

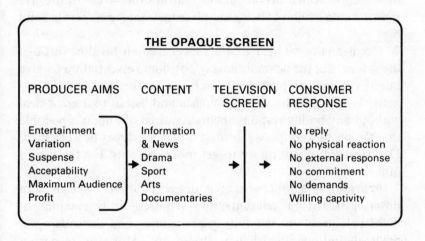

THE OPAQUE SCREEN

PRODUCER AIMS	CONTENT	TELEVISION SCREEN	CONSUMER RESPONSE
Entertainment	Information		No reply
Variation	& News		No physical reaction
Suspense	Drama		No external response
Acceptability	Sport		No commitment
Maximum Audience	Arts		No demands
Profit	Documentaries		Willing captivity

prove, but nevertheless it is a substantial argument. Is the place that television holds in family and communal life damaging socially? The researcher cannot answer the question, because he cannot establish the criteria by which to judge, but many families and individuals can, on the basis of their own more *ad hoc* criteria. The more difficult issue concerns the effect on the audience of what is seen, and here we note that there is a tendency to a rather behaviourist, stimulus-response orientation to viewing. If the viewer is fed violence or sex, how will he respond? It can be argued that this framework is defective and amoral, and that the viewer has a right to say, 'that should not be shown', as the Viewers and Listeners Association has repeatedly pointed out. Nevertheless, for the time being, we shall adopt this posture and suggest some more subtle ways in which the viewer may be affected. Evidence is impossible to obtain, but the arguments *may* be important.

1. There is a major difference between the real and the viewing world. When a baby bangs himself with a rattle it hurts, and the association is very real. When a gun fires on television, nothing really changes. All that happens on the screen changes nothing in

reality and the viewer may therefore be taught patterns of dissociation which become important in other areas of life. He may develop a habit of being cut off from what is going on around him.

2. Occasionally we hear that a viewer has put his shoe through the screen, but the normal viewing position is essentially a passive one. Even talking back to the screen is rather an unrewarding activity. Thus, if the viewer watches and listens to a great deal without any bodily response being required of him, it is possible that the physical response to what is perceived may be weakened. Dad, instead of getting up to get more coal, just lets the fire go out.

3. Learning is a process that is done at different speeds with different kinds of concentration required; it is cumulative, involves correction and testing procedures and depends upon prior definitions of what is significant. However television presents people with a great deal of unsystematic and varied data which have to be received at a given speed without any possibility of recall. It is interesting how slow a formal education programme is, like an Open University broadcast, compared with 'normal' television. The viewer may be adopting unhelpful and temporary learning patterns, which impair some of his abilities.

4. The clarity of a television screen, even with the clearest possible definition, is poor and fairly limited. It is possible that the television pattern of perception weakens the development of people's perceptual understanding and responsiveness. They may see, but not see, except in a television perceptual sense.

5. It is a normal part of thinking and communication that a particular subject is followed up by a person who is interested in it by conversation, reading and investigation; a person becomes 'absorbed' as we say, in that subject. Study and other important personal activities have this obsessive quality. The contrast between this important aspect of human action and interaction and the pattern of television where the programmic nature of the experience militates against any continuity of interest is quite marked. It is possible that the continual change of subject forestalls any abiding concern on the part of some viewers with any one subject. Indeed, it is possible to meet avid viewers whose thought processes correspond to a news bulletin in that they seem

to move from one subject to another purely on the pattern established in a news report without any other link being apparent.

How one views these and other potential effects depends on the attitudes to life which one holds. However, our analysis thus far should at least enable us to question one of the great myths of our time: that homogeneous television is a neutral phenomenon which is an incontrovertible part of life, the effects of which we merely have to monitor. In reality there are many different, possible forms of television, guided by very different perspectives on communication. The fact that one ethos, involving mass audience appeal, centralized production control and centralized financing has, and is, dominant (although there are regional variations and differences between BBC and ITV) tends to prevent a consideration of some of the other possibilities. The Annan Report has to some extent opened the door to considering these possible forms, but it could be argued that it has largely accepted the production model rather than the free communication model which we shall develop in more detail later. However, before we move on to look at a well-tried alternative, we shall briefly consider other media forms which have developed a similar structure and ethos.

The other mass media

The development of newspaper communication in Britain has been dominated by what has come to be called the 'Northcliffe Revolution' which took place just before the turn of the century. Its main characteristic was a switch to dependence on advertising revenue. The emphasis was on mass circulation in order to attract advertising and this in turn provided the funds for mass circulation. This process enabled the main publishers to become large-scale combines able to eliminate competitors and move into a situation of oligopolistic control. Thus as a matter initially of policy and later of necessity mass readership became the key to modern newspaper production. The incredible power of the print unions, the scale of the rotary press and the very low cost of paper cemented the pattern. However, the pattern has not been an undiluted success. Gradually the commitment to local newspapers is growing and the national press is facing falling sales. At the same time the meaning of written news has changed because of the development of television news. Thus, although the readership of daily newspapers in Britain is one of the highest in the world, the mass production model is tottering.

The policy of seeking a mass audience is also reflected in a variety of ways in the content of newspapers. Often news is made to focus around one personality to give it human interest. Reports of criminal and sexual offences, scandalous happenings and sensational events tend to predominate. Articles are kept short. Sport is given excessive coverage. Suspense is often drummed up, and competitions and letters are used to focus newspaper loyalty. When the viability level of sales is about 1 million for a quality and 2 million for a popular newspaper, the editor and staff are often under extreme pressure to hold their audience.

However, it is not only the readership that is wooed, but also the advertisers. It is interesting, for example, to see the way in which the business sections of all newspapers have expanded over the last few years, and it is evident that the motive for this development was the lucrative business advertising revenue. Also, the motive and strategy for the development of colour supplements in Sunday and daily papers was the tapping of advertising revenue. Similarly the various consumer pages, holiday guides and car supplements are clearly providing a format for the advertisers. This dependence on advertising puts a question-mark against the independence and freedom of parts of the press. Can the motoring, woman's, travel and film correspondents stay independent when so much advertising revenue is tied to their subject matter? Thus, it could be argued that the subject matter of much of the press is subservient to its existence, security and continuation. That this structure of self-interested organization is often assumed to be normal shows how difficult it is to move out of this perspective.

The cinema is another medium which has been fighting to hold a mass audience, but with less success. Admissions have fallen from over 1350 millions per year in 1950 to 116 millions in 1975, largely as a result of competition from television. The only substantial audience that the cinemas have is among the young, who can afford it and for whom it is part of the extraparental orbit; apart from them the audiences are very thin. In the face of this enormous contraction, the film industry has used a variety of techniques to try to hold a larger audience. These include the cultivation and projection into orbit of stars who command audience loyalty or, at least, interest, and also the production of spectaculars, each more lavish than the last. Every possible form of suspense and agony has been exploited to the full—the white knuckles clawing at the edge of a tall building, the rising water, the chase in cars or helicopters over mountains, through rivers, over roofs, under water, *etc.* The variations are endless, but in the end they are all the same, because the basic aim is to hold an audience in suspense; the formula has priority over the communicated content. The use of sex and violence in more and more extreme and inhuman forms is the weakened thrashing of a dying industry. At the same time it is destructive, especially to the young, because it is consumer sex saying, 'Buy this; this is what you want', and, 'Watch this violence, this will give you an experience you'll want more of'. This is an industry in which the actors and actresses are used to buy audiences, as many others besides Marilyn Monroe could testify.

The financial structure of the industry tends to favour this kind of development. Normally banks lend money for the films, but only against collateral, which is usually provided by 'selling' the project to one of the big film distributors, who agree to pay a certain sum on completion of the film. Thus the distributors, whose primary concern is box office returns, tend to be the arbiters over which films are produced and which are not. They are, of course, extremely few in number and consequently films are normally generated by the crude criteria of box office success of a few distributors. Film units also are professional production units, which means that there is, again, an inherent tendency to use mass production methods for an activity which ought to be a process of unique personal communication. The communal language of films is so impoverished simply because films have become consumption goods, not free media communication. The whole structure of this aspect of our life needs to be radically redefined.

The issue involved can be further explored by looking at advertising which is carried out on television, in newspapers and in cinemas. Mass advertising tends to be relatively contentless with little detailed description, costing or details of manufacture. The emphasis is rather on some method of making people take notice, usually by some form of visual manipulation. There is often an image in the advertisement which seems desirable, but which has no obvious connection with the item to be sold. Frequently products promise intangible benefits like poise, glamour, peace of mind, *etc.*, which they could not possibly bring about. Psychological exploitation is often involved, focusing on people's needs, weaknesses, hopes and fears in order to sell. The principles on which advertisements are based include flattery, greed, laziness, snobbery, lust, pleasure for its own sake, possessiveness and other very unchristian motives. The process that is taking place is obvious, the requirements of mass production and selling have led to the exploitation of this form of communication, so that rather than the wants and choices of the consumer being respected and cared for, he is manipulated into buying decisions. The basic norms of free communication like respect and honesty are so frequently twisted and destroyed by the advertising industry that it is *normal* for people to expect twisted communication.

Diagnosis

In all these media forms which we have examined there has been a common pattern. It is that the communicators' main aim is predominantly that of capturing and holding a mass audience, because the institution depends on this for its success, growth and profit. As we have seen, the content of the medium is shaped to this end, and the guiding principles of the media tend to be ones like popularity, interest, sensational value, excitement and impact. These carry greater weight than norms like truthfulness, accuracy and personal respect. Although this is often accepted as normal, it is a substantial breakdown in the meaning and integrity of the media. Instead of their acting as a means of free communication on a large scale within a national community, they are manipulating and controlling communication to their own ends. Raymond Williams comes to a similar conclusion,

'The ownership of the means of communication, old and new,

has passed, or is passing, in large part, to a kind of financial organisation unknown in earlier periods, and with important resemblances to the major forms of ownership in general industrial production. The methods and attitudes of capitalist business have established themselves near the centre of communications ... All the basic purposes of communication—the sharing of human experience—can become subordinated to this drive to sell ... The organisation of communications is then not for use, but for profit, and we seem to have passed the stage in which there is any pretence that things are otherwise ... The irony is that the only practical use of communication is the sharing of real experience.'[1]

As the media have processed content to their own ends, we find ourselves living in a world of double talk and double think. The powerful media world dominates communication about the substantially different, real world we live in. The suspense that exists in the darkened, flickering room does not exist in the rest of the house. The pornography is not about sex, but about luring money or attention from people. The news item that dominates a paper today will disappear tomorrow when its news value dies, because it has no intrinsic importance. The feature article on Italian holidays says very little, but is surrounded by travel advertisements. The report of the court case abhors the crime but revels in the details. The television hero escapes magnificently to reappear week after week. Political statements, sought out by news-hungry reporters, flood the news bulletins. The ceaseless propaganda of build-ups of personalities, events and programmes goes on. A new colour world is created to excite the eyes. What is being communicated? It is valuable, honest, respectful and open? Or is it inevitable that the mass media should eat up communal communication and put it out in its own processed form?

Is it also inevitable that in all the different areas of communal activity and communication we should be pushed towards elitism? For the centralized mass audience-seeking media require, create and establish elites, which are able to communicate successfully to mass audiences. But the elites have a slightly

[1] R. Williams, *Communications* (Penguin, 1968), pp. 31–32.

different character from other forms in that they are performance elites. The ability must lie in performance to a mass audience. Thus, for example, it is Magnus Magnusson, a media man, not an archaeologist, who prepares an important series on biblical archaeology. Moreover the elitist pattern confers authority on the elite performer, because he has mastered the medium. As yet it has not been realized that the new elitism of the media is gradually sucking the vitality from many areas of national life. Sports like cricket, tennis, athletics, football, *etc.*, are now becoming media performances dominated by 'stars', not communal games. Pundits have emerged whose wisdom the rest of the nation is expected to follow. The political stars absorb most of the limelight while the whole complex system of politics is left in the shadows. Thus again it could be argued that the mass media create a new unreal but real system of elites, which create communication in their own image.

The economics of the media

Crucial to the problem we have been analysing is the economic structure of the media. One of the most important reasons why television is watched so much is because it is so cheap to watch an extra programme. The only marginal cost is that of the electricity required to run a set, which, since the set also provides warmth, is minimal. Similarly, newspapers, by raising money through advertising and selling at relatively low prices, are able to operate on a scale which takes full advantage of low marginal costs. In this situation, which is not uncommon in industry too, the cost structure has important implications in making large-scale output an obvious strategy.

Also, *all* the costs incurred by television, are fixed costs in the sense that there is no extra outlay which is dependent on more people watching television. This means that there is no way in which the costs incurred in producing programmes can be related to consumption in the market, and all costing must therefore be made by overall executive decisions. The tendency therefore is for there to be little constraint on costs, and every emphasis on gaining and holding a mass audience. So the situation exists where large audiences are necessary to support the rather lavish production systems, and lavish production is deemed necessary to support large audiences.

The revenue pattern also has peculiar effects on the service provided. The BBC is in the rather anomalous position that everybody buying a television set has to have a BBC licence. Thus, provided television sets, especially colour ones, are bought, the consumer has absolutely no economic impact on the BBC at all. There is zero economic accountability of the BBC to the public. The ITV companies receive no money directly from the public, but they are indirectly dependent in that the advertisers' main concern is audiences. The duopoly, as Annan calls it, is undoubtedly competitive, but the competition is not based on any direct form of market dependence. The economic structure of television is a legally established one, and it could be changed. It would be possible for example to relate payment to the BBC to the metered yearly viewing of BBC programmes. That would certainly be fairer to the viewer and to ITV. However, it is arguable that the whole economic structure needs to be rethought, for what the present pattern does is to provide a *consumption* pattern rather than a *communication* pattern, and we would argue that the latter is what television (and perhaps the newspapers) need. In the communication structure what becomes important is that various groups in the community commission and finance the production of their own television programmes, so that funding does not take place through the consumption process, but by underwriting the production of programmes. The public is not simply at the receiving end but acts in and funds the process of communication. Fortunately there is a well tried example of this process on our doorstep, the Dutch broadcasting system, although it was more or less ignored by the Annan Report.

The Dutch alternative

The country is small in size and the resources available to television are therefore much more limited than in Britain. However, the Dutch have long taken seriously the issue of *pluralist* mass communication, and the structure which has been set up reflects this. Responsibility for most of the programmes does not lie with one overall authority, but with a number of independent television companies. The programmes contributed by these different companies are co-ordinated by a public foundation, made up of government and private representatives. This foundation lays down certain standards which a broadcasting company must meet if it is to be eligible to broadcast. It must have as its main purpose the provision of radio and television broadcasting; it must be prepared to present a complete and balanced schedule, covering all kinds of subjects; it must not be commercially orientated; and it must have a minimum of 15,000 licence holders as contributing members. A key element in this structure is that programme time is allotted according to the membership of the broadcasting companies, which means that smaller groups regularly get time to broadcast, and also that the companies where the public put their money and their membership votes get more air time than others. That the system is representative can be gauged from the fact that half of all Dutch families are represented in the six largest broadcasting societies, which reflect various dominant, political and religious opinions in the country. Nine of the political parties in the Chamber of Deputies are able to broadcast, including, since 1965 the small Communist Party. Thus the system has established many independent contributors, which have their roots in various Dutch communal groups, and allows them to communicate nationally in a variety of programme forms. The actual responsibility which the companies have to their members, and the fact that they are economically dependent upon them for maintaining their programme time, means that a very firm system of pluralist accountability is established.

In view of this well-established example it is somewhat sad to see how the Annan Report gropes towards the idea of an Open Broadcasting Authority,[1] financed partially by advertising and sponsorship. The openness of the channel consists of a vacuum into which it is hoped independent producers will come, and the emphasis apart from being educational seems to be on 'novelty'. The conviction emerges throughout the report that there is a need

[1] *Report of the Committee on the Future of Broadcasting* (HMSO, 1977, Cmnd. 6753), pp. 229–241. See also Andrew Quicke, *Tomorrow's Television* (Lion, 1976).

for broadcasting which is not dominated by the producers, but the recommendation lacks awareness of the kind of pluralist, communal communication which the Dutch system exhibits, and which I have experienced from Dutch television. Direct communication by a number of different groups is more refreshing than neutral entertainment, even if it means that more people turn the set off for programmes they do not like. We would argue that this system deserves careful consideration as part of the British system.

Such issues seem to pass most Christians by. They see a clergyman on television and realize that what he is saying does not quite fit, but do not see that the medium is being used in a way which prevents the issues from being considered properly. They have also been slow to understand that most of what passes for religious broadcasting consists of institutional church affairs rather than Christian communication, so that the Christian life seems from the media to consist of little but services. Believers do not notice that they spend three hours a week in church, and twenty with the mass media, or that their children spend twenty times as many hours watching television as they spend at Sunday school. Tremendous amounts of time and energy are given to decorating a church, but rarely any to writing a programme script.

Generous help is given to churches, but support of Christian films, newspapers and broadcasting is rarely thought of. There are signs of change, but most Christians are still soaking up the output of the media without any critical awareness or alternative action entering their horizons.

However, although the institutional structure is important, the present situation is not just an institutional product, but is also related to a crucial cultural development which we must now examine.

Humanism and communication

Earlier we discussed the free media as an introduction to an analysis of the mass media. Now we must also recognize that the mass media tend to get their inspiration from the free media; there is a steady filtering of ideas, thoughts and attitudes from the stage

271

and the arts into mass forms. The producers are hungry for new material, and they know where to look. However, we suggest that the cultural perspective in the free media has led to the disintegration of audiences and to many different artistic languages, and we now need to consider how this basic perspective affects the mass media.

The dominant humanism of the West is, as we have seen, strongly individualistic, and the impact of this on the processes of communication has been pervasive. When man is the starting point for thought, it is easy for each individual to develop his own criteria of what is true. Despite the many attempts to develop a rational, objective, scientific, or universal view of the world, there has been an inherent tendency for a culture to develop where individuals are arbiters of their own 'truth'. Subjectivist movements like romanticism, impressionism and expressionism signal a significant switch from a concern for establishing true and false to the statement, 'This is the way I see things. What does it look like to you?'[1]

The crucial, spiritual crisis of this process was the development of existentialism which, although it had grown into a movement long before, became public in the 1960s. The two important points made by Sartre and Camus were, firstly, that it was absurd for the humanist to believe in any transpersonal truth and, secondly, that communication was a problem about which one could only despair, because one person's existence was totally other to another person. The influence of this movement was very great, because no humanist could refute the central arguments, but cultural development moved on from this position. If it was not possible to talk in terms of what was true of man, relationships and morality, then it was necessary to concentrate on at least achieving some kind of communication.[2] The desperate air conveyed by playwrights of the era, like Ionesco and Pinter, artists like Giocometti and Francis Bacon, and musicians like Bob Dylan, passed. On the stage the concern was with establishing an identity with the audience through situations or common points of identification. Artists have either worked in an

---

[1] See F. Schaeffer's 'The Line of Despair' in *The God Who Is There* (Hodder and Stoughton, 1968).

[2] M. Esslin. *The Theatre of the Absurd* (Pelican, 1968).

idiosyncratic, semi-private style, or else sought for items of meaning that will span the vacuum between artist and audience. The focus has switched from what is communicated to the fact that 'communication' has been made. Philosophy switched its emphasis from epistemology to the study of language as a means of communication at the same time. This radical change has filtered through to the mass media during the last two decades, and shapes many of the responses that we examined earlier. For example, popular music has used rhythm and noise as a technique for conveying the impression that communication is being made. Similarly, there is a resurgence of historical plays and films, because these offer common forms of identification with the past which can be used to span the chasm of communication. Further, the importance of allowing the viewer to identify with television characters signals another attempt to bridge the gap. We are into the era where it does not matter what we say as long as we talk to one another. The chasm which humanism and existentialism have created between one man and another is being bridged electronically by television images, but the bridges are not strong enough for people to walk over. Mass media communication is at root a problem of humanism and man's inability, without God's help, to know himself and his fellow men.

Chapter 11

British politics and parties

Faith and parties

There are many important areas in British political life, but the contribution made by political parties to government and legislation is undoubtedly a critical one. But what is a party? The impression given by day-to-day events is that parties are concerned with policies, publicity, power and popularity, but these aspects do not really identify the body to which some are committed and others are not. Often party members disagree on specific policies, and yet the party stays intact. What really holds a party together, it could be argued, is a *political faith*. If a group is merely concerned with certain specific policies or supports a particular interest group, it does not move beyond pressure group politics, but when it has an integrating faith which has implications for most areas of politics, it becomes a party.[1]

The idea of a political faith needs elaboration. It tends to be generated out of a more basic religious or social outlook—a philosophy of man and society which is far broader than merely political. Thus, political Liberalism is based on a philosophy of human freedom which goes beyond the sphere of politics alone. (At the same time some philosophies offer a *political* interpretation of man and society, *e.g.* Nazism and Communism.) The actual political faith must necessarily provide answers to basic

---

[1] See H. Dooyeweerd, *A New Critique of Theoretical Thought* (Presbyterian and Reformed Pub. Co., USA, 1953) Vol. III, pp. 605–24 for a closer analysis of the nature of political parties.

political issues: a theory of the state, a philosophy of law, punishment, a definition of the scope and competence of government, a definition of legitimacy, the political unit, the aims of the state and its guiding principles. Various forms of political faith can be identified as Nationalism, Socialism, Conservatism, Liberalism, Gaullism, *etc.* Following from these perspectives are the actual policies supported by the parties. It is important at this stage to recognize that an apparent single principle, like the principle of equality, is actually a range of fundamentally different principles depending on the underlying perspective. Thus there are radically different, individualist, collectivist, materialist, pluralist, liberal and socialist definitions of equality. Principles are often used as political glow-words to attract widespread support, so this point tends to be overlooked.

The conclusion, therefore, is that a party is a voluntary organization which coheres around a political faith and operates at all these different levels:

Religious faith, philosophy of man and society, political perspective, political principles, political programme, political priorities and political practice.

In actual practice it is even more complex than this, but the political perspective or faith may offer an incisive point of understanding for modern party politics, and we shall therefore try to enunciate some of the strands in the political faith of the three main British parties.

The Labour Party The Labour Party has from its inception included a number of strands in its credo. The first element is the radical tradition, beginning with the support in Britain for the French revolutionaries and later finding expression in Chartism, which involved a faith in the common people and their participation in politics through the electoral process, especially as the franchise was widened in the late 19th/early 20th century to include the working classes. Secondly, there is the kind of optimism associated with Robert Owen, which centred on the idea that if people are given the right conditions they will be good or ameliorate. The paternalist responsibility of leaders is therefore to improve conditions. Thirdly, there was a range of Christian influences, including the Christian Socialist movement under

F. D. Maurice and C. Kingsley, which put emphasis on the brotherhood of man and self-governing economic units, and also the Nonconformist and Presbyterian moral concern with social and economic injustice. Another emphasis was the romanticism of William Morris, which suggested that work needed to be redeemed from capitalist alienation, possibly through a return to pre-industrial craft patterns of work. This was an idealization of working class culture, and was not of much long-term importance. However, these issues were not really battling for the heart of the Labour Party as were the three following political systems of belief.

The first element was Fabianism, associated with figures like Sidney and Beatrice Webb, Graham Wallas, George Bernard Shaw, Clement Attlee, Hugh Gaistskell, Anthony Crosland and Shirley Williams. The faith of the Fabians was that the State, directed by a Socialist Party, would act as a paternalist reforming unit which would gradually help the working class out of its exploitation and subjection. The key to this process was the education of the workers, who would then be able to achieve the kind of independence and equality they had not had. The state also needed to provide for other causes of poverty and unhappiness by organizing systems of care and protection. This element tended to be the more 'intellectual' and middle class wing of the party, and was very strong in the post 1945 era.

The second of these major strands saw the Labour Party as the political defender of the trades unions. This was a vital factor in its origins, has been the Party's financial backbone, and was especially important in the period following the formation of the MacDonald National Government in 1931. The belief is that the main issue is economic, and that the unions are therefore the key institution for getting rid of exploitation and improving the lot of the working class. The Labour Party must therefore defend and support the work of the unions. Attitudes have tended not to be socialist in any strong political sense, but to be more concerned with the practical material improvement in the lot of their members. At the same time, the fact that they represent 'the workers' has given the Labour Party its basic group identity, although the unions themselves provide no coherent *ideological* perspective for the party.

The third position is that of non-revolutionary Marxist socialism. This is a more doctrinaire class perspective which puts no faith in a process of gradual amelioration. What the workers gain, they gain by power and the hope is that, by controlling the state through normal electoral processes, capitalism and exploitation could be eradicated. State control would effectively eliminate exploitation and emancipate the working class from their historical bondage. Marxism as such was anglicized so that there has never been much question of revolution in the classical sense; however, the major theorists like Harold Laski argued that, in order to achieve the end of exploitation and the beginning of equality, a period of unqualified state control might be necessary. This view of the Labour Party was most strongly evident in the Independent Labour Party and Kingsley Martin, in his biography of Laski, feels that after 1931 'it became dominant, not yet in action, but as a matter of increasingly accepted theory.'[1] Whether it was or not, it was certainly one of the three most important political perspectives in the party.

The Conservative Party   The political faith of the Conservatives is difficult to define, because it is more implicit and has a longer history, but the following elements are undoubtedly important. There is first of all the belief that the wisdom accumulated in the institutions of society over the centuries is greater than that available at any one instant. This Burkean theme leads to the conclusion that institutions and political practices should be changed only circumspectly, and that reaction is always a valid policy. Another element is the belief in an establishment, namely that a group of people emerges in society who are bearers of what is good in our culture and it is therefore right that the leaders should come from this group in the nation. The Conservative tradition also includes a belief that the party is above class divisions and is therefore able to cement national

[1] Kingsley Martin, *Harold Laski* (Gollancz, 1953), pp. 81–82. See also Henry Pelling, *A Short History of the Labour Party* (Macmillan, 1961); George Lichtheim, *A Short History of Socialism* (Fontana, 1975); P. Anderson and R. Blackburn (Eds.), *Towards Socialism* (Fontana, 1965); Bernard Zylstra, *From Pluralism to Collectivism* (Van Gorcum, Netherlands, 1970) for further background.

unity. The vision of unity has changed from Disraeli's imperialist form, through a Churchillian sense of national destiny to the meritocratic, classless conception of Edward Heath, but it has been constantly present. Then again there is some dependence within the party upon Christian values; the long-standing links with the Church of England have led to an emphasis on personal moral values being upheld politically.

Another nexus of Conservative belief is related to faith in free competitive markets and material progress. The party has been committed to capital, growth, expansion and minimal interference by the state in economic affairs. It has also seen wealth as a sign of success and a key to progress. This attitude has been allied with a belief that, through processes of competition, those with high levels of achievement should emerge and be available to lead. Thus an elitist attitude tends to dominate, which sees leadership largely as an issue of competence and ability to be decided by technical criteria, rather than one which puts emphasis on ideological commitment. Finally, going back to its strong monarchist commitment, the party tends to believe in the exemplary leadership of those with legitimate political authority. This may explain the deferential behaviour which, as some claim, is shown by the rank and file towards the leaders.

It has been suggested that the Conservative Party is agnostic, and merely waits for the mistakes of the other parties to make it an attractive alternative.[1] Some leaders like Salisbury and Baldwin seem to have been close to this position, but it would not account for the continuance and coherence of a major party for a century or more. The Conservative faith, although less crusading, is no less present than that of the Labour Party in substantial numbers of British citizens.

The Liberal Party The Liberal Party has tended to centre its political faith on the individual and his freedoms. The focus of concern has changed at different periods, for example, property rights, civil rights, minority rights, *etc.*, but the key concept is that the individual should be free to do whatever does not impinge on

---

[1] See R. Blake, *The Conservative Party from Peel to Churchill* (Fontana, 1972) for a discussion of this issue.

the freedom of others. Following from this belief is a general support for free economic enterprise without restrictions on trade and the development of monopoly power. At the same time the normal framework of reference and appeal to the electorate is through rational self-interest, because, it is held, people understand what is good for them in the long run. It could be argued that Liberalism also tends to understand most important institutions in society in terms of contractual relationships among individuals, and the aim of institutional reform is therefore to redefine those relationships in terms of what the individuals want. Another important element in this nexus of beliefs is that dissenting minorities need to be protected. The pattern could be said to have begun with the support of Nonconformists in their battles with the established church, and it has extended to regional, religious and local issues. This party is also the strongest supporter of decentralization, and has repeatedly moved to bring politics down to the level of the individual. Indeed, in an attempt to politicize a perspective which is often rather apolitical, local participation politics has been emphasized as a way of involving the public in Liberal politics.

The theory of the state associated with Liberalism has evolved considerably over the last hundred years. The basic perspective is that the state should interfere as little as possible with the freedom of individual citizens, as long as their freedom does not interfere with that of others. It was therefore a minimalist view of the scope of state activity which was dominant in the Gladstonian era, as it dovetailed neatly with belief in private enterprise. This perspective was modified, especially by Joseph Chamberlain, who emphasized that modern political power was based on organized mass democratic support, and by the time of Lloyd George a more positive philosophy of the state had been put alongside the minimalist one. This saw it as the duty of the state to provide for the welfare of individual citizens in a range of areas where need became evident. This point is often ignored in modern political debate; the theory of the welfare state, although influenced by the Webbs, was originally a Liberal political faith, and was considerably modified after World War II by the Labour Party. The Liberal conception was that insurance and the state should provide for the welfare of individual citizens. The Labour conception was that the state should control the agencies that provide services for citizens; thus, the health service, education, social work, *etc.*, become state agencies.

The eclipse of the Liberal Party for the half century before 1974 can be explained at various levels. It can be argued that modern parties cannot split, as did the Liberal Party under Asquith and Lloyd George, without serious electoral consequences. It can be explained in terms of the organization of the trades unions and the backing they gave to the emergence of the Labour Party. It can also be noted that the Liberals had a decided aristocratic, and working class, split among its supporters which became an obvious weakness. However, it can also be explained in terms of a fundamental weakness in Liberal political philosophy which became more serious, although not openly expressed. It was that the Liberal emphasis on individual freedom precluded the development of any philosophy of corporate institutions. A firm, a family, a trades union or a community is more than the individuals who comprise it, and an individualistic approach to politics therefore tended to ignore many of the most important issues in an increasingly corporate society. The problem already existed in the era of Gladstone and Lord Rosebery, but had not been faced properly until well into the 1960s.

There is, however, a great deal in these political faiths that requires respect and careful analysis. Although it is the aim of this chapter to open up the possibility of a Christian political faith, the considered reflection of these three major political parties is of great importance in the formation of a political perspective, and in each of the parties there are elements of implicit Christian thinking which are directly relevant to the task of rethinking a political commitment. But this analysis of the political parties is an incomplete one, because ideologies are overlaid by other perspectives which are part of the culture of the age, and radically affect actual political life in Britain.

Power and parties

Some people consider that political power is a very simple matter; either you have it or you don't. In reality the situation is much more complex. Problems immediately arise about the basis of power (whether it is money, technology, physical force, influence, popularity or democratic elections), how long it lasts, and whether or not it is accepted by those over whom it is exercised. Political power contains many paradoxes. Some political leaders would claim, quite rightly, that on a whole range of issues they have little room for manoeuvre or cannot do anything at all. Power does not always lie at the top and is not always exercised there. Richard Crossman describes in his diaries how the Prime Minister was incapable of making an independent decision in Cabinet.[1] The subject is surrounded by illusions, and some of these are built into our political system.

The first illusion is created by our electoral system. The process of representation of single member constituencies leads to the situation where the government is normally formed by a party elected on a minority vote of, say, 40 per cent. The illusion, as Lord Hailsham pointed out in his 1976 Dimbleby Lecture, is to believe that the fact of being elected gives some kind of mandate for carrying out all of the policies advocated by the successful party during the election. The actual situation is that only a small proportion of the 40 per cent supporting the winning party will agree on all the measures suggested by it. Furthermore, the choice offered to the electorate is extremely limited because of the tendency of the British system to polarize parties. Thus an election becomes a very crude and insensitive way of expressing the electorate's loyalties and opinions, and leads parties systematically to over-emphasize their political authority.

The second illusion concerns the way in which power is sought. The electoral process is sometimes described as the 'first past the post' system, where the strong parties, especially the winner, tend to be over-represented in the House of Commons, while the weaker parties are under- or unrepresented. The temptation created by the system, therefore, is to seek power by whatever methods are available. However, this is where the problems lie. One of the necessary prerequisites for power is said to be electoral popularity, and the route to electoral popularity is lined with concepts like mass appeal, party image, electoral promises and

[1] R. Crossman, *The Diaries of a Cabinet Minister*, Vol. 1, 1964–66 (Hamish Hamilton and Cape, 1976), p. 591.

solidarity. Parties are also continuously tempted to a form of infallibility, whereby their own views and predictions must always be presented as correct and those of their opponents as incorrect. The charting of electoral popularity through opinion polls, and the construction of a basis for popular appeal, have thus led to a situation where the need to gain or retain power directs the stance of parties as much as does their underlying political faith.

There follows from this another constraint upon the party. It is organized primarily for power and this means that the voluntary faith community in politics becomes an organization in which the whips and the party machine exercise tight control, in which internal dissension is artificially suppressed in parliamentary voting, and in which groups fight within the parties for power in a similar, second order struggle. The constraints arise from the fact that, within this framework, power must be bought. Something must be given to groups whose electoral support is courted. The various pressure groups which can give resources to the parties also require compensation. Even though the transactions are not normally financial or corrupt, they involve a set of obligations which are often heavy, complex, incompatible and even impossible. Thus, at the very point where a political party thinks that it has achieved power, it may have incurred so many obligations that it is impotent. That Edward Heath came to power in June 1970 with a promise round his neck to 'cut the rise in prices at a stroke' meant that he was already locked in a credibility gap.

Another effect of this search for power is that there is a tendency to confuse and manipulate the electorate. In a consumer society where the aim is to sell goods on an opportunist basis, it is also possible for politicians to set their sights no higher than getting the votes of the electorate. The faithful bond between party and party supporters can become a question of instant salesmanship. The beginning of this pattern was evident during the 1950s. It was presumably no accident that the Conservative governments of 1955, 1959, and 1964 had elections at times when the fiscal policy of those governments had encouraged substantial economic booms. The fact that the British Prime Minister chooses the time when Parliament is dissolved has led to some manipulation of the electorate in that the voter is 'presented' with the right answer. In March 1977 Mr. Callaghan preferred an agreement with the Liberals to holding an election when the voter might have got the 'wrong' answer. It is also a common pattern for politicians to claim credit or impute blame for that which is inevitable. In 1970 the improvement in the balance of payments was primarily the result of the recession during that period, yet the Labour Government claimed it as a major vindication of their tenure of office.

The pattern is developed still further. The key to the hearts of the electorate, it is argued, is economic success. In 1959 Harold Macmillan told the nation, 'You've never had it so good', and the people laid their votes at his feet. The hidden assumption is that the government is responsible for the economic welfare of the nation. This illusion was created by the short-term Keynesian manipulation that occurred, but the illusion continued to make its demands. 'What was the government doing about the economy?' became an insistent chorus which every government faced. This illusion became so strong that in 1972/3 the Chancellor of the Exchequer engineered a boom which was crazy from the viewpoint of most economists who remained sane, but which was based on the idea that the government could generate take-off into high level growth. It is not fanciful to say that Anthony Barber's failure was a direct judgment on the earlier opportunism of his party under Harold Macmillan. But the materialist appeal has not been limited to one party, and the electorate still has all kinds of false expectations about what the government can do, which enslave the party in power and commit it to inappropriate responses. Are not the major parties even now queuing up to take the credit for the oil bonanza? The illusion shows no sign of weakening, and it is, incidentally, a major motive for the expansion of the public sector.

Thus we glimpse the paradox of political power. Those who seek it and think they have it are already committed to that which is their weakness. The ethos of gaining power and manipulating it creates a culture of demands, of distrusting authority, of illusions leading to destruction. The voices of the leaders become as the bleating of lambs. What becomes evident to those who can see is that the initial starting point in the approach to power is wrong. In the Bible we see Isaiah and the other prophets continually developing the same point to their own generations. The key issue comes in the New Testament when Jesus, wearing a crown of thorns, stood before Pilate, representative of the Roman Empire. Pilate pointed out his absolute power over the life or death of Jesus:

> "'You will not speak to me? Do you not know that I have power to release you, and power to crucify you?" Jesus answered him, "You would have no power over me unless it had been given you from above; therefore he who delivered me to you has the greater sin"' (Jn. 19:10–11).

Then Pilate wanted to release Jesus, but was powerless to do so. Thus the crucial point that Jesus made about power, shortly before his death and resurrection, was that *it is given by God and it is not possessed by men*. Those who think they possess power or who commit themselves to gaining it are committed to an illusory view of power which ends with weakness and enslavement. This principle has significance for all kinds of situations, but we now bring it to an understanding of the true relationship between a political party and power.

The argument is that a political party should not seek power. It should merely seek to witness to what it believes to be true in terms of political principles and policies. This commitment is the overriding one, and it may just as well lead away from power as towards it. Only when power is *given* by God is it not manufactured and enslaving. Accepting this fundamental Christian principle has more immediate results in a range of different areas. More specifically it is only when parties present their beliefs honestly that the electorate has a fully meaningful choice. When the electorate is presented with what it wants to hear by the various parties, then the choice becomes a fuzzy one. A Christian conception of authority changes not only the stance of parties, but also leads to a rethinking of the processes whereby holders of office are chosen. An office is a position of responsibility subject to various norms which allows service of others; it is not a reward for past favours, a pay-off or a recognition of the power of a potential adversary. It is not an incidental fact that because of the constraints of internal party organization a Prime Minister selects his Cabinet from a pool of about 40 people.

The current political expedients

Political parties fill a crucial position in the political scene because they offer a political faith, which in the end is what differentiates a Communist, a Liberal, a Socialist or a Gaullist political system. Despite the weight of technical expertise which a civil service carries, the need for a directing political faith is experienced the world over. It is sometimes claimed that the technocrats run the system, and this theory may well have local validity, but nowhere has a civil service or administrative party been elected to power, because there must always be a rationale or faith which guides the technical decisions to be made. The argument of this section is that in the postwar era there has been a new fluidity in political ideology which is in part the result of weaknesses in the classical Conservative, Liberal and Socialist positions, and is in part the result of current cultural attitudes.

How has the faith changed? Mainly because political realities are now viewed not so much in terms of values and principles, but *pragmatically*. Goudzwaard describes pragmatism in this way:

'In its most simple sense "pragmatism" indicates a movement which desires to be led by facts (*pragma* = fact) alone, without the so-called "bias" of specific convictions or principles. Purely on the grounds of a healthy and businesslike weighing of facts one attempts to arrive at a political position. On a somewhat deeper level the word "pragmatism" is used to indicate that movement in Western thought which denies that there is *one* norm for truth which binds all people. Only that can be "true" and "correct" which is useful for the factual, practical goals which one has established. If a certain pronouncement or measure brings you closer to this practical goal, that pronouncement or measure is true or correct.'[1]

Pragmatism has thus become a widespread, cross-party, political faith—a faith in the satisfactory nature of short-term solutions, a faith in problem-solving by techniques, a faith in one obvious, incontrovertible way of doing things, and a faith in the practical men of politics, *i.e.* those for whom principles do not create too many problems.

[1] B. Goudzwaard, *A Christian Political Option* (Wedge, Toronto, 1972), pp. 17–18.

The pragmatic position is, of course, a lie. Facts cannot be isolated from values, and they cannot of themselves generate policies, but the political version of this position, untenable though it is, still carries weight. The immediate practical decisions are made, and the values that are a necessary part of those decisions become evident later. Or alternatively, some form of technical apparatus is set up to monitor the problem and to provide channels through which a solution can be found. Again, a common stance is for one party to claim that its position is reasonable, commonsense, realistic, and down to earth, while that of their opponents is ideological. The net result of this position is obscurity and lack of clarity. It is not obvious where politicians stand, not just because the issues are complex, but because they do not accept that their positions are value-based. Let us look at an example, one of many which could be chosen, which exposes the issue. The National Enterprise Board is a well funded, supposedly pragmatic institution set up to help invest-ment. But what kind of investment? What criteria are used for lending? What control is exercised within the firms to which funds are lent? A single case, that of British Leyland, brings all these value judgments into the open. Should jobs be saved, exports protected, or should strict criteria of profitability be used? Thus pragmatism, otherwise defined by Harold Wilson as 'steering by the seat of your pants', creates a bogus fluidity which strongly affects the ideological stances of the parties.

This preoccupation with the immediate can be seen in some of the most important rallying points in postwar elections. In 1964, the focus of Wilson's appeal was technology and science. The purpose of the technology was not considered and, not surprisingly, the resulting educational boom produced a large number of highly trained, unemployed scientists and technol-ogists. The next emphasis, spearheaded by George Brown and the new Department of Economic Affairs, was planning. But this was not planning designed to specific *ends*; rather it was a national plan establishing guidelines and setting an amorphous national growth target. The target was a projection based on current economic facts, and soon proved to be unrealistic. The next emphasis was growth, the key to economic success, but, again, few openly questioned what growth was for, or towards what end, or for whom. The example of our European neighbours was so compelling; they were running so fast that we could not stop to ask where we were supposed to run to. Similarly, in the attempt to cure inflation the emphasis on the month by month reduction in the figures has often obscured any consideration of the way in which institutional structures encourage inflation. Immediate pragmatic solutions are all that is needed. The emphasis on technology, planning and growth shows how the most important, recent ideologies have been pragmatically based. This is not to deny that many important political decisions are made on the basis of authentic values, whether of the Right or the Left; the danger is that these are being eclipsed by pseudo-pragmatic ideologies which, by their supposed neutrality, eliminate the possibility of principled opposition.

The present weakness of parties

From this analysis we can draw the conclusion that the parties are getting weaker. Let us look at this systematically.

Firstly, if we examine the most important elements in the Labour Party philosophy we note the following problems. The Fabian perspective is geared to the amelioration of the lot of the working class through the provision of various facilities by the state. However, this paternalism fits into the pattern of middle-class control and working-class dependence that we have already considered, and it is easy for the most well-intentioned measures to end by establishing new middle-class forms of control. Thus one element in the Labour Party is part of a socialist political establishment. The second element that acts as a political supporter of the trades unions is still operating within the control/dependence class nexus, but aims to use collective power to maximize the rewards of the unions. The third element, emphasizing various forms of Marxist socialism, aims at the elimination of capitalism by state control. The conflicts among these three elements are serious and long-standing but they are not at the level of specific policies so much as at the level of political perspective and underlying philosophy. We would argue that, increasingly, what keeps these elements together is not a natural political community, but the necessity of maintaining a cohesive party machine if 'power' is to be retained.

The Conservative Party, although its responses are also complex, faces a similar long-term problem. It is that the long-term support given to free enterprise and capital has been uncritical, and has never allowed the party to develop sound policies for a non-exploitative economic order. The policies developed by other parties in office have often been retained, but no party can be nationally credible without facing this issue. At the same time, the freedom granted to the owners of capital to play the markets has now effectively to be granted to trades unionists to do the same in the labour market when they achieve the organized power. The historical weaknesses of capitalism remain with the party that supported it. Also, a party which has a largely traditional basis for its values is often condemned to a largely reactionary stance in an era of rapid change. When, in addition, the Conservatives have found that the traditional business/finance/ landed/ public school/ Oxbridge establishment has in part been superseded by a new Socialist establishment, it is clear that they find it difficult to have confidence in the historical, political faith of the party.

It is in the context of these weaknesses that the pressures of gaining power and of a pragmatic approach to politics have had their effect. The normal exposure of the electorate to issues through the mass media, and the simplistic stance the major parties are often forced to adopt, further add to the feeling of 'disillusion' among the electorate, which could be better described as a lack of certainty about the meaning of political parties. Symptoms of this situation are already appearing in the substantial increase in the number of floating voters. It now seems that one-third of the electorate is undecided about its party commitment until very late in an electoral campaign, and that voters are turning to the growing minority parties in increasing numbers, often perhaps in protest against the performance of the major ones.

The fact that there is no Christian political tradition in Britain is not widely seen as a problem, but in view of the situation in most of Europe it is surprising that the pattern has excluded a Christian party. In Germany, France, Holland, Italy, Belgium, Switzerland and Austria there have been strong Christian parties, combined often with strong trade union movements and a distinctive social philosophy. They have often obtained a majority and been significant in terms of the political development of the nation. The differences in these parties are considerable and worth careful study. Some are rooted in Roman Catholic and others in Protestant Christianity. Some have developed quite radical policies of political reform while others have been more conservative.[1] However. at present our concern is merely the contrast with the British pattern. Why has Britain not developed a Christian political party?

[1] See M. P. Fogarty, *Christian Democracy in Western Europe 1820–1953* (Routledge and Kegan Paul, 1957) for a very good exposition of this tradition.

Chapter 12

A Christian view of the state

In this chapter we shall begin by considering the form and limitations of Christian political involvement up to the present day. We shall then look at some of the basic principles by means of which the Christian understands the position of the state in society. We cannot, unfortunately, move on to consider specific Christian policies, because these are beyond the scope of the book, but it will be evident that much material in other chapters will be relevant to Christian policy formation.

Christian involvement in politics

We have already noted that Britain does not have a Christian political party as do most other countries in Europe. It is also evident that Christians have been divided about exactly what implications, if any, their faith has for political life. Let us therefore consider why this is so.

A crucial starting point is the mediaeval Roman Catholic perspective of nature and grace. This involved a dualism between an area of life governed by Christian faith and God's grace on the one hand, and on the other an area which was subject to what was 'natural' and could be discovered solely by human reason. It grew from the time of Thomas Aquinas (1225–1274) and reached its peak in the 16th century with the impact of Platonism on Roman Catholic thinking.[1]

[1] For a fuller analysis of the nature/grace framework see F. A. Schaeffer, *Escape From Reason* (IVP, 1968), chapter 1, and E. L. Hebden Taylor, *The Christian Philosophy of Law, Politics and the State* (Craig Press, 1966), chapter 4.

This dualist view affected politics. It was strongest in the period when the Roman Catholic church was seeing the steady erosion of its sphere of influence from almost total control of society to the situation where secular influence was dominant. As a rationalization of this process of 'secularization' Catholic thinking came to identify the Church with what was 'sacred' or 'religious' in society, while on the other hand politics, economic life, *etc.*, were seen as secular, natural and of no significance in matters of faith. The pattern that resulted from this perspective, especially where absolute monarchs asserted their position, tended to be a kind of contractual division of influence where the church held sway over what was 'sacred' or 'spiritual', and the state over 'secular' or political affairs.

This view dominated Roman Catholic thinking about politics and led to two perspectives. The first was that politics was in some way unholy or degrading, and therefore something from which Christians should withdraw. The second was to see involvement in politics as necessary to protect the interests of the Catholic Church. This view has been behind the formation of most of the clerical parties of Europe; for example, the Centre Party in Germany was formed to defend Roman Catholic institutions under attack by Bismarck in the Kulturkampf. Thus involvement in politics became ecclesiastical, rather than the result of Christian *political* principles. However, this perspective was not only Catholic. Luther's response to the tremendous changes in Germany was to see politics in ecclesiastical terms and to work for the establishment of the Lutheran Church in the various German states. In reaction, the Anabaptists, apart from those involved in the peasants revolt at Munster in 1534–35, chose the path of withdrawal from politics; they often refused to accept any civic office, to go to law, or to engage in any political activity. Thus the attitudes of ecclesiastical politics and political withdrawal were carried through into Protestantism.

In Britain this dualist attitude has taken a unique form which it is worth trying to sketch. The tale begins with the Act of Supremacy in 1534, whereby Henry VIII became the Protector and only supreme Head of the Church and Clergy of England, as well as being Head of the State. This alliance between church and state, very similar to the Lutheran perspective, was essentially an *institutional* alliance. It created the situation where, apart from a brief period in the middle of the 17th century, the established church supported the political establishment and *vice versa*. Consequently the dominant church in England has automatically had a conservative slant in its political thinking as it necessarily supported the established viewpoint, and it also saw politics in ecclesiastical terms. The quip about the Church of England being the Tory Party at prayer does have some historical evidence behind it. The attempt to defend the Anglican Church politically often led to partiality against other denominations, and by the beginning of the 19th century this had created a good deal of resentment. At the same time there was a dearth of Christian political thinking and discussion in the church, since that was left to the political establishment. The Nonconformists, who were debarred from political office from 1660 right through to the beginning of the 19th century, tended on the other hand to be strongly influenced by Anabaptist teaching, and thus completely forgot the habits of political involvement.

There were some other factors which encouraged and cemented this pattern of non-involvement. The first was that during the period of the Commonwealth, although there were many changes that were for the good, there were also some serious failures in terms of justice, peace and toleration, and withdrawal was the natural reaction to these failures. Secondly, evangelical Christians rightly reacted against the political movements which arose during the French Revolution, which offered some form of political salvation, but sadly they reacted by withdrawal.[1] Thirdly, the nature/grace dichotomy often appealed to the Bible for interpretations which were other-worldly and which therefore excluded political action. Thus, for example, Christ's words, 'My kingship is not of this world' (Jn. 18:36), are interpreted as a justification for non-involvement in politics rather than (as seems to be the meaning from the context) as a statement that Christ's kingdom is not based on human power and support, with the added idea that Christ's mission was not a political one. In course of time, then, reaction against any kind of involvement in politics became quite common.

[1] By contrast, in the Netherlands, Groen van Prinsterer and Abraham Kuyper formed the Anti-revolutionary Party.

With the Methodist and evangelical revivals, however, a new kind of interest in politics sprang up. One of its characteristics was a dependence on conscience or moral concern. When Christians saw an obvious social evil they acted to eradicate it, forming pressure groups to achieve that specific end. There was a number of outstanding individuals in the 19th century like Wilberforce, Shaftesbury and Gladstone who stood out as Christians in politics, but they never formed a tradition of Christian politics. For a while the Christian Socialists from a more liberal theological position tried to develop a Christian political consciousness with the series 'Politics for the People', but they fought shy of any party organization and their influence faded. Gradually, as the parties became more organized towards the end of the century, the effectiveness of individual Christian political witness became less noticeable. One interesting development was the bias shown by denominations towards certain parties. Anglicans had natural links with the Conservatives, Nonconformists with the Liberals and, later, Methodists with the Labour Party. Certainly, there seemed to be a merging of any distinct Christian political stance into the normal party loyalties and ideologies, to the extent that for many decades there has been no strong evidence of Christian political thought and practice. Some see it as unspiritual or secular, and therefore to be avoided; some as detracting from the church's primary task of evangelism. Others have a limited interest in what are considered to be moral matters or church related issues, but have no concern outside these areas. Another group expresses concern and emphasizes social justice, but in terms of whatever secular ideology is suitable. Others are involved in politics as Christian individuals within the existing party groups, which they hope to influence in a Christian direction. It has not yet become a matter of conviction among Christians that an explicit Christian political faith and biblically rooted principles are desperately needed in our political culture.

In the rest of this chapter we shall draw together some of the basic Christian principles which define and structure the state as a first step in articulating a Christian political position. It is only a part of the full development of Christian politics which can and will occur within the context of a Christian political party, but it will be evident to the reader that the implications of what is sketched here are very very wide.

A biblical perspective of the state

When we look in the Bible for an understanding of the principles on which the state is structured we do not see a natural, created, institution like marriage, the family, or work, which is integrally bound up with man's created nature and his relationship with the environment. Rather we see a different kind of institution, which was gradually established and took different forms under God's guidance in response to a definite social weakness and need. Let us briefly look at the development of this institution as the Bible presents it, so that we have a background from which to look in more detail at some of the structural principles.

Long before the state, or any kind of political form, appeared we see issues of *justice* continually occurring, for example in Cain's dealings with Abel (Genesis 4), in Jacob's with his sons (Genesis 27), Jacob's with Laban (Genesis 30 and 31), in Joseph's treatment by his brothers (Genesis 37), Judah's relations with Tamar (Genesis 38), Joseph's with Potiphar's wife (Genesis 39), and eventually the important issue of justice in how the Egyptians treated the Israelites (Exodus 1–5). In those situations the true dealings of a man with his fellows in various relationships were perverted, and hurt was caused. It is clear in all of these cases that, with sin dominant in the heart of man since the Fall, these issues of injustice were a permanent part of social life. When the children of Israel left Egypt and formed a new national community, injustices continued to occur. In response to this Moses begins, under the authority of God, to administer justice to the nation when a person has been wronged and his father-in-law, Jethro, advised him how this could be done more efficiently by a process of delegation (Exodus 18). Shortly after this, at Sinai, the Israelites were given in the Ten Commandments and other laws a definitive statement of what should be the true dealings of a man with his God and fellow men, and they were also given detailed teaching about this institution of justice: procedures in trials and details of punishment. The teaching on justice, and the development of a political institution continued, despite the rather anarchic period of the Judges, through to the times of the Kings, and it is the theme of much of the teaching of the prophets up to, during, and after the exile. It is this background which is assumed in the New Testament and lies behind much of Christ's teaching as he interacts with the various rulers like Caesar, Herod and Pilate, and political groups like the Sadducees and the Zealots. Later, even though the apostles and early Christians are on the fringe of political life simply because of their small numbers, this teaching is upheld and continued.

Even from this short survey it is obvious that politics is presented as an integral part of human life which cannot be ignored or pushed aside, and that the central truths of the Christian faith have political implications. At the same time, and this is very important for our subsequent analysis, it is clear that the Bible does not present us with a direct political blueprint, but rather with a deep understanding of the meaning of politics and of the principles which should be embodied in the state. We now turn to examine some of the principles shaping the way politics should be seen.

God's sovereignty The truth that God is sovereign over political life is basic. This truth is fundamental to an understanding of politics and the state and the Bible shows it to be true in two ways. When it is accepted, the fruits of this understanding are shown; when men deny it and assert themselves as sovereign, God vindicates himself in the confusion and perversion of politics that results. We shall begin by looking at this latter case. Often the state or the ruler has been worshipped in some form or another. Instead of politics being seen *within* a Christian religious perspective, it has been made a religion in itself. The Bible gives many examples of this fundamental perversion, and we shall now consider some of them.

Perhaps the first example is Pharaoh, who was in effect the deified ruler of the Egyptians, and who set his face against God and against just treatment of the Israelites; in the early chapters of Exodus we read of his defeat. Not surprisingly the great victory song of Moses and the Israelites ends with the words 'The Lord will reign for ever and ever' (Ex. 15:18). Another example involving the ruler of an empire was Nebuchadnezzar, who made himself an object of worship (Daniel 3). He was led by God to acknowledge that 'the Most High rules the kingdom of men, and gives it to whom he will' (Dan. 4:32). Many times, when the kings of Israel began to form ideas of their own sovereignty and to assert their own will, we find that they are warned and punished; Saul and Ahab are obvious examples. An example from the New Testament is that of Herod. When he was given adulation and praise by the people and took to himself the flattery of their words, 'The voice of a god and not of man!', we read that 'he was eaten by worms and died', because he did not give God the glory. These examples involve the downfall of rulers who were arrogant and claimed worship and ultimate sovereignty, and the lesson is clear. However, there is a far wider principle involved in this teaching which we must try to formulate.

It is that the kingdom of God cuts at the roots of all human kingdoms which claim absolute sovereignty and therefore try to provide a religious framework for society. This is the meaning of the great prophecy in Daniel 2. The historic statement is that, with Christ's coming, there will be a radically new situation.

'And in the days of those kings the God of heaven will set up a kingdom which shall never be destroyed, nor shall its sovereignty be left to another people. It shall break in pieces all these kingdoms and bring them to an end and it shall stand forever'

(Dn. 2:44).

This prophecy was fulfilled with the fall of great Babylonian, Persian and Greek Empires, and finally after the coming of Christ with the fall of the Roman Empire. The rule of Christ, the Prince of Peace, meant a radically new principle of politics. It was no longer the ultimate framework, as in the Roman Empire, and the ruler was no longer completely sovereign and an object of worship, as with the later Roman Emperors, but he was subject to a higher authority and politics was part of a greater framework; it was subject to the rule and law of God. This issue was and is fundamental. Are the state and politics the ultimate framework for society, as the Babylonians, Greeks and Romans thought, or is the state to be seen *within* a perspective where God is sovereign and the state is *subject* to various principles? This is the main issue of European politics over the last three thousand years and, as

Hitler and Stalin remind us, the issue is not dead. Thus, before we go on to look at a positive understanding of this principle, let us spend some time looking at this perspective of a *religion of politics* in its historical development.

Apart from the ancient civilizations which we have already mentioned, this pattern had a very strong hold in the Far East, where society tended to be dominated by emperor worship and a vast system of state bureaucracy. Confucianism was not so much a transcendental religion as an ethical system which operated within the political framework. It has been noted by many commentators that a similar form of religion of politics has existed in modern China with the near worship of Mao Tse Tung and the high level of centralized party control. This would need to be examined in detail, but there seems to be a strong continuity in perspective.

However, if we look nearer home, the civilizations which have had a more immediate effect on our political culture are those of the Greeks and Romans. Professor Ernest Barker writes of Greek society:

> 'Religion was an aspect of the political life of a political society: it was no other life and it entailed no other society. The sphere of the Greek city was not limited by existence of an association claiming to be its equal or superior.'[1]

The structure of the Greek *polis* (hence our 'politics') was basically political: this was even reflected in the state organization of religious worship. There was a state organized and paid priesthood which supervised the worship. This focused on the main temple, called the Acropolis, where the god or goddess of the state was worshipped. The most famous example of course, is the worship of Athena on the acropolis at Athens, but the pattern was repeated throughout Greece. In some communities this political orientation took a particularly militaristic form, as at Sparta. The variations have been widely discussed. However, our point at present concerns the common element that within this culture man was seen primarily as a political animal and society was seen as a political organization. Plato's *Republic* is very much

[1] E. Barker, *Greek Political Theory* (Methuen University Paperbacks, 1964), p. 9.

a product of such a political culture. This perspective has been one of the tap roots of later European political philosophy and practice.

As we have already suggested a similar perspective grew up also in the later Roman Empire. However, with the collapse of that great structure there was a gradual and imperceptible movement away from a religion of politics, as Christian thinking slowly penetrated political life. We cannot now look at all the developments of this long era but, following our theme, we must pass on to our recent history, where it is possible to see again in our post-Christian culture the emergence of this belief that politics is the ultimate framework. Nor is just a question of belief. Nazi and Communist systems have both utterly repudiated Christianity and have also established ideologies in which man is seen in predominantly political terms and where the state is the total framework for society. Against this it is not difficult to see that, in the countries which have a Protestant (mainly Calvinist) background like Switzerland, Holland, Britain, and North America, the state tends not to assume this predominant role and these countries have been notable for the absence of totalitarian or autocratic governments. This pattern is perhaps now one of political habit, as these countries have become less Christian, but the importance of the principles is no less: that the state is subordinate to God and his laws.

Thus far we have been concerned with the vindication of this truth when it has been denied. However, it has positive implications. First of all it removes the idea of sovereignty from the institution of the state or the ruler. The state is not the ultimate authority, but is responsible before God to exercise certain limited functions. It is an institution which serves God and the populace, not a dominating force. Secondly, it is necessarily subject to laws which have their origin with God, and is not an institution which creates laws on its own authority. Law is rooted in morality, which is rooted in religion, and is not the arbitrary creation of the state. Thirdly, the principle eliminates all totalitarian views of government. The state has no right to shape and direct people's lives; they live before God and not before the state, and their responsibility to the latter is defined and limited to matters of justice. Lastly, it involves acknowledging that all power and authority derives from God and is given by God, and that the present pattern of rule can be seen critically in the light of more ultimate principles. These points will be elaborated later.

The state is instituted because of sin   We have already seen how sin and injustice required the creation of the office of judge and how this developed in the nation of Israel into an institution which we would recognize as a state. This foundation for the state is very important. In Judges we read of the anarchy and violence that existed when everybody did what was right in his own eyes and sought revenge rather than being subject to someone in the office of judge. The power of sin to disrupt and hurt, to cause strife, violence and divisions, and to break down economic, marriage and family relationships is incalculable. More than this, there is a kind of causal chain of evil; the desire to retaliate is very strong in the human heart, and unless it is checked evil and injustice are necessarily perpetuated. It is also true that, in a sinful society, the laws and standards of true dealing in human relationships are upheld institutionally, they are forgotten and disregarded, and the whole society becomes disordered and unprincipled. It is for those reasons that the state, the institution of justice, is established under the authority of God, as we see from the time of Moses onwards. This theme is reiterated in the New Testament as well. For example, Peter writes about rulers being sent by God 'to punish those who do wrong and to praise those who do right' (1 Pet. 2:14). This is always the context of the state's activities.

This principle is crucial for a Christian understanding of the state, and contains a number of implications. Firstly, it allows no utopian view of politics, whether anarchist or communist, which preaches that the state may or will wither away and leave people to live in freedom. The state will continually witness to the sin and injustice that is part of man's nature, and it cannot be dismissed. Secondly, it allows no utopian view of the state which would claim that the state can eradicate or cure sin and injustice. Politics and state action is no solution for social evils and offers no hope of salvation. The state has the practical, specific task of maintaining the law and upholding public justice; this is its area of competence and responsibility. To go further and to seek to direct and control human action and motives is to go too far into totalitarian control. The Christian sees no ultimate solution for sin except in man's relationship to his creator.

This principle also points to a further fundamental tension that exists within the body politic: that *both the ruler and the ruled are sinful men*. This means two things. Firstly, we can have no intrinsic faith in rulers. We see this truth exemplified when the Israelites ask for a king to govern them.(1 Samuel 8).They hope much from a king and put their faith in him, but Samuel in the name of the Lord warns them that they will find that their ruler oppresses them and extorts from them. Yet, contrary to this insight, a nation often puts all its faith in a ruler and believes that he can do no wrong. The most obvious modern European example is that of Hitler, but there are other charismatic figures who have been put in such a position, such as Lenin, Mussolini, Mao, Nkrumah, Nasser, and perhaps even Amin. One notes how the American President almost has to be an infallible, charismatic figure.

Over against this view of the ruler, a mature, Christian, political perspective recognizes the weakness of the ruler and provides institutional solutions which prevent this weakness from becoming disastrous. Just as Nathan, the prophet, is able to point his finger at King David, when he has abused his position (2 Samuel 12), so in our polity the opposition, the press and the electorate need to be able to point the finger. Critical opposition is an absolute necessity in a mature political system.

A second and no less important point is that *neither can the people be the object of faith in the political system*. They too are sinful, weak and fallible. This view stands over against a very strong political tradition which dates back at least to the French Revolution. It has its roots in the assertion by Rousseau and others that man is good. If this is true, the main problem of politics is merely that the rulers are cut off from the people, who are the infallible final authority in all matters. The answer is therefore direct participation of the people in politics; the will of the people assures that the right thing is done. Thus it was that Robespierre dreamed of an assembly hall with a public gallery large enough to contain twelve thousand spectators. This theme, that the people can do no wrong, has been a tremendously strong motive in politics since the French Revolution. Marxism has transmuted it into the basic assumption that the workers can do no wrong. Mass politics, populism, propaganda and politics have all toyed with this idea. The truth is just the opposite. The people can and have done wrong. They have oppressed minorities, chosen leaders who are evil, and perverted justice. With devastating accuracy the Old Testament shows how fallible the will of the people is in situation after situation. This lesson comes home with shattering force when we read in the New Testament of what happened to Christ:

'And the crowd came up and began to ask Pilate to do as he was wont to do for them. And he answered them, "Do you want me to release for you the King of the Jews?" For he perceived that it was out of envy that the chief priests had delivered him up. But the chief priests stirred up the crowd to have him release for them Barabbas instead. And Pilate again said to them, "Then what shall I do with the man whom you call King of the Jews?" And they cried out again, "Crucify him." And Pilate said to them, "Why, what evil has he done?" But they shouted all the more, "Crucify him." So Pilate, *wishing to satisfy the crowd*, released for them Barabbas; and having scourged Jesus, he delivered him to be crucified'

(Mk. 15: 8–15, italics added).

The people did this to Jesus. They too cannot be the object of political faith.

Thus the Christian rejects both these viewpoints. Each of them has the same characteristic—that of putting faith in man; both are humanist. The conclusion that seems inescapable is that neither ruler nor people can be the repository of political faith; both are weak, sinful and unstable. The Christian believes that faith is not to be rooted in man, but in God, and that in politics, and in every other area of life, sin needs to be faced realistically, repented of, and rooted out *before God*.

Apart from these basic conclusions there are one or two other points which grow out of this principle which are worth mentioning. Firstly we can deduce that the state is continually a *responsive* institution. It is in a situation where new injustices appear in different forms (racial, class, technological, educational, in industrial relations, *etc.*), evils wax and wane, and the state's relationship with them is necessarily dynamic. Secondly, it follows that a basic characteristic of state legislation is its involvement in situations where evil and injustice have been committed. The purpose of legislation is to affirm and uphold justice *relative to the specific situation*. This means that state law has a different character and purpose from what we could call the law of God. We shall take up this point later.

The state and justice   The guiding principle of the state is that of justice. We have mentioned several times already the predominance of the principle of justice in the state, and have seen how it developed as an institution which legitimately administered justice from the time of Moses onwards. It is worth referring by comparison to the illegitimate act of justice by Moses in Exodus 2:11–15. We see this emphasis on justice in the charge given to the judges who were appointed in 2 Chronicles 19:6, 7:

> 'Consider what you do, for you judge not for man but for the Lord; he is with you in giving judgment. Now then, let the fear of the Lord be upon you; take heed what you do, for there is no perversion of justice with the Lord our God, or partiality, or taking bribes.'

This theme continues throughout the Old Testament. Constantly the prophets cry at the rulers who have been seduced away from justice.

It is worth looking for a while at what the Bible teaches about justice. Justice is not only political; it is far wider than that; it involves God's evaluation of all our actions, motives and thoughts and our facing what we deserve for what we have done. It is God's radical judgment of our lives. God is no respecter of persons; he is not partial, and as our Creator he relativizes all the advantages and disadvantages that we put so much weight on, and sees us as we are. From Adam onwards we read of God's judgment, or just evaluation, of men, and nobody except Christ comes out of that analysis uncondemned. Political justice is derived from this total framework of justice in which we are all accountable to God. It is judgment by the state of public actions of injustice. At its best it involves, as we have seen, fear of God, impartiality and no perversion of justice. It means a clear and consistent statement of which public actions are wrong and which are right. This is an awesome task, and when Solomon faced it it led him to pray: 'Give thy servant therefore an understanding mind to govern thy people, that I may discern between good and evil; for who is able to govern this thy great people?' (1 Ki. 3:9).

This derivative view of justice is very different from the view that tends to be current today. Justice is not that which judges all men; rather it is something which men create by their own reason, which they use, and which they identify with their own opinions. More especially it is what is upheld by social consensus. Almost inevitably the situation arises where the dominant class shapes justice to its own interests. The landowners hanged people for stealing sheep and legislated for enclosure; the Revolutionaries hanged people for being aristocrats; the *bourgeoisie* prohibited the workers from combining into trades unions; and white people discriminate against blacks. There are innumerable regimes and political systems which stand convicted under this principle. It is very difficult for man-centred justice to be impartial.

Further, this principle does not *identify* the ruler or the state with justice. The ruler is subject to God and his justice; 'he is', as Paul says, 'God's servant' (Rom. 13:4). The State can be dangerously unjust, and especially when it sees what it decrees as being *ipso facto* just. This kind of autocracy has been present in the statist tradition in Germany and also in the concept of the divine right of kings in the absolute monarchies of the 17th and 18th centuries. It was one of the great constitutional victories of our history that the Puritans fought this view, and to a large extent prevailed over it.

Finally, a Christian perspective stands over against natural justice or justice based on reason. Man in his sin is not capable on his own initiative of discerning what is just and what is unjust. His own partiality is bound in the end to lead him astray and what seems to be naturally just will be false. True justice is only to be seen in relation to God and his judgment.

The state and coercion   The state is given sole authority to use the power of the sword subject to the norms of justice. This authority is something that has been accepted from the time of the giving of the Mosaic law onwards. Punishment and the use of force is to be the prerogative of the state. Thus murder is forbidden, but we read, 'if a man willfully attacks another to kill him treacherously, you shall take him from my altar, that he may die' (Ex. 21:14). Killing in execution of justice by the state is legitimate. Thus David, although continually wronged, does not lift the sword against Saul, and Christ, although unjustly arrested, tells Peter to put away his sword. Paul states the principle in the following terms: 'But if you do wrong, be afraid, for he (the ruler) does not bear the sword in vain; he is the servant of God to execute his wrath on the wrongdoer' (Rom. 13:4). Many centuries later Max Weber made the principle his definition of the state:

> 'A compulsory political association with continuous organization will be called a "state" if and in so far as its administrative staff upholds a claim to the monopoly of the legitimate use of physical force in the enforcement of its order.'[1]

Christians have often focused on the apparent weakness of this political doctrine, namely, that it forbids trying to overthrow an unjust regime, and have become entangled in interminable arguments. They miss the main point, for the purpose of this doctrine is to restrict the use of physical force and violence to the institutional framework where it is subject to the norms of justice. The state can only *legitimately* use the sword subject to justice; it does not have a 'right' to use physical force. Legitimate physical force against an attacker, to restrain violence and to punish, is different from the arbitrary use of force. Christians are called therefore to respect and support the legitimate use of force by the state, and not to use violence outside the authority and framework of the state where it is used subject to justice. Even if the principle is not respected, Christians are still to uphold it. If they find it necessary to disobey the state or the laws because they conflict with the higher claims of what they believe God requires of them, they still submit to the state powers and face the consequences of their action. Suffering and punishment are a witness which can lead to the reform of injustice without

[1] M. Weber, *The Theory of Social and Economic Organization* (Free Press, 1964), p. 154.

disrespect to the God-given authority of the state. Revolution cannot but enthrone naked force in the place of force subject to justice. This pattern means neither compromising with a regime, nor compromising Christian political principles in opposing a regime. This issue is of current concern in Northern Ireland. If the Christians were prepared to use force, even in response to the illegitimate violence of the IRA, they could not rightly claim to be Protestant or Christian in their actions.

This principle strikes against another view of politics: that power is the basis of politics and is what politics are all about. This view which is normally traced back to Machiavelli and the *condottiere* of the Renaissance, reappeared in Italy with the Fascists. It also grew up out of Social Darwinist ideas about the survival of the fittest into Nazi political philosophy. However, although these are the most extreme forms, there is scarcely any political system in which power, control over other people, threats, *etc.*, do not operate. The power may be economic, military, social or charismatic, but inevitably it sets up a rival system of relationships to the legitimate authority of government, which obscures and complicates political processes. It leads to situations where informal power relationships stand alongside the legitimate structures and rival them, so that manipulation, power struggles, coups, the elimination of rivals, *etc.*, replace legitimate procedures. It also inevitably undermined justice with the counter principle that might is right. The Christian stands firmly against this principle and seeks to eradicate it from all parts of the political structure. Especially he seeks to make sure that the military remains a servant of the state rather than in any way becoming its guiding force.

The state and law In one of the great passages of the Mosaic law we read of the procedure when Israel comes to have a king as ruler. 'And when he sits on the throne of his kingdom, he shall write for himself in a book a copy of this law, from that which is in charge of the Levitical priests; and it shall be with him, and he shall read in it all the days of his life, that he may learn to fear the Lord his God, by keeping all the words of this law and these statutes, and doing them; that his heart may not be lifted up above his brethren, and that he may not turn aside from the commandment, either to the right hand or to the left; so that he may continue long in his kingdom, he and his children, in Israel' (Dt. 17:18–20). The ruler is subject to the rule of law; he has no higher status than the rest of his fellows except that he has the task of administering the law, and in this task he is to submit himself to the law of God. This principle is taught time and time again throughout the Old Testament, perhaps most beautifully in Psalm 119 when we see the writer's love and concern for the law of the Lord. It is the law that defines what is just; it defines the true dealings of man with his fellows, and even the ruler is subject to it.

We have already suggested that political legislation is different from the law of God. It is necessarily involved in the evils and injustices of a given situation. It is not so much concerned with motives and thoughts as with public actions. Nevertheless, this point, which requires a great deal of careful analysis, does not detract from the more fundamental one that, for the Christian, political legislation is dependent upon and responsive to the law of God. This is its only true source. Political legislation is not a separate, self-subsistent set of rules, but is bound up in the norms for living that are given in the Word of God. This is the standard under which political legislation is to be formulated.

It is arguable that in countries where Puritanism was strong, this doctrine of the rule of law over the state has been accepted and built into the structure of the state. One thinks of Switzerland, Holland, Britain and the United States as the prime examples. A *constitutional* form of government is the conventional way in which this principle is expressed. There was certainly a marked change from the autocracy of the Stuarts in the style of the monarchy after 1640 and again after 1688, and one suspects that the change can be partly represented by the clash of ideologies in this reported interchange between the puritan Lord Chief Justice, Sir Edward Coke, and James I.

"'True it is, please your Majesty, that God has endowed your Majesty with excellent science as well as great gifts of nature: but your Majesty will allow me to say, with all reverence, that you are not learned in the laws of this your realm of England ... which is an art which requires long study and experience before a man can attain to cognisance of it. The law is the golden met-wand and measure to try the causes of your

Majesty's subjects, and it is by that law that your Majesty is protected in safety and peace." King James in a great rage said, "Then am I to be under the law which is a treason to affirm."

The Chief Justice replied, "Thus wrote Bracton, 'The King is under no man save under God and the law.'"[1] This was part of the process of excluding arbitrary rule from British Government, a task which, of course, is not yet completed.

There is much more that we could consider under this principle, but we shall leave it until we come to look at more specific issues of legislation. Here we are more concerned with the status of law with respect to the state than with the detailed content of legislation.

Political office   When Moses found himself the political leader of the Israelites, he was not left with an unstructured job, but his duty was laid down in norms and statutes which he had to obey. His position was an office; it was structured, and as we have seen (Dt. 17:20) it was not one which gave him higher status than his fellows, or any intrinsic merit; rather it was a position which involved responsibility before God. It was the norms and standards of the office that were definitive, not the incumbent, who was a sinner like everyone else. The responsibility of the office meant that he was serving God in this role; in no way was the office to be used in a self-serving way. Indeed, this was expressly forbidden (see Dt. 17:14–17 and the warning of 1 Sam. 8:10–18). The ruler was to administer justice, uphold the law, remain impartial and in every way to submit to the norms of his office. At this time in the early history of the Israelites the offices were relatively simple. Indeed, Moses' political office was not differentiated from the other positions he held. Later things became much more complex, and to-day we have a vast number of interrelated offices in our political structure, each with its own specific authority and responsibility.

Yet the principle and the warning apply even more forcibly in this complex situation. Men must hold office with the right motives—of service and of fulfilling the norms of office rather

---

[1] Quoted in Shaftesbury Project Crime, Law and Punishment Study Paper *Sir Edward Coke* by Philip Turl.

than of self-seeking and wanting to maintain their position and privileges. At least half of the nations of the world have faced obvious problems of corruption of office over the last few years. It would be vain to deny that one of the main motives in British politics, perhaps even the main motive, is a desire to achieve office, or to stay in office; the position is seen as an end in itself, rather than as a means of service. This view of office leads, perhaps more quickly than anything else, to the degeneration of the political system.

Impartiality We have already touched on this principle in connection with justice, but there is much more that needs to be said about it. Impartiality is continually commanded in the Old Testament. Judgment should not favour either a majority group or the rich (Ex. 23:2, 3). Impartiality is the key to political stability. 'If a king judges the poor with equity his throne will be established for ever' (Pr. 29:14). Quite clearly the ruler is not to be identified with, or favour, any particular group or sector. He is to judge principially. Time and time again the prophets are forced to declaim against this evil. 'Their partiality witnesses against them' (Is. 3:9). It is part of the destruction of the nation.

The process of development towards universal suffrage in Britain has often been explained in terms of the participation of the people in the government of the country; in other words, in terms of a crude idea of democracy stemming from the French Revolutionary idea of faith in the people. Not only is the idea an illusory one (the people just do not participate, and cannot in any complex society), but it also seems to obscure what was in fact a more important motive in the process of enfranchisement, namely, that of achieving impartiality. It is clear that since the beginning of the 18th century, first the landowners and then the capitalist classes tended to be partial to their own situation and interests. This was the issue behind the immediate one of suffrage; it was a very good way of ensuring that a privileged section of the community did not govern the country partially. However, universal suffrage was not an ultimate solution to the problem, for it now faces us in a new form, namely that of *interest politics*.

If, and this is a major premise, people see politics primarily as a process of securing their own interests (that is, they have an egocentric perspective on politics), then politics tends to become a process in which different interest groups are vying for the privilege of office. In this situation the political parties tend to reflect these interest groups and inevitably government is caught in all kinds of partiality. It is probably true that the Conservative and Labour parties are more known for the interest groups which they represent than for the principles they stand for. In this framework, office holders represent various interest groups and the principle of impartiality becomes severely compromised.

Redistribution of resources   It was a fundamental tenet of the Mosaic law that as people naturally became poor through various processes, some accidental and some involving exploitation, they were to be helped. They were not only to be helped through various neighbourly activities, but also through state activity. In the Mosaic law this was far more radical than anything we would envisage now. It was basically a redistribution of *wealth*, especially land, whereas we tend to limit redistribution to income and leave wealth relatively untouched. (*cf.* Leviticus 25 and Deuteronomy 15). This was a matter of law and of state control, and it seems inevitable that Christians who take the biblical teaching about the poor seriously must be committed to a fairly radical view of wealth redistribution through legislation and the state. This will be examined more fully in chapters 13 and 14.

Limitations on the activities of the state   The biblical perspective, as we have seen is not a 'religion of politics'; politics is not the total framework for society but a perspective in which the state, alongside other institutions, has a specific function which it alone can perform, namely that of maintaining justice and equity. This function necessarily involves the state in these other institutions as upholders of justice, but this does not mean that the state is to take them over; rather it should respect their integrity. Thus the family, marriage, education, economic institutions, church, *etc.*, are all institutions which have their own integrity before God, as we have seen, and they are not part of the state mechanism. We can see a practical example of the principle in Peter's First Letter where, in advising the Christians on social issues, he says, 'Be subject for the Lord's sake to every human institution' (1 Pet. 2:13). He then goes on to mention government (noting that it should not induce a spirit of political slavery), economic institutions, marriage and church life. Government is *part* of God's normative order for society, not the whole.

There are various issues which we could discuss in this context, such as the rule of the State in education, but one which highlights what we are saying is that of nationalization. This policy was undertaken to prevent injustices which arose out of the monopoly position of those great concerns, and it was an understandable response. Nevertheless, one issue which has now arisen and which poses something of a dilemma is that the state finds itself acting both as employer and as arbiter or judge in industrial disputes; in other words, by going outside its specific function the state finds itself compromised in its essential role, since it becomes judge in its own cause. Governments came up against this problem several times in the early 1970s without it being clearly articulated. However, what for us is a relatively minor problem can become more acute; for example, in Russia trades unions are more or less ideologically impossible. It is not easy to see what the scope of politics should be in specific areas, yet our perspective makes us aware of the problem, and as with the previous issue of the scope of economics, certain answers seem more Christian than others.

Religious toleration In the past this has caused problems as a result of a naive reading of the Old Testament. The Israelites were a chosen nation which grew out of God's promise to Abraham. Part of this covenant relationship was that they were to be religiously pure. In this they were unique and thus were not a normative standard for other nations. In the New Testament, the chosen nation became the chosen people from all nations and races, and no hint of the Old Testament situation remains in the multi-faith context in which the early church emerged. The attitude was rather that of emphasizing the just treatment of all, irrespective of religion (see Acts, *passim*). Needless to say, in the Roman Empire neither the Jews nor the Christians were treated in this way.

What framed the approach to the issue of toleration for a long while was the claim of the Roman Catholic church to embrace all types of society. This perspective is religiously intolerant. For

310

example, one of the *Syllabus of Errors* of 1864 was that 'it is no longer necessary that the Catholic religion be held as the only religion of the State, to the exclusion of all other modes of worship.'[1] It was carried over to Protestant churches in the idea of the established church, and it was a long while before the truly different functions of church and state were sorted out. A measure of the confusion can be seen in the situation in Britain at the end of the 18th century. The Nonconformists were campaigning for the repeal of the Test and Corporation Acts by which the Anglicans had intolerantly excluded them from political office, but the Nonconformists still wanted to exclude the Roman Catholics (who were presumably themselves intolerant, given the chance), so the situation did not reflect much credit on any of the three parties. The truth surely is that the state should never interpose in a man's relationship with God. In that central relationship man is to be free to choose his own direction. Further it is the function of the state to be impartial among various religious groups in every way. This is the Christian perspective on this issue, and one which we should want to see upheld. Any other view overstates the function of the state.

Peacemaking In 1 Kings 3:16-28 we read how two harlots came to Solomon with a quarrel and how he judged wisely between them. This situation is of the essence of politics; most political issues are, at least in part, a quarrel between people or groups or institutions. Often there is no ground between the two sides. Often the issue has been left unresolved for too long and the problems have festered and require urgent attention. The state has as part of its task the function of bringing these opposed and antagonistic groups together under the rule of law and justice. This is no easy task, but if justice is established between them, peace can be restored on a lasting and sound basis. Paul asks that prayers be made for rulers 'that we may lead a quiet and peaceable life' (1 Tim. 2:2). This is a major commitment.

However, peace is an easy word. The prophets warn us about those who use the word but deny the reality of peace. What is

[1] H. Bettenson, *Documents of the Christian Church* (Oxford Univ. Press, 1943), p. 381.

involved is a reinstatement of what we have called the true dealings of a man with his fellows, and the prime way in which this is achieved, as judged by the life and teaching of the Prince of Peace, is by returning good for evil. At the same time it is clear that there is also a place in the process of peacemaking for law and justice. When these are upheld rather than power, self-interest, self-righteousness, violence and retaliation, there is some hope of peace. There are many areas where this needs to be worked through. One thinks of industrial, racial and international unrest, where all too often the pattern is to talk of peace, and use threats. Can this be changed? The answer involves deep religious issues, in that peace seems only to occur when it is in the self-interest of the warring parties and not on principle, but from a Christian viewpoint this must be a serious, principal aim of the state. Peace is established on God's terms, not man's.

The principles that we have outlined show that Christians are committed by their faith and the teaching of the Bible to a specific view of the state. It will be clear by now that this view is not based on transplanting texts, or even political systems or practices from the Bible to our own situation, but rather on a full religious perspective. These principles still have an important place in our British constitutional structures, seen in terms of precedent, convention or political habit. However, the present practice may be based on a serious misunderstanding, which makes the continuance of these principles more precarious than it might seem.

The normal rationale for Western liberties, such as they are, is in terms of the word *democracy*, which is normally identified with the principles of the participation of all adult citizens in the process of representative government. Yet our analysis suggests that this might be a secular rationalization of a number of principles which are far more complex and are not directly associated with the French Revolutionary idea of participation of the populace in government. Democracy involves the principles of the rule of law, the absence of sovereign and autocratic government, the recognition of checks on the sinfulness of government and governed, the doctrine of office as service of God and man, the principles of impartiality, toleration, and peace, the rise of state coercion only within a framework of justice, and so on. When democracy is so poorly understood and now that the underlying faith out of which it grows is largely absent, it is unlikely that the development of those principles will take place unless there is a new, overtly Christian, political movement which will witness to their validity. Its full articulation must take place elsewhere.

Chapter 13

Economic perspectives

There are several areas of secondary sociology which study aspects of people's economic lives—the sociology of work, organizations, industrial relations—and it is to the study of some of these that we now turn. However, we cannot just deal with them in sociological terms, because these activities are economically qualified and directed. The questions raised by an economic study of these activities must shape our sociological grasp of the issues. A woman's behaviour in a supermarket is social, but it is primarily to be understood in terms of economic consumption. Thus, although our concern with industrial organizations, work and consumption will be sociological, we must be prepared to consider some important general economic issues first.

The study of economics is no less fraught with problems than is that of sociology. There has tended to be an orthodoxy in economics which has regarded the subject in two philosophically contradictory ways. On the one hand the subject is *positive*, that is, it is factual and empirical, building knowledge from the data produced by economic behaviour. On the other hand, it is *a priori rationalist*, in that it assumes that people will respond in certain ways which allows logico-mathematical deductions to be made about what will naturally happen. As a result the theoretical development of economics has had a very peculiar structure.[1] In

---

[1] See R. G. Lipsey, *An Introduction to Positive Economics* (Weidenfeld and Nicholson, 1973) for just that and A. B. Cramp, *Notes towards a Christian Critique of Secular Economic Theory* (Institute of Christian Studies, 1975) for a very good investigation of the assumptions of various secular economic schools of thought.

the first place, the supposed positivist basis of this economic theory makes it ill-equipped to prescribe—you cannot move from an 'is' to an 'ought'—and yet it is constantly required to be the basis for policy (economic and political). Secondly, the *a priori* and supposedly neutral stance eliminates differences in motives and attitudes to economic life which undoubtedly exist but which, because of the power of orthodox policy, are under extreme pressure. Actually, orthodox economics is often 'totalitarian'; the descriptions and explanations of how the economy works are so ubiquitous as to have the effect of decreeing how people *should* react and taking steps to elicit that reaction. Thirdly, because economics has tried to establish its autonomy and independence, it has isolated itself from other disciplines like sociology. Insofar as it is not recognized that the discipline depends upon a religious and philosophical view of man, the coherence of economic and other social studies cannot be realized. There are of course many economists working in the borderline (or interface) areas with other disciplines, but in doing so they are necessarily at odds with much theoretical economics. Lastly, economics, as so conceived, is not critical, in the sense that it is not thought possible to evaluate analysis, unless *imported* assumptions are used.

Consequently, the discipline of economics has a very strained relationship with the practitioners. In some ways, the theoreticians' work often seems inhuman, and out of date and unrelated to what is actually going on. Events like the occurrence of 'stagflation' surprises them because they produce new behavioural and institutional reactions. The theoretical framework can be quickly modified to incorporate the new case, but because normal behavioural assumptions are so out of true with much of what is going on in industry, there is an obvious credibility gap between the theorists and the practitioners. Sometimes the discipline seems to enshrine the orthodox tenets of faith that constitute current economic practice among certain middle-class groups in the population. A revolt that is not merely an internal squabble makes news, as Schumacher has shown.[1] Yet there are harsh conflicts between what the economists prescribe and the obvious personal needs of ordinary people. Thus, it is not

[1] E. F. Schumacher, *Small is Beautiful* (Sphere, 1974).

enough merely to look at the discipline of economics; one needs to consider the dynamic of the relationship between the practitioners and the professionals.

These crucial issues cannot be adequately considered unless the religious roots of economic practice and the discipline of economics are examined more thoroughly than usual. Joan Robinson has written 'It does not seem that religion has ever had much to do with our own economic ideology'.[1] In this chapter we shall look at ways in which she might be wrong in this judgment. Firstly, we shall consider some of the Christian religious attitudes that predated the Industrial Revolution by several hundred years. It may be that the assumption that economics began in 1776 with the publication of *The Wealth of Nations* has cut us off from a set of religious attitudes which were actually foundational in our economic development, but which have since been lost. Then we shall look at the way the religious attitude of humanism reshaped economic practice and theory. This introduction will provide a way of uncovering some of the deeper problems in our economic development.

Christian foundations of modern economics

The development of the British economy into the 19th century has been one of the most thoroughly studied aspects of history, because of the subsequent world-wide significance of industrialization. However, the conclusion that there is one process of industrialization or economic development is open to question, and even though we cannot begin to study the economic history of Britain in detail, we shall consider an issue which uncovers the fundamentally different economic perspectives that have existed and still do exist.

In *The Protestant Ethic and the Spirit of Capitalism* Max Weber suggested that the capitalist form of production which was characteristic of industrialization owed something to the Protestant culture of Northwest Europe and especially Britain.[2]

[1] J. Robinson, *Economic Philosophy* (Pelican, 1974), p. 19.
[2] See discussion in H. F. R. Catherwood, *The Christian in Industrial Society* (IVP, 1964), pp. 114–26.

Weber argued from the Puritan doctrines of election and calling, and suggested that with the asceticism that was also practised, economic growth was more or less inevitable.[1] The argument is oversimplified, and has been subjected to criticisms which we shall examine later, but because it is important to establish the relationship of faith to economics, we shall look at some possible links between Protestantism and the development of economics. These arguments are speculative and diffuse; they present attitudinal and institutional preconditions which might have some significance for British economic development.

The first is the necessity of normative or moral economics. The normative teaching of Roman Catholicism, centring on the just price, broadened into a Protestant perspective which saw all economic activities as carried out under the eye of God, and therefore to be done scrupulously and with zeal. Prices, contracts, employment, trade, lending and patterns of tenure were therefore all subject to intense moral examination, and the conscience of economic man directed very firmly. The proposition is that this was a fundamental, necessary precondition for the growth of markets beyond interpersonal contract and haggling. Wider markets needed a structure of agreed norms and *trust*; without it there was no basis for the *free* communities (which markets are) to develop reliably. The respectable merchants, strongly affected by and embodying these values, may therefore be said to have provided an important key to translocal and transnational exchange development.

Secondly, the Protestant world view gave an independent rationale to economic activity. Previously it had tended to be seen as a ritualized, habitual pattern of obtaining subsistence, or as a routine excluded from the sacred aspects of life. The new perspective recognized that a person lived his life in faith before his Maker, and that the work to which he was called, his *vocation* was an integral part of his faith. Thus the form of employment

[1] It is worth noting that Weber and countless dependent authors have completely misunderstood the puritan doctrine of election. Worldly success through work could be neither validation nor proof nor grounds for election. Puritans believed in a covenant of sovereign grace based on God's promise and any trust in human success would have been a denial of the cherished grounds of their faith. See M. Weber, *The Protestant Ethic and the Spirit of Capitalism* (Allen and Unwin, 1930).

was a choice which was consciously made and the work involved prayer, reflection, commitment and creative effort. The doctrine that work was service of God and of one's fellow men meant that in principle, and sometimes in practice, work was not constrained to immediate self-interest. The meaning of work was greater than just obtaining wealth, or drudgery, and economic activity became potentially valid in a new and unfolding way.

The crucial doctrine around which this new orientation to work unfolded was that of *stewardship*. The great mandate to mankind in Genesis to fill the earth and have dominion over it was the key to a new understanding of man's relationship with his environment, namely that of responsible care and control. This was incorporated into the new view of scientific activity outlined in chapter 3, and also into a new consciousness of the possibility of technology—creating tools by which the earth could be subdued and used. A recognition of the incredible creativity of God, evident through new scientific instruments like the microscope and telescope and by careful observation, was likely to lead to a creative response, and that is what seems to have happened in all kinds of areas. Moreover, this development of control was not directed to aristocratic ends (or practised mainly by the gentry), but to the more immediate and mundane aspects of life—the making of soap, bricks, pots, yarn and cloth, the production of coal and iron, the building of roads and the growing of food. The doctrine of man's stewardship of the creation was an important part of the background of these changes.

It is one of the great jokes of economics that a perspective which warns against the accumulation of wealth and riches should give birth to a new dimension of wealth. The asceticism of the Puritans, and also of the later Christians during the Wesleyan revival was based on the understanding that faith in material goods was misplaced and a denial of man's true purpose. Thus the idea that the creation of wealth was for one's own satisfaction or for conspicuous consumption was out of the question. As a result, those who gained wealth tended to channel it back into enterprise. Capital accumulation was therefore financed internally and the wealth was *useful*. There are many civilizations where the accumulated wealth is channelled into political or plutocratic glorification, and monuments to this pattern litter the world; in contrast, the this-worldly asceticism, as Weber calls it, of the Protestants tended to produce more practical monuments.

We have just referred to the process of creating capital or investment, and it is worth noting another element which might have been significant in relation to the process of investment. This could be described as an act of faith, in that it involved a long-term commitment of resources in the hope that rewards would eventually be obtained. Such a step of faith for an early entrepreneur would often be considerable. It could be argued that a Christian who was accustomed to committing his ways to the Lord and trusting in the faithfulness of his God would not find this kind of investment of time, money and work out of character. His true horizons would be long ones. The attitudes of the Pilgrim Fathers and other early North American immigrants show a similar quality. Life, the Puritan fathers taught, was not a process of immediate rewards, and long-term economic commitments would therefore be congruent with their religious attitudes.

Lastly, we note that Puritanism in its emphasis on the independent status of economic activity before God and the limited spheres of responsibility of church and state began to create a pluralist social system in which neither church nor state exercised control over economic activity by chartering monopolies and trade restrictions. In its secularized form in the late 18th century, this perspective became known as *laissez-faire*, but it had had a long slow process of genesis in the independence of people who did not see why they should be controlled in their work by the politicians.

These points may throw some light on the ways in which Protestantism contributed to the rapid economic development associated with industrialization. Whether this is so or not, the congruence of Protestantism and capitalism was not as immediate as crude interpretations of Weber often suggest, as, of course, Tawney has pointed out. The actual development of industrial capitalism was characteristically the result of the philosophy of the Enlightenment which led to a radical discontinuity with the earlier Christian perspective. Elton put the issue thus:

'It was not Calvinism that freed man from the restraints of the traditional moral concepts in economics, but emancipation from religion and theology in general, which enabled men, pursuing the logic of palpable economic fact, either to ignore the thunders of their clergy or ultimately to persuade some clergy to come to terms.'[1]

This fundamental revolution in economic perspectives is crucial. We find that the actual development of the Industrial Revolution was directed to a considerable extent by the philosophy of the Enlightenment, rather than being shaped by a Christian culture. However, this does not mean that these foundational, normative perspectives were, or are, obsolete. We shall suggest later that they have a great deal to teach us about the problems that beset our economic development now.

Post-Christian economic perspectives

Property The view that man was a creature subject to economic norms was slowly eaten away and replaced by several different ideologies, which to some extent represented the class interests of the day. One of these was the belief that property was an inalienable right of man, which was often taught by the philosophers, who had the landed gentry as patrons. It is interesting that this position had a long prehistory. Tawney recounts how a group called the Commonwealth Men, headed by Latimer, led opposition to the accumulation of land that followed the appropriation of abbey, guild and chantry land by the Crown in the early 16th century. The Commonwealth Men's view of trusteeship and stewardship was pitted against those who preferred private gain to the public zeal. Tawney comments:

'Their enemy was not merely the Northumberlands or Herberts, but an idea, and they sprang to the attack, less of spoliation or tyranny, than of a creed, which was the parent of both. That creed was that the individual is absolute master of his own, and within limits set by positive law, may exploit it with a single eye to his pecuniary advantage, unrestrained by any obligation to postpone his own profit to the well-being of his neighbours, or to give account of his actions to a higher authority. It was, in short, the theory of property which was later to be accepted by all civilised communities.'[2]

[1] G. R. Elton, *Reformation Europe 1517–1559* (Fontana, 1963), p. 317.
[2] R. H. Tawney, *Religion and the Rise of Capitalism* (Pelican, 1938), p. 151.

This dominant view of property, to be contrasted with that found in the Mosaic law, was consolidated by the victory over the Commonwealth Men, and became the orthodoxy of the 18th and 19th centuries. The philosophers and moralists sponsored and patronized by the landed gentry not unnaturally became apologists for the inalienable right of private property. The results that following from its more or less universal acceptance are worth noting, for they have had a very significant effect on economic development.

Firstly, the privatized right of property, as expressed in the enclosure movements and especially that at the end of the 18th century, played a major part in creating the propertyless worker who had only his labour to sell.[1] The importance of this cannot be overestimated. Instead of the propertyless worker being seen as abnormal, he became accepted and used (compare with the Mosaic view), and the control of the worker on the basis of this dependence became endemic to the capitalist system. Further, the economic theory based on the division into the factors of production of land, labour and capital has its origins in the creation of the propertyless worker. The many models, from Ricardo's onwards, which incorporate it, are often formalized justifications of privatized ownership and rewards. Most productive processes necessarily involve raw materials, work and equipment in an interdependent relationship, and this privatized kind of analysis is therefore a very artificial kind of special pleading. Marx's special pleading for labour was an inevitable reaction to that which had gone before.

Secondly, the privatized view of land was translated to a privatized view of capital and profit. It was this conception which tied 19th century capital in many of its exploitative forms. Without the dominance of the privatized property idea it would have been impossible for the slave trade and slave owning pattern to have developed as it did. Thus, the expropriation of profit as the reward of the private capitalist was merely a continuation of the landed ethos.

The doctrine also prevented any consideration of the regular

[1] See N. L. Hammond and Barbara Hammond, *The Village Labourer 1760–1832* (Longmans, 1920).

redistribution of wealth, such as was established in the Mosaic law. In a market economy it is inevitable, because of market fluctuations and because the rich can choose when to buy and sell, that there will be accumulation of wealth. When property is considered as an absolute private right, the idea that it is a communal responsibility regularly to share out accumulated wealth is ruled out. The process of accumulation becomes more and more serious as the possession of wealth means the growth of economic power in the hands of a few, and the problems thus created are more difficult to handle than the original inequalities. The right to property becomes the right to grossly unequal economic power.

Finally, we note that the ethos of privatized property has created a peculiar structure of property in Britain. There has been an almost complete obliteration of common property from the face of the country since the 18th century. Our towns are almost completely devoid of it, because they are the product of a post-privatized era, and in the country the occasional common has been mercifully supplemented by the National Trust. What is lacking is any concept of communal property. The state, which now owns 44 per cent of total national wealth is an institution of control and does not provide free communal land or property, and we therefore have a situation where people are heavily bounded by other people's private property. Another aspect of this situation is that whatever wealth property has brought, whether through coal, minerals, oil, building rights or appreciation has been regarded as a private reward, and it is only recently that this kind of windfall profit has been seen in more communal terms. This privatization has also obscured the pattern of obligations and interdependencies which is a necessary part of economic life. Rather than being co-operative, the stance that is encouraged by the privatized property idea is anti-pathetic.

Self-Interest The importance of the concept of self-interest as an Enlightenment dogma which has become basic to economics cannot be overrated. The 18th century faith in the individual was formalized in the economic man who was guided by the rational self-interest. In the context of Adam Smith's 'invisible hand' it became a macroeconomic philosophy, in that rational self-interest worked for the economy as a whole. However, at this point we need to clarify the exact meaning of the 'invisible hand'. Originally, the Christian perspective was of the order which is created and upheld by God, but this was secularized into a perspective which saw the economy as a self-sustained natural system ordered by natural laws. The sin of avarice now became the fuel that kept the system turning. The strength of this system grew with a steady accretion of subsidiary ideas and became the basic model adopted into economic theory.

The first stage was the formalization by Jeremy Bentham and his followers of the notion of self-interest into a hedonistic calculus whereby the individual lived in a continuous (and quantifiable) calculation of pleasure and pain. The religious weight of this position needs to be felt; the entire stress in economic decision-making (and in life generally) was narrowed down to the autonomous self-seeking individual. This was both a lie, in that people would not consistently live like that, and also a very powerful ideology in that people could be persuaded and convinced that all wider economic issues than their own pleasure or self-interest could be excluded from their decision-making. Utility became a measure of all things, and one that could be quantified at that.

This key concept of utility, self-interest or pleasure is still at the centre of modern economic life, but it is worth noting in passing how economists have tried to extract it from their theory. The original utilitarian form functions fairly explicitly in the work of Mill, Jevons and Marshall. However, towards the end of the 19th century, this overt ideological commitment became rather embarrassing. (Marshall went through his *Principles of Economics* crossing out and changing his definitions of utility in later editions.) Various economists, notably Edgeworth, Fisher, Pareto, Slutsky, Hicks and Allen, tried to eliminate the concept from economics by various theoretical refinements, which tended to lead to this kind of result.

'Thus, the consumer's market behaviour is explained in terms of preferences, which are in turn defined only by behaviour. The result can very easily be circular, and in very many formulations undoubtedly is. Often nothing more is stated

than the conclusion that people behave as they behave.'[1]
Joan Robinson observes as follows:

'Before going any further, we must sadly observe that all the modern refinements of this concept have not freed it from metaphysics. We are told nowadays that since *utility* cannot be measured, it is not an operational concept, and that "revealed preference" should be put in its place. Observable market behaviour will show what an individual chooses. Preference is just what the individual under discussion prefers; there is no value judgement involved. Yet, as the argument goes on, it is clear that it is a Good Thing for the individual to have what he prefers . . .'[2]

Thus, although the value judgments are pushed to the edge, they will not fall over it, and economists find themselves dependent upon values they fear are shaky, but which they dare not question for fear of rocking the boat.

Meanwhile, we observe how the ideology of self-interest was spread. One of the areas of missionary activity was among the workforce. The use of pain and pleasure incentives, fines, physical punishment, *etc.*, on the one hand and piece rates and bonuses, on the other, could reduce the meaning of work to calculations about self-interest and gain. They could be made into pawns, which could be manipulated by carrots and sticks, to perform in the larger games which the entrepreneurs were playing. The pattern was by no means general, but it was very influential. In the face of economic growth, competition, rapid turnovers, *etc.*, the easiest way of controlling a workforce seemed to be by the stimuli of self-interest. Often the motives were prejudged, but people learnt what was expected of them. When work became more complex and a different kind of motivation was required, new stimuli were developed, such as the company car and expenses. But, whatever the variations, the understanding often remained that the basis of the employer/employee relationship was a self-interested hedonistic calculation. The destructive nature of this imposed attitude on a person's vocational life can scarcely be assessed, for it involves no less than a prostitution of a basic aspect of a person's

[1] P. Samuelson, *Foundations of Economic Analysis* (Harvard Univ. Press, 1963), p. 91.
[2] J. Robinson, *Economic Philosophy* (Pelican, 1964), p. 50.

life—his call to work with integrity before God and for his fellow men.

Another area where self-interest was proselytized was in consumption. The motives for consumption are complex, including elements like necessity, use, love, status, security, comfort, greed, addition, care, aesthetic qualities, *etc.* A Christian perspective would suggest that these motives are subject to moral evaluation and need to be considered carefully. However, the dominant thrust of much commercial persuasion is to appeal to whatever motives will most easily sell goods. The articulation of this pattern has become well-entrenched not only in people's consumption responses, but also in the production patterns that are developed. One characteristic of many modern goods—cars, aeroplanes, housing, roads, *etc.*—is that they are mutually destructive because they are developed mainly for sale rather than for use. That this is the root of a range of ecological problems becomes evident as the problems arising from use are uncovered.

For the entrenchment of self-interest in economic activity undermines the social aspect of this activity, for self-interest is never an adequate basis for social relationships, and this is very relevant to our later analysis. Thus, there is a whole range of situations in which the primary economic direction of self-interest can be seen to undermine the secondary social relationships. The joke image of hoards of women scratching at each other to get to the sale counter posits the problem in an extreme form!

Blind natural evolution Another crucial religious step in economic development rests on the idea of a natural order in economics. The 'invisible hand' constituted a faith that the system would naturally grow on the basis of self-interest. As a result it became an article of faith that no normative direction of economic activity should exist, but that people should leave the system to establish things naturally. This natural, anormative perspective underlay the thinking of most early economists. Malthus came to gloomy conclusions about the tendency of the masses to fall naturally to subsistence level. Others began to see competition as a key natural process whereby the best evolved into a dominant position. Adam Smith had spent several chapters in the *Wealth of Nations* trying to determine what was the natural as opposed to the market price of commodities, and when Marx came to criticize the system, he did it in terms of the argument that the natural and inevitable development of the system would undermine capitalism.

This philosophical perspective was therefore a fundamental abdication in that the entrepreneur and banker were not required to ask deeper questions, but were assured that as long as they continued pursuing their own ends all would be well. At the same time, the slant of economic theory became different, in that normative economic behaviour was treated in terms of natural economic forces and laws. Instead of man being responsible for his economic life, the natural law perspective developed into the idea that economics, as a law system, controlled man. It is not without significance that the discipline of economics before the work done by Keynes, seemed to be unable to make a responsible analytical response to the problem of cyclical depression; this was the result of subjection to the natural order and abdication of responsibility to it. Natural market forces were the process by which equilibrium had to be re-established in the economy.

The effect of this perspective on the discipline of economics has been, and is, very dangerous. The search for laws and regularities shapes the kind of economic knowledge that is sought, and human behaviour is thereby squeezed into narrow mechanical prototypes which misrepresent what is actually happening. Thus, the assumption that economics is just looking at the interplay of economic forces in a value-free positivist way grows out of this naturalist perspective. On this basis the simplified models of consumption and the profit-maximizing firm have been made into an orthodoxy which begs a thousand questions. Economic orthodoxy therefore opens the way for practitioners to become unconcerned about a range of normative issues for which they are necessarily responsible. Their job, it seems, is just to produce a profit and no more, although of course many managers do not slip into this pattern.

The main thrust of this naturalist perspective in Britain and the USA was in terms of the beneficent process of competitive evolution. Competition, it was argued, weeded out the sub-standard firms in a way similar to that in which species became

326

extinct. This meant that the best remained, and that there was a continual process of economic amelioration. By the end of the 19th century it was beginning to be apparent that this doctrine always appealed to the species that did evolve, and that there were weaknesses in it. By the time of Marshall, it was evident that much of the economy in Britain and other advanced countries was post-competitive in a variety of senses.[1] However, the naturalist interpretation was not in danger, although shaken by the great depression, because Galbraith was able to declare that counter-vailing power had come to replace competition. Moreover, it was a self-generating force which again freed people from any responsibility in the economic process. The prestige of the profitable, the successful and the fittest who survive was guaranteed for another generation.[2]

However, the fact is that no natural system will guarantee a stable economy; the abdication of responsibility will not work, and it is perhaps worth pausing to consider why the idea of competition is weak. In any market it is true that buyers can discriminate between various goods and the vendors will become aware of the values and preferences of the purchasers as a result of their choices. Nevertheless, this is not competition, because the goods usually appeal to different kinds of purchasers, the vendors are often prepared to accept different rewards, and the marketing situation of different producers and vendors always creates some element of monopoly. If, as we shall argue later, the main aim of a producer should be to serve his customers, this does not require him to try to eliminate all rivals. Indeed, in areas where the products of different firms are homogeneous all that is required is that the market is regularly cleared. Thus a *respectful* analysis of marketing shows that the idea of competition need play very little part in it. Conversely, it is also evident that the idea is often, and has often been, very wasteful. Competitive railway lines and postal services, for example, are an obvious waste of resources. The situations where competition is strong tend to be those where large windfall profits are available, where much is to be gained by the elimination of rivals, where advertising allows a market to be

---

[1] See A. Marshall, *Industry and Trade* (Macmillan, 1919).
[2] J. K. Galbraith, *American Capitalism: The Concept of Countervailing Power* (Pelican, 1963), pp. 122–48.

monopolized or resources are likely to be under-utilized. As a dominant norm for the market it is often very destructive and unnecessary.

This points to the fact that the real impetus behind the concept comes from the survival of the fittest. The debate is really about economic power, and often the basis of competition has been not the provision of the best or cheapest goods or services, but who is the most ruthless in exploiting a monopoly, engineering discrimination against other producers or taking over producers of similar goods. The supposed equation between the exercise of self-interest and the public good through the link of the survival of the fittest just does not work. The point about the exercise of economic power is that it aims to restrict or channel the free choice of consumers in the market. Even the Galbraithian formula does no more than cover a multitude of sins by putting them in two heaps. What is actually happening is that the structure of agreed norms and trust which underlie marketing, which is ignored by more scientific, quantitative analysis of markets, breaks down in practice because the exercise of economic power and the gospel of private cost efficiency positively encourage it to do so.

Thus we see that the Enlightenment idea of a natural economic order has been a basis for abdicating economic responsibility, both in analysis and practice, and it has also provided a cloak for a range of immoral acts which have often seriously damaged our development.

Neutrality, power and socialist economics   The retreat from the normative or moral perspective of pre-industrial Protestant-ism into a belief in 'the system' and its ability to generate progress has had another long-term effect. The supposed neutrality of economics has encouraged the view that whatever is possible is legitimate, and only legal constraints define what it is right to do. Moreover, there has been little firm and positive thinking about the legal constraints. The laws of 1856 and 1862 establishing incorporation and limited liability were typical in that they were a late reaction which validated the anonymity of capital, and subsequent laws have tended merely to define particular aspects of company practice rather than to grasp the structure of the company in the modern world. In this *laissez-faire* environment where the major normative character of economic activity has tended to be ignored, permissiveness has changed the emphasis to economic power.

What is meant by economic power? It can simply mean command over resources, but its meaning in this context is different. We take it to mean that, as economic dependence increases, it is possible for one economic group to exploit the dependence of others to attain its own ends. Contrary to the Galbraithian view, we see the use of economic power as profoundly immoral. The important point is that it tends to break down the trust upon which an interdependent economy is based, and encourages retaliation and mutual destructiveness. The history of this immoral use is long: it involves capitalist exploitation of worker dependence, firms exploiting market dependence and workers exploiting their own scarcity. However, the crucial fact is that the opportunities for using economic power have increased with the complex division of labour and production we practise, and the problem is therefore potentially becoming more acute. The major power confrontation between the trades unions and company managers, in which the power varies with the various economic indicators, is but one of the areas of power competition and leverage. It has become a major thought form of British industry in the late 20th century, and its exercise encourages its proliferation, in that the weak cannot remain weak without facing extinction.

There is, however, an answer which has been extensively used. Initially the answer of socialism was directed mainly against the power of monopolies. The argument has the form that if state power supersedes economic power, the exploitation of economic power disappears. Without denying that there are elements that are valuable, it is also possible to argue that this response leads to new deeper problems. Firstly, the involvement of state is likely to be partisan in terms of investment, pricing and conditions. Secondly, the state cannot identify the forms of immoral economic power that are operative without a thorough understanding of the moral structure of a firm or industry. Yet the socialist analysis of capitalist industry is far too narrow and ignores many of the important dimensions of economic power.

Thirdly control cannot eliminate the exploitation of economic power, because everybody is dependent, especially the controllers. Therefore either the form of control becomes more and more totalitarian and bureaucratic or it becomes ineffective. Fourthly, control which reduces responsibility induces an anomic response and alienation in the workforce and therefore tends further to erode the internal moral order of an organization. Again, there is a qualitative difference between political and economic responsibility which makes it very difficult for politicians to guide an economic organization with economic authority and effectiveness. Lastly, the engorged socialist state is so complex and exercises so many forms of control that the pattern of occasional elections offers no hope of effective democratic participation in the running of state economic enterprises. Thus, the answer to economic power and its misuse is not, we suggest, political control.

The alternative we shall explore in later chapters rests in an understanding of the internal normative structure of organizations and markets. Economic standards and principles are detailed and complex, needing to be constantly worked out in countless decisions in the hearts of those in factories, offices, shops and boardroom. One sweeping act of transfer cannot penetrate to people's moral economic commitment unless it opens up economic freedom for them, rather than establishing a different pattern of control. Probably the most difficult form of investment is in people's economic responsibility, and their free normative commitment to an enterprise. Yet it is precisely the failure to carry out this investment by substituting effective control and mechanical incentives that has created many of the antagonisms that disrupt work communities. Communities are based on freely shared norms, and the current impoverishment of economic structures in Britain reflects the anormative approach of industry and academic economics.

Changing the system   The humanist viewpoints which we have already discussed have recently surfaced in another interesting but illusory form. The belief in the economic system as a naturalistic, mechanistic system has been allied with a democtatic socialist faith in the state to produce the conclusion that the state

330

is able to make the system work or to put it right by the appropriate manipulation. The working of the economy is a matter of technical adjustment, similar to the kind required in mending a watch. It is more than a little interesting to follow the history of this development.

Keynes wrote *The General Theory of Employment, Interest and Money* as a Liberal seeking to correct the tendency to underemployment in the economy, and he attached no particular significance or foresight to the state other than some new forms of guidance.

'Thus, apart from the necessity of central controls to bring about an adjustment between the propensity to consume and the inducement to invest, there is no more reason to socialise economic life than there was before.'[1]

Nevertheless, there has developed over the years a faith in macroeconomic manipulation by the State, which has partly been fostered by economists, with their belief in their own omniscience, and has partly been the necessary result of the politicians' claim that they can put the economy right. The winning slogan, 'You've never had it so good' in 1959 was part of a long process in which the state was seen to be, in the right hands, the key to economic success. One of the effects of this academic and political *hubris* was to produce some very bad economics.

For it would now be generally acknowledged that the various manipulative strategies that were adopted to create economic success, like technological growth, a national plan, export-led growth and the '72–'73 'take-off' were economically naive. Moreover, the traditional post-Keynesian manipulative macro-economics ignored the importance of the transfers and changes involved in these kinds of manipulations. Not only was the effect of the public sector borrowing requirement on the government's monetary policy more or less ignored, but also the economy was expected to respond in ways and at a pace which were physically impossible, although they seemed eminently sensible to the system managers. Also, people's attitudes to various aspects of their economic life were expected to change overnight in response

---

[1] J. M. Keynes, *The General Theory of Employment, Interest and Money* (Macmillan, 1936), p. 379.

to some simple incentive when all their experiences pointed the other way. Moreover, the quality of transfers was ignored; investment could be replaced by government expenditure as a source of expansion in the economy, but what was the nature of that expansion? Thus, the form of abstraction in much macroeconomic reasoning covered a range of problems which are continually present and are more and more obvious.

Consider one aspect of this development. The Conservative governments of 1955, 1959, and 1964 engineered excessive expansion in the economy to coincide with the elections of those years. These acts were immoral and they have created certain historical patterns of fluctuation in our economy which are very difficult to eradicate. Sales of consumer durables are inherently spasmodic, investment tends to be short-term and speculative; there is a high marginal propensity to import, because British goods will not be available and predictions about the future are less reliable than in many other countries. Manipulation will not solve this problem, although a careful macroeconomic policy is obviously important, for it is at root a moral issue, and until the initial hypocrisy and the attitudes engineered by British fluctuations are faced, there is little hope of the pattern changing in this decade. Indeed, we now face the unedifying spectacle of politicians calculating how they can use the oil boom to their electoral advantage.

This confusion, where there is on the one hand faith in the state as guardians and manipulators of the economic system and a changing trust in political parties to put the economy right, and on the other disillusion with the way politicians and academic economists actually perform, is therefore yet another presentation of the underlying religious malaise.

Means and ends The final dimension we shall consider is the purpose of our economic activity. If, as we have suggested, the aim of production and marketing is primarily to serve one's neighbours through that activity, this must be reflected in the structure of economic organizations. When, however, the organization becomes self-serving, the needs of others become instrumental to the growth and progress of economic organizations. In course of time, this development can be quite serious, in that the 'servants' grow out of the norm of service, and other motives begin to shape the economy.

The strong emphasis given to the interests, profitability and growth of companies, rather than to their ultimate purpose as servants, has produced a range of interesting characteristics, which have often been noted. Firstly, the emphasis is often on the form of production which brings the most profit rather than that which suits the consumer. Secondly, the firm tends to minimize its own private costs even if that means incurring severe social costs. Indeed, although most economists treat 'externalities' as things that 'just happen', most profit-maximizing firms have a strong incentive to turn their costs into externalities: pollution rather than proper disposal, centralized marketing which puts the onus of distribution largely on the consumer, and planned obsolescence, will all tend to maximize profits. Many 'economies of scale' are similarly calculated on private costs, ignoring the heavy external or social costs which they involve. Thirdly, firms seek market security and immunity by various forms of market manipulation. Again, technology is often aimed at technological supremacy over rivals and tends therefore towards constantly increasing complexity. Then there is also a fairly constant trend towards takeovers, mergers and financial consolidation, as companies develop a complex strategy for security and growth. The net effect is that there is a momentum, which comes from within the company itself, which focuses on the needs of production, finance and marketing, and it is this momentum which dictates, to a large extent, to the consumer.

A similar emphasis comes from labour. What is considered important is that jobs are saved here or that redundancy is not created there. The purpose of labour seems to be extrinsic to the goods being produced and to lie primarily in the pay. Regulations and the establishment of positions of power become the immediate concern. Qualifications are more for the purpose of creating labour scarcity than for doing the job properly. The emphasis again tends to be immediate, self-interested, and unquestioning, in the sense that the deeper questions such as the kind of goods which can and should be produced, and how they can best be made, are outside the normal framework of vision.

This pragmatic immediacy is strangely blinkered. Many have

raised the issue of how the economy will need to adapt itself radically in the coming decades, because our understanding of man's position in the world has radically altered, but the means to production are now ends in themselves, and the ability to change is therefore seriously in question.[1]

Conclusion

These points can do no more than illustrate some of the ways in which the direction of economic development is shaped by underlying humanist religious motives. If, as we suggest, these directions have a fallacious basis, there is a need for an alternative normative perspective, which has some connections with the pre-industrial, puritan perspective briefly discussed at the beginning of the chapter. The next chapter will therefore be concerned with the Christian perspective on economic life.

[1] For a thorough Christian critique on this dimension see J. Ellul, *The Technological Society* (Cape, 1964) and E. F. Schumacher, *Small is Beautiful* (Sphere, 1974).

Chapter 14

A Christian economic perspective

It is very difficult when we are immersed day by day in a complex economy to draw back and look at this vast structure in perspective, especially when it seems to be so firm an autonomous area with its own rules and *raison d'être*. It seems self-evident that the purpose of economic activity is to increase wealth, or to make money or to produce more, while the aim of firms is to increase profits and efficiency and to grow in size. Men and women work in order to earn money, which is the measure of the value of goods and services, while at the same time the value of money is established by the goods and services it can buy. Thus economic life takes on the character of a closed system which is only to be seen in terms of itself. However, if the analysis of the last chapter is at all valid, this supposed autonomy is a lie and economic life is riddled with values and is necessarily bound up with the rest of life. Economic activity may be differentiated from other aspects of life, but it is religious; it involves the basic issues of life at every turn.

In this chapter we therefore attempt to look at a Christian definition of the meaning of economic life. Since most economies most of the time have been relatively simple compared with our own, the chapter begins with a look at undifferentiated economic principles, and only in the later sections are the more complex issues presented. It will be evident that our biblical understanding of basic principles needs to be tentatively extrapolated to more immediate modern conditions, but because the character of economic reality is not fundamentally changed, but rather elaborated, the task is both possible and very necessary.

The biblical meaning of economic life

The religious nature of economic life Economic life needs
to be placed in context. The Christian understands that mankind
was placed by God in a creation which would support him and
sustain his life, and his whole historical development from his first
garden environment has taken place before God, and has
crucially involved his relationship with God. Economic blessing,
judgment, freedom and care, the meaning of work and rest are all
shaped by, and shape, mankind's relationship with God. Nothing
is irrelevant to this central relationship. Thus, the Mosaic law
contains precepts like 'You shall not muzzle an ox when it treads
out the grain' (Dt. 25:4), because even these specific aspects of
economic life matter to God. When a man came to Jesus burning
with a sense of economic injustice, he was asked by Jesus to put
his concern in the context of his relationship with God (Lk.
12:13–21). The truths of the Christian faith interpenetrate all
aspects of economic life. 'Are you anxious about food, clothing
and drink? But consider, your Father knows that you need them'
(Lk. 12:22–31). 'You cannot serve God and mammon' (Mt. 6:24).
There is, in this perspective, not one iota of room for economic
autonomy.

Economic blessing The central relationship between God and
man is initially established in terms of God's blessing and
providence.
>'Thou visitest the Earth and waterest it,
>   thou greatly enrichest it;
>The river of God is full of water;
>   thou providest their grain,
>   for so thou hast prepared it.
>Thou waterest its furrows abundantly,
>   settling its ridges,
>   softening it with showers,
>   and blessing its growth.
>Thou crownest the year with thy bounty'
>   (Ps. 65:9–11).

This great original blessing (Gn. 1:28) is continually repeated to
all mankind, and in the Mosaic law a feast lasting for a week, the

feast of booths, is instituted, when the people can have joy in their food and drink. The joy in receiving the goodness God has given is lost to many in the rapacity of modern living, but it is basic to our existence. At the same time, the provision of God for man has only slowly been revealed down the centuries, as new and wonderful possibilities in the creation have become evident and been tapped.

'Know that the Lord is God!
It is he that made us, and we are his;
We are his people, and the sheep of his pasture.
Enter his gates with thanksgiving, and his courts with
praise!
Give thanks to him, bless his name!
For the Lord is good;
His steadfast love endures for ever,
and his faithfulness to all generations'

(Ps. 100:3–5).

This is the ultimate context of economic life.

Stewardship The relationship is also defined for mankind by God in terms of the great mandate to have dominion over the earth (Gn. 1:28). This responsible office of stewardship is part of the greatness to which man has been called by God, in that in partnership with his Creator he is invited to this kind of control of the natural world.[1] The historical development from primitive agriculture to the modern forms of dominion is therefore to be seen (critically) within this norm of stewardship. It is not without significance that dominion opened up most fully in the Bible-saturated culture of Northern Europe, as people have entered, in part, into this truth about our economic existence. This responsibility is far greater than what we now understand by 'work', which is often narrow and routine, and it involves a whole range of economic norms which are developed in Scripture. At this stage, we recognize that one of the greatest answers to the question, 'What is man?' is that God has

'given him dominion over the work of his hands;

[1] See B. Goudzwaard, *Economic Stewardship versus Capitalist Religion* (Institute for Christian Studies, Toronto, 1972) for a full articulation of this.

he has put all things under man's feet,
all sheep and oxen, and also the beasts of the field,
the birds of the air, and the fish of the sea . . .

                                    (Ps. 8:6–8, paraphrased).

One of the principles of stewardship is of economic care. It was ordained that the land should be fallow during the seventh year to allow wild animals their place and to rest the land (Ex. 23:10, 11), and the domestic animals were to be rested on the Sabbath (Ex. 23:12). There was great care over food and hygiene (Leviticus 11), and respect for that which was consumed: 'You shall not boil a kid in its mother's milk' (Dt. 14:21). There was also care for the species, a respect which did not allow thoughtless extinction (Dt. 22:6, 7). Thus stewardship meant a care of the whole of the natural order—land, animals, birds, fish and trees, and this approach to life contrasts with the humanist concept of unrestrained exploitation, which has tended to be the dominant modern response.

Economic judgment   We also recognize that human sinfulness and attempted independence has led to a fundamental judgment on man's economic situation. Adam's attempt at independence and self-sufficiency led to a curse on his environment which made the position of stewardship continually a problematic one.

"Because you have listened to the voice of your wife,
and have eaten of the tree of which I commanded you,
'You shall not eat of it',
cursed is the ground because of you;
in toil you shall eat of it all the days of your life;
thorns and thistles it shall bring forth to you;
and you shall eat the plants of the field.
In the sweat of your face you shall eat bread
till you return to the ground, for out of it you were
taken;
you are dust,
and to dust you shall return"

                                              (Gn. 3:17–19).

These chilling words define the futility of man's hope for his own economic self-sufficiency, and the breakdown of the created harmony and blessing of the true relationship. The falseness of man's response has engendered an inherent pattern of economic frustration in man's history, and it is possible that we in the West are now beginning to reap another crop of the bitterness of years of economic pride. The lie of independence does not change character when there is economic plenty, as Christ's parable of the rich fool illustrates, but for most people, most of the time, their economic situation is circumscribed enough with toil and frustration for them not to pat themselves on the back and bask in their unmitigated success. The alienation that comes with sin is highlighted by the Preacher.

'Then I considered all that my hands had done and the toil I had spent in doing it, and behold, all was vanity and a striving after wind, and there was nothing to be gained under the sun.'

'Then I saw that all toil and all skill in work come from a man's envy of his neighbour. This also is vanity and a striving after wind.'

'All the toil of man is for his mouth, yet his appetite is not satisfied.'

(Ec. 2:11; 4:4; 6:7).

The economic judgment of man, and the various forms it takes will be examined more fully later.

Economic rest   When we come to look at the great structural principles of economic life, one of the most central is related to the doctrine of the Sabbath. It can be summed up by saying that work has meaning within life, but it is not the meaning of life. In Genesis 2:2, 3 we read:

'And on the seventh day, God finished his work which he had done, and he rested on the seventh day from all his work which he had done. So God blessed the seventh day and hallowed it, because on it God rested from all his work which he had done in creation.'

It is scarcely possible to grasp the meaning of this great supracosmic rest, but it does have a message for God's human stewards, in that they too are commanded to rest. The Sabbath is a holy rest day for everybody (Ex. 20:8–11). Without the work of the week, rest is relatively meaningless, but given the normal demands of work, rest is a practical realization of the principle that man is not a slave to his work, and that life is not to be equated with work. It is also a recognition that we are not only made to serve God, but also to rest and enjoy him.

In Hebrews, the writer takes up the Old Testament theme of a Sabbath rest, and contrasts the restlessness that follows from disobedience, which is exemplified by the wanderings of the Children of Israel in the wilderness, with the rest of obedience which allows people to cease from their labour (Hebrews 4). We would argue that the forms of economic commitment in which we live and the approach to work often current to-day are destroying our knowledge of peace and rest, replacing it with patterns of turmoil and insecurity which are destructive. The implications of this point will be developed later.

Economic independence   Yet another of the economic themes of the Bible is that of economic freedom. In Genesis 37 we read that Joseph was sold by his brothers to the Midianites, and this set in train a process whereby the children of Israel were slaves in the land of Egypt. The oppression led to God's intervention and deliverance of his people, and the establishment of their religious and economic freedom. God's message to them was:

   'I am the Lord your God, who brought you forth out of the
   land of Egypt, that you should not be their slaves; and I have
   broken the bars of your yoke and made you walk erect' (Lv.
   26:13).

To maintain this principle, the Israelites were given a legal system and an economic structure which eradicated permanent slavery from the nation. The distribution of land was such that each family was given, and could not be permanently alienated from, a means of livelihood. The requirement that a poor person should be lent what he needed and have a release from credit every seven years meant that he would not easily be forced into bankruptcy (Dt. 15:1–11). At the same time, a person who was not self-sufficient was still not forced into slavery, but was to become a hired servant (an employee), which seems to have been considered a relatively satisfactory economic situation in a predominantly agricultural community (Lv. 25:39–46). Thus, with a few exceptions where the institution of marriage was involved, the principle of a free labour force not bound to others was strongly established in the Israelite nation. The vehemence with which the principle is upheld is evident in the following legal ruling:

'If a man is found stealing one of his brethren, the people of
Israel, and if he treats him as a slave or sells him, then that thief
shall die; so you shall purge the evil from the midst of you' (Dt.
24:7).

The principle is, however, not merely the limited and negative
legal one of abolishing slavery. It is exciting to follow the process,
beginning with Paul's pleading to Philemon that Onesimus should
no longer be a slave but a brother to Philemon, leading to the
eradication of the various forms of slavery present in the Greek,
Roman, Spanish and British empires; but the *basis* of this process
was the principle of economic freedom. The key argument echoed
throughout scripture, is that God has made man, and he therefore
owns and has redeemed man. For any human being to claim ownership of another person is therefore a falsehood, for we are God's. A
person's economic independence before God was therefore a
major concern of the Mosaic law and there was a strong emphasis
on not using economic weakness to push a brother into a position
where he could be exploited (Dt. 15: 7–11; 24: 10–15, 19.) or made
dependent. In a situation where the early Christians were trapped
in a system of slavery, Paul reiterates the key principle:

'Slaves, be obedient to those who are your earthly masters,
with fear and trembling, in singleness of heart, as to Christ; not
in the way of eyeservice as men-pleasers, but as servants of
Christ, doing the will of God from the heart, rendering service
with a good will as to the Lord and not to men, knowing that
whatever good anyone does, he will receive the same again
from the Lord, whether he is a slave or free. Masters, do the
same to them, and forbear threatening, knowing that he who is
both their Master and yours is in heaven, and that there is no
partiality with him' (Eph. 6:5–9).

People have sometimes described passages like this as condoning
or supporting slavery, but this simplistic response not only
ignores the power of the principle, but also fails to recognize the
patient, non-aggressive method of social change which is
characteristically Christian, and which was established by Christ
in many situations, including the similar one where he stated that
the children of God were free of the Roman yoke, but then freely
paid the tribute money (Mt. 17:24–27). The principle is therefore

to be lived out in the lives of Christians and to take root in economic structures. Later, we shall look at some of the more specific implications of this principle which could be established in our system.

Social acquisitiveness   Another fundamental antithesis growing out of the biblical perspective is rooted in two of the commandments: 'You shall not steal' and 'You shall not covet your neighbour's house; you shall not covert your neighbour's wife, or his manservant, or his maidservant, or his ox, or his ass, or anything that is your neighbour's' (Ex. 20: 15, 17). The principle here is that economic possessions are not to be a source of division, envy and strife between people; they are merely what each person owns. This, of course, was very different from the 18th century assertion of property as a natural right, for that was possessive and without any framework of economic justice and communal care. The Mosaic law, with its provision of a firm and fair system of distribution of wealth and income forbids stealing and the motive of coveting. Stealing means more than taking someone else's goods; it also means engineering into your own possession what another had owned (Dt. 19:14.). The principle is evidenced in the precept which allows a person to eat the grapes of another, but not to appropriate the crop (Dt. 23:24, 25). The contrast is between peaceable possession with sharing and fairness, and the alien motives of economic gain, self-interest and greed. The watershed is perhaps most clearly seen in the action taken by Abram, when there was strife between his and Lot's herdsmen. Abram made the choice which avoided the well watered Jordan valley and the strife, while Lot in his thirst for gain committed himself to a decadent and dying culture (Genesis 13). We read that God's blessing was given to Abram, while Lot suffered in a rapacious society. The normative principles are therefore laid down for a non-acquisitive economic order, and the fact that coveting has become an established attitude in Western economic life therefore needs to be critically analysed.

Economic fairness   The Mosaic law also laid down that in all forms of economic exchange or transaction, scrupulous fairness was to be observed.

'You shall do no wrong in judgment, in measures of length or weight or quantity. You shall have just balances, just weights, a just ephah, and a just hin: I am the Lord your God, who brought you out of the land of Egypt (Lv. 19: 35, 36).
The same applied to wage transactions, borrowing, lending, cases of neglect, *etc.* The meaning of economic exchange was not to be found in the individualist idea of personal gain, but in mutual care and regard; it was not antisocial, but was meant to parallel mutual respect. We, of course, have moved into all kinds of anonymous exchange relationships, but this still requires us to recognize the wider implications of fairness in transactions.

The economic community   This brings us to the two basic characteristics of this perspective on economic life. God's command to man that he shall love his neighbour as himself is the normative framework for economic activity. Personal respect and care is exhibited in precept after precept.
'When you make your neighbour a loan of any sort, you shall not go into his house to fetch his pledge' (Dt. 24:10)
exhibits the way in which people are not to be pushed by economic pressures. It has frequently been noted that the Mosaic law downgrades punishment for property offences and emphasizes offences against people. This then is the theme throughout; the conduct of economic activity is shaped by, and in no way compromises, love one for another. To say this is not to deny that the children of Israel often disobeyed this command in their economic life. The prophets spent much of their time making this very point. However, departure from these normative standards was to be understood, as the prophets again emphasized, as sin, and required repentance, recompense and forgiveness. The economic relationships of property and exchange were to be shaped by love, and only in this context could they properly be understood.

Normative economics   The other basic characteristic is that all economic activity, guided by normative principles, was and is carried out responsibly before God. Obedience to God brought blessing and disobedience to these basic norms brought a curse, not only because God's judgment was directed against those who disobeyed him and harmed others, but also because attempts to defy the created structure of economic life and relationships necessarily brought evil (Deuteronomy 28). The prophets raise a mounting crescendo of voices stating God's concern at, and impending punishment of, economic exploitation.

'Woe to those who devise wickedness and work evil upon their beds!
When the morning dawns, they perform it, because it is in the power of their hand.
They covet fields and seize them; and houses, and take them away;
they oppress a man and his house, a man and his inheritance.
Therefore thus says the Lord:
Behold, against this family I am devising evil, from which you cannot remove your necks;
and you shall not walk haughtily, for it will be an evil time'
(Mi. 2:1-3).

Thus, whether it is recognized or not, the process of economic judgment goes on. There is much that we do not understand about God's judgment on exploitation and empire building, but we are fools if we believe that, economically, we are laws unto ourselves rather than being stewards in God's creation. It behoves us to try to understand carefully our situation and its problems.

A Christian economic philosophy

The initial study of a biblical understanding of economic life directs us into the development of a Christian economic philosophy. The latter is necessarily speculative as it moves into the major issues of a modern developed economy, but our aim is to make sure that it is directed by biblical norms, principles and understandings. It is also important that we recognize the developmental nature of this philosophical analysis. Complex patterns of analysis cannot be carried out until the more basic points have been established, and the argument will, therefore, often postpone discussion of second and third order issues. The perspective will be developed within major, typical areas, although many issues cannot be neatly confined in one topic.

Work We have already covered a number of crucial points in relation to work. The central meaning is rooted in man's steward relationship with God and the blessings given to man by God. Thus, at root, the Marxist idea that independent human labour is the source of all value is a lie. Even the form of the labour theory of value, which states that all the value added to free goods is the result of labour, ignores the fact that much value exists and is appropriated as property without work taking place. Free goods are therefore only limiting examples of goods, much of the value of which is given. Work, therefore, is basically a dependent activity, and to isolate it from its creational context, and the blessings which people enjoy from the creation, is to be involved in a fundamental falsehood.

Further, we note that because man is given dominion over the creation, and his work is creative, he is not in subjection to nature. It is noteworthy that in cultures where nature is worshipped, like the animist cultures of pre-colonial Africa south of Muslim influence, people tended to be subject to the gods or spirits of nature which they worshipped or manipulated through magic, and the economy remained dominated by the natural environment. Animals were often seen as sacred, which inhibited their economic use. In other cultures, like that of India, the creative relationship between man and nature is lost, for nature is seen as illusory, and the life of contemplation or aesthetic withdrawal is valued above that of active work. This perspective, with its roots in Upanishadic Hinduism, is recognized by many to be a major obstacle to development in Hindu and Buddhist cultures. Another common cultural perspective is that which makes work only a necessary means to the end of pleasure, leisure, enjoyment and conspicuous wealth. In these cultures a leisured, economically parasitic elite has tended to emerge, which has undermined the economic stability of a civilization. In this case work, rather than being normal, is what the unsuccessful do, but if too many people are successful, the system crumbles. This is part of the classical interpretation of the downfall of the Roman Empire, and it cannot be easily dismissed. It may have considerable relevance to our own civilization, as we shall see later. A Christian perspective, however, sees work as a normal and creative aspect of man's relation to nature, and it is essentially within this ethos that economic development has taken place in the Western world.

Thus, in a primary sense, the meaning of work is intrinsic. In the Scriptures, the creation is often described as the work of God's hands; Genesis 1 is set out like a work schedule. We therefore live in a creation where work, production and manufacture make sense, and where, just as God looked on his creation and saw that it was very good, so we can look on our work and see that there is something good in it. This experience is important and most people recognize it, either in their paid employment or in activities like gardening, decorating or making clothes. However, many people do *not* experience this in their daily work, and it is worth asking why. One reason is that when man is independent of God, his view of work is not a harmonious one; frustration and tension are involved. His relationship with the material world becomes that of tyrant over nature, and the intrinsic meaning is lost because nature then becomes merely a pawn in the hand of man, and the exploiter cannot have any respect for that which he exploits. Work can also become a means to status, power or reward. It may be, also, that for many people the work they are actually doing has no intrinsic meaning, in that it is, in their opinion, a misdirection of effort.

There can be a variety of reasons for this. One is the product; it must be difficult to get much satisfaction from manufacturing cigarettes or a product which is badly made. Another possibility is that a person has withdrawn from his work and sees it merely as a meaningless process which allows him to achieve the level of material satisfaction he desires. Another is that the job definition of a worker makes his specific task inappropriate for, or even insulting to, him. Again, it may be possible for a worker to act mechanically and ritualistically in an occupation, without there being much significant interaction. In large organizations the meaning of specific jobs can be lost, simply because the structure is confused. Clearly many of these reasons relate to the economic organization in which the work takes place, but a key question is always, 'Does the worker believe in his work?', and this issue of individual vocation is one which requires radical rethinking, simply because the size of organizations tends to swamp the issue. The cog is not given the chance to do what he believes he can do which is of value. There are some practical ways of remedying

346

this. One is school apprenticeships, whereby 14- and 15-year-olds are apprenticed to workers in a wide variety of occupations for a week or a month to see and assess what a job involves. Another is a wider use of probationary work, and another is the use of workers in schools giving direct vocational education.

Another way in which the meaning of work tends to be evaluated, especially among the middle classes, is the concept of career. The idea is that the worker is on a ladder which involves successively higher levels of responsibility, significance, reward, status and satisfaction, and the concept is often strongly built into the organizational structure by those for whom the career concept seems to make sense, namely those at the top. The result of this ethos can easily be that work becomes a continual pattern of deferred gratification; it is a way of getting on, to the extent that its intrinsic meaning is lost or distorted. It is possible for those who have lived on this deferred gratification ideal, but who do not 'succeed', to feel very disillusioned and unhappy, and similarly for those who do 'succeed' to overrate their ability, importance and the scope of decisions they are competent to make. We shall argue later that organizations reflect career egoisms more than most managers would care to admit. The Christian view of work scythes through this elitist concept. Our vocation is that which we are called to do before God, and he is totally interested in what each of us is doing. Indeed, those who notice find it disturbing how carefully their work is monitored by God, how thorough their training is, and how shallow their own career plans were.

Another perspective on work, beloved by economists, but which is fundamentally at odds with a Christian view, is that which sees the entrepreneur as making decisions and organizing the factors of production: land, labour and capital. In this model, which has dominated economic thinking from the early 19th century, labour is made a part of the production process and is seen as excluded from decision-making and responsibility. The idea is that the workers' labour is being used by the entrepreneur rather than contributed by the workers. A corollary of this is that decisions can be made about substituting capital for labour which effectively by-pass the worker and dismiss his work contribution. The passive and reactionary stance of the trades unions means that this problem has rarely been faced. Many workers would not even begin to think about improving their own work, let alone being allowed to do it, because the ethos of an organized factor bears upon them. This attitude reflects the normal capitalist definition of the firm, and we shall look later at ways in which it can be modified. The standard to which we appeal is that economic activity should not treat people as pawns, but should be *their* activity. To take people's work from them, in the sense that what they do is not theirs, is one of the most serious and common forms of human degradation.

We note as well that the motives for work can often be fundamentally sinful. The Preacher declares 'Then I saw that all toil and all skill in work came from a man's envy of his neighbour. This also is vanity and a striving after wind (Ec. 4:4), and makes the point very clearly. A major motive in the development of various skills and forms of expertise is that of self-glorification. The desire is to impress, and implicit superiority has become a system, in that diplomas and qualifications are often part of a process of job enhancement or professionalization that is clogging educational institutions at all levels. Moreover, when the wrong motives become established in an organization, the work community can be shattered into vicious power-seeking cliques who are prepared to use one another. Motives never remain hidden, and when they emerge, they have already had substantial effects on the work situation. Moreover, there are not many people who cannot analyse their own work motives very accurately and see exactly where they diverge from the aim of doing a worthwhile job well.

Although there are many more aspects of work which deserve examination, we shall at this stage look at work and wages or recompense. It is assumed throughout the Scriptures that there is a close, real and moral link between work and wages. James states 'Behold the wages of the labourers who mowed your fields, which you kept back by fraud, cry out; and the cries of the harvesters have reached the ears of the Lord of hosts' (Jas. 5:4). To some this pre-theoretical moral norm might seem inadequate in a modern economy, but this is partly because some of our own concepts are inadequately conceived. The idea that a person's output or the value of his marginal product can be strictly calculated as the result of his work is entirely misconceived except in a few individual cases. Most work is necessarily interdependent, and output is crucially dependent on the equipment which a worker is able to use. Indeed, it is one of the most serious problems of the era that workers, through no effort on their part, use or are responsible for vastly varying quantities of capital. It can be argued that decisions which put certain workers in control of millions of pounds of capital, to which they have not themselves contributed, not only give those workers excessive power but also lead to an undervaluation of less capital intensive forms of work. We are therefore in the situation where no rigorous productivity theory of wages is valid, and where analysis of markets for labour begs the issue of how those markets are organized and controlled, for so they are by professional organizations, employers, the state and trades unions. Because of the habit of using market power which the unions have acquired, they have even begun to use the argument that a worker, unionized or not, owes his wages to the efforts of the union. Normally a worker is paid for *his* work, and the unions, apart from their special pleading, ought to consider whether they are aiming to achieve the wages the workers deserve, or to exploit the temporary power they may have. We therefore conclude that there is no substantial substitute for a system of wages which is based upon a moral evaluation of desert, especially in our highly structured economy. For example, we need first to realize that what a person 'earns' is the result of the productivity of the country at large. People in India and the USA performing identical tasks receive radically different wages because, with the division of labour, each person is dependent on all, or most of, the others, for his wage and standard of living. If we are members one of another in this way and if, with the division of labour, it is not possible to establish productivity, especially when it might reflect high levels of investment or monopoly prices, the idea of desert in the actual job is all that remains. There are obvious factors which lead to higher levels of recompense, like danger, long hours, poor working conditions, unpleasant job, uninteresting job, short holidays and more responsibility and others which deserve the reverse, like a safe job, short hours, a pleasant, interesting job, *etc*. Essentially, however, it is to some kind of moral evaluation on these terms that we are all forced to return. The solicitor gets higher pay than the bricklayer because he charges more and firmly controls his market, not for any 'objective' reasons. Interestingly, occupational status also has often been very important in shaping wages differentials and elevating the white-collar jobs and professions. Given our large-scale pattern of employment, there is a need to have a moral evaluation which allows shared establishment of desert.

Surprisingly, this approach is the only possible one, and the major problem is still making sure that the powerful do not grab the loot and justify it technically. The last word perhaps comes from Christ's parable of the vineyard. Although the parable is applicable to the whole of life, it is perhaps not wrong to reapply it to the employment situation. In the kingdom of God there is room for pay which is not just calculated desert, but is also a gift to those who need help.

'Take what belongs to you, and go; I choose to give to this last as I give to you. Am I not allowed to do what I choose with what belongs to me? Or do you begrudge my generosity?' (See Mt. 20:1–16).

Property An analysis of property cannot properly be carried out without making a distinction between personal consumption property and productive property, and there is a clear biblical perspective in both these areas.

Consumption property, or personal wealth, is seen as a danger for a variety of reasons. First, it is seductive. 'Where your treasure is, there will your heart be also, so do not lay up for yourselves treasures on earth' (Mt. 6:19–21). It is easy for a person's trust, ambition, pleasure and time to focus on wealth rather than on God; 'You cannot serve God and mammon' (Mt. 6:24). In case he has not been understood, Jesus makes the same point more forcefully: 'Again, I tell you, it is easier for a camel to go through the eye of a needle than for a rich man to enter the kingdom of God. When the disciples heard this they were greatly astonished, saying, "Who then can be saved?"' (Mt. 19:24, 25). The second danger is that the desire for wealth is a strong temptation to wrongdoing. From the cows of Bashan to the false prophets of Jeremiah, the pattern is continually revealed.

'From the least to the greatest of them, everyone is greedy for unjust gain;

and from prophet to priest, every one deals falsely.

They have healed the wound of my people lightly,

saying, "Peace, peace," when there is no peace' (Je. 6:13, 14). Adding field to field, the acquisitive instinct, is seen in biblical terms as a totally destructive motive, both individually and in social terms.

The contrary attitude which the Scriptures present is clear. Firstly, personal consumption property is to be respected as belonging to the owner. Stealing and coveting is forbidden. The result is that possessions are not to be allowed to come between or dominate interpersonal relationships. Secondly, it is expected that property will be used to help family and neighbours who have need. The precept that the Israelite was to lend to his brother who was in need (Dt. 23:19, 20) was part of the pattern in which a person's possessions were available to others, and not seen in a privatized and right-centred perspective. Thirdly, and most important, personal wealth was to be understood as a gift from God and this entailed both thanksgiving, a real gratitude that prosperity is given of the Lord, and also a willingness to give back to God and to others in the form of tithe and offering.

This perspective is in fundamental contrast with the perspective growing out of the 18th century landed gentry, which emphasized the *right* of a person to wealth and property. This view builds defences for the individual to protect himself against claims on his property and his giving, and it was used in this way throughout the 19th and early 20th centuries. The very slow and inadequate development of wealth taxes in Britain is substantially due to the fact that although income was later seen as being subject to redistribution, wealth was and is regarded as sacrosanct. At the same time it is this view of wealth that has contributed to the accumulation of capital into ever larger units which can be organized by the direction of those who own capital wealth. What is interesting is that the Mosaic pattern seems to have the opposite emphasis. Redistribution of wealth through the jubilee and other laws is given rather more weight than the redistribution of income, although the latter is present. We shall consider this more thoroughly as we look at productive property.[1]

[1] See A. B. Atkinson, *Unequal Shares* (Pelican, 1974); *The Economics of Inequality* (Clarendon Press, Oxford, 1975).

Today, property, land, capital and investment funds are all seen in different senses, but for the sake of this argument, we can use a more basic and primitive term, namely productive property. By this we mean that which enables a worker or a community to earn their living, the means of livelihood. In the Israelite and most pre-industrial societies, this would consist of land, cattle, sheep, *etc.*, while in more industralized economies, it would be predominantly forms of capital. The Mosaic law and the pattern of distribution of land described in Joshua 13–20 were such that the means of livelihood, the productive property, land, was equitably distributed among the population, and could not be permanently alienated from any family. The law of jubilee meant that throughout the country there must be a redemption of the land and a return to the original owners (Leviticus 25 and Numbers 36). There was also careful legislation about buying back land that had been temporarily sold (leased) to someone else, and the seven-yearly release from credit (Dt. 15:2) also prevented capital debts from accumulating. Thus the whole structure of distribution and legislation actively prevented the emergence of a stratum of poor people cut off from a means of livelihood. The hired servant (the employee or wage labourer) was meant to be relatively uncommon, and the emphasis throughout the law was towards helping families to achieve an independent means of livelihood, and against the accumulation of productive property.

This perspective is normative in principle for us to-day. The situation is changed in that what constitutes the means of livelihood has now become largely the complex and massive production units of modern industry, rather than familial or isolated ownership. We would argue that this trend is the result of the use of economic power as much as of criteria of efficiency, and that steps should be taken to see that it is reversed and a less anonymous pattern of ownership encouraged. Nevertheless, even this new form does not mean that families should not have productive property rather than being solely dependent on wage labour, which is the contemporary norm. We shall consider how this principle could be rearticulated in connection with the firm, and at this stage we shall merely look at the pathological nature of our present situation.

The socio-economic structure of Britain has been shaped by a number of periods of concentration of wealth and some of redistribution. In the 16th and 18th centuries the enclosure movements resulted in a slow eclipse of the yeoman and other independent landed groups, and by the early 19th century there were several developments of even greater significance. The unpropertied wage-labourer was becoming part of the economic order; economic power was being used by dominant firms to eliminate competition and concentrate capital; floating capital accumulated by the wealthy was on the move looking for lucrative rates of return. These developments were set in the context which, as George Goyder has pointed out, fundamentally distorts the meaning of capital—namely the right to a perpetual dividend which share capital has established for itself.[1] Thus, despite the more widespread diffusion of savings through redistribution and the development of institutional forms of investment, the holding and conception of capital has been considerably at variance with the Christian perspective in being more concentrated and more temporally absolute. The reforms that could be envisaged in the position of productive property will be considered later.

Economic freedom We have already looked at the central meaning of economic freedom, namely that man's open responsibility before God is not to be circumscribed by systems of slavery and control. Now we shall look at the concept in more analytical terms. First of all we note that economic life can exercise freedom or slavery over other aspects of life. Thus if politics is riddled with bribery and corruption, political freedom is lost to economic control. Similarly if marriage is dominated by brideprice or economic transactions, marital choice is circumscribed. However, economic development can also be a means of opening up freedom in these other areas. Welfare provisions only become possible with a certain level and kind of economic development. Freedom in marriage is strongly affected by housing. It is therefore crucial whether economic life develops by

[1] See G. Goyder, *The Future of Private Enterprise* (Oxford Univ. Press, 1951); *The Responsible Company* (Oxford Univ. Press, 1961).

exercising control over other aspects of life and starving them of resources, or whether it really does open up freedom in these areas. We have already considered, in chapter 9, the effects of the economy on family life.

It is also possible for other aspects of life to exercise control over economic life. Thus, the Roman Catholic church before the Reformation, through its ecclesiastical rules and payments, tried to exercise such a control. The absolutist system, identified with mercantilism, tried to do the same politically, and Adam Smith marks a breakaway from the tyranny of the idea that what is good for the state is good for the economy as a whole. Another more current example is that provided by specialist patterns of economic development. The evidence is difficult to assess, but there seems to be a large number of politically led development plans which have revealed major weaknesses later.[1] The political impetus behind Concorde is an example of a politico-economic flop. It seems that the attempts by Russian and other socialist states to take central political decisions about the economy weaken its effectiveness because all kinds of levels of economic freedom which are seriously needed are rendered inoperative. Conversely the state can hinder economic freedom by not providing the right legal framework in which companies, markets, *etc.*, can operate.

If we leave these external aspects of economic freedom and look at the internal aspect, we face one of the crucial issues of the day. Freedom in buying, in work or in design, is freedom from control (not freedom from discipline, effort, normative standards or responsibility), but increasingly economic systems are eliminating it by control because they believe this is the only viable way in which to operate. For example, much advertising aims to eliminate consumer freedom, as does much marketing. There are many examples of producers aiming to reduce the freedom of other producers by eliminating competition. Many unions aim to circumscribe the freedom of workers by establishing a closed shop. Many managers operate as tight a system of control over the workforce as they can; incentives, bonuses, pensions,

---

[1] See A. J. Storkey, *A Christian Perspective on Development and Aid* (Shaftesbury Project, 1973).

promotion, perks, all operate to make sure that the employee does what he should. This nexus is not the same as the traditional democratic/authoritarian antithesis because *formally* democratic systems may have very strong control elements, if the latter ethos is the dominant one. We would argue that there is less and less trust in personal responsibility and freedom, and more recourse to control mechanisms. It has already been shown that this is essentially a middle-class response based on the motives of fear, distrust and guilt (chapter 7), and one suspects that the trend will be for a continual erosion of the scope of freedom.

The meaning of freedom within an economic community needs to be defined. Workers who voluntarily agree to join a firm normally come under an authority structure which at present derives from the ownership of shares. Although this form of definition of work relationship, akin to the Old Testament hired servant, can be and often is, a fair one, we would argue that it is defective in that the basic standpoint of the Mosaic law is that of encouraging independence and economic freedom. Joining an economic unit should therefore be seen as akin to joining an economic community of free relationships, rather than joining an institution with an authority structure based on property. It is true that the community then establishes an authority structure, but this is based on the expertise of different groups of workers in performing their functions, not on *a priori* property rights. A firm which utilizes expertise at all levels is established on a much sounder basis than that which emphasizes property-based authority. It is clear that this perspective leads quite naturally to the idea of worker directors and patterns of common ownership, but it is important to define on what basis they are needed. They are not a power bloc defending the interests of one group, but they are a responsible part of an economic community where expertise-based authority is very necessary. Sadly, the history of industrial relations in Britain does not suggest that such a perspective can easily take root, although the spiritual vision of some has already led in this direction.[1]

---

[1] Christian Industrial Enterprises Ltd. has, for example, formed a common ownership group which radically breaks away from these existing patterns towards a Christian pattern of work.

We note finally that economic freedom is not self-serving indulgence. There is a tendency for the economic ideal of many to be maximum leisure and minimum work, with the goals of pleasure, comfort and material well-being. The search for amusement is endless; indigestion, hangovers and boredom become major problems in life. It is not only that people *do* behave this way sometimes, but that utilitarianism and other theories of consumption assume that this is the way people do and should behave. This individualist fallacy, powerful though it is in our society, is completely at odds with the Scriptural view of economic freedom, which is freedom to serve God and other people, and which involves self-discipline, responsibility, competence, hard work, efficiency and frustration. The West is littered with the secularized remains of the Protestant work ethic, and few seem to realize that the best test of the authentic value of their work is not their pay, but what they actually contribute to the welfare of others over the years. That the development of a parasitic self-serving attitude severely restricts the economic freedom of others is obvious.

The firm and production   It is easy for the central meaning of production in firms to get lost, for few people can accurately define what it is. In principle, it is *not* to maximize profits, or growth, or to establish a secure position, but it *is* to provide goods and services for other people. Production comes within the scope of loving one's neighbour as oneself. His needs are defined in various markets and the firm produces to meet that need. This principle, has, however, been ignored for a long while and, as a result, various developments have occurred which affect the structure and direction of firms. It is often argued that because firms can only succeed if they meet the needs of the public successfully; the end result is the same as if service had been the main motive; but this is not the case.

The dominant conception of the firm in the West has been capitalist in the sense that the unit has been identified with the shareholders, the providers of capital, and their interest. Their interest has in turn been seen as the maximization of profit and therefore of dividends. This view of the firm was dominant until the 1930s and its effects were as follows. Firstly, the power of shareholding capital was enhanced over the productive process, because capital/finance was the key to industrial control. Secondly, the conception of the firm which identified it with the shareholders, and which narrowed the policy goals to their self-interests, created a backlash among worker organizations which aimed to establish power over the employers by utilizing productive power. Thirdly, it led in the late 19th century to a drastic increase in the size of companies, as firms sought for monopoly power and control of (falling) prices by creating monopolies. In the 20th century, this pattern has in part been superseded, but it could be argued that these three characteristics still continue in a different form in the modern corporation. The power of finance, the management/worker antithesis and market control are key facets of it.

The changes that have taken place derive essentially from the preceding ethos. Thus, the managerial revolution, first identified by Berle & Means in 1932,[1] although it marked a change of emphasis in that managers were more closely allied with the productive process, was also a continuation of the capitalist-financial ethos; managers were quite sure that they were primarily there to fulfil certain well-defined financial aims. Again, the form of financial control has changed. After the 1930s the pattern of holding companies and pyramids began to wane, and there was a sense in which finance went within the company. Take-over and conglomerates meant that rather than a shareholder arranging his portfolio of companies, boards of directors were involved in arranging their portfolio of production enterprises. At the same time the development of the big institutional investors, like pension funds and insurance companies, meant that the financial logic which they required was largely followed by the board. Again, although growth has been identified as the modern corporate goal, it is largely because it is so closely associated with profits. Thus the importance of the key financial indicator has not diminished, even though non-major share-holders are passive in most corporations; it is now the rate of return on capital.

[1] A. A. Berle and G. C. Means, *The Modern Corporation and Private Property* (Commerce Clearing House, N.Y., 1932).

But how is this defined? Is it the residue after fixed costs like raw materials, wages, *etc.*, are taken from revenue? Is it the difference that investment makes to output and revenue? Should it be discounted by the rate of interest at which funds are borrowed, and if so, should variations in that rate be taken into account? The fact is that there is no satisfactory way of isolating investment decisions from the full production process. Whatever the managers and financiers might think, they are undertaking a full corporate production decision in which capital plays only a part, and they are making the decision on the basis of faith in the workforce, the product, the technology, the state of the market, and a range of other factors. In other words, there is often a commitment to purely financial analysis and calculation of a spuriously rigorous kind, transposed from financial markets where funds can easily be moved around, which is merely a sophisticated version of the old profit motive. However, in reality investment decisions are very much more firmly rooted in relation to a workforce, plant, product and market. Yet, given the pattern of control, firms are able to act as if capital was an isolated factor in their accounting and their relations with shareholders. Part of the problem lies with the structure of the capital market: the fluctuations that can occur in capital values and dividends, the exclusive power of share ownership in company control and the way in which the return of capital is isolated. What is needed therefore is a redefinition of the meaning of capital within the structure of the firm and within the Stock Exchange, and this we shall attempt later.

The second area of change, but also of continuity, is the bifurcation of the working community into employers and employees. The change has largely been one of the growth of the power and organization of the trades unions. Here we face a failure of the unions to understand their historical significance. The 19th century unions were born into an economic situation where economic exploitation of the workforce was widespread. Their *raison d'être* was economic justice. Apart from the Co-operative Movement, there was little attempt at independent economic activity, and the unions therefore grew up dependent on the property-owning and managerial groups in industry, but increasingly powerful in relation to them. By the mid-1970s it was evident in some industries that the level of wages was so high that losses were being made and substantial government subsidies were needed to pay the wages. Given this situation, it is possible to envisage that the unions' role as defenders of economic justice preventing the exploitation of the workforce is largely a passive one.

But what then is their *raison d'être*? It could be argued that the most obvious way forward is for the unions to seek to establish a more communal pattern of industrial organization which supersedes the capitalist model and to dissolve into it, or at least radically redefine its institutional role. However, the unions are too well-developed institutionally to begin to dissolve, and they are also too reactionary in the sense that their policies have for decades been reactions to management rather than based on any positive normative model of the firm. We are therefore now in an era when the Bullock Report crystallizes the problems which our industrial system has generated for decades. The failure of both groups to be able to visualize and realize the meaning of an economic community is predictable because of the patterns of self-interest, control and power manipulation which have been internalized.

The monopoly aspect of firms has shown a similar pattern of development. The capitalist emphasis on maximizing profit produced the old monopolist problem that a price was charged in excess of the average cost of the product (including return on capital). Attempts were made to create various systems which could contain the problem, especially systems for ensuring competition, but these have had very limited success. The failure is partly related to the fact that a positivist approach confuses size and monopoly (firms which are big enough to create a monopoly position do not necessarily act as monopolies) and partly because the firms do not play the competitive games they were asked to, or play and win. The crucial point is that monopoly is not a technical, positive situation which can be eliminated by engineering, but it is a *motive* which has and can surface in innumerable different forms. Guilds, trading companies, churches, and railroads have all tried to engineer different kinds of monopoly and then exploit it, but all the attempts to control various forms, important though these are, do not get close to the root motive.

This is no different from the motive which is supposed to operate under perfect competition, the aim of maximizing one's own profit, except that perfect competition assumes identical conditions, but the monopoly motive involves exploiting a *unique* economic situation, or creating a situation which the firm can exploit. The definition of monopoly therefore requires a careful delineation of what constitutes fair or unfair uses of unique economic situations, and this is an underdeveloped branch of economics because of the classical emphasis on positivist, *general* economic statements.

The practices that come within this definition are recognized by those in the situation. They include pre-emptive take-overs, using locational advantages, control of raw materials, equipment, retail outlets, deliberate over-production to eliminate rivals, temporary underpricing, dual or multiple pricing systems, restrictive agreements, inducing market under-production, engineering technological monopolies, payments to persons rather than for goods and services, monopolizing advertizing, creating tied customers, exploiting the potential economic inconvenience of others, using weaknesses of consumers, and using political, social and even legal methods of obtaining an advantage. These practices, with careful definition, need to be categorized as unfair, and the normative issues in a firm's activities faced.

However, reform cannot be predominantly legal, because the root problem is the guiding internal motive of the firm. The true motive, we have argued, is the service of others by the provision of goods and services, which is an economic extension of the great command to love one's neighbour as oneself. Motives cannot be changed by structural reforms, but structures can represent certain motives. In the October 1974 General Election, the Christian Party Manifesto suggested that public companies should be required to elect one-third of their board from representatives chosen by the consumers. It would be possible for interested consumers to choose their directors at annual meetings in a parallel form to the shareholders meeting, and for these representatives to have substantial authority within the company to reinstate the norm of service and keep prices down. We would argue that in an era when monopolies are more and more inevitable, giving consumers authority within a company is the obvious way to prevent an eclipse of the consumer's concerns.

As well as a redirection of the basic motive, there is also a need to break through the antagonism of capital and labour caused by the pattern of control that developed especially in the 19th century. This means that the communal nature of an enterprise has to be structurally expressed. Authority within a firm rests on the agreement of a community (*i.e.* some degree of permanence is involved) to allow direction of their economic activity. It is therefore obvious that both workers and providers of capital should elect their representatives to the directing board. However, and this is perhaps the weakness of the Bullock Report, this movement is different in a radical way from the capital/labour antagonism, and it also marks the end of trade unionism as it is conventionally understood. It must be emphasized that it should be the working members of the economic community who elect representatives, and not the trades unions, for the latter are often not representative, deny the communal principle and are constructed as *external* pressure groups.

It would seem, therefore, that a more soundly principled directing structure for a public company than that which exists at present is a tripartite board with one third of its members elected by consumer's associations, one-third by employees and one-third by providers of capital.

It is worth noting that this pattern would not only tend to reduce the controlling position of finance, weaken the labour/capital antagonism and curb the excesses of monopoly power, but it would also change one of two other patterns within the firm. One common complaint of shareholders is that they are often expected to take all the risks of enterprise, but are begrudged the rewards of taking the risk. In the next section we shall look at ways in which the structure of the stock market can be reformed, and we also suggest that there is nothing particularly virtuous in the speculative gambling which results from massive changes in the capital value of shares. However, it is also true that employees, as members of an economic enterprise sharing in decision-taking, should share in risk. At present, the risk is only the terminal one of redundancy, but there is no reason why, either through a system of worker shares or through wage variations, employees should not share risks more than they do at present.

It still needs to be remembered that the formal structure of the firm cannot guarantee a serving economic community. It needs also forgiveness, a concern for fairness, the breakdown of fear, patterns of control, manipulation and opposition, and an education into the meaning of free responsibility and the norms of educational activity. Much in our culture actively thwarts this possibility.

Capital We have already described capital as productive wealth, and it is evident that there is much in a Christian perspective on economic life which predisposes people to use wealth productively rather than ostentatiously or for self-gratification. Exercising dominion over the creation involves using tools, stewarding, patiently waiting, maintenance and manufacture and it is natural within a perspective of faithful stewardship that 'capital' should develop. But here we notice the fallacy of monolithic 'capital', plastic and with established rates of return. Monolithic capital does not exist for the following reasons. Firstly, embodied 'capital' is as heterogeneous as is imaginable; apart from their intermediary role, there is nothing that a spade, grain, an aluminium smelter, a van, a filing cabinet and a tree have in common. Moreover, it is absolutely impossible to convert one into the other. Secondly, 'capital' itself needs to be created, and this presupposes capital goods industries, which are again specific and rarely able to convert their production. Each of these, whether it is a separate sector of an industry or whether it is part of the firms operating within that industry, constitutes a body of specific knowledge, expertise, experience and theory which is unique and rich in ways which the monolithic capital concept completely misses. It is in this area that the faith underlying an industry finds expression as decisions are made about the development of one technical possibility or another. The variations and possible variations are limitless. Which ones are taken up cannot be decided by a simplistic concept like the rate of return on capital, for this concept absolves the economic unit of all positive responsibility in deciding where to commit its resources, and assumes that that which the market rewards is right. Again, we note that the wealth available for investment has tended to be concentrated in relatively few hands, and this gives a spurious impression of a homogeneous body of funds available as liquid 'capital'. Apart from the issue of redistribution, which we looked at under the heading *property*, this begs several different questions. In the first place owners have the freedom to decide whether to use their resources themselves or to commit them to others, and they also have the freedom to decide to whom and on what terms they are prepared to pass over their resources. This involves far more than variations in the term of loans and the risk involved. Its importance is considerable. Ignoring these facts has tended to make our capital markets spuriously liquid and therefore very unstable.

For the economic reality is that the commitment of resources to a particular economic enterprise is a serious long-term act of faith. However, the present financial mirror of this is of a distorted, liquid, unstable gambling joint. The structure of the Stock Exchange is a perversion of the nature of the 'capital' enterprise. There are a number of reforms which would correct this situation. One, growing out of George Goyder's important Christian analysis,[1] is the recognition that the life of a share should be limited to something like the life of the capital which it represents. The share has no right to immortality, and the claims of the owner who committed the resources should die at roughly the same time as the resources themselves. This would have the effect of reducing the capital value fluctuations of most shares and putting more weight on the dividend payments—a great improvement on the present situation. However, there is another change which needs to be made, for the responsible use of capital necessarily implies personal involvement rather than anonymity. It is the establishment of a rule which restricts the liquidity of share capital, for the commitment of funds should be deeper than the present system involves. There are several possible restrictions, for example that shares should be held for a minimum of one or two years, and/or that six months or some other period of notice should be required for share transactions. Also the cost of share transfer could be substantially increased. The point is that the possibility of funds flooding in and out of the share market needs

[1] G. Goyder, *The Responsible Company* (Oxford Univ. Press, 1961).

to be severely restricted, so that it corresponds with the responsible investment decisions that are made in industry. There are, of course, many people in the City who could not see beyond their immediate requirements and interests to this deeper meaning of capital, but the meaning matters most.

'Capital' is wasted on an enormous scale. Millions of pounds are spent on plant which is obsolete, redundant or unutilized. At the same time there is a poverty of resources that is glaringly apparent in various areas. This instability and unevenness in the use of resources points to a variety of elements that are awry in investment patterns. One is that competitive, high technology often leads to an over-commitment of resources. Another is that there are often periods when companies reap high profits and there are therefore massive funds which are available for investment and are used. Again, given the constant fluctuations, investment often has to be short-term and immediate, with the result that the accelerator principle accentuates the fluctuations.

The pattern that has built up constantly puts pressures on managers to make defective investment decisions. Yet to some extent the instability in capital markets, levels of effective demand trade patterns and which create these problems can be minimized, since they are often caused by economic obsession with profit and growth which can be put in a longer-term, less obsessive context if, for example, the Stock Exchange were more stable in its capital values and risk was more widely shared.

A final point of importance in relation to 'capital' is that the present structure of the Stock Exchange is that of a market for dead capital, in that it merely absorbs funds into old issues, which do not provide any new funds for the actual investing companies. This means that at various periods there are substantial funds which are sunk into the inflated values of dead capital and which give no direct help to the firms themselves whose capital the shares represent. It is true that high share values make it easier for them to raise funds, but it is difficult to pretend that this market for dead capital operates with the greatest efficiency or responsibility. There is therefore good reason for a substantial redefinition of the meaning of 'capital' and a reform of the structure of shares and the share market.

Markets and exchange   The common view of the market in the West is of a free competitive system in which buyers can bid for the lowest prices and sellers for the highest. The emphasis is individualist, all participants are assumed to be acting from self-interest and the framework is anomic; it is merely a technical means of transfer. The classical contention is that such free markets, where each buyer or seller pursues his own self-interest, result in the greater good of all, since there is a motivation to produce better commodities, more efficient production and lower prices. This classical, literal view is still the basic rationale of the Western market system, even though it is evidently no more than a half-truth and, despite the abundant weaknesses of this perspective, few liberal economists appeal to any other.

However, there is an alternative which is rooted in the biblical view of exchange and which was developed in some depth by the Schoolmen and the Reformers.[1] Exchange is seen in the Scriptures in normative terms as a transaction undertaken for the good of both parties which is to be marked by fairness—just balances and no control of one party by the other. Contemporary economic theorists have tended to look at the Schoolmen and Reformers for a labour theory of value, but one of their main concerns was a normative understanding of the more anonymous markets which were then developing. This, then, is the crucial element. Although in modern markets the relationships are anonymous, they are no less normatively qualified. Seller is serving buyer, and sellers are to be scrupulously fair in relation to one another. There is no simple doctrine of the just price, because a complex of issues bears upon the free transactions of buyers and sellers, but it remains a key concern in any market. When we realize that a market is a community, *i.e.* a free association of people who permanently join together under various norms, we can see that the normative structure of markets is really the concern of all who are involved in them. Thus there is a whole range of moral issues which need working out at local, national, and international levels. What about prices in markets with big

---

[1] See J. A. Schumpeter, *A History of Economic Thought* (Oxford Univ. Press, 1954) and also M. N. Rothbard, 'Late Mediaeval Origins of Free Market Economic Thought', *The Journal of Christian Reconstruction*, II, 1975, pp. 62–75.

natural variations in supply and inelastic demand? Can stocks be used to create greater stability? Are consumers or producers establishing control over the market to their own ends? Where large natural surpluses exist for some producers, how should these be distributed? Does one nation put a higher priority on the output of one set of producers than comes from world markets, and why? Are markets fair and service-orientated? To what extent do power and control limit the freedom of the market community? Should the weakness of the third world countries to command high labour and other costs allow low market prices to be established, or is there a moral commitment to international standards of reward? What size should markets be: can they be too small and too big? What obligations upon buyers and sellers does membership of a market community involve? There are many more such issues which need to be carefully considered with full moral integrity.

The natural situation that exists in the West, however, is that many markets are fundamentally corrupt. It is not only the outright bribery that has become evident recently in the aircraft, automobile and armaments industries, but also the systematic attempts of many major companies to subvert markets to their own ends. This constitutes a major crisis of the so-called free market economy of the West and, sadly, academic economists have contributed to it by insisting on an anormative positive approach to markets which implies that any self-interested manipulation of them is legitimate. The state of play in different markets varies, but in many of them managers find that the jungle has replaced any kind of normative order. Another fundamental defect in Western, humanist, economic life continues to fester.

At the same time, general market analysis ignored crucial differences in the structure of markets for different goods and services. The housing market, where the annual output is about one-fiftieth of the total stock, is very different from the market in soft fruit. Further, there are substantial differences in markets where demand is from high or low income groups, from mobile or immobile consumers, and is frequent or irregular. Also, whether demand is rooted in addiction, need, is instrumental, pleasure-based, or subject to fashion changes the meaning of the market further. In most markets, there are experienced people who can see the structure of the market and the way normative principles can be applied in that particular one. This kind of generic knowledge is valuable and there is a need for standards and norms of operation to be established within the various markets through its application. In some cases this already obtains, but in many the need is great.

Money   There was a time when money was seen as the standard of value, against which all goods and services could be measured. In our inflationary era, we are apt to forget that the value of money in terms of other goods and services, although it fluctuated significantly, actually rose during the 19th century. The gold standard, where the legal tender circulation was mainly sovereigns and gold-backed notes, also gave this feeling of objectivity to money. A quite recent text-book could still describe it in these terms:

> 'Money is not only the *thing* with which we pay for goods and services; it is also the scale in which we measure their value. Money provides a scale of pounds, shillings and pence by which we can make comparisons of value, just as a thermometer provides a scale of degrees centigrade by which we can make comparisons of temperature.'[1]

This kind of statement now sounds very dated. Inflation means that money is not the criterion of value, but is valued less and less each year. Moreover, it is obvious that there is a market for money in which its price fluctuates like that of any other commodity which changes in supply and demand.

This change, although it is by no means a new phenomenon, poses an interesting dilemma for economists. As long as money could act as some kind of absolute standard of value, with the same kind of objective status as the centigrade scale, it was possible to see economics as an autonomous discipline, because it contained an inherent standard of values. However, when money no longer has this status, the autonomy of economics is threatened, because it is apparent that values are imported from outside, and that the discipline is dependent on these values. Thus the autonomous science wobbles.

[1] A. Cairncross, *Introduction to Economics* (Butterworth, 1966), p. 443.

However, for people generally, the development is disconcerting, for their faith in money as some kind of absolute standard is shaken, and they are only left, it is generally assumed, with the alternative of relativism. It is easy to feel that, since there are no firm standards of economic valuation, values are merely what a buyer or seller can get in a particular market. There is little doubt that this kind of attitude, which often gains currency during periods of high inflation, because it attacks people's understanding of economic value, is extremely corrosive. It is not only that accountants find themselves having to make impossible decisions, but that the general feeling develops that prices are ephemeral and do not reflect normative values. The process of creating anormative markets is speeded up. Thus the dire warnings that are repeatedly made about inflation are not without foundation; fundamental economic relativism is dangerous.

Yet the alternatives of an absolute standard of value and relativism are both false, and until money is conceived on a different basis, there is little hope of a better situation. The initial point is a recognition that money is not *the* standard of value. It is not the basic element in economics, and has no claim to any absolute status. Rather, we need to recognize that money gets its meaning at the exchange interface. It is a standard of *exchange* value. In an economic community, where people's valuation of goods and services differs widely, money is used to reflect exchange values in anonymous exchange relationships. Prices mediate communal values, and they must necessarily be *fair* prices in normative markets. Thus, the value which money represents is not inherent, but is derived from the attitudes, preferences, priorities and commitments of the community at large. In passing, it is worth remembering how Christ was prepared to dismiss the absolute value of money when he observed the poor widow putting her two small coins into the treasury. His comment was:

'Truly, I say unto you, this poor widow has put in more than all those who are contributing to the treasury. For they all contributed out of their abundance; but she out of her poverty has put in everything she had, her whole living' (Mk. 12:43, 44). Christ's absolute standards put the standard that we are looking at very much in context.

If we return to consider the fairness of money exchange, it is clear that this depends considerably on who creates money and how much they create. The automatic constraints of a gold standard have been removed since World War I, and recently we have seen two other motives affecting monetary policy apart from the desire to maintain fair exchange relationships. One is the aim of using monetary policy to stimulate the economy into higher rates of growth, and the other is that of increasing the resources available to the public sector without immediately facing the cost in terms of taxation. For when money is created, the creator through exchange has access to resources which have effectively cost him nothing. Thus we have had the situation recently where the state, which has the primary function of maintaining fairness and justice, has actually undermined fair exchange relationships because its monetary policies were biased towards the public sector.

It is also worth noting the significance of the banks in this process of money creation. Although they are subject to constraints, the banks are able to create and amortize money on a large scale. Moreover, their ability to do so has been considerably enhanced since the introduction of Competition and Credit Control in 1971 reduced the reserve ratios they need to hold. It is arguable that the banks have no more right to create money than private citizens, and that the extent to which the present system allows this gives a great sectoral advantage to the clearing banks which is scarcely fair. They should, perhaps, be taxed on the basis of this money/credit they create, so that they do not continually reap this windfall which is especially high during inflationary periods.

At the same time the emphasis on credit-based transfer which the banks give to the economic system creates another range of socio-economic problems. One is that people receiving credit are predisposed to inflation. Another is that credit has tended to be channelled in certain directions—consumer durables, property, appreciating stock and raw materials—with the effect that fluctuations of demand and often of prices tend to be great in these areas. The extent to which our economy is based upon credit is an important index which is not considered carefully enough today.

Consumption   The contrast between the biblical injunction to be content with what you have (Heb. 13:5) in the confidence that, 'Your God will provide all your needs', and the acquisitive, limitless wants of utilitarianism and materialism has been often recognized. Christ's message was, 'Do not be anxious about material things' (Matthew 6) but the message of our culture is, 'Be anxious above all about material things.' What is the difference between the Christian perspective and that of this other perspective? The key, it could be argued, lies in the meaning of pleasure and happiness. When a person aims to get pleasure from the consumption of goods and services, and when he sees the pleasure obtainable as proportional to the goods and services which he can appropriate, a subtle change takes place in his relationship with material goods. First, the meaning of the goods and services is egocentrically defined—they are for my pleasure—and the result of this process is that the subject cannot consider or be aware of their intrinsic value in his concern with what pleasure they will give him. Further, *possession* becomes vital within this framework, because it is the way of making sure that the object yields its pleasure to me (and by implication, only me). Thus, in the end, this philosophical and practical motive yields only dust. The search for pleasure which is religiously self-centred and possessive prevents enjoyment because the intrinsic and independent value of what is appropriated gets lost. It is amazing how many people one can see trying to enjoy forms of consumption which they feel they should enjoy, especially in view of the cost, and failing miserably. This point is beautifully analysed by the Preacher; without losing his wisdom he said to himself, '"Come now, I will make a test of pleasure; enjoy yourself" But behold, this also was vanity' (Ec. 2:1). There is little doubt that much of our economic culture is in the grip of this pleasure motive. People's hearts are sold to pleasure, however costly the process, and the search is inevitably one that is frustrated. Again, they come up against the underlying humanist weakness: man cannot independently make his own pleasure, he can only receive from the hand of God.

For the fact is that although we receive many good gifts from God and from other people, they are only enjoyable as gifts from God, and when they come to hold any central place in a person's life, replacing the centrality of his relationship with God, they both restrict the subjective identity of the person—an addict is a pathetic example of this—and also the object or gift is expected to have characteristics which are beyond its nature. Conversely, when we recognize that God is the giver of all, there is no need to appropriate, we merely receive from him what he has given, and the gift implies thankfulness and praise. This point is a repetition of what Christ said so incisively in the Sermon on the Mount: 'Blessed are the meek for they shall inherit the earth' (Mt. 5:5). One aspect of this teaching is perhaps that those who do not appropriate and grab, but receive from God what he gives, do in fact inherit the earth. It is not the great landowner who enjoys the view, the rich who enjoy the warmth or the lazy who enjoy sleep.

At the same time we now have to recognize that the present Western ethos of consumption will have to change, in that the demands on resources made by the way we want to live just cannot be met. Britain may experience a reprieve through North Sea oil, but she is a dependent nation needing in the long-run a substantial redefinition of her pattern of consumption. A Christian alternative has been opened on one front by John Taylor's study, *Enough is Enough* (SCM Press, 1971) but there is a range of other problems involved here which are more structural. One is that the consumers are continually under pressure within our economy as the great passive force. They are the least organized sector of the whole economy, and as a result, their decisions are essentially *post facto* decisions to buy or not to buy existing commodities or services. The added weight of advertizing and marketing techniques, which practise various techniques of consumer captivity, make the passivity even more emphatic. In addition, in a high technology, specialized economy, much consumption is interdependent; buying X necessarily involves buying Y, and the consumer's freedom is further restricted. Again, there is a great deal of consumption which is addictive; indeed, this seems to be the aim of many producers, and it is not easy for a single consumer to defeat these forces. The productive side of the economy and its organization also involves the consumer in a range of necessary forms of consumption like travel to work, status costume, wining and dining, *etc.* Moreover, some of the most wasteful forms of consumption take place in corporate rather than individual forms, especially as a form of evasion of direct taxation. Another problem is that for various reasons related to the organization of recycling techniques, the prices of 'waste' resources are often too low and the cost of disposal is also artificially low. These issues need tackling, not only by giving consumers powers within companies, but also by deinstitutionalizing wasteful forms, and using the price system with an eye to social rather than private costs.

For the key problem with the traditional approach to free market transactions and patterns of consumption is that the assumption that they are isolated, individual choices just does not hold. This has recently been highlighted by the skateboard craze in Britain. A person buys a skateboard from the manufacturer at a price, but should the manufacturer not also provide safety equipment and skateboard parks for their use within the sale price if the social costs of that transaction are not to fall on other areas? At a more important level there is a whole range of goods the consumption or use of which has important effects on the lives of others. Cars have effects on noise, safety, pollution, the size and organization of cities and neighbourhoods; those having holidays in Spain are indirectly creating noise and fear for those living near an airport, and people who enjoy motor boats and water skiing effectively ruin fishing and swimming for others. Thus a substantial number of consumption decisions constrain the way in which other people live. Moreover, the rich are very adept at avoiding the unpleasant aspects of their own and other people's consumption, while the poor tend to finish up with the noise, lead, smoke, danger and constraints. The problem is a complex one, but one way in which it could be tackled, which respected consumer choice and took account of these social and environmental effects, is to levy indirect taxes which are seen as compensatory. For example, a tax on skateboards to cover hospital costs and the cost of parks, or on cars to provide relatively safe bicycle transport. The problem is that at present consumers get many goods too cheaply, considering the real costs they involve for others.

There is another aspect to our personal attitude to consumption which creates a further blockage. A corollary of the view of consumption which sees it as conferring positive utility is the attitude to work which sees it as involving negative utility. In other words, the attitude to consumption is part of a process in which work is evacuated of meaning. The studies of Goldthorpe *et al.* show the extent to which an instrumental view of work was operative in the factories studies.[1] However, the process is two-way; if work is meaningless for a worker, he will tend to retreat into extra-work leisure and consumption for satisfaction, and the drive towards higher consumption will therefore be stronger. It is possible that the consumption ethos current in the modern urban environment is partly rooted in the conditions and structure of work that many people experience.

Thus, in all these areas that we have investigated, a Christian perspective leads in new and different directions, and the assumed neutrality of much contemporary economic thinking is merely a statement that these views are dogmas which are seen as beyond criticism. With this groundwork on a Christian perspective on the economy, we shall briefly consider the relationship between the economy and other sectors of life.

The economy and the state

We are now in a position to define more carefully the relative positions of the state and the economy within this perspective. The state's God-given role, it was suggested in Chapter 11, was to exercise justice in other areas by law, judgment and punishment. The method of operation was not that of control, but through law upholding people's responsibility to one another. Within this framework, law does not limit freedom except the freedom of evil, but provides proper protection for people's social and economic relationships with one another. The authority of the law rests on God's laws for his creation, and the agencies of the state are merely forming and administering the positive law to which they are also subject.

At the same time we have outlined how the economy is also a normative order, where man exercises his responsibility before God and to his fellow-men. Corresponding to this normative

---

[1] See J. H. Goldthorpe *et al.*, *The Affluent Worker* (Cambridge Univ. Press, (1968–9).

order, there is a proper legal basis for economic institutions, which lays down the good and fair economic relationships that should obtain between institutions and individuals. Responsibility and freedom in economic activity is responsibility before God, and is not to be seen as subject to the control of other people or of other institutions like the state.

However, what we actually experience in Britain is a serious distortion of this relationship. Because of the historical weight of a *laissez-faire* view of economics, there has been a very weak development of the legal structure of economic institutions. This has been true of firms, especially, and also of trades unions, who still seem to consider freedom from legislation as a right. There has also been weak legislation on the redistribution of wealth, the definition of capital, the creation of money and the structure of markets. The net effect of this legal vacuum has been that the strong have gained over the weak and economic power has tended to eclipse the economic freedom.

However, it has also produced a well-intentioned but misguided reaction. The state has been used as a countervailing power against the large economic corporations, and through the take-over of nationalized industries and firms has tried to put right the misuse of monopoly powers. That the state can run an industry more efficiently and that state support is necessary to ailing industries have also been used to justify this intervention.[1] At the same time the state (government) has been held increasingly responsible for the state of the economy, and has been expected to intervene and control not only macroeconomic fluctuations, but also strategically to offer incentives and disincentives in all the different corners of the economy.

Thus relations between the economy and the state are hung on a false antinomy: either Conservative *laissez-faire* or Socialist state intervention. An alternative which has been historically ignored is legal definition but not control. It is disturbing how widespread is the acceptance of the idea of state control, simply because most people see no alternative to private (capitalist) or public (state) control. Yet the fact that representation of consumers by *legal* right on the board of say British Rail or the

[1] See pp. 328–30 for parallel discussion of this.

Post Office is a much more efficient system of public account-ability than the tenacious links through elections, Prime Ministers, Cabinets and Ministers, suggests that the alternative could be developed.

At the same time we need to see that the economy can wrongly intrude into the process of legislation and administering justice. The political system can be made corrupt by the misuse of economic power. Thus, in the USA, the size and power of giant corporations has led to a series of world-wide political scandals involving political corruption. The attitude, 'What's good for General Motors is good for the country', can easily lead to this kind of involvement. At another level, it is surely a problem that when most political parties must in theory aim for some kind of impartiality, many of them are so closely tied to a major economic interest. Again, when Britain was deciding to enter the Common Market (and to remain in it), it was noticeable that the large multinational corporations were the groups showing most enthusiasm for the change and arguing the case most articulately. Their activity was entirely legitimate, but it was evident that the Common Market framework would give them greater freedom from national constraints and would change the relationship between large-scale capital and the British political institutions. It is easy for a dual system of understanding to operate when economic interests are strong in politics; at one level economic groups decide what is in their interest, and at another level a propagandist rationale is given to the poor fools who vote. The long-term damage this does is incalculable.

There are other points that arise involving the scope of economics. A few years back there was a debate about selling arms to South Africa, but few have questioned the practice of selling arms for commercial reasons. Britain is a large-scale supplier of arms, often to both sides of a local confrontation, provided that the buyers are able to pay for them. Yet if the manufacture and use of arms is by its very nature a political issue, because they are only to be used in defence of just relationships, it would seem that the commercial marketing of arms is in principle wrong. It is possible that within a few years we shall witness large-scale international murder carried out with British-made weapons. It is sad that the political principle is so easily overridden by commercial zeal and our weak balance of payments position.

One final point is that it is very easy for a state to form its international policy on the basis of economic expediency and interests, rather than on political principle. That this was patently the case during the colonial period is obvious, and it can be argued that World War I was born out of the conflict of colonial economic interests. More recently, we saw how all the European countries except Holland responded to the third Arab-Israeli war purely on the basis of their dependence on Arab oil. Internal economic weakness can easily lead to the burying of political principles.

The economy and society

The degree of penetration of economic activities into various areas of social life also differs, and it is not easy to understand how the two spheres are related in principle.

We have already looked at marriage and the family in relation to economics, and have seen that money cannot buy love and that exchange relationships are excluded from these institutions. The same kind of principle operates in other areas.

In a neighbourhood, if somebody wants to borrow a lawnmower, there is no question of asking him to pay for it, because the social norm is one of mutual help and the response will therefore be, 'Yes or no', not, 'How much will you pay?' A community therefore operates on a different normative principle from the economy; rather than exchange, the principle is one of personal care and concern. The issue therefore is the extent to which a community is prepared to share its resources and the extent to which it is open. Often the individualism which dominates much of British social life is wasteful; for example, it is not uncommon for an estate of 400 houses to have spent £80,000 on gardening equipment, when with a little consultation they could easily have saved £40,000 of that. Thus, a key issue is the extent to which a community is prepared to share resources freely. However, it could be argued that the present debate in this area has been oversimplified and insensitive, partly because the principle of communal care has been inaccurately identified with the activity of the state. The concept of the welfare state is a misnomer; it really means that there is communal support for various forms of care which have therefore been given a permanent legislative basis.

Let us consider an example which outlines some of the issues in this area. If we regard care in sickness as part of the love which we ought to have for our neighbour (and in view of Christ's own life and example and the parable of the good Samaritan, it is difficult for the Christian to do otherwise), then the formation of a National Health Service is meaningful and natural. It would be wrong for the community to allow health services to be provided on a market exchange basis. We note that this principle is rather different from the more individualistic one of health insurance practised in the USA. However, we also note that the National Health Service is not the *state* Health Service for to identify with the state is to miss the point; it is not a *political* institution, but an expression of social care, staffed by those trained to serve in this way and funded communally. The criticism could be made that the occasional inappropriateness of the state system of ministerial control, and the uneasy status of the Health Service as a public corporation, reflect some of this confusion. At the same time there is pressure to pull the health service into the market sector, with doctors and nurses preferring private practice and clients who pay, and private abortion clinics making huge profits. (What are the salaries of doctors in private abortion clinics?)

Another area where the same kind of confusion occurs is education. This is described as *state* education, but as we have already suggested, education is a family-based institution. To some extent it was and is a market service in that some people were prepared to pay for private education and schools developed to meet this demand. However, there was a strong tradition which goes back to John Knox's *Fifth Book of Discipline* which sees education as something which should be freely available for all, irrespective of whether they could afford it or not. Other reformers, like Shaftesbury with his Ragged Schools, recognized later that education is not something just for the rich who can afford it, but that a normal part of communal care is the provision of education for all. When funded schools did at last arrive in Britain, it was largely within the framework of a state system of control. However, it is arguable that there are many other possible systems of accountability and funding than those which involve state control.

Since this area of secondary economics is often rather neglected, it is worth considering ways in which communal enterprises can be funded. Donations, covenants, subscriptions membership fees, levies, flat or graduated rates are all used to support organizations which have a primarily social aim, and which are only secondarily economic. The contributions may be, and need to be, legally imposed, but this does not change their character from being communally rooted. Traditionally, many Christian organizations have this social basis and are not part of the market exchange economic system, and it is important that Christians should be quite clear about the foundation and structure of these non-commercial, but communally supported institutions.

We see therefore that the issue of the scope of exchange and market economic activity is a crucial one. It is easy for commercial, i.e. primarily economic forms, to extend their scope, as for example they have done in one sport after another, without people understanding in principle the difference between economically based and communally based activity. Professional sport is a service of entertainment to the consumers, while amateur sport is a communal activity. Because the consumer is so weak, he is easily led into abandoning communal activities to the economic sphere, and he is then surprised that his communal life is so impoverished.

Chapter 15

The institutional church

In this last aspect of secondary sociology which we have chosen to consider, we move into an area where quite a few Christians have already felt tensions. Some have felt quite rightly that, since the church is a social institution, it is right to open it up to critical analysis, so that it shall not wallow in its own errors. Others, equally correctly, have felt that judgments passed by secular sociologists on the Christian church are not binding or valid, and that the sociological perspective tends to see the church simply as a social institution. The latter claim is not normally made explicitly by sociologists of religion, but since in practice they just study the social aspects there is a strong tendency in this direction. However, we are now in a situation to see our way through this issue, for we see that the churches are social institutions, but not primarily social; that their primary meaning is as expressions of *faith*, and we therefore recognize that they must be understood in their primary aspect before the social aspect is analysed. Moreover it is evident that the guiding norms and principles for this institution are to be taken from the Scriptures not from secular sociology. Indeed, it is one of the weaknesses of secular studies of churches that the standpoint from which the critical analysis is made is not made explicit. Thus, if it is soundly done, a Christian sociology of the churches can be a valuable aid to understanding and church practice. This we now do, limiting our attention to Christian churches.[1]

[1] See articles by R. Furbey and D. Lyon in *Christian Commitment and the Study of Sociology* (Ilkley Study Group/UCCF, 1976).

The New Testament church

It would seem arrogant to try to summarize briefly what the New Testament reveals about the meaning of the church, when so much has been written on it. But it could be argued that much of what has been written has been biased in that it has been an ecclesiastical interpretation of the Christian faith carried out by professional (in the modern rather than the original sense) members of the church, namely clergymen and theologians. It is possible that we may be culture-bound in our view of the New Testament in that we read back into it the vast institutional structures which are now part of Christendom. If we try not to do that, we may get a slightly different perspective from that which is current now.

Let us therefore look at the picture of the church that we get from the Acts and the Letters. At first, after the disciples had been blessed and filled with the Holy Spirit at Pentecost they were constantly together; they formed a simple community where all things were held in common. This was partly in reaction to the persecution to which they were subject, but mainly it was to share what they now knew of Jesus Christ, the risen Son of God, their Lord and Saviour. Quickly the numbers of disciples grew as the authorities were confused by the resurrection of Christ and people realized what had happened. Christ's teaching was carefully passed on to the new disciples, and those who were especially close to Jesus before his death were, as apostles, given special authority to pass on and record their witness of his life and teaching. As the new way of life spread, all kinds of issues began to arise: Christians found that they clashed with the political authorities; they faced questions of economic redistribution and racial differences, and they also faced a whole range of issues involving the implications of their new faith for different areas of their life such as marriage, family life and work. In this situation we can see the apostles giving authoritative teaching about the Christian faith and applied teaching as to how all these different areas of life were to be lived in obedience to God. Thus the number of people who heard about Jesus and committed themselves to be his disciples grew, and they worked out their faith in fear and trembling and in the joy of the Lord.

So far, no picture of a specific institution called a church appears in the relatively undifferentiated lives of the early believers. Nevertheless, the necessity for this institution was absolutely compelling, because it was the natural consequence of their faith that the believers would want to worship, pray, preach, learn, praise, share and commune together. The Christians were committed to meet together to break bread by their obedience to Christ and they were bound together in the one Spirit who was able to overcome all their differences. Gradually, as well, the organization of this institution developed. There was an early differentiation between preaching and administering funds (Acts 6), and this was further developed later as the need was revealed for vital tasks to be fulfilled. Soon there was preaching, partaking of the Lord's supper, teaching, healing, prophesying, organizing missionary activities, worship, financial support and other aspects of church life, in which the members of the churches ministered to one another. Elders were appointed to exercise discipline in specific churches as the Gospel spread and bore fruit.

This development was marked by one or two characteristics which were not just incidental, but were structurally normative. The first was that the institution was nothing in itself; the early Christians did not go about talking about institutional church with a capital C, because in all its activities the institution pointed beyond itself to Christ and to the new life lived in obedience to him. Thus organizationally it was instrumental, shaped to fulfil the purposes of God in the lives of Christians. 'Let all things be done for edification' (1 Cor. 14:26) says Paul, and again in directions to Timothy he says 'For to this end we toil and strive, because we have our hope set on the living God, who is the Saviour of all men, especially of those who believe' (1 Tim. 4:10). Thus the institution was a by-product of the Christian faith and the saving power of God, and did not claim to itself importance and glory. As a result there was a flexibility of response to the Holy Spirit, high mobility and a responsiveness in the churches. The elders of the Ephesian Church readily travelled 30 miles on foot to meet Paul (Acts 20:17, 18), a Jew who could help was channelled into a situation where he could meet and confute Jews (Acts 18:24–28), and all kinds of places—households, beaches, halls, riversides, *etc*—were used for meeting. The church was not, and could not be, a self-orientated institution.

Secondly, we also get from the New Testament a vivid awareness of the way in which the institutional church was woven in with the total lives of faith of the early Christians. The Acts and Letters document the sins, weaknesses and mistakes of the early churches very thoroughly, but they give no evidence of a split between church and secular areas of life. Their church life and teaching, as judged by the Letters, was directive for their whole lives. It was a melting-pot to which they brought all the day-to-day issues for God's refining work to be done on them, not a retreat from those issues into another world. There was no question of ecclesiastical *apartheid* when the Gospel was at work. In Romans, Corinthians, Ephesians, Colossians, Hebrews, James and the letters of Peter, the churches are bombarded with issues, principles and advice from all areas explaining the full implications of the new life in Christ.

At the same time the institutional church, to be distinguished of course from the church seen as the whole body of Christian believers, the body of Christ (Eph. 4:15, 16), is seen as having a divine purpose and a key place among the institutions that we have looked at. The reason is that it is the institution founded upon the Gospel and the establishment of the kingdom of God, for worship, communion, preaching and other vital central aspects of the Christian faith. Teaching and admonition in the faith takes place within the church, but it is parents, children, husbands, wives, employers and employees who are responsible for working out their faith in these areas of their lives. The teaching of the institutional church was that life was to be Christ-centred, not church-centred, but the church was the key institution of faith.

Another aspect of early institutional church life is the kind of authority that is manifest there. After the resurrection Jesus came to the disciples and said to them. 'All authority in heaven and on earth has been given to me. Go therefore and make disciples of all nations, baptizing them in the name of the Father and of the Son and of the Holy Spirit, teaching them to observe all that I have commanded you; and lo, I am with you always, to the close of the age' (Mt. 28:18–20). Thus the authority of Christ over the church was and remains the key to its structure. 'He is before all things, and in him all things hold together. He is the head of the body, the church' (Col. 1:17, 18). Moreover, Christ had already laid down the pattern of authority which was to exist in the church. The leader was to be one who served, and the offices in the church were therefore positions of care. Those in authority are to be servants, and other views of authority—hierarchic, elitist, institutionalized—have no place. At the same time Christians are asked to be subject to one another because, as they are given varieties of gifts (1 Corinthians 12), they are able to minister to one another. Thus the pattern is a dynamic one, in a way which should at least raise some questions in our minds about contemporary churches. However, there is also a great deal of emphasis on defending the authority and truth of the gospel, and one of the areas where the elders and others were expected to exercise discipline was in making sure that the truths of the gospel were not compromised by human pride and disobedience.

Finally, we note that the early churches did not try to use institutional power to further the gospel. At the centre of their corporate life was the awareness that it was only God's power working in them that produced anything of worth, and to rely on institutional power or wealth or wisdom was to depart from God's ways, for God chose what was foolish, weak and despised to bless and use. Thus, what was completely alien to the church's foundation was to try to build itself up, become influential, use its power and bring human pressures to bear on other institutions. Its glory was its weakness.

In view of these points about the ordained structure of the church in the New Testament, what is the situation in the present-day churches?

The church as 'sacred' institution

In chapter 4 we looked at the effect of the sacred/secular division on the thinking of Christians. We noted the roots of this dichotomy in the Roman Catholic tradition and the way it has been continually reinforced. The labels 'secular' and 'sacred' became commonplace, and were the framework into which people's thinking automatically fitted. Issues of faith were *ipso facto* issues concerning the church, and secular institutions were beyond Christian concern. Shortly, we shall consider all kinds of ways in which this framework affects the institutional church in Britain, but first we shall look briefly at the way in which the concepts have been used in the sociology of religion, so that the weaknesses of key sociological concepts are evident, and they are not used uncritically.

The concepts 'sacred' and 'secular' were imported into the sociology of religion by Durkheim, who was brought up and educated in the Roman Catholic church and therefore naturally thought in these terms. So, he states:

'All known religious beliefs, whether simple or complex, present one common characteristic: they presuppose a classification of all things, real and ideal, of which men think, into two classes or opposed groups, generally designated by two distinct terms which are translated well enough by the words *profane* and *sacred*.'[1]

This initial assumption is then directed at the process of decline evident in the churches, which is then described as a pattern of secularization. The religious and the secular are then two characteristic social phenomena which can be analysed in interaction.[2] Usually, the definition of 'religious' or 'sacred' is in terms of the church which is in turn involved with that which is sacred. In other words, the definitions are circular. In fact the Christian doctrines of creation, sin and redemption cut across any such dichotomy and make it meaningless.

Nevertheless, the churches have allowed this divide to create a barrier between church life and the rest. There is the divide between Sunday and the rest of the week, with a total association of worship, prayer, Bible reading and praising God with church on Sunday, and none of these can take place during the rest of the week. There is also a barrier between those professionally associated with the institutional church, the clergy, and those who are outside the area of the 'sacred', the laity. Language is often split between sacred and liturgical and ordinary everyday forms. The church buildings develop all kinds of sacred motifs which

[1] E. Durkheim, *The Elementary Forms of Religious Life* (Free Press, 1961), p. 52.
[2] *e.g.* B. R. Wilson, *Religion in Secular Society* (C. A. Watts, 1966).

make them at odds with much other architecture. The form and structure of meetings comes to have a ritual significance; they are something in themselves which cannot be changed. What takes place in church on Sundays has little relation to the events, problems and situations of the week. Church members know little of the daily lives of those who sit beside them. People wear different clothes for church, and some events like marriage and burial are given a sacred aura. Some 'high' churches tend to emphasize these elements, but the grip of the sacred/secular divide is now an iron one, simply because the pressure during the rest of the week is overwhelmingly secular. Even when the churches try to break out of this pattern, they sometimes do so by having more institutional church activities, more sacred meetings. Because there is no penetration of issues outside the circumscribed sacred area the study of churchmen becomes increasingly 'theological' in the sense of picking over ecclesiastical or doctrinal issues.

There are other ways in which the influence of this dichotomy is felt. One is that the Scriptures can be, and are, 'spiritualized', so that the more sublime elements of the gospel are cut off from any significance for everyday behaviour. Another is that when the Christian tries to change the secular, he does it by adding a bit of sacred, a bit of moralizing perhaps, or morning assembly in schools. At the same time, the non-Christian does not expect any interference from the sacred area; he does not need 'religion' and cannot see what relevance it has for him. As we noted in chapter 4, the church has walked into this straightjacket, this *cul-de-sac*, through a process of self-justification and self-vindication. In defining its own territory, its own area of influence, it has denied the fulness and the cosmic proportions of the gospel. What is so pathetic is that the church has deserted the power of God for its own institutional power.

The church institutionalized

The view of the church as a sacred institution has an almost inevitable corollary. It is that the church as an institution becomes self-centred and self-serving. Because the church is sacred and the sacred is an end in itself, the church becomes an end in itself. It is possible for churches which deny this doctrinally (and of course, the Reformation involved a fundamental rebellion against the self-serving of the mediaeval Catholic church) to slip into this pattern of activity in various ways. Nobody is immune if there is not a direct living response to the gospel which fixes the attention of the church beyond itself. Let us look at some of the ways in which this can happen.

Church loyalty Institutional church loyalty is still quite a strong force in Britain. Most of the adult population identify themselves, even loosely, with some church or another, and it seems that many people go to church intermittently out of a sense of loyalty. People have been taught from birth that they ought to go, and have often been asked to go. Townsend reports that:

> 'Most people rarely, if ever, went to church. They often expressed guilt at not going. When asked whether they went to church they often said, "We've got to tell the truth, we don't."'[1]

These people did not go to church, others did. The important point, however, is that the whole nexus of loyalty, obligations, duty, expectations, moral pressure, *etc.*, is binding. It is clear that when churchgoers see and know little of each other, and where the gospel does not live strongly, then institutional pressures can creep in. People can be given all kinds of jobs to do to keep them involved. Leaders can use loyalty to try and maintain falling congregations. Yet when at the heart of the gospel is the believer's response to God's free gift of grace, this kind of second-order loyalty cannot but deaden. The focus has moved from Christ to the church.

Ecumenism The dominant church attitude towards ecumenism is that it is the manifestation of a spirit of love and reconciliation, which is drawing together churches that have been historically divided. This 'success-story' view is not the only one that can be taken. Bryan Wilson's conclusions are rather different:

> 'Ecumenism, then is a response which might save the churches from becoming sects, since "from church to sect" would

---

[1] P. Townsend, *The Family Life of Old People* (Pelican, 1963), p. 143.

appear to be the order of the day for religious organisations in secular society . . . The forces of ecumenism are clerical forces and the forces of the new ritualist movement are clerical forces. We witness the struggles of a profession for survival in the Protestant countries of Europe.'[1]

On this view ecumenism is a professionally organized and engineered reorganization to protect the clergy in a situation where they seem vulnerable, and the stated view is merely a hypocritical piece of double talk. Which view is correct? It is not possible to assess this, but we note that the clergy were more ready for the Anglican–Methodist reunion than the lay representatives were. Is it possible that institutional organization is the dominant concern of those with authority in the church? Again we stand back from this issue and recognize that the development of a community of Christians depends totally upon the power of Christ bringing love, peace, patience, and care, and chasing out fear, pride and distrust. To pre-empt the powerful working of God by putting faith in reorganization is just to play with symptoms again.

Denominational commitment   At the same time we recognize that the pattern of Christian commitment in Britain tends to be dominated by denominational loyalties. Many of the barriers between churches tend to be of this form, since there are often more important issues of doctrine and principle within churches in the same denomination than those which divide the denominations. Often there is a traditional commitment to a set way of doing things and no habit of intercourse between the various churches. There is no sense of Christian security outside the home church, and the tendency is to an ingrown, culture-bound community. This is expressed especially in the rural confrontation between church and chapel, or in the more complex urban pattern of exclusivism.

It is worth considering for a moment just when a church is gripped by exclusivism, for it is easy to misidentify. A church is a community of faith, and the community is only as wide as the faith is shared. Thus to say that a church or group is exclusive

[1] B. Wilson, *Religion in Secular Society* (Watts, 1966), pp. 225–6.

because it will not ignore parts of its living creed is to miss the point, because being subject to the truth of the gospel means being exclusive of error and also because the *basis* of community is that living credal faith. When my Christian brother and I know that we are saved by grace and not by our own works, then self-righteousness and achievement fixations are cleared from between us. When each of us knows that we are seen through and through by God, status loses any meaning. When we have both experienced God's love and patience with us, the relationship will be 'for better or for worse'. When we know that we cannot lie to God, we shall not lie to one another. Thus exclusivism is not to be identified with holding to Christian truths which provide a basis for true communal relationships. These truths are big enough to include everybody.

Rather, it could be argued that there is another motive behind exclusivism. It occurs when people, rather than being *subject* to the truth, to the work of God's Spirit, *identify themselves with the true faith*. When this kind of spiritual pride is evident, others, rather than being invited to share the faith, are seen as outside it. An institutional form of this has been the idea that exclusion from a certain church meant exclusion from the Christian faith. The prototype of this position was the mediaeval Catholic church with its anathemas, but it was also transmitted to other churches and has become common in the various sects. This attitude, a mixture of pride and fear, creates division simply because it focuses on *who* is right or wrong, not on what is true or false. It is interesting to see how Paul defuses the same problem in the Corinthian church and redirects the Christians there to the only grounds on which they can boast (1 Corinthians 1). He turns their eyes away from themselves to the God whose foolishness is wiser than men's wisdom.

The congregation Many churches in Britain have been faced with lower attendances in recent years and have seen this as their most burning problem. Yet it will be evident after a moment's thought that a church is in a spiritual rut if it sees falling attendances as its most pressing problem. It means that the only vision present is the vision of a full church singing lustily and listening to a good, interesting sermon. Evangelism is often directed by, and contained within, this institutional framework, with the result that fewer people are reached.

Most citizens are suspicious of the institutional church. In part they hear the rattle of collecting boxes and in part they know that what most clergy want above all is to have their churches full. Moreover, they suspect that the clergy want to fill their churches at any cost. Implicitly the ethos is established that people are needed and used to support the institutional church, and there is nothing that is likely to make people run faster in the opposite direction. Again, we see that the churches cannot grow through social pressure and self-concern; their strength is in the power of the gospel or it does not exist.

Finance When churches become large institutions, all kinds of financial considerations necessarily arise. However, when the energies of the people in the churches are primarily directed towards keeping the institution going financially, clearly its faith life is weakened. Yet this is precisely what is happening in many areas.

Especially in rural areas many churches are scarcely self-supporting. As a result, what tends to happen is that village fetes, coffee mornings, 'bring and buy' sales and bingo sessions provide the revenue and soak up the energies of many of the congregation. Church economics takes up a high proportion of the discussion at PCC meetings. At a national level a similar pattern of constraints seems to operate. The Church of England, for example, has for a long time been unable to meet its basic costs from current contributions and has become organized economically in a more and more commercial way. Apart from being one of the largest land and property owners in Britain, the Church Commissioners hold something like £300 million of shares. There has been a movement based on the idea of Christian stewardship over the last few years which has involved using firms of professional fund-raisers, and this has substantially increased the Church of England's income from gifts, but it still only about equals the income from shares. Thus the historical situation means that this church is living on capital, which in turn means that issues of economic maintenance and survival of the institution tend to move to the centre of church life. It is very easy in this situation for economic pressures to bring change, rather than strategic, prayerful decisions, and for the survival of the institution to be the dominant concern.

The functional church   When Durkheim first formulated his theory that religions were a totemic form of worshipping the society, he was substantially wrong about Protestant Christianity. The Nonconformist and sectarian character of much Christianity defy analysis in these terms, and its origin was completely outside any such framework. However, the argument has often been repeated, for example by Bocock:

'In fact, we can only say that the believer is not deceived when he believes in the existence of a moral power upon which he depends and from which he receives all that is best in himself: the power exists, it is society.' [1]

As it stands the statement is just false, but nevertheless there is a sense in which it is significant. How is it possible, clergymen and others ask in anguish, for the church to be relevant in modern society? What place has the sacred in an overwhelmingly secular society? The answer comes that the church must be *useful* in a secular society; it must fulfil whatever functions the secular society asks of it. If this position is adopted the institutional church therefore becomes a repository of secular needs and requirements. Its *raison d'être* is established in terms of secular society and not in response to God. One example of this development was the worker-priest movement, which was in the end seen as being disloyal to the Roman Catholic church because its identification with the secular work scene was so complete. [2] However, less dramatic forms are available in Britain. One, for example, is the way the churches put a halo over the births, marriages and deaths of non-Christians. Another is the way many clergy become a kind of amateur social work agency, meeting an obvious secular need. Yet another is the way some churches aim to become community centres, providing a social focus for the

[1] R. Bocock, *Ritual in Industrial Society* (Allen and Unwin, 1974), p. 27.
[2] See E. R. Wickham, 'The Worker–Priest Movement in France, and a consideration of its validity in the British Scene' in *Encounter with Modern Society* (Lutterworth, 1964), chapter 8, pp. 96–125; and Gregor Sieler, *The Church and Industrial Society* (Darton, Longman and Todd, 1964).

area. The institution has a rationale in secular society, but it is no longer a unit which is responsive to God.

The institutional church professionals   What is the place of the clergy in the church? The long traditions of priests, clergy and ministers tends to obscure the fact that this question is problematic. The early church was largely non-professional in the sense that many church leaders had jobs, but the need for some Christians to use their gifts for the full-time building up of the church was recognized as part of the general mutual dependence of all church members on the gifts of others. It was also immediate in that it was a calling to a specific task in a certain church. Further, there was clear recognition that the churches needed a variety of ministries, and no identification of 'the ministry' as a separate professional vocation. With the later growth of the churches a tendency for the clergy to try to regularize their position developed. One way in which this was done was to identify the priesthood with the sacraments and to mystify them. Although many Christians especially Roman Catholics, would dispute this, I suggest that most of the mystique surrounding the simple Supper of Remembrance has been induced by the professionals who administer it. Another form has been the development of liturgical expertise; if only the clergy can master the complex liturgy, their place is secure (Latin played a key role in this area). The more normal Protestant regulation of the ministry was fulfilled in preaching.[1] The importance of this ministry is very great and several preachers have given me more than I could ever express, but the fact remains that all clergy are not preachers, and have therefore been trapped in this regularization of their role. One final justification is described by Werner Stark in this way:

'There existed in this manner a division between the common run of men and religious specialists (this ugly term will, it is hoped, be forgiven) who made the realization of the counsels of perfection their business, so to speak, their profession, their function. It is with this separation of a minority in active

---

[1] D. M. Lloyd-Jones, *Preaching and Preachers* (Hodder and Stoughton, 1971), for a statement of its importance.

pursuit of sanctification and a majority more passive in relation to religious values, that Protestantism had a serious quarrel, especially in its earliest, perfectionist days.'[1]

There are, it could be argued, serious distortions possible as a result of this position. One of them, is that holiness becomes a process of withdrawal from day to day events, and another is that lay people associate the idea of holiness with the institutional church professionals, and never with themselves.

For these and other reasons the place of the clergy in the churches has therefore become quite problematic. The general form which the problem takes is that the minister is associated with what is sacred and the congregation to some extent with what is secular. This division is reinforced in a number of ways. The clergyman is the only person who can handle the liturgy and the organization of the church building. He is assumed to be the one to take the dominant role in most proceedings. His vestments act as a kind of professional uniform. Many clergy have spent a lot of time and energy struggling to demolish this sacred–secular barrier which predefines their role, but they have had very limited success.

Indeed, it is not inaccurate to say that a pattern of minister-dependence can grow up in which the minister is invested with faith and Christian understanding which the congregation lives *on,* without living and growing in. He is seen as the faith person on whose faith others can rely. The minister is expected to carry the faith of the congregation while they live their normal everyday lives. This situation can impose a tremendous strain on the clergy, and means that the vicarious faith of the congregation is brittle and fragile.

Quite a few churches have emphasized lay participation in church government in recent years and there is a good deal of rethinking going on about the relationship between clergy and congregation, but the problem is a peculiar one in that there is no organizational solution to it. If the church, professional and lay, is merely concerned with keeping the institution going and making it more efficient, it has no *raison d'être* and will decay. If, on the other hand, a church represents a living response to God,

---

[1] W. Stark *The Sociology of Religion: Vol. IV Types of Religious Man* (Routledge and Kegan Paul, 1969), p. 231.

the organizational problems can be solved in the context of the need.

This contrast is therefore the basic one which emerges from these examples. The emphasis on church loyalty, ecumenism, denominational barriers, a concern with numbers, finance and the secular functions of the church and its professional organization can all be symptoms of a church turning in upon itself and developing an ecclesiastical faith. There is an ever present danger as soon as it turns from openness to Christ and actively walking in faith; immediately, one of these patterns awaits it. Just how relevant this diagnosis is to specific churches is best analysed by the reader. The need for self-diagnosis is great, especially in view of the self-sufficiency which is easily present. The words to the Laodicean church were:

'For you say, I am rich, I have prospered, and I need nothing; not knowing that you are wretched, pitiable, poor, blind, and naked. Therefore I counsel you to buy from me gold refined by fire, that you may be rich, and white garments to clothe you and to keep the shame of your nakedness from being seen, and salve to anoint your eyes, that you may see. Those whom I love, I reprove and chasten; so be zealous and repent' (Rev. 3:17–19).

Secular divisions within the churches

It might seem at first that the barrier between the sacred and the secular would keep the churches immune from the effects of secular social life. That, after all, was part of the function of such a barrier. However, there is a great deal of evidence that all kinds of social forces affect and even structure institutional churches. Let us consider some of these.

Class If we consider denominations in relation to class, quite a clear pattern emerges. The Church of England has a traditional identification with the upper and middle classes, although it also has a very wide pattern of membership. The United Reformed churches tend to be upper middle, the Baptist middle and the Methodist lower middle, while the Roman Catholic and Pentecostal Churches tend to be working class. However, there are also strong regional variations which need to be taken into account. The Anglican Church tends to be numerically stronger in the South, the Methodist in the North, the Presbyterian in Scotland, the Roman Catholic in the Northwest and Scotland, and the Baptist in the Southeast. Moreover it needs to be remembered that, in principle, churches are open communities and that most churches have a mixed class membership, even if one class tends to predominate, so that the pattern is rather more complex than is often suggested.

Nevertheless, if we consider churchgoing, irrespective of denomination, in relation to class, it is predominantly a middle class habit. The upper class has a nodding acquaintance with the church, but the working class family is less likely to go. There are several explanations for this. One is the Catherwood development of Weber's thesis.[1] It argues that those who join the churches tend to be upwardly mobile in economic and class terms, because their faith implies vocation, service, hard-work and non-indulgent living. In terms of our previous class analysis it means converts moving out of a position of dependence and subservience into responsibility. This is probably quite important historically, and the basic truth that the Christian faith provides all men with an identity which is not rooted in dependence on others has probably been a stronger liberating force than is generally recognized. However, this is only part of the answer. The provision of churches in the city areas where the working classes migrated and multiplied was completely inadequate; the fixed institutional forms of the churches simply could not cope with the pace of urban change.

However, there are other explanations which are more disturbing. The first is that the churches have been used by the upper and middle classes as agencies of control. This is a different argument from the Halévy thesis which suggested that the Methodist revival, and the changed attitudes it brought, prevented any revolutionary movement in England. It suggests that there was deliberate manipulation. An obvious example is an early 19th century catechism:

[1] H. F. R. Catherwood, *The Christian in Industrial Society* (Tyndale Press, 1964).

'Is it honest for workmen to waste and destroy the materials which they make use of? (Answer, No.)
Who do these things belong to? (Answer, Their Master.)
Whose eyes see you when your master is not by? (Answer, God's.)
Who sees people when they are pilfering tea and sugar and such things? (Answer, God.)
Does God approve of such actions? (Answer, No.)
What will God do to thieves of all kinds? (Answer, Punish them.)'[1]

Was this kind of manipulation widespread? The important place of landed patronage in the provision of livings suggests that it was in the 18th and early 19th centuries, but this factor has become less important in a more urban community. At the same time there was a dependence on middle class funds for building churches, as the custom of pew rents shows. Thus, dependence for funds would have made the churches more sensitive to a middle class message. This raises the most serious explanation of class church-going habits, namely that a middle class version of Christianity was, and is, lived in Britain.

It could be argued that there are many aspects of conventional Christianity which are at root middle class rather than biblical. Vocation is generally seen in terms of a successful career judged in terms of status, income and reputation. There is very little critical teaching against affluence and the pursuit of material possessions, in spite of all the biblical teaching on this theme. If this teaching is mentioned, great play is often made of the distinction between the love of money being the root of all evil, and having money, which is all right. Issues of social justice and redistribution tend to be ignored and righteousness and holiness are identified with individual moral behaviour. There is also a high valuation of social affluence, and a tendency to try to work within the establishment. Privacy, a middle class characteristic, tends to inhibit Christian fellowship in many churches; the patterns of fear, distance, distrust, reserve. which we have seen are all an important part of middle class orientations and tend to structure

[1] Quoted in R. Bendix, *Work and Authority in Industry* (Harper Torchbook, 1963), p. 67.

relationships in many churches. Achievement is valued highly. The church is organized in a managerial way. Church members retain their independence at all costs rather than being members of one another. The financial position of the church and the growth of capital assets assume great importance. The church is activity-orientated. Importance is attached to clothes. Words predominate in social relationships. Emotions are limited to a certain range of expression. Time is carefully rationed and timetables strictly adhered to; a modern affluent life-style is a very time-consuming one, and the church cannot overstep its demands in terms of time. These are merely guesses at the way elements of church life may be influenced and shaped by class attitudes in, for example, the great ring of churches that surrounds London in the commuter zone. However, there is another element that is of crucial importance. To whatever extent Christian attitudes and living are established in the church, they still face an incredible barrier which prevents them from penetrating to the middle class behaviour of weekday life. Thus far and no further is a likely response to the demands of Christian living.

At the same time it is worth noting that identification with working class values is not a valid Christian response either. The dependence of Christians on one another is different from the structural dependence of class relationships. Other-directed solidarity is not a basis for Christian fellowship, nor are commonly held attitudes to pleasure, conscience, authority and education easily assimilated into a Christian life. It may well be true that the absence of wealth means that the barriers to accepting the Christian faith are less among the working class, but a tendency towards a middle class church should not be 'corrected' by another form of identification. The great need is for the Christian faith to redeem areas of passivity and dependence in the lives of many who have been subdued by our class system.

Status We have already defined status in terms of comparing and grouping people on the basis of external characteristics. Thus it is a more subtle form of grouping than that of class, and the patterns may be less predictable from situation to situation. Especially since it almost necessarily involves self or group glorification, it is something that ought to be fully eradicated from the Christian community. Yet it is doubtful whether this is what happens. For example, the conventional status accorded to education is adopted in churches; the clergy are expected to be highly educated, including often some requirement about classical languages, and their training is very similar to that associated with the professions. The question needs to be asked whether this kind of educational background and training is necessary for all full-time ministers within the church, or whether it merely gives the institution a status bias which cuts off certain groups from communion. Certainly, I have learned a tremendous amount from formally uneducated Christian teachers.

The issue is also important when we consider the internal relationships of a church. What is the pattern of communication and friendship? Are there several relatively autonomous groups which have much in common internally, but are segregated from other groups? How much are people sensitive to status, reputation and position within the church? To what extent do the patterns of intercourse which exist in the neighbourhood infiltrate the church and become established there? Do various activities tend to glorify certain church members or groups and show disrespect to others? These are all questions which cannot be answered except in the context of a specific church, but if such problems do exist, they are serious. Patterns of status are fundamentally at odds with the development of a community founded in God's grace.

Sex The relations between the sexes often have an unusual pattern in churches. The problem to some extent arises because clergymen do their job mainly when most other men are working, and it is more than likely that most of their meetings, contact and help during this period will be dominated by women. It is not uncommon for a church to have a preponderance of women in the congregation and to be largely run by them. This has contributed to a feeling that churches are unmanly institutions. This situation is further reinforced by having a system of sexual segregation in meetings which is fairly rigid. Women only, and men only meetings are standard in many denominations. Given that the clergy are almost always men, and that women rarely have positions of authority, the potential is present for patterns of misunderstanding to build up. Often, of course, relationships are sufficiently healthy for there to be no major problem. Nevertheless, the issue is important, and it is noticeable that Paul spent a good deal of time over the different roles of men and women in the church.

Race Another aspect of church life which shows how secular standards have automatically become accepted has been the response to immigration. The West Indians came from predominantly Christian backgrounds, and about three-quarters of them were regular churchgoers before coming to Britain. When they arrived here 90 per cent of them stopped coming to church, although the same denominations existed in both Britain and the West Indies. Those who did go often went largely to West Indian sect churches which developed and flourished in immigrant areas. This pattern stands as a monument to the conventional attitudes of indifference and occasional prejudice that occur within churches in Britain.[1]

It is possible, therefore, that despite the great divide between the sacred and the secular, these secular attitudes and divisions have made substantial inroads into church communal life, and has compromised basic aspects of Christian teaching. If we recognize this and repent of it, then we shall be given the means of changing the situation.

The Christian warfare

Thus far our analysis has been mainly concerned with the institutional church, but now we come to the central point of this chapter, namely an understanding of the effect of the sacred–secular framework on the overall witness of the church. The Scriptures teach that the Christian life is a battle between the rule of God and the rule of the world in the form of various forces, powers and principalities which deny God or subvert the Christian's discipleship. In Ephesians 6 Paul describes the rather

[1] See D. Humphrey and G. John, *Because They're Black* (Penguin, 1971), pp. 66, 70.

unconventional weapons that the Christian is to use in this battle, in which, as Paul makes clear, the Christian is involved with his whole life.

If we, so to speak, step back from the battle, climb a hill and look strategically at the situation, we soon become aware that the sacred-secular view has left the Christian in an extremely weak position. If we look at the battlefield in institutional terms it might look something like this:

THE RULE OF THE WORLD		THE RULE OF CHRIST
MARRIAGE	⚙→	MARRIAGE
FAMILY	⚙→	FAMILY
NEIGHBOURHOOD	⚙→	NEIGHBOURHOOD
ECONOMY	⚙→	ECONOMIC LIFE
MASS MEDIA	⚙→	MASS MEDIA
EDUCATION	⚙→	EDUCATION
POLITICS	⚙→	POLITICS
THE ARTS	⚙→	THE ARTS
	←⚙	CHURCH

The situation is that the secular forces, the rule of this world, hold sway in all the major institutional areas, and many Christians are not even aware of what is going on in these parts of the battlefield. Of if the Christian is under attack, he finds himself on the defensive as an individual with very little armour. He is the only Christian in his workplace, struggles through a non-Christian form of education, and is confronted by media which constantly pump non-Christian themes at him. The secular forces are not under attack in most of these areas, they have free play and range the battlefield. At the same time, Christians tend to have massed all their forces in the *sacred* institution, the church. However, it is just at this point that there is no secular counterpart, except perhaps the liberal theologians, so the counter attack has very little impact. It is aimed at an outcrop of rock with no troops behind it. It is just this impossible strategy to which the Christian church has become committed.

The obvious answer is that the Christians should meet the challenge of secular forces in all these other areas. This conclusion is not just a matter of expediency, but involves recognizing the rule of God in all areas of life, as the early church did. However, meeting the challenge means attack in the peculiarly Christian sense of using the weapons of peace, faith, prayer, truth and love, not those of power, propaganda and domination. The challenge may be met within existing marriages, families, workplaces, or it may involve setting up a Christian marriage advisory service, garage, political party, magazine or playgroup. As the church allows Christian truth to penetrate freely those areas of our lives, so the conflict will lose some of the unevenness that characterizes it at present, and Christians will be able to use their unlimited resources.

That the institutional churches have allowed themselves to become culture-bound and fixed in institutional patterns, which are the result of normal sinful motives, has been evident for many decades. Perhaps the weaknesses of the church are now so evident that the trust in institutional power and influence will decay, and be replaced by trust in the power of the gospel and of God. 'But we have this treasure in earthen vessels, to show that the transcendent power belongs to God and not to us' (2 Cor. 4:7).

Chapter 16

Conclusion

The historical situation

In the previous chapters our main concern has been to gain a Christian understanding of various social issues and problems, and it may now be valuable to return to a more general analysis of the historical situation in Britain and the Christian response to it. There are many lessons to be learned.

All the areas which we have examined have shown how humanism, man's belief in himself, has tended to shape his social life and attitudes. There is little doubt that this religious perspective is dominant in Britain, even if there are some places where it does not hold sway. It is present not only in and through the great social and economic philosophies like capitalism, Marxism, liberalism and racialism, but also in the small day-to-day relationships of marriage, family, neighbourhood and through the media. What in the 18th century was an elitist movement of faith has steadily become the background perspective of our culture. It is automatically accepted and rarely questioned that thinking and action should be man-centred. Many people are unaware that the attitudes they breathe and grow up in are humanist, simply because the faith is so implicit and pervasive. All the social classes are caught up in this cultural pattern.

However, it would be a mistake to see our culture as *unified*; it cannot be, for humanism does not lead to one coherent view of man, but rather to a whole range of divergent views. Thus what we see is humanism fragmented into a range of different forms. The first great division is between the individualist and collectivist forms, which, as we have seen, is a tension throughout our society. Secondly, all kinds of ideology make one aspect of man absolute or autonomous, and so distort an understanding of the whole man. For example, sexual relationships are seen in biological or natural terms, economics in terms of 'economic man' or politics in terms of power. Thirdly, in our culture, there are all kinds of humanist faith which sweep across the scene and hold people's imagination for a time; apart from the youth cults there has been a vast increase in non-Christian religious sects in recent years. Thus at all kinds of different levels our culture is severely fragmented, but at the same time there is this underlying faith in autonomous man, the Enlightenment ideal.

If this is the key fact of the historical situation, what of the Christian response to it? Sadly, we have to acknowledge that many Christians have just not understood it; they have sheltered behind the myth of a Christian culture in Britain and have been lulled into attitudes that are a compromise of their faith. The great Christian revivals of the late 18th and 19th centuries changed people's lives, but the Enlightenment ideal still remained unchallenged in many areas and only in a limited sense could there be said to be a reformation of social life. Gradually Christianity has been pushed out of much of economic life, politics and education, and often it was the Christians who were most prepared thus to impoverish and limit their faith. For many, Christianity became a series of cultural habits or established practices, of brittle moral values or activities associated solely with the institutional church. At the end of the last century, the real vehicles of faith in Britain were movements like nationalism, socialism, and evolutionary thinking, and Christian faith was privatized or weakened. Later, A. J. P. Taylor could describe this process at a further stage of development as follows,

'More broadly, religious faith was losing its strength. Not only did church-going universally decline. The dogma of revealed religion—the Incarnation and the Resurrection—were fully accepted by only a small minority. Our Lord Jesus became, even for many avowed Christians, merely the supreme example of a good man. This was as great a happening as any in English history since the conversion of the Anglo Saxons to Christianity . . . England remained Christian in morality, though not in faith.'[1]

Here he was describing the period around 1922 but clearly, in succeeding decades, the morality became more and more hollow and has been modified by the growing man-centred outlook. However, most Christians have been decades behind in their diagnosis of this process, and it is only in the present era when the brittle shell of morality has cracked wide open that they have been forced to recognize the non-Christian nature of the dominant faith. This almost deliberate blindness has done much damage and is still causing problems, as we can see if we look at some of the current Christian responses.

In the face of this vast change, some members of the established church still cling to the myth of establishment and baptism figures as signs of Christian religiosity. This kind of optimism is so unrealistic as to be pathetic. Other Christians have focused on the most obvious symptoms of the change, issues like divorce, pornography and drugs, and have waged a moral campaign against them. This reaction is right and valuable, as long as it does not ignore the great weight of cultural attitudes which are behind these changes and try to reinstate the brittle moral shell which has already cracked. Although legal reform, *etc.*, is important, these moral issues are primarily, as we have shown, rooted in the religious outlook of people in our society, and they must needs be treated at this deeper level. Another characteristic response, especially among Nonconformists, is to concentrate on issues of *private* morality and to ignore the whole range of broader economic, social and political issues which equally involve questions of justice and righteousness, but which have been pushed outside Christian concern. Yet another reaction is to retreat from the secular world into the churches. Others attempt to justify Christian morality in terms which will be acceptable on humanist presuppositions, hoping that this will stem the pattern of changes in behaviour. Perhaps the saddest response is from those who have tried to synthesize the Christian faith with various forms of humanism to win it a temporary popularity, or have

[1] A. J. P. Taylor, *English History 1914–45* (Oxford Univ. Press, 1965), pp. 168–9.

pretended that people accept the Christian faith by deliberately ignoring important differences of attitude and belief. Thus we see that the reaction has been a confused one, and it is still hampered by lack of awareness. For example, many Christians still believe that Christianity is taught in schools and have not realized that most of the curriculum is usually either implicitly or explicitly humanist. These kinds of illusion ill-equip Christians to face the current situation.

The confrontation

If we say that the situation is most aptly described as one of confrontation, we are not talking about confrontation between Christian and non-Christian people. The confrontation is not *antagonism*; it cannot be that without compromising the gospel of peace and love. Rather it is a recognition of the radical difference between the dominant faith perspective of our age and the Christian faith. This has been obscured at several different levels, and it is time that there was a change.

The first level is that of *faith*. Some of the ways in which Christianity has been clouded are beyond the scope of this book, including, for example, various theological attacks on Christian truth. However, there are others which have a social origin and these need to be considered. Thus we need to ask why theology, unlike the Bible itself, has developed such a specialized vocabulary which is out of contact with day-to-day issues. Have theologians in many cases been an overeducated and isolated group bent on creating their own specialized knowledge and thus justifying their existence? Of course this charge will often be unjustified, but the question needs to be asked. In the last chapter we looked at a whole range of ways in which the institutional church obscured the gospel. Has faith been transferred to the institution or to the clergy? It is vested in a set of ideas, in certain patterns of behaviour or right ways of living? Has there been a nominal, habitual, conventional or traditional pattern of allegiance which has obscured the difference between Christian and non-Christian in the churches? Has faith retreated into the churches and into a 'sacred' corner of people's lives, and therefore become partial and unreal for six days each week? All these questions and many others need to be asked urgently by the churches. Yet another whole area of concern is with the groups which are out of contact with the Christian gospel, either because it is not available in their cultural form, or because there just is no Christian contact. There is now an awareness of this problem and things are changing, but, for example, the average working class family is still almost completely out of range of the Christian faith.

For this to be changed, there needs to be a new obedience to the Holy Spirit and a new purity of faith among Christians, involving full discipleship rather than part-time commitment, so that men and women are ready to be changed by God. We seek and pray that this will happen.

Yet there is also another side to this confrontation, and it is the faith of non-Christians. Here we enter an area of widespread haziness. Very many people are just not aware of what their own faith and attitude to life is; they have not reached this level of self-consciousness. Various important views are accepted passively or absorbed via cool communication and subsequently shape lives and people's destinies. Attitudes and ideas swirl around so rapidly that the chance to evaluate is rare. At the same time the greatest effort in time and money is lavished on the most trivial forms of communication like advertising and entertainment, and it is not possible to discern what is important and what is not. In this cultural atmosphere, where at the same time people's energies are mainly absorbed in the immediate tasks of earning and consumption, it is not surprising that few people stop to consider their faith and the meaning of their lives. At least this is what it seems like. It is probably nearer the truth to say that a great deal of heart-searching and wondering goes on, but that for many the background noise is deafening and distracting. If this is the situation, there is an obvious need for help. Instead of the high pressure there is need for shelter.[1] There is also need to bring this haziness of faith out into the light, so that people do not trust that which has no foundation.

The second level at which this confrontation has to be made clear is at the level of understanding. In chapter 2 we saw how,

[1] See E. Schaeffer, *L'Abri* (Norfolk Press, 1969) for one statement of what this means.

through the use of terms like 'scientific', 'empirical', and 'value-free,' an appearance of neutrality was given to various faith perspectives in the social sciences, although the idea of neutral knowledge just did not stand up under analysis. What we have found in the social sciences could also be found in many other areas of knowledge. We have to acknowledge that in these social, political and economic areas there has been an abdication of Christian thought. Instead there has been a passive, uncritical learning of 'neutral' knowledge, or a synthesis with non-Christian thought. We have seen Christians swim with the current tides of thought, even when these have been humanist. In a revolutionary era, some Christian scholars get to work to try to show that Christ was a Zealot. In a very telling test case we see the way in which most German Christians were unable to confront the ideology of Nazism in any effective way. In Britain there is painfully little that could be described as Christian social, political and economic understanding. When Paul writes in Romans 12:2: 'Do not be conformed to this world but be transformed by the renewal of your mind . . .' it strikes painfully into our present situation.

That there is this continual compromise with non-Christian ways of understanding is not surprising in view of the dominant attitude towards education, especially among evangelical Christians. David Martin describes it thus:

'It is worth enlarging a little on the evangelical attitude to education. Obviously literacy is essential to meditation on Scripture and for adequate daily refreshment of the soul. On this point Puritan and Jewish values are identical. Literacy is also essential to achieving or sustaining a decent, probably non-manual job, and security for one's family: particularly was this the case some fifty or more years ago. Thus education served spiritual and secular vocations alike, but it was still not specially valuable in itself . . . Hence evangelicals persistently attempted to restrict the scope of experience to a context of religious discipline . . .'[1]

The outcome of this rather utilitarian attitude is that there is scarcely a single institute, college or department in higher education in Britain which is committed to a Christian

[1] D. Martin, *A Sociology of English Religion* (Heinemann Educational, 1967), p. 61.

understanding of a particular discipline or area of study that is not theological. In some areas of study there are very few individual Christians who are so committed. In view of the vast resources that are poured into education to-day, this is rather astonishing. Christian understanding, we must conclude, is only valued in areas which are narrowly theological, and outside those areas Christians are on the whole prepared to accept the teaching of our culture and work to get good jobs. Thus in this area the confrontation has scarcely begun. The Shaftesbury Project is one early attempt. There should be-many others.

The third level we need to consider is that of *action*. Quite a few Christians are becoming concerned at the lack of social involvement, and it might be helpful to begin by asking why there has been no active Christian social confrontation. Why has the normal pattern been one of relative non-involvement? One explanation is that which we considered in the last chapter, namely the way in which the Christian faith has gradually been excluded from political, educational and other public areas of concern, and how Christians have come to accept a secular–sacred split in their lives. The hold of this perspective clearly severely inhibits Christian social involvement. Another explanation is that present-day evangelical Christians tend to be middle class and relatively affluent, and this can lead to privatized, home-centred living, conservatism and conformity. The extent to which this explanation is valid can be judged by the reader.

Yet another explanation which we must look at more fully is that most Christians have lost the ability to act collectively outside the context of the institutional church, because the Christian faith is seen individualistically.

In other words, the humanist breakdown that we examined in chapter 1 has influenced Christian faith and doctrine. For example, it is assumed that Christ's precept 'You are the salt of the earth . . .' is to be taken individualistically. It talks of the Christian in industry, politics, the teaching profession, the trade union or elsewhere *as an individual*. To suggest that Christians act together in industry, housing, banking or any other socio-economic activity is to talk of something strange. Although, for example, the letters of Peter, Paul and John are full of exhortations about various forms of Christian communal activity, this is still seen as something that is mildly heretical. Yet this individualism is supported by Christians in a society where, outside marriage and family life, nearly all important decisions are made within communal corporate or institutional structures. To approach these structures individualistically is to be automatically ineffective, to fail to be salting salt. The individual manager rarely touches company policy, the individual Christian MP depends on the party and effects nothing of importance, and the single Christian teacher often finds what he teaches compromised by others on the staff. If this explanation has validity, and if the pattern is both unbiblical and ineffective, then the obvious conclusion is that we should break away from it, and Christians should learn to work, pray and think together in all these so-called secular situations.

However, there is a further step which needs even more decisive action. It is one thing to work and pray with Christians in a particular institution, but it is also possible to create an institution which aims to be Christian *as an institution*. Some Christians might find this an alien idea, while forgetting that they wholeheartedly accept Christian marriage. However, with the dominant culture becoming more and more non-Christian, it is possible that this will increasingly become a practical necessity. If the only union in the industry is Trotskyite, then the Christians would have to form their own union if they were not to capitulate. If the main political parties became continually more and more non-Christian in their principles and policies, then perhaps Christians would eventually be pushed towards forming a political party. If banks and other lenders of private funds to those in need deny the biblical principle of usury, then rich Christians ought to think of forming another lending institution. If popular newspapers become even more unchristian in their content and news-slant, then perhaps Christians will begin to think of an alternative tabloid. However, we are thus far speaking in very negative terms. We are talking of trends pushing Christians into action. But this is really to see things the wrong way round. Rather than being pushed into action, the vision should already be present as a positive force. Shortly we shall again see how biblical teaching, and especially that of the Lord Jesus Christ, demands and gives that vision.

The idea of a Christian newspaper, political party or trade union is so new to some people that, to avoid misunderstanding, a few points need to be discussed. The first is that what is created would not be the perfect institution which would always be right and Christian at every point. Perfection is impossible, but Christians do not cease to live individual Christian lives because they are not perfect and always right, nor do Christian marriages cease for the same reason. Such communal ventures will often be weak and full of mistakes but nevertheless, as they attempt to be faithful in thought and action to the Word of God, they have a radically different direction from that of other groups. They can, as communities or institutions, be a light set on a hill, just as individuals can. A second point is that ventures of faith will not be better just because *Christians* are involved; this is not magic. Christians can make as much of a mess of them as anyone else. Whether it is a marriage or a political party, it is essential that the relevant Christian principles are understood and respected. Nor, for example, in politics is the understanding of various issues easy; it may take years of prayer and thought and faithful action. Christian marriage is more than the marriage of Christians and Christian politics is more than individual Christian politicians. The key issue is the outworking of faith and Christian truth in that particular area of life. Another misunderstanding arises from the traditional view of what it means to be 'in the world', which is that Christians should bury themselves one by one in the world as isolated grains of salt, and that collective action is separatist. Yet the Christian newspaper, trade union or arts centre are no less in the world. They could be isolationist, just as individuals can be (and often are when they are lonely and unsupported), but this is unlikely. They are merely in the world in units which can act effectively rather than units which cannot. One final point is that we have not said that Christians should or should always act collectively as Christians; there is no mechanical rule. It is just that in our highly organized world this individualism outside the institutional church may be less helpful.

This kind of collective action is an immediate possibility. The resources of finance and manpower which could be available are considerable. The problem is Christian quietism. In some areas there would be a need for much more study and understanding but this would inevitably accompany action. So that we may be practical and specific, let us look at some of the ventures that might be possible and in some cases are already. We are talking of Christian (not church) newspapers, housing trusts, marriage guidance centres, film companies, firms, professional practices, educational centres, garages, shops, schools, arts centres, broadcasting groups, builders, political pressure groups or parties, hostels, farms, publishers, banks, estate agents, Old People's Homes and so on. The list is endless. The alternative to this kind of corporate action is sobering. Without this kind of development it is inevitable that many Christians will live essentially secular and humanist lives for most of the week. In many important ways their lives will be compromised by non-Christian practices and policy. When they shed their secular coats at the end of the week to worship God, their faith will have been weakened and assaulted. It therefore seems that corporate social responses of faith are important if Christians are to confront the dominant faith of our era in a realistic and consistent way.

The kingdom of God

We cannot finish by discussing these corporate forms of activity as though they were the key issue. They may well be important in the present situation, but the perspective in which they are seen needs to be a bigger and more biblical one. It would be easy for them to degenerate into social activism for its own sake, or into the hope that social reform is the key to human betterment and progress. We could even begin to judge various activities by criteria of success and failure which are borrowed from secular institutions. There is so much that could go wrong. If this social action does not have the right foundation it will be just another human reaction. When tested by fire it will be seen to be just wood, hay or stubble, that which has no eternal significance. Therefore we need to ask again what is the basis for truly Christian action. We have discussed norms, institutions and all kinds of issues that need to be understood, but we must finally consider in relation to the teachings and life of Christ the key to Christian action. It is *that the Christian has entered into a kingdom where his life is governed in a totally new way*. This we learn from Christ himself.

Often so much attention is paid to the great events of Christ's life, death and resurrection, or to the indelible sayings of the Sermon on the Mount, that the main and continual thrust of Christ's teaching is passed over. The central message was of the coming of the kingdom of God, or more accurately, the rule of God. Christ's coming was to make possible the rule of God in men's hearts and lives in a totally new way. He proclaimed this right from the beginning of his teaching (Mt. 4:17) through until after his resurrection (Acts 1:3). It was clear that the coming of the kingdom of God was a radical and 'violent' message to bring (Matthew 11), and also that to submit to the rule of God involved a total commitment and was costly (Mt. 13:44, 45 and Lk. 14:25–33). It also required a change of heart, a conversion from man-centredness to God-centred living; 'unless one is born anew, he cannot see the kingdom of God' (Jn. 3:3). Thus to enter the kingdom, people could not come on their own terms; they had to become like little children (Mt. 18:1–4), and there were certain kinds of attitude, like trust in wealth (Mt. 19:23), or importance (Matthew 23), which made it impossible to come into the kingdom where God rules and where men must be humble. It was not only in his teaching that Christ declared this message, but also in his life and actions. He submitted himself completely to the will of God, and did what the Father commanded him (Jn. 14:31). In him it was possible to see the rule of God present among men, and those around him marvelled at what they saw.

For those who by faith entered the kingdom of God, life was turned upside down. A totally new way of living was involved. Suddenly true happiness was seen to dwell with those who were poor, sad, hated, pure and meek, while the rich, popular and satisfied were storing up trouble for themselves (Matthew 5 and Luke 6). Authority was no longer a matter of human power and intrigue, but was found in the quiet and gentle man, who commanded them that the person in authority was to be the servant of others and claim no status (Lk. 22:24–27). There was to be a new heartfelt respect for all of the Old Testament law and an obedience to its commands which was never to be compromised by circumstances (Matthew 5). Various kinds of subordination and status were to disappear (Mt. 18:1–4). The disciples learnt that in the kingdom of God human views of desert and reward were lost in the sight of what God gives (Mt. 20:1–16); rather the pattern was that 'to him who has will more be given, and he will have abundance; but from him who has not, even what he has will be taken away' (Mt. 13:12). This new way of submission to God meant a community where forgiveness was obligatory and love of one another was the central commandment given by Christ (Mt. 18:21–35 and John 15). All this was involved in being subject to the rule of God and, not surprisingly, it was the babes, rather than the wise and understanding, who entered the kingdom and became Christ's disciples (Mt. 11:25.).

The new way of life stood out against the dominant culture of the time. Then, as now, the dominant faith was of men in themselves, even though it was tinged with Old Testament practices and precepts. Various groups and individuals believed in their knowledge and wealth, power, status, righteousness and birth, and Christ's teaching and life soon provoked their antagonism and hostility, or perhaps more accurately, revealed it. 'And this is the judgment, that the light has come into the world, and men loved darkness rather than light, because their deeds were evil' (jn. 3:19). Gradually the groups that were stung by Christ's teaching gathered against him, and worked for his death. This they achieved through a series of intrigues, and on their interpretation this marked the victory of human power and influence. Bit there was another interpretation of Christ's sinless life and the obedient and deliberate walk to the cross, and with Christ's resurrection and appearance to hundreds, this was totally vindicated and the scene completely changed. The way of life which involved submission to God was not overwhelmed, but rather was established for ever. Paul describes the event thus: 'He disarmed the principalities and powers and made a public example of them, triumphing over them in him' (Col. 2:15). With his resurrection Christ proclaimed his own total authority and the new obedience to which his disciples in all nations were called (Mt. 28:19, 20), and they, after they had received the gift of the Holy Spirit, lived and proclaimed this new way.

The early Christians were in no doubt that the whole of their lives was to be lived in obedience to God and through faith in

Christ. They taught each other the commands and words of Christ and the precepts of the law, which were then applied with prayer in all the areas of their lives. So much of the Acts and the Letters is filled with teaching about all kinds of specific social issues and problems which were being faced in obedience to God. Even when the Christians were a tiny sect in the mighty Roman Empire, politics was seen as under the rule of God (Romans 13). It was natural that all these areas of life should be part of kingdom-living; there was no restriction of Christianity to 'church' affairs. The Christians worked out their salvation socially in fear and trembling, for God was at work in them. Various forms of social action, including evangelism, were not additional to their faith, but integral, as God recreated them in the order of the creation.

The teaching of the kingdom was not a blueprint of a perfect society. Christ made it clear that the wheat and tares would grow together until the end of the age (Mt. 13:24–43). Nevertheless, the rule of God was established by Christ to grow like a grain of mustard seed into the greatest kingdom ever known to mankind (Mt. 13:31, 32). It is with this growth of the rule of God rather than the rule of man that this book is chiefly concerned.

Index